The Christian
Bed & Breakfast
Directory

1994-1995 Edition

The Christian Bed & Breakfast Directory

1994-1995 Edition

Edited by Karen Carroll

A BARBOUR BOOK

ISBN 1-55748-459-7

Published by Barbour and Company, Inc.
P.O. Box 719
Uhrichsville, Ohio 44683

Table of Contents

How To Use This Book

Have you ever dreamed of spending a few days in a rustic cabin in Alaska? Would you like to stay in an urban town house while taking care of some business in the city? Would your family like to spend a weekend on a midwestern farm feeding the pigs and gathering eggs? Maybe a romantic Victorian mansion in San Francisco or an antebellum plantation in Mississippi is what you've been looking for. No matter what your needs may be, whether you are traveling for business or pleasure, you will find a variety of choices in the 1994-1995 edition of *The Christian Bed and Breakfast Directory*.

In the pages of this guide you will find over 1,200 bed and breakfasts, small inns, and homestays. All of the information has been updated from last year's edition, and many entries are listed for the first time. Although every establishment is not owned or operated by Christians, each host has expressed a desire to welcome Christian travelers.

The directory is designed for easy reference. At a glance, you can determine the number of rooms available at each establishment and how many rooms have private (PB) and shared (SB) baths. You will find the name of the host or hosts, the price range for two people sharing one room, the kind of breakfast that is served, and what credit cards are accepted. There is a "Notes" section to let you know important information that may not be included in the description. These notes correspond to the list at the bottom of each page. The descriptions have been written by the hosts. The publisher has not visited these bed and breakfasts and is not responsible for inaccuracies.

It is recommended that you make reservations in advance. Many bed and breakfasts have small staffs or are run single-handedly and cannot easily accommodate surprises. Also, ask about taxes, as city and state taxes vary. Remember to ask for directions, and if your special dietary needs can be met, and confirm check-in and check-out times.

Whether you're planning a honeymoon (first or second!), family vacation, or business trip, *The Christian Bed & Breakfast Directory* will make any outing out of the ordinary.

KAREN CARROLL, EDITOR

Alabama

FOREST HOME

Pine Flat Plantation Bed & Breakfast

P.O. Box 33, Route 1, 36030
(205) 471-8024; (205) 346-2739

Pine Flat Plantation Bed and Breakfast was built in 1825 by an ancestor of the present owner. This country comfortable home has recently been lovingly restored and warmly decorated with cheerful fabrics and interesting antiques. Located just minutes off I-65 between Greenville and Pine Apple, Alabama, this plantation home provides a relaxed, romantic country setting for weary travelers, hunters who want more than just a hunt, or city folks looking for a peaceful place to unwind.

Hosts: Jane and George Inge
Rooms: 5 (3PB; 2SB) $60-75
Full Breakfast
Credit Cards: None
Notes: 2, 7, 10, 12

LEEDS

B & B Birmingham

Route 2, Box 275, 35094
(205) 699-9841

This is a reservation service for the state of Alabama with bed and breakfasts in Anniston, Decatur, Fort Payne, Huntsville, Birmingham, Arab, Franklin, Spanish Fort, and Muscle Shoals. Meals vary. Horse boarding, stalls, pasture, and trails on property in Birmingham area only. Kay Redhorse, coordinator.

Country Sunshine Bed and Breakfast

Rt. 2, Box 275, 35094
(205) 699-9841

Four and one-half acres secluded retreat with quiet country atmosphere. Elegant surroundings; each room decorated differently. Barn and pasture to board your horses. Ranch-style house with four bedrooms and four baths. Western Cowboy, Indian den with fireplace for TV watching. Formal dining room, country dining room, or outdoor screened patio for your dining needs. Full breakfast included and additional meals on request for an additional charge. Cater to holidays and family reunions. Guided fishing and camping in the area, horseback riding available at these places. Children over thirteen welcome. No alcoholic beverages or smoking allowed on the premises. Daily, weekly, monthly rates available. Reservation service for bed and breakfasts throughout the state of Alabama also available at this phone number.

Hostess: Kay Redhorse
Rooms: 4 (2PB; 2SB) $50-65 (off season rates available)
Full Breakfast
Credit Cards: None
Notes: None

MONTGOMERY

The Lattice Inn
1414 South Hull Street, 36104
(205) 832-9931; (205) 264-0075 (FAX)

The Lattice Inn Bed and Breakfast is Montgomery, Alabama's quiet way to relax in southern comfort. Located in the Historic Garden District, this turn-of-the-century home has been lovingly restored to provide a comfortable retreat for today's traveler. The beautiful guest rooms have private baths and fireplaces and are furnished with high postered beds and family antiques. Bountiful breakfasts are served, and the guests are urged to enjoy the pool and decks. We promise to pamper you!

Host: Michael Pierce
Rooms: 3 (PB) $50-60
Full Breakfast
Credit Cards: None
Notes: 2, 5, 7, 9, 10

Red Bluff Cottage
551 Clay St., P.O. Box 1026, 36101
(205) 264-0556; (205) 262-1872 (FAX)

This raised cottage, furnished with family antiques, is high above the Alabama River in Montgomery's Cottage Hill district near the state capitol, Dextor Avenue, King Memorial Baptist Church, the first White House of the Confederacy, the Civil Rights Memorial, and Old Alabama Town. It is convenient to the Alabama Shakespeare Festival Theater, the Museum of Fine Arts, and the expanded zoo.

Hosts: Mark and Anne Waldo
Rooms: 4 (PB) $55
Full Breakfast
Credit Cards: A, B
Notes: 2, 5, 7,12

Red Bluff Cottage

Alaska

ANCHORAGE

AAA Homestay at Homesteads

Mailing address: Box 771283, Eagle River, 99577
(907) 272-8644; (907) 694-8644; (907) 274-8644 (FAX)

Homestay at the Homesteads throughout Alaska features delightful folks who open their homes to you from wilderness to downtown. We know Alaska; where to go, what to do, how and when to do it. Let us make all your travel arrangements and bed and breakfast reservations. Sharon Kelly, coordinator.

Hillcrest Haven B & B

1449 Hillcrest Drive, 99503
(907) 274-3086; (907) 276-8411 (FAX)

The recipient of several awards for exceptional service from Anchorage's visitor bureau, this European-style guest house is blessed with the finest views of Anchorage, Denali Cook Inlet, and spectacular sunsets. Located in a secluded wilderness setting, it is convenient to downtown, buses, restaurants, shopping, and airport.

Hostess: Linda M. Smith
Rooms: 5(2PB; 3SB) $56-68
Continental Breakfast
Credit Cards: A, B, C, D, E
Notes: 2, 5, 8, 9, 11

Hospitality Plus

7722 Anne Circle, 99504-4601
(907) 333-8504

A comfortable home, delightful and thematically decorated rooms, caring and knowledgeable hosts, sumptuous breakfasts elegantly served, a mountain range within reach, a profusion of wildflowers and moose in the yard. Add to that years of various Alaskan adventures, a Hungarian refugee's escape story, exceptional tour and guiding experience, an avid fisherman, storytelling experts and artistic achievements, and then sum it all up in one word: HOSPITALITY. It doesn't get better than this!

Hosts: Charlie and Joan Budai
Rooms: 3 (1PB; 2SB) $50-75
Full Breakfast
Credit Cards: None
Notes: 2, 5, 7, 8, 10, 11, 12

DENALI NATIONAL PARK

McKinley Wilderness Lodge

P.O. Box 89, 99755
(907) 683-2277

Large, private sleeping cabins, up to four

welcome; 7 Children welcome; 8 Tennis nearby; 9 Swimming nearby; 10 Golf nearby; 11 Skiing nearby; 12 May be booked through travel agent

people per cabin, located on Caulo Creek, thirteen miles south of entrance to Denali National Park, Alaska. Barbeque area, picnic area, assistance with wildlife tours, rafting, flightseeing. Transportation for people arriving by train or bus. Restaurants located nearby. Snacks available. Gift shop, friendly personal service. Family-run business.

Hosts: Mike and Deb Planty
Rooms: 11 (SB) $82
Continental Breakfast
Credit Cards: A, B
Notes: 2, 3, 7, 12

DOUGLAS

Windsock Inn Bed and Breakfast
P. O. Box 240223, 99824-0223
(907) 364-2431

Only three families have owned and occupied this historic home built in 1912 in the heart of Douglas, five minutes from downtown Juneau. Pioneer hosts are now retired and spend a portion of the winters south but return each spring to share their Alaskan experience and hospitality with bed and breakfast clientele from all over the world.

Hosts: Julie and Bob Isaac
Rooms: 2 (SB) $50-55
Full Breakfast
Credit Cards: None
Notes: 2, 7, 8, 9, 10, 11, 12

FAIRBANKS

Alaska's 7 Gables Bed and Breakfast
P. O. Box 80890, 99708
(907) 479-0751; (907) 479-2229 (FAX)

Historically, Alaska's 7 Gables was a fraternity house. It is within walking distance of the University of Alaska, Fairbanks campus, yet near the river and airport. The spacious 10,000 square-foot Tudor-style home features a floral solarium, a foyer with antique stained-glass and an indoor waterfall, cathedral ceilings, wedding chapel, conference room and dormers. A gourmet breakfast is served daily. Other amenities include cable TV and phones, library, laundry facilities, jacuzzis, bikes, canoes and skis. Suites are available.

Hosts: Paul and Leicha Welton
Rooms: 9 (4PB; 4SB) $45-95
Full Breakfast
Credit Cards: A, B, C, D, E
Notes: 2, 5, 7, 9, 10, 11, 12

GUSTAVUS

Glacier Bay Country Inn
P.O. Box 5, 99826
(907) 697-2288; (907) 697-2289 (FAX)

Set in a clearing by lush, green rainforest and a majestic mountain backdrop, the Glacier Bay Country Inn will capture your heart at first sight. Its unique architecture includes multi-angled roofs, dormer windows, log-beamed ceilings, and large porches. Meals feature freshly baked breads and desserts, garden-fresh produce and local seafood—crab, halibut and salmon. Some of the best whalewatching in the world (humpbacks and orcas), kayaking, hiking—and time to just relax!

Hosts: Al and Annie Unrein
Rooms: 9 (8PB; 1SB) $218
Full Breakfast (lunch and dinner included)
Credit Cards: None
Notes: 2, 3, 4, 7, 12

Glacier Bay Country Inn

HOMER

Homer Bed and Breakfast/ Seekins

Box 1264, 99603
(907) 235-8996; (907) 235-2625

Spectacular panoramic view of beautiful Koclenar Bay, glaciers and mountains. Yummy breakfasts served in our rustic Alaskan home, with art—native doll collection. Truly Alaskan. Each unit has cable TV, kitchens with pots, pans, dishes, popcorn poppers, popcorn, coffee and tea. Daily maid service. Outdoor wood-heated sauna, occasional moose, birds at feeder, flowers. We are also a referral service for other apartments, suites, and cabins. Fishing, boats, and land sightseeing

available. Hosts moved here from Wisconsin and Minnesota in 1969.

Hosts: Floyd and Gert Seekins
Rooms: 8 (6PB; 2SB) $65
Full Breakfast
Credit Cards: A, B
Notes: 2, 5, 6, 7, 8, 9, 10, 11, 12

JUNEAU

The Lost Chord

2200 Fritz Cave Road, 99801
(907) 784-7296

Twelve and one-half miles from Juneau, located in a beautiful setting and home on Auke Bay across from Alaska Marine Highway docks with a private beach. Warm Alaskan hospitality. Binoculars, spotting scope, fishing equipment, kayak rental could be part of your vacation.

Hosts: Jesse and Ellen
Rooms: 4 (1PB; 3SB) $45-75
Full Breakfast
Credit Cards: None
Notes: 2, 5, 6 (by arrangement), 7, 8, 9, 10, 11, 12

Pearson's Pond Luxury Bed and Breakfast

4541 Sawa Circle, 99801
(907) 789-3772

Private studio/suites on scenic pond. Hot tub under the stars, rowboat, bicycles, BBQ, guest kitchenette. Complimentary cappuccino, fresh breads, gourmet coffee, popcorn. Near glacier, fishing, rafting, skiing, ferry, airport and Glacier Bay departures. Smoke-free. Quiet, scenic, and lots of privacy in fully equipped studio with private entrance and deck. In-room dining and TV, VCR and stereo—tapes provided. Hosts will make all travel, tours, excursion arrangements. Guests say it's a definite "10". . .where expectations are quietly met. Winner of AAA three-diamond award and ABBA three-crown award.

Hosts: Steve and Diane Pearson
Rooms: 3 (1PB; 2SB) $69-148
Full (self-serve) Breakfast
Credit Cards: A, B, E
Notes: 2, 5, 8, 9, 10, 11, 12

KETCHIKAN

Boardwalk Wilderness Lodge

P.O. Box 6440, 99901
(800) 327-9382; (907) 225-8530 (FAX)

Family-owned-and-operated Boardwalk Wilderness Lodge is located on picturesque Prince of Whales Island in Southeast Alaska. This "dream home" was turned into a beautiful log cabin lodge for eight guests. All-inclusive package provides float plane trip from Ketchikan; crabbing and fully-guided saltwater and freshwater fishing for salmon, halibut, steelhead and rainbow trout; as well as all meals served family-style and use of outdoor spa. Boardwalk is a haven for couples and families.

Hosts: Sid and Kathy Cook
Rooms: 4 (4SB) 4 day/3 night package $2,225 per person
All Meals Served
Credit Cards: A, B, C
Notes: 3, 4, 7, 12

SEWARD

The White House Bed and Breakfast

P.O. Box 1157, 99664
(907) 224-3614

This 5,000-square-foot home is surrounded by a panoramic mountain view. One-half of the home is for guest use. Country charm abounds with quilts and hand crafts. Guest TV room and fully equipped kitchen is in common area. Breakfast is self-serve buffet in guest dining area. The Historical Iditarod Trail close by. Also the famed Kenai Fjords National Park is accessed by road or boat.

Hosts: Tom and Annette Reese
Rooms: 5 (3PB; 2SB) $40-55 (winter) $55-75 (summer)
Expanded Continental Breakfast
Credit Cards: A, B
Notes: 2, 5, 7, 11, 12

SITKA

Karras Bed and Breakfast

230 Kegwonton Street, 99835
(907) 747-3985

A warm welcome will be yours at our bed and breakfast overlooking Sitka Sound, the picturesque fishing fleet, and the Pacific Ocean. You can walk to Sitka's main historic attractions, dining and shopping areas. Bus service is available from the airport or ferry to our home. We have a room for lounging, reading, visiting, and watching the endless marine traffic.

NOTES: Credit cards accepted: A MasterCard; B Visa; C American Express; D Discover Card; E Diners Club; F Other; 2 Personal checks accepted; 3 Lunch available; 4 Dinner available; 5 Open all year; 6 Pets

Hosts: Pete and Bertha Karras
Rooms: 4 (4SB) $30 plus tax
Full Breakfast
Credit Cards: C
Notes: 2, 5, 7

VALDEZ

Alaskan Flower Forget-me-not Bed and Breakfast

P.O. Box 1153, 99686
(907) 835-2717

Prince William Sound hospitality at its best. We know you will enjoy your visit with us. Relax in one of our luxurious guest rooms. Enjoy our informal breakfast. Year-round service. Write for free brochure or call for reservation and information.

Hostess: Betty Schackne
Rooms: 4 (1PB; 3SB) $65-75
Expanded Continental Breakfast
Credit Cards: None
Notes: 2, 5, 7, 8, 9, 11, 12

Best of All Bed and Breakfast

Box 1578, 99686
(907) 835-4524

Relax in a home-like atmosphere with Asian and Alaskan decor. Downtown location. Each of our rooms has its own personality with TV, VCR. Continental breakfast available before 7:00 am and special breakfast served between 7:00-9:00 am. No smoking in the house. A thirty percent deposit for advance reservations, refundable with a cancellation within 3 days of day of arrival. Accommodations in Valdez are limited, reservations highly recommended.

Hosts: Barry and Sue Kennedy
Rooms: 4 (1PB; 2SB) $55-70
Full Breakfast (after 7:00 am)
Credit Cards: None
Notes: 5, 7, 8, 9, 11, 12

WASILLA

Yukon Don's

1830 E. Parks Hwy, Suite 386, 99654
(907) 376-7472; (907) 376-6515 (FAX)

This 10,000-square-foot converted cow barn is one of Alaska's finest bed and breakfast inns and has been selected as one of the Top 50 Inns in America by *Inn Times* in 1991. Located near the old town site of Matanuska and just 40 minutes from Anchorage, we offer the finest view in the Matanuska Valley. Each of our rooms is theme decorated. A full-color brochure is available on request.

Hosts: Don and Karen Tanner
Rooms: 5 (1 PB; 4 SB) $50-80
Continental Breakfast
Credit Cards: None
Notes: 2, 5, 7, 9, 10, 11, 12

welcome; 7 Children welcome; 8 Tennis nearby; 9 Swimming nearby; 10 Golf nearby; 11 Skiing nearby; 12 May be booked through travel agent

Arizona

FLAGSTAFF

Comfi Cottages
of Flagstaff

1612 N. Aztec, 86001
(602) 774-0731; (602) 779-2236

Near the Grand Canyon, great for families. Five individual cottages with antiques and English country motif. Three cottages are two bedroom, one bath; one is a one bedroom honeymoon cottage; one is a large three bedroom, two baths. Fully equipped with linens, towels and blankets. Kitchens have dishes, pots, pans, coffee pot, etc. Ready to prepare breakfast foods in fridge. Color cable TV and telephone. Bicycles on premises, washer and dryer available, and picnic tables and barbecue grills at each cottage.

Hosts: Ed and Pat Wiebe
Rooms: 7 (PB) $65-185 (for entire cottage)
Guest-Prepared Full Breakfast
Credit Cards: A, B
Notes: 2, 5, 7, 8, 9, 10, 11, 12

PRESCOTT

The Cottages. . .Prescott
Country Inn

503 S. Montezuma, 86303
(602) 445-7991

Twelve charming American, English, or French country cottages near the heart of Ol' Prescott, all with queens/kings, handquilted comforters, some fireplaces, private baths and entrances, TV, direct dial phones, and fresh flowers. Most unique is the deluxe continental breakfast brought to guests to be enjoyed in the privacy of their cottage or patio. A "one free with one" dinner coupon at a choice of seven top restaurants is included. AAA and Mobil rated.

Hosts: Morris and Sue Faulkner
Rooms: 12 (PB) $89-125
Continental Breakfast
Credit Cards: A, B
Notes: 2, 5, 7, 8, 9, 10, 12

The Graham Bed and Breakfast

The Graham B & B

150 Canyon Circle Drive
(602) 284-1627; (800) 228-1425;
(602) 284-0767 (FAX)

The Graham Inn is an impressive contemporary Southwest inn with huge windows allowing great views of Sedona's red rock formations. Each guest room has a private

---

NOTES: Credit cards accepted: A Master Card; B Visa; C American Express; D Discover Card; E Diners Club; F Other; 2 Personal checks accepted; 3 Lunch available; 4 Dinner available; 5 Open all

balcony and some have a jacuzzi and fireplace. All rooms have many individual features which make each unique and delightful. Pool and spa invite guests outdoors. Mobil four-star award 1988-1993. Sedona's finest; "like going home."

Hosts: Carol and Roger Redenbaugh
Rooms: 6 (PB) $90-190
Full Breakfast
Credit Cards: A, B, D
Notes: 2, 5, 7, 8, 9, 10, 11, 12(no fee)

Territorial House, An Old West Bed and Breakfast

65 Piki Drive, 86336
(602) 204-2737

Our large stone and cedar house has been tastefully decorated to depict Arizona's territorial era. Each room is decorated to recall different stages of Sedona's early history. Some rooms have private balcony, jacuzzi tub, or fireplace. An enormous stone fireplace graces the living room and a covered veranda welcomes guests at the end of a day of sightseeing around Sedona. A full hearty breakfast is served at the harvest table each morning. All of this served with western hospitality.

Hosts: John and Linda Steele
Rooms: 4 (PB) $90-130
Full Breakfast
Credit Cards: A, B
Notes: 2, 5, 7, 8, 9, 10, 11, 12

Mi Casa Su Casa (sample)

TEMPE

Mi Casa Su Casa Bed and Breakfast

P. O. Box 950, 85280-0950
(602) 990-0682; (800) 456-0682 reservations;
(602) 990-0950 (FAX)

Our reservation service has over 160 inspected and approved homestays, guest cottages, ranches, and inns in Arizona, Utah, New Mexico, and Nevada. In Arizona, listings include Ajo, Apache Junction, Bisbee, Cave Creek, Clarkdale, Dragoon, Flagstaff, Mesa, Page, Patagonia, Payson, Pinetop, Phoenix, Prescott, Scottsdale, Sedona, Sierra Vista, Tempe, Tombstone, Tucson, Yuma, and other cities. In New Mexico, we list Albuquerque, Algodones, Chimayo, Los Cruces, Silver City, Sante Fe, and Taos. In Utah, listings include Moab, Monroe, Salt Lake City, Springdale, St. George, Tropic. In Nevada, we list Las Vegas. Private and shared baths range from $35-150. Full or continental breakfast. Ruth Young, coordinator.

TUCSON

Bonnie's Bed and Breakfast

5902 E. 9th, 85711
(602) 747-8943

This beautiful ranch-style home is located near the Tucson International Airport, University of Arizona, library, and shopping. It is a home where families are welcome and couples will find it quiet and relaxing. Bonnie and Lee have an extensive Christian tape, video, and book library available. You will be served fresh

year; 6 Pets welcome; 7 Children welcome; 8 Tennis nearby; 9 Swimming nearby; 10 Golf nearby; 11 Skiing nearby; 12 May be booked through travel agent

citrus picked from our back yard with your choice of breakfast. Offering a three-room suite or a fully furnished guest cottage. Visit Old Tucson movie location, Desert Museum.

Hosts: Bonnie and Lee Myers
Rooms: Cottage and three-room suite (PB) $35-75
Full Breakfast
Credit Cards: None
Notes: 2, 7, 8, 9, 10, 11

Bonnie's Bed and Breakfast

Casa Alegre
Bed and Breakfast
316 E. Speedway 85705
(602) 628-1800; (602) 792-1880 (FAX)

Casa Alegre is a distinguished 1915 craftsman-style bungalow, located minutes from the University of Arizona and downtown Tucson. Each of the four guest rooms has been lovingly furnished with unique pieces that reflect the highlights of Tucson's history. Every morning, guests awaken to a scrumptious full breakfast and spend their relaxing time in the Inn's serene patio and pool area or by the rock fireplace in the formal living room during the cool winter months.

Hostess: Phyllis Florek
Rooms: 4 (PB) $70-85
Full Breakfast
Credit Cards: None
Notes: 2, 5, 8, 9, 10, 11, 12

El Presidio
Bed and Breakfast Inn
297 North Main Avenue, 85701
(602) 623-6151; (501) 297-8764 (at night)

Experience Southwestern charm in a desert oasis with the romance of a country inn. Garden courtyards with Old Mexico ambience of lush, floral displays, fountains, and cobblestone surround richly appointed guest house and suites. Enjoy antique decors, robes, complimentary beverages, fruit, snacks, TV's, and telephones. The 1880's Victorian adobe mansion has been featured in many magazines and the book *The Desert Southwest.* Located in a historic district; walk to fine restaurants, museums, shops, and the Arts District. Close to downtown. Mobil and AAA three-star rated.

Hostess: Patti Toci
Rooms: 4 (PB) $75-105
Full Breakfast
Credit Cards: None
Notes: 2, 5, 8, 9, 10, 11, 12

Old Pueblo Homestays
Reservation Service
P.O. Box 13603, 85732
(602) 790-2399; (800) 333-9776 reservations;
(602) 790-2399 (FAX)

A B&B reservation service featuring accommodations in individual homes in southeast Arizona and Sedona, ranging from very modest to luxurious, including continental to gourmet breakfast. Brochure free with SASE. William A. Janssen, coordinator.

NOTES: Credit cards accepted: A Master Card; B Visa; C American Express; D Discover Card; E Diners Club; F Other; 2 Personal checks accepted; 3 Lunch available; 4 Dinner available; 5 Open all

Arkansas

EUREKA SPRINGS

Bonnybrooke Farm atop Misty Mountain

Rt. 2, Box 335A, 72632
(501) 253-6903

If your heart's in the country...or longs to be... we invite you to come share in the sweet quiet and serenity that awaits you in your place to come home to... Five cottages, distinctively different in their pleasure to tempt you: fireplace and jacuzzi in two, full glass fronts and mountain top views, shower under the stars in your glass shower, wicker porch swing in front of the fireplace and a waterfall jacuzzi ...you're gonna love it!

Hosts: Bonny and Josh
Rooms: 5 cottages (PB) $85-125
Continental Breakfast
Credit Cards: None
Notes: 2, 5, 9, 10, 12

Bonnybrooke Farm atop Misty Mountain

The Brownstone Inn

75 Hillside Ave., 72632
(501) 253-7505

A present part of Eureka's past. A historical site located on trolley route with luxury Victorian accommodations, private entrances, private baths, gourmet breakfasts, and a personal touch. Featured in *Best Places to Stay in the South*.

Hosts: Marvin and Donna Shepard
Rooms: 4 (PB) $85-95
Full Breakfast
Credit Cards: A, B
Notes: 2, 5, 10, 12

Ellis House at Trail's End

One Wheeler (end of Wall Street), 72632
(800) 243-8218

Secluded estate offering acres of privacy, panoramic view overlooking downtown historic district, Ozark Mountains, historic Crescent Hotel. Beautiful gardens and wildlife enhance this elegant Tudor home featuring fireplace, luxury suites, king- and queen-sized beds, CATV, giant whirlpools, private baths. Bountiful breakfast served in elegant dining room; evening desserts. Come to the Ellis House for

welcome; 7 Children welcome; 8 Tennis nearby; 9 Swimming nearby; 10 Golf nearby; 11 Skiing nearby; 12 May be booked through travel agent

weddings, honeymoons, family reunions, romantic getaways.

Hostess: Jan Watson
Rooms: 4 (PB) $79-129
Full Breakfast
Credit Cards: A, B, C, D
Notes: 2, 3, 4, 5, 7, 8, 9, 10, 12 (10%)

The Heartstone Inn and Cottages

35 Kings Highway, 72632
(501) 253-8916

An award-winning inn. All private baths, private entrances, cable TV. King and queen beds. Antiques galore. Renowned gourmet breakfasts. In-house massage therapy studio. Golf privileges. Large decks and gazebo under the trees; great for bird watching. Recommended by: *New York Times, Country Home Magazine, America's Wonderful Little Hotels and Inns, Recommended Inns of the South,* and many more.

Hosts: Iris and Bill Simantel
Rooms: 10 plus 2 cottages (PB) $63-110
Full Breakfast
Credit Cards: A, B, C, D
Notes: 2, 5 (Closed Christmas through January) 9, 10, 12

Ridgeway House

28 Ridgeway, 72632
(501) 253-6618; (800) 477-6618

Prepare to be pampered! Sumptuous breakfasts elegantly served, luxurious rooms, antiques, flowers, desserts, quiet street within walking distance of eight churches, five-minute walk to historic downtown, trolley one block. Porches, decks, private jacuzzi suite for anniversaries/honeymoons. All my guests are VIP's!! Open all year.

Hostess: Linda Kerkera
Rooms: 5 (3PB; 2SB) $69-109
Full Breakfast
Credit Cards: A, B, C
Notes: 2, 5, 7, 12

Singleton House

11 Singleton, 72632
(501) 253-9111

This old-fashioned Victorian house with a touch of magic is whimsically decorated and has an eclectic collection of treasures and antiques. Breakfast is served on the balcony overlooking a wildflower garden and fish pond. Walk to the historic district, shops, and cafés. Passion Play and Holy Land tour reservations can be arranged. A guest cottage with a jacuzzi is also available at a separate location.

Hostess: Barbara Bavron
Rooms: 5 (PB) $65-75/ Cottage, No Breakfast, $95
Full Breakfast
Credit Cards: A, B, C, D
Notes: 2, 5, 7, 9, 10, 12

Singleton House

FAYETTEVILLE

Hill Avenue Bed and Breakfast

131 S. Hill, 72701
(501) 444-0865

This century-old home is located in a residential neighborhood near the University of Arkansas, downtown square, and Walton Art Center. This inn is the only licensed Bed and Breakfast in Fayetteville. Comfortable common areas and a large porch are available to guests. Breakfast is served on the porch or in the formal dining room.

Hosts: Cecila and Dale Thompson
Rooms: 2 (PB) $40-50
Full Breakfast
Credit Cards: None
Notes: None

GASSVILLE

Lithia Springs Lodge

R1, Box 77A, HWY 126 North, 72635
(501) 435-6100

A lovingly restored early Ozark health lodge, six miles southwest of Mountain Home in north central Arkansas. Fishing, boating, canoeing in famous lakes and rivers. Scenic hills and valleys, caverns. Silver Dollar City, Branson, Eureka Springs within driving distance. Enjoy the walk in meadow and woods and browse through the adjoining Country Treasures Gift Shop.

Hosts: Paul and Reita Johnson
Rooms: 5 (3PB; 2SB) $40-45
Full Breakfast
Credit Cards: None
Notes: 2, 8, 9, 10

HARDY

Olde Stonehouse Bed and Breakfast Inn

511 Main St., 72542
(501) 856-2983

Historic, native Arkansas stone house with large porches lined with jumbo rocking chairs provides the perfect place to relax and watch the world go by. Each room is individually and comfortably furnished with antiques. Central heat and air, ceiling fans, queen beds, private baths. In-town location, block from Spring River and the unique shops of Old Hardy Town. Three country music theaters, golf courses, horseback riding, canoeing and fishing nearby. Attractions: Mammoth Springs State park, Grand Gulf State Park, Evening Shade, AR, Arkansas Traveler Theater. Breakfast is a treat, like Grandma used to make, gourmet but hearty! Evening snacks. Special occasion packages available. Murder mystery dinner parties and packages. Gift certificates. Approved by AAA and ABBA.

Hosts: David and Peggy Johnson
Rooms: 7 and 2 suites (PB) $55-85
Full Breakfast
Credit Cards: A, B, D
Notes: 2, 3, 4, 5, 8, 9, 10, 12

HELENA

Edwardian Inn / Allin House

317 Biscoe, 72342
(501) 338-9155

Two elegantly restored National Register

welcome; 7 Children welcome; 8 Tennis nearby; 9 Swimming nearby; 10 Golf nearby; 11 Skiing nearby; 12 May be booked through travel agent

buildings, the 1904 Victorian Edwardian Inn and the 1858 Italiante Allin House have the beauty and charm of the past with all the conveniences of the present. The Inn is large and very imposing, filled with quarter-sawn oak paneling, wooden mantels, wood flooring, and brass hardware—all still in excellent condition. The Allin House is smaller, but just as beautifully decorated with the look and charm of New Orleans.

Hostess: Jerri Steed
Rooms: 18 (PB) $49-99
Continental Breakfast
Credit Cards: A, B, C, E
Notes: 2, 5, 6 (small), 7, 8, 10, 12

HOT SPRINGS

Dogwood Manor

906 Malvern Hwy., 71901
(501) 624-0896

Lovely three-story Victorian—National Registry. An architect's dream: Five gables, lead-glass, gingerbread trim. Custom draped; array of wonderful wall coverings built in China. French prism sconces adorn the fireplace. Den features eight-foot marble-top L-shaped bar. Four entries, five bedrooms, seven baths. Six blocks from famed Bath House Row. Great assortment of antique furnishings.

Hostess: Lady Janie
Rooms: 5 (PB) $50-85
Continental Breakfast
Credit Cards: A, B
Notes: 2, 5, 6, 9, 10, 12

Vintage Comfort Bed and Breakfast Inn

303 Quapaw, 71901
(501) 623-3258

Situated on a tree-lined street, a short walk from Hot Springs' historic Bath House Row, art galleries, restaurants, and shopping. Guests enjoy a comfortably restored Queen Anne house built in 1907. Four spacious rooms are available upstairs, each with private bath, ceiling fan, and period furnishings. A delicious full breakfast is served each morning in the Inn's dining room. Vintage Comfort is known for its comfort and gracious Southern hospitality.

Rooms: 4 (PB) $60-80
Full Breakfast
Credit Cards: A, B, C, E
Notes: 2, 5, 7 (over 5 years), 10, 12

Wildwood 1884

808 Park Avenue, 71901
(501) 624-4267

Wildwood 1884 was a dream of the original owners Dr. Prosper and Sarah Ellsworth. It took six years to build at a cost of fourty-thousand dollars. The woodwork is of native Arkansas trees—cherry, walnut, sweetgum—all hand-rubbed to a beautiful shine. Owners/innkeepers Randy and Karen Duncan have lovingly restored this grand mansion. Whether sitting on one of the many verandas or quietly relaxing in one of the parlors, the magnificence of this Victorian estate, listed on National Register of Historic Places is unsurpassed.

Hosts: Randy and Karen Duncan
Rooms: 5 (PB) $75-85
Full Breakfast
Credit Cards: A, B
Notes: 2, 5, 7 (over 10), 8, 9, 10, 12

NOTES: Credit cards accepted: A Master Card; B Visa; C American Express; D Discover Card; E Diners Club; F Other; 2 Personal checks accepted; 3 Lunch available; 4 Dinner available; 5 Open all year; 6 Pets

California

ALAMEDA

Garratt Mansion

900 Union St., 94501
(510) 521-4779

This 1893 Victorian halts time on the tranquil island of Alameda. Only 15 miles to Berkeley or downtown San Francisco. We'll help maximize your vacation plans or leave you alone to regroup. Our rooms are large and comfortable, and our breakfasts are nutritious and filling.

Hosts: Royce and Betty Gladden
Rooms: 6 (3PB; 3SB) $75-125
Full Breakfast
Credit Cards: A, B, C, E
Notes: 2, 5, 7, 8, 9, 10, 12

ALBION

Fensalden Inn

P.O. Box 99, 95410
(707) 937-4042; (800) 959-3850

Overlooking the Pacific Ocean from twenty tree-lined pastoral acres, Fensalden Inn offers a quiet respite for the perfect getaway. A former stagecoach way station, the inn offers a restful, yet interesting stay for the traveler. There are eight guest quarters; some are suites with fireplaces and kitchens; all have private baths with showers or tubs; and most have beautiful ocean views. Come and whale watch, join the deer on a stroll through our meadow, or just relax and enjoy!

Hosts: Scott and Frances Brazil
Rooms: 8 (PB) $95-140
Full Gourmet Breakfast
Credit Cards: A, B
Notes: 2, 5, 8, 9, 10, 12

ANAHEIM

Anaheim Country Inn

856 S. Walnut St., 92802
(714) 778-0150; (800) 755-7801

Step back in time and enjoy our Anaheim Country Inn. This large, beautiful Princess Anne home was built in 1910 by John Cook, prominent landowner and former mayor of Anaheim. The Inn is graced by bevelled, leaded glass windows and charming turn of the century country furnishings. Anaheim Country Inn is located on spacious grounds in the midst of a quiet residential neighborhood—very near the Disneyland/Convention tourist area. Ample off-street parking is provided.

Hosts: Lois Ramont and Marilyn Watson
Rooms: 8 (6PB; 2SB) $55-80
Full Breakfast
Credit Cards: A, B, C, D
Notes: 2, 5, 7, 12

welcome; 7 Children welcome; 8 Tennis nearby; 9 Swimming nearby; 10 Golf nearby; 11 Skiing nearby; 12 May be booked through travel agent

ANGWIN

Forest Manor

415 Cold Springs Road, 94508
(707) 965-3538, (800) 788-0364;
(707) 965-3516 (FAX)

Tucked among the forest and vineyards of famous Napa wine country is this secluded 20-acre English Tudor estate, described as "one of the most romantic country inns ... a small exclusive resort." Enjoy the scenic countryside near hot air ballooning, hot springs, lake, and water sports. Fireplaces, verandas, a 53-foot pool, spas, spacious suites (one with Jacuzzi), refrigerators, coffee makers, home-baked breakfasts. Hosts are former medical missionaries.

Hosts: Harold and Corlene Lambeth
Rooms: 3 (PB) $99-179 off-season;
$119-199 in-season
Full Breakfast
Credit Cards: None
Notes: 2, 5, 8, 9, 12

APTOS

Apple Lane Inn

6265 Soquel Drive, 95003
(408) 475-6868; (800) 649-8988

This secluded 1870's Victorian is set on a hill overlooking acres of gardens, meadows, orchards, a romantic gazebo, and flowering gardens. Each room is unique with period antiques, quilts, and authentic decor. A lavish country breakfast is served in the parlor. Enjoy the game room, darts, croquet, horseshoes, and player piano. Pick apples to feed the horses or gather fresh eggs and produce from the gardens. Walk to the beach. Just minutes from Santa Cruz.

Hosts: Douglas and Diana Groom
Rooms: 5 (3PB; 2 SB) $70-150
Full Breakfast
Credit Cards: A, B, D
Notes: 2, 5, 12

Mangels House

570 Aptos Creek Rd., 95003
(408) 688-7982

Beautiful Italiante Victorian house on four acres of formal garden. Large sitting room and library with couches and grand piano. Six large bedrooms with high ceilings and long, double-hung windows, all with private baths and individual decor. Less than a mile from Monterey Bay and bordering a ten-thousand acre redwood park with hiking trails. Peaceful.

Hostess: Jacqueline Fisher
Rooms: 5 (PB) $98-125
Full Breakfast
Credit Cards: A, B, C
Notes: 2, 5 (except one week over Christmas),
7 (over 12), 8, 9, 10, 12

CALISTOGA

Calistoga Wayside Inn

1523 Foothill Blvd., 94515
(800) 845-3632; (707) 942-5357 (FAX)

A warm, inviting Mediterranean-style home, built in the 1920s, situated in a secluded garden setting. Rooms have king or queen beds, private baths. Enjoy the relaxing hot tub, patio, or curl up by the

---

NOTES: Credit cards accepted: A MasterCard; B Visa; C American Express; D Discover Card; E Diners Club; F Other; 2 Personal checks accepted; 3 Lunch available; 4 Dinner available; 5 Open all year; 6 Pets

fireplace. Savor a Calistoga country breakfast, afternoon refreshments, herb tea in the evening. Restaurants, shops, and spas nearby. Gift certificates.

Hosts: Pat and Carmine
Rooms: 3 (PB) $95-125
Full Breakfast
Credit Cards: A, B, C
Notes: 2, 5, 7, 8, 9, 10, 12

Foothill House

3037 Foothill Blvd., 94515
(707) 942-6933; (707) 942-5692 (FAX)

"The romantic inn of the Napa Valley," according to a *Chicago Tribune* travel editor. In a country setting, located in the western foothills just north of Calistoga, the Foothill House offers spacious suites individually decorated with antiques. All suites have private baths and entrances, fireplaces, small refrigerators and air conditioning. Some have jacuzzis. A luxurious cottage is also available. A gourmet breakfast is served each morning and appetizers and refreshments each evening.

Hosts: Gus and Doris Beckert
Rooms: 3 (PB) $115-220
Full Breakfast
Credit Cards: A, B, C
Notes: 2, 5, 8, 9, 10, 12

Hillcrest Bed and Breakfast

3225 Lake County Highway, 94515
(707) 942-6334

Hilltop, rambling country home filled with antique silver, china, art work and furniture. Rooms have balconies with breathtaking views of lush Napa Valley. Swim-

ming, hiking, and fishing on forty acres. Guests have use of trampoline, spa, and barbeque area.

Hostess: Debbie O'Gorman
Rooms: 6 (4PB; 2 SB) $45-90
Continental Breakfast
Credit Cards: None
Notes: 2, 5, 6, 8, 9, 10, 12

Quail Mt. B & B

4455 North St. Helena Hwy., 94515
(707) 942-0316

A secluded, romantic B & B located on 26 heavily wooded acres 300 feet above Napa Valley. All king size beds, private baths, and decks. A swimming pool, hot tub, and picnic facilities on premises. A full breakfast is served in the guest common room, decks that wrap around the house, or in winter, in the formal dining room that has a fireplace. Reservation deposit required.

Hosts: Alma and Don Swiers
Rooms: 3 (PB) $100-130
Full Breakfast
Credit Cards: A, B
Notes: 2, 5, 8, 10, 12

Scarlett's Country Inn

3918 Silverado Trail, 94515
(707) 942-6669

This secluded 1890 farmhouse set in the quiet of green lawns and tall pines that overlook vineyards has three exquisitely appointed suites, one with a fireplace. Breakfast is served in your room or by the woodland swimming pool. Close to win-

welcome; 7 Children welcome; 8 Tennis nearby; 9 Swimming nearby; 10 Golf nearby; 11 Skiing nearby; 12 May be booked through travel agent

eries and spas, we offer private baths, queen beds, private entrances, air conditioning, and afternoon refreshments.

Hosts: Scarlett and Derek Dwyer
Rooms: 3 (PB) $95-150
Continental Breakfast
Credit Cards: None
Notes: 2, 5, 7, 8, 9, 10, 12

CAMBRIA

The Pickford House Bed and Breakfast

2555 MacLeod Way, 93428
(805) 927-8619

Enjoy antiques, clawfoot tubs with showers, only seven miles from Hearst Castle. Three rooms have fireplaces; all rooms have in-room TV's and king or queen beds. Evening refreshments and wine served at 5:00 pm each day. Near beaches. Gift certificates available. Third person any age $20. Reservations needed. Well-behaved children welcome. Check in after 3pm, check out 11 am.

Hostess: Anna Larsen
Rooms: 8 (PB) $85-125 plus tax
Full Breakfast
Credit Cards: A, B
Notes: 2, 5, 7

CAPITOLA-BY-THE-SEA

The Inn at Depot Hill

250 Monterey Avenue, 95010
(408) 462-3376; (408) 462-3697 (FAX)

Located in quaint, Mediterranean beachside resort, this award-winning inn is

the next best thing to a romantic European escape. The rooms are named and beautifully decorated to resemble different parts of the world: The Cote d'Azur room captures the essence of a chic auberge in St. Tropez; Paris, a romantic French hideaway; Portofino, an Italian coastal villa; Delft, a summer home on the coast of Holland; Sissiinghurst, a traditional English garden room. Five rooms have patios with private hot tubs. All rooms have fireplaces, TV's, VCR's, stereo systems, white marble baths, phones and bathrobes.

Hostess: Suzie Lankes
Rooms: 8 (PB) $155-250
Full Breakfast
Credit Cards: A, B, C
Notes: 2, 5, 8, 9, 10, 12

CARLSBAD

Pelican Cove Inn

320 Walnut, 92008
(619) 434-5995

This romantic inn is located 200 yards from the beach and features eight rooms all with: private baths (some spas), feather beds, down comforters, fireplaces, and TVs. An extended continental breakfast that can be enjoyed in your room, the gazebo, or the oceanview deck is included. Excellent restaurants and shopping are within walking distance.

Hosts: Scott and Betsy Buckwald
Rooms: 8 (PB) $85-175
Full Breakfast
Credit Cards: A, B, C
Notes: 2, 5, 8, 9, 10, 12

NOTES: Credit cards accepted: A MasterCard; B Visa; C American Express; D Discover Card; E Diners Club; F Other; 2 Personal checks accepted; 3 Lunch available; 4 Dinner available; 5 Open all year; 6 Pets

CARMEL VALLEY

The Valley Lodge

Carmel Valley Road at Ford Road, Box 93, 93924
(408) 659-2261; (800) 641-4646;
(408) 659-4558 (FAX)

A warm Carmel Valley welcome awaits the two of you, a few of you, or a small conference. Relax in a garden patio room or a cozy one- or two-bedroom cottage with fireplace and kitchen. Enjoy a sumptuous continental breakfast, our heated pool, sauna, hot spa, and fitness center. Tennis and golf are nearby. Walk to fine restaurants and quaint shops of Carmel Valley village, or just listen to your beard grow.

Hosts: Peter and Sherry Coakley
Rooms: 31 (PB) $95-135; $155 one-bedroom cottage; $235 two-bedroom cottage
Expanded Continental Breakfast
Credit Cards: A, B, C
Notes: 2, 5, 6 (extra fee), 7, 8, 9 (on premises), 10, 12

CLOVERDALE

Abrams House Inn

314 N. Main, 95425
(707) 894-2412; (800) 764-4-INN;
(707) 894-2412 (FAX)

1870s Victorian home with four unique bedrooms, and three parlours filled with historic family memorabilia. A wicker decorated porch overlooks flowers, fruit trees and herb garden, a gazebo, plus a covered deck. We are minutes from Lake Sonoma, the Russian River, Sonoma and Mendocino wineries. We accommodate small weddings and seminars.

Hosts: Betsy Fitzgerald and Patti and Ray Robarts
Rooms: 4 (2PB; 2SB) $65-115
Full Breakfast
Credit Cards: A, B, C
Notes: 2, 5, 9, 12

Ye Olde' Shelford House

29955 River Road, 95425
(707) 894-5956; (800) 833-6479

This 1885 country Victorian is located in the heart of wine country, with six beautifully decorated rooms with family antiques, fresh flowers, home-made quilts, and porcelain dolls by Ina. A gourmet breakfast is served in our delightful dining room. We will make reservations for you at one of the many good restaurants nearby. Before you retire, you can enjoy the many games in the recreation room, then get into the hot tub to relax after a busy day. Pool and tandem 10-speed bicycles available. Air conditioned.

Hosts: Ina and Allen Sauder
Rooms: 6 (PB) $85-110
Full Breakfast
Closed January
Credit Cards: A, B, C, D
Notes: 2, 7, 8, 9, 10

COLUMBIA

Fallon Hotel

Washington Street, 95310
(209) 532-1470; (209) 532-7027

Since 1857 the Fallon Hotel in the historic Columbia State Park has provided hospitality and comfort to travelers from all over the world. It has been authentically re-

welcome; 7 Children welcome; 8 Tennis nearby; 9 Swimming nearby; 10 Golf nearby; 11 Skiing nearby; 12 May be booked through travel agent

stored to its Victorian grandeur, and many of the antiques and furnishings are original to the hotel. We welcome you to come visit our Fallon Hotel, Fallon Theater, and old-fashioned ice cream parlor for a taste of the Old West.

Host: Tom Bender
Rooms: 14 (13PB; 1SB) $50-90
Continental Breakfast
Credit Cards: A, B, C
Notes: 2, 5 (weekends only Jan-March), 7, 8, 9, 10, 11, 12

ELK

Elk Cove Inn

6300 South Highway 1, P.O. Box 367, 95432
(707) 877-3321

This 1883 Victorian is nestled atop a bluff overlooking the ocean. Enjoy wide vista views amid the relaxed and romantic setting of a rural village. Behind the main house are four cabins, two with fireplace and skylights. The main house, where a full breakfast is served in the dining rooms, has three large ocean-view rooms, a parlor, and deck. There is access to a driftwood strewn beach and numerous scenic trails for hiking and biking nearby.

Host: Hildrun-Uta Triebess
Rooms: 8 (PB) $98-148
Full Breakfast
Credit Cards: None
Notes: 2, 5, 8, 10

The Daly Inn

EUREKA

An Elegant Victorian Mansion

1406 C Street, 95501
(707) 444-3144

Exclusively for non-smokers: An 1888 National Historic Landmark of opulence, grace and grandeur offering deluxe lodging and world-class service. Authentically restored Victorian interiors, family antiques; flower gardens. Gourmet breakfast. Secured garage parking, laundry service, bicycles, sauna; best mattresses in the world. Near ocean, redwoods. Complimentary bay cruise. AAA and Mobil rated.

Hosts: Doug and Lily Vieyra
Rooms: 4 (2PB; 2SB) $90-125
Full Breakfast
Credit Cards: A, B
Notes: 5, 8, 9, 10

The Daly Inn

1125 H Street, 95501
(707) 445-3638; (800) 321-9656

1905 Colonial Revival surrounded with generous grounds and Victorian gardens. The home has been beautifully restored with modern conveniences tastefully added. This bed and breakfast mansion is truly one of the finest examples of turn-of-the-century elegance on California's North Coast.

Hosts: Sue and Gene Clinesmith
Rooms: 5 (3PB; 2SB) $75-125
Full Breakfast
Credit Cards: A, B, C, D
Notes: 2, 5, 8, 10, 12

NOTES: Credit cards accepted: A MasterCard; B Visa; C American Express; D Discover Card; E Diners Club; F Other; 2 Personal checks accepted; 3 Lunch available; 4 Dinner available; 5 Open all year; 6 Pets

Shannon House B & B

2154 Spring Street, 95501
(707) 443-8130

The Shannon House is an 1891 Victorian that has been lovingly restored by the owners. It features period wallpapers and antiques throughout. The inn is situated on a quiet residential street in Eureka, a town of about 25,000. The town offers a walk through history with its various museums featuring Indian history, logging, working steam engines, and maritime history. Within short distance are miles of trails running through old growth redwood forests and along secluded beaches.

Hosts: David and Barbara Shannon
Rooms: 3 (1PB; 2SB) $55-75 + tax
Full Breakfast
Credit Cards: C, D
Notes: 2, 5, 7, 8, 9, 10, 12

A Weaver's Inn

1440 B Street, 95501
(707) 443-8119

A Weaver's Inn is the home and studio of a fiber artist and her husband. The home is a stately Queen Anne Colonial Revival house built in 1883 and remodeled in 1907. Placed in a spacious fenced garden, it is airy and light, cozy and warm even when veiled by wisps of fog. Arriving early, you might visit the studio, try the spinning wheel before the fire, or weave on the antique loom, before having refreshments. The Victorian parlor offers a piano and elegant relaxing.

Hosts: Bob and Dorothy Swendeman
Rooms: 4 (2PB; 2SB) $60-85
Full Breakfast
Credit Cards: A, B, C, D
Notes: 2, 5, 6, 7, 8, 10, 12

FAWNSKIN

The Inn at Fawnskin Bed and Breakfast

880 Canyon Road, P.O. Box 378, 92333
(909) 866-3200

Beautiful custom log home with knotty pine interior located on the quiet north shore of Big Bear Lake on an acre of land among towering pine trees. Living room with big rock fireplace, and comfy furniture. Library. Game room with 30-inch wide-screen TV, full size pool table, movie library, and game table. Full, delicious, home-made breakfast served in front of another brick fireplace. Four lovely guest rooms.

Hosts: G.B. and Susan Sneed
Rooms: 4 (2PB; 2SB) $75-155
Full Breakfast
Credit Cards: A, B
Notes: 2, 3, 4, 5, 8, 9, 10, 11, 12

FERNDALE

The Gingerbread Mansion

400 Berding Street, P.O. Box 40, 95536
(707) 786-4000; (800) 952-4136

Trimmed in gingerbread and surrounded by a formal English garden, the Gingerbread Mansion, circa 1899, is an elegant Queen Anne Eastlake-style Victorian. Completely decorated in antiques, the Victorian theme is carried throughout the four parlors, dining room, and nine guest rooms. The Gingerbread Mansion is located in the state historic landmark village of Ferndale, offering three blocks of shops, galleries, a

---

welcome; 7 Children welcome; 8 Tennis nearby; 9 Swimming nearby; 10 Golf nearby; 11 Skiing nearby; 12 May be booked through travel agent

repertory theater, and museum. The coast, redwoods, hiking trails, and more are nearby.

Host: Ken Torbert
Rooms: 9 (PB) $85-185
Full Breakfast
Credit Cards: A, B, C
Notes: 2, 5, 10, 12

Shaw House
Bed and Breakfast

703 Main Street, P.O. Box 1125, 95536-1125
(707) 786-9958

1854 Carpenter Gothic built by the founder of Ferndale for his bride. Listed on the National Register of Historic Places, Shaw House is the second oldest building running as a B&B in California. One-half hour from Avenue of the Giants trees. Five hours north of San Francisco and 15 minutes south of Eureka. In Victorian Village on one acre, one-half block from businesses and restaurants.

Hosts: Ken and Norma Bessingpas
Rooms: 6 (PB) $75-125
Continental Plus Breakfast
Credit Cards: A, B, C
Notes: 2, 5, 12

FORT BRAGG

Grey Whale Inn

615 Main St., 95437
(707) 964-0640; (800) 382-7244 (Reservations)

Handsome four-story Mendocino Coast Landmark since 1915. Cozy rooms to expansive suites, all have private baths. Ocean, garden or hill, or town views. Some have fireplaces, TV, one has jacuzzi tub, all have phones. Recreation Area: Pool table/library, fireside lounge, TV theater. Sixteen-person conference room. Full buffet breakfast features blue-ribbon breads. Friendly, helpful staff. Relaxed seaside charm, situated 6 blocks to beach. Celebrate your special occasion on the fabled Mendocino Coast!

Hosts: John and Colette Bailey
Rooms: 14 (PB) $82.50-160
Full Breakfast
Credit Cards: A, B, C, D
Notes: 2, 5, 7, 8, 9, 10, 12

Pudding Creek Inn

700 North Main, 95437
(707) 964-9529; (800) 227-9529

Two lovely 1884 Victorian homes adjoined by a lush garden court offer comfortable and romantic rooms all with private baths. Your stay includes buffet breakfast with fresh fruit, juice, main dish, and tantalizing home-made coffee cakes served hot. Antiques, fireplaces, personalized sightseeing assistance. Near scenic Skunk Train excursion, beaches, dining, shops, galleries, hiking, tennis, and golf. Mention this book for a 15% discount off room rate.

Hostess: Jacque Woltman
Rooms: 10 (PB) $65-125
Full Breakfast
Credit Cards: A, B, C, D
Notes: 2, 5 (by prior arrangement), 8, 9, 10, 12

NOTES: Credit cards accepted: A MasterCard; B Visa; C American Express; D Discover Card; E Diners Club; F Other; 2 Personal checks accepted; 3 Lunch available; 4 Dinner available; 5 Open all year; 6 Pets

GEORGETOWN

American River Inn

P.O. Box 43, Main at Orleans St., 95634
(916) 333-4499; (800) 245-6566

Innkeepers Will and Maria Collin carry on the century old tradition of graciousness in a setting far removed from the fast pace of modern living. You are invited to cool off in a beautiful mountain pool or relax in the spa. Some may choose a day of bicycling amid the colorful breathtaking daffodils, iris and the brilliant yellow-gold scotch broom. The bicycles are provided.

Their historic Queen Anne Inn can provide the ideal setting for your corporate off-site meeting or retreat. All meeting necessities and food catering services are available. The inn can accommodate up to 35/40 participants. Please call for detailed information for your group.

Hosts: Will and Maria Collin
Rooms: 18 (12PB; 6SB) $85-115
Full Breakfast
Credit Cards: A, B, C, D, E, F
Notes: 2, 3, 5, 7, 8, 9, 10, 11, 12

American River Inn

GEYSERVILLE

Campbell Ranch Inn

1475 Canyon Road, 95441
(707) 857-3476

A 35-acre country setting in the heart of the Sonoma wine country offers a spectacular view, beautiful gardens, tennis court, swimming pool, hot tub, and bicycles. We have five spacious rooms with private baths, fresh flowers, fruit, king beds, and balconies. Full breakfast is served on the terrace, and we offer an evening dessert of home-made pie or cake.

Hosts: Mary Jane and Jerry Campbell
Rooms: 5 (PB) $100-165
Full Breakfast
Credit Cards: A, B
Notes: 2, 5, 10, 12

GILROY

Country Rose Inn
Bed and Breakfast

P.O. Box 1804, 95201
(408) 842-0441

Featured in *Country Inns*—Dutch Colonial Manor. Spacious rooms, bridal suite, cozy and friendly. Rural setting, relaxing, with baby grand piano. Big trees nearby and a wonderful gourmet breakfast and turn-down service. Near wineries, hot air ballooning, outlet shopping. Pivotal location for the ocean, Silicon Valley and San Francisco. It is unexpected, a surprise at the end of the lane.

Hostess: Rose Hernandez
Rooms: 5 (PB) $79-169+tax
Full Breakfast
Credit Cards: A, B
Notes: 2, 5, 10, 12

welcome; 7 Children welcome; 8 Tennis nearby; 9 Swimming nearby; 10 Golf nearby; 11 Skiing nearby; 12 May be booked through travel agent

GUALALA

North Coast Country Inn

34591 South Highway 1, 95445
(707) 884-4537; (800) 995-4537

Picturesque redwood buildings on a forested hillside overlook the Pacific Ocean. The large guest suites feature fireplaces, decks, minikitchens, and authentic antique furnishings. Enjoy the romantic hot tub under the pines and the beautiful hilltop garden with gazebo. Near beaches, hiking, golf, tennis, horseback riding, state parks, and restaurants.

Hosts: Loren and Nancy Flanagan
Rooms: 4 (PB) $135
Full Breakfast
Credit Cards: A, B, C
Notes: 2, 5, 8, 10, 12

HALF MOON BAY

Old Thyme Inn

779 Main Street, 94019
(415) 726-1616

The Inn has 7 guest rooms, all with private baths. We are a restored 1899 Queen Anne Victorian, located on historic Main Street in the downtown area. Some rooms have fireplaces and double size whirlpool tubs. The theme is our English-style herb garden; all rooms are named after herbs. Atmosphere is friendly and informal. We serve beverages in the evening and a hearty breakfast each morning. Nearby activities include: Golf, whale-watching, tidepools, shopping. Many fine restaurants are close-by, some within walking distance.

Hosts: George and Marcia Dempsey
Rooms: 7 (PB) $75-210
Full Breakfast
Credit Cards: A, B
Notes: 2, 5, 7, 8, 9, 10, 12

Old Thyme Inn

HEALDSBURG

Healdsburg Inn on the Plaza

110 Matheson Street, 95448
(707) 433-6991; (800) 491-2327

A quiet place in the center of town where history and hospitality meet. This historic 1900 brick Victorian, once a Wells Fargo Express building, now houses our nine-room bed and breakfast. Rooms done in sunrise/sunset colors feature fireplaces, queen beds, private bathrooms, fluffy towels, and a rubber ducky. Breakfast is served in our sun-filled solarium. Enjoy browsing through our art gallery, bakery and gift shops on the first floor.

Host: Genny Jenkins
Rooms: 9 (PB) $115-160 (midweek rates discounted)
Full Breakfast
Credit Cards: A, B
Notes: 2, 5, 8, 9, 10

NOTES: Credit cards accepted: A MasterCard; B Visa; C American Express; D Discover Card; E Diners Club; F Other; 2 Personal checks accepted; 3 Lunch available; 4 Dinner available; 5 Open all year; 6 Pets

HOMEWOOD

Rockwood Lodge

5295 West Lake Boulevard, 96141-0226
(916) 525-5273 or (800) LE TAHOE; FAX (916) 525-5949

Set back in the tall trees on the wooded west shore of Tahoe, the lodge blends in with its surroundings. There is history and elegance in this region, and Rockwood is a remnant of the "old Tahoe" and has all the requisites for a special sojourn: knotty pine walls, huge stone fireplace, sitting room, and an intimate atmosphere. Homey touches add to the enjoyment of a stay at Rockwood. This is the way a mountain chalet ought to be.

Host: Louis Reinkens
Rooms: 4 (2PB; 2 SB) $90-200
Full Breakfast
Credit Cards: None
Notes: 2, 5, 8, 9, 10, 11,12

IDYLLWILD

Wilkum Inn
Bed and Breakfast

P.O. Box 1115, 92549
(909) 659-4087

Come home to warm hospitality and personal service in a friendly mountain ambience. The two-story shingle-sided inn is nestled among pines, oaks and cedars. Warm knotty pine interiors and a cozy river rock fireplace are enhanced by the innkeepers' antiques and collectibles. Expanded continental breakfasts of special fruits and breads, such as crepes, Belgian waffles or abelskivers, fortify guests

for a day of hiking or visiting unique shops and art galleries.

Hosts: Annamae Chambers and Barbara Jones
Rooms: 5 (3PB; 2SB) $65-95
Expanded Continental Breakfast
Credit Cards: None
Notes: 2, 5, 9, 12

IONE

The Heirloom

214 Shakeley Lane, P.O. Box 322, 95640
(209) 274-4468

Travel down a country lane to a spacious, romantic English garden and a petite Colonial mansion built circa 1863. The house features balconies, fireplaces, and heirloom antiques, along with a gourmet breakfast and gracious hospitality. Located in the historic gold country, close to all major northern California cities. The area abounds with antiques, wineries, and historic sites.

Hosts: Melisande Hubbs and Patricia Cross
Rooms: 6 (4PB; 2 SB) $55-90
Full Breakfast
Credit Cards: None
Closed Thanksgiving and Christmas
Notes: 2, 5, 9, 10, 12

JENNER

Timber Cove Inn

21780 North Coast Highway One, 95450
(707) 847-3231; (707) 847-3704 (FAX)

Located 15 miles north of Jenner on Coast Highway One. Timber Cove Inn offers you a rustic setting in which you may enjoy the beauty of the wild Sonoma Coast.

Situated in 26 oceanfront acres. Nearby public parks and redwood forests offer unlimited exploration. The essence of Timber Cove Inn is that it is a place of beauty, a place to forget worry, a place to get to know yourself again, a place to think, and not least, it is a place to be in love.

Host: Richard Hojohn
Rooms: 49 (PB) $78-325
Call for details on breakfast
Credit Cards: A, B, C, E
Notes: 2, 3, 4, 5, 7, 10, 12

JULIAN

Butterfield Bed and Breakfast

2284 Sunset Drive, Box 1115, 92036
(619) 765-2179; (619) 765-1115 (FAX)

Our cozy five-room inn is located in the historic mountain community of Julian. We pamper our guests with romantic suites and a whimsical Christmas cottage. The garden gazebo provides a beautiful setting for our country gourmet breakfast and afternoon weddings. Terraces with waterfalls and fountains let you relax in the serene setting. Romantic candlelight dinners and culinary workshops are a specialty of Chef Skalada of *The Chef's Palate*. Holidays are most special at Butterfield's.

Hosts: Ray and Mary Trimmins
Rooms: 5 (PB) $79-119
Full Breakfast
Credit Cards: A, B
Notes: 2, 4, 5, 7, 8, 10, 12

KERNVILLE

Kern River Inn B & B

P.O. Box 1725, 119 Kern River Dr., 93238
(619) 376-6750

A charming, classic country riverfront B&B located on the wild and scenic Kern River in the quaint little town of Kernville within the Sequoia National Forest in the southern Sierra Mountains. We specialize in romantic getaways. All bedrooms have private baths and feature riverviews; some with whirlpool tubs and fireplaces. Full breakfast. Walk to restaurants, shops, parks, museum. A short drive to giant redwood trees. An all-year vacation area with fishing, skiing, hiking, biking, whitewater rafting, Lake Isabella.

Hosts: Mike and Marti
Rooms: 6 (PB) $69-89 + tax
Full Breakfast
Credit Cards: A, B
Notes: 5, 9, 10, 11, 12

LAGUNA BEACH

Eiler's Inn

741 South Coast Highway, 92651
(714) 494-3004

Twelve rooms with private baths and a courtyard with gurgling fountain and colorful blooming plants are within walking distance of town and most restaurants; half block from the beach.

Hosts: Henk and Annette Wirtz
Rooms: 12 (PB) $100-130
Full Breakfast
Credit Cards: A, B, C
Notes: 2, 5, 8, 9, 10, 12

NOTES: Credit cards accepted: A MasterCard; B Visa; C American Express; D Discover Card; E Diners Club; F Other; 2 Personal checks accepted; 3 Lunch available; 4 Dinner available; 5 Open all year; 6 Pets

LAKE ARROWHEAD

Bluebelle House Bed and Breakfast

263 South State Highway 173, P.O. Box 2177, 92352
(714) 336-3292; (800) 429-BLUE-California

The cozy elegance of European decor in an alpine setting welcomes you to Bluebelle House. Guests appreciate immaculate housekeeping, exquisite breakfasts, warm hospitality, and relaxing by the fire or out on the deck. Walk to charming lakeside village, boating, swimming, and restaurants. Private beach club and ice skating are nearby; winter sports 30 minutes away.

Hosts: Rick and Lila Peiffer
Rooms: 5 (3PB; 2 SB) $75-110
Full Breakfast
Credit Cards: A, B
Notes: 2, 5, 9, 11

Romantique Lakeview Lodge

28051 Hwy 189, 92352
(909) 337-6633

Victorian inn featuring antique furnishings, luxurious baths, Victorian fireplaces, VCR's and silver screen classics. Continental breakfast with "sinful" cinnamon rolls. Special midweek rates. Strolling distance from numerous restaurants and shops.

Hosts: Megan Edrick and Linda Fischer
Rooms: 9 (PB) $65-225
Full Breakfast
Credit Cards: A, B, C
Notes: 2 (within two weeks), 5, 7 (some restrictions), 8, 9, 10, 11, 12

Storybook Inn

28717 Highway 18, P.O. Box 362, 92385
(909) 336-1483

An elegant, classic bed and breakfast with nine bedrooms and private baths. All rooms are professionally decorated around the theme of a book with designer linens and abundant pillows. Many have private sitting areas and glass porches. A separate rustic "Call of the Wild" cabin has a stone fireplace, deck and three bedrooms and two baths. A nightly social hour features an array of hot and cold hors d'oeuvres, refreshments, hot chocolate chip cookies and milk to top off your day. Mornings full breakfast can be served to your room, or eaten on our oval dining table enjoying our spectacular 100-mile alpine view or in fine weather one can breakfast al fresco.

Hosts: Kathleen and John Wooley
Rooms: 9 (PB) $98-175 (cabin is $200)
Full Breakfast
Credit Cards: A, B, C, D
Notes: 2, 3, 5, 7, 8, 9, 10, 11, 12

Storybook Inn

LODI

Wine and Roses Country Inn

2505 W. Turner Rd., 95242
(209) 334-6988; (209) 334-6570 (FAX)

Nestled in a secluded five-acre setting of towering trees and old-fashioned flower gardens, our inn is a beautiful, charming, and romantic 92-year-old historical estate that has been converted to an elegant country inn with 9 guest rooms and a special two-room suite with terrace. Hand-made comforters, antiques, collectibles, fresh flowers, library, evening refreshments, delightful breakfasts. Full restaurant featuring "wine country" dining for lunch, dinner, and Sunday brunch. Lake with boating, swimming, fishing, golf, tennis, shopping, museum, zoo within five minutes. Delta Waterways, Old Sacramento Gold Country within 30 minutes.

Hosts: Kris Cromwell, and Del & Sherri Smith
Rooms: 10 (PB) $79-125
Full Breakfast
Credit Cards: A, B, C
Notes: 2, 3, 4, 5, 7, 8, 9, 10, 12

LONG BEACH

Bed and Breakfast of Los Angeles— A Reservation Service

3924 E. 14th Street, 90804
(310) 498-0552 (voice and FAX); (800) 383-3513

B&B of Los Angeles helps travelers make reservations anywhere in California. Our accommodations include private homestays in San Diego, Los Angeles, Santa Barbara, Malibu, Cambria and San Francisco. We also work with historic inns, guest houses, and ranches. Rates range from $45-95 per night, including a full breakfast. Our KIDS WELCOME program is geared toward family travel. These homes emphasize comfort, hospitality and affordability. Please call for information or to order a directory.

Lord Mayor's Inn

435 Cedar Avenue, 90802
(310) 436-0324

An award winning historical landmark, the 1904 home of the first mayor of Long Beach invites you to enjoy the ambience of years gone by. Rooms have 10-foot ceilings and are decorated with period antiques. Each unique bedroom has its private bath and access to a large sundeck. Full breakfast is served in the dining room or deck overlooking the garden. Located near beaches, close by major attractions, within walking distance of convention and civic center and special events held downtown. The right touch for the business and vacation traveler.

Hosts: Laura and Reuben Brasser
Rooms: 5 (PB) $85-95
Full Breakfast
Credit cards: A, B, C
Notes: 2, 5, 7, 9, 12

LOS ANGELES

California Home Hospitality

P.O. Box 66662, 90066
(310) 390-1526 (voice and FAX)

Situated in a quiet residential area, this

NOTES: Credit cards accepted: A MasterCard; B Visa; C American Express; D Discover Card; E Diners Club; F Other; 2 Personal checks accepted; 3 Lunch available; 4 Dinner available; 5 Open all year; 6 Pets

hilltop home enjoys a spectacular view of the Santa Monica mountains including Beverly Hills, Westwood, and Century City. Just 15 minutes from the beach at Santa Monica and adjacent to Marina del Rey Yacht Harbor and Santa Monica Municipal Airport. Hosts stress comfort, cleanliness, secure surroundings, and lots of TLC! Don and Helen are both native to Southern California. Customized sightseeing tours of the city and to Santa Barbara are available.

Hosts: Don and Helen Bourquin
Rooms: 1 (PB) $45
Full Breakfast
Credit Cards: None
Notes: 2, 3, 4, 5, 8, 9, 10

LOWER LAKES

Big Canyon Inn
P.O. Box 1311, 95457
(707) 928-5631

A secluded and peaceful home on a hilly 12 acres of pine and oaks beneath Cobb Mountain, the Big Canyon Inn offers its guests local beauty and recreational activities. Hike on property and search for Lake County diamonds. See wildflowers in the spring, changing colors and crisp air in the fall, or perhaps in winter an occasional snowy landscape. Enjoy fishing and boating on nearby Clear Lake. Our guests stay in a bedroom suite with private porch, private bath and kitchenette.

Hosts: John and Helen Wiegand
Rooms: 2 (PB) $65
Continental Breakfast
Credit Cards: None
Notes: 2, 5, 7, 8, 9, 10

MARIPOSA

Finch Haven
4605 Triangle Road, 95338
(209) 966-4738 (voice and FAX)

A quiet country home on nine acres with panoramic mountain views. Birds, deer, and other abundant wildlife. Two rooms, each with private bath and private deck. Queen and twin beds. Nutritious breakfast. In the heart of the California Gold Rush Country near historic attractions. Convenient access to spectacular Yosemite Valley and Yosemite National Park. A restful place to practice Mark 6:31 and to enjoy Christian hospitality.

Hosts: Bruce and Carol Fincham
Rooms: 2 (PB) $65
Continental Plus
Credit Cards: None
Notes: 2, 5, 7, 8, 9, 11, 12

Oak Meadows, too Bed and Breakfast
5263 Highway 140 North, P. O. Box 619, 95338
(209) 742-6161; (209) 966-2320 (FAX)

Just a short drive to Yosemite National Park, Oak Meadows, too is located in the historic Gold Rush town of Mariposa. Oak Meadows, too was built with New England architecture and turn-of-the-century charm. A stone fireplace greets you upon arrival in the guest parlor, where a continental-plus breakfast is served each morning. All rooms are furnished with hand-made quilts, brass headboards, and charming wallpapers. Central heat and

---

welcome; 7 Children welcome; 8 Tennis nearby; 9 Swimming nearby; 10 Golf nearby; 11 Skiing nearby; 12 May be booked through travel agent

air-conditioning.

Hosts: Frank Ross and Karen Black
Rooms: 6 (PB) $69-89
Expanded Continental Breakfast
Credit Cards: A, B
Notes: 2, 5, 11, 12 (10%)

MENDOCINO

John Dougherty House
571 Ukiah Street, P. O. Box 817, 95460
(707) 937-5266

The historic John Dougherty House was
built in 1867 and is one of the oldest houses
in Mendocino. Located on land bordered
by Ukiah and Albion Streets, the inn has
some of the best ocean and bay views in
the village. Steps away from great restaurants and shopping, but years removed
from 20th-century reality. The inn is furnished with period country antiques. Cottages, cabin, and water tower.

Hosts: David and Marion Wells
Rooms: 6 (PB) $85-165
Full Breakfast
Credit Cards: None
Notes: 2, 5

John Dougherty House

The Jabberwock

MONTEREY

The Jabberwock
598 Laine Street, 93940
(408) 372-4777

Once a convent, The Jabberwock has
retained the warmth of its historic flavor
with antique beds, down comforters and
pillows, lace-trimmed sheets, and fresh
flowers in all guest rooms. Each morning
the enticement of snarkleberry flumptious
or burndt blumbleberry lures everyone
down for a full breakfast by the fireplace in
the dining room. At five o'clock, hors
d'oeuvres are served on the enclosed
sunporch looking out over the bay and
gardens. Finally, Vorpal Bear tucks everyone in bed with cookies and milk before snuggling under the comforter. Spend
a memory at The Jabberwock.

Hosts: Jim and Barbara Allen
Rooms: 7 (3PB; 4SB) $100-180
Full Breakfast
Credit Cards: A, B
Notes: 2, 5, 8, 9, 10, 12

NOTES: Credit cards accepted: A MasterCard; B Visa; C American Express; D Discover Card; E Diners
Club; F Other; 2 Personal checks accepted; 3 Lunch available; 4 Dinner available; 5 Open all year; 6 Pets

MT. SHASTA

Mt. Shasta Ranch Bed and Breakfast

1008 W. A. Barr Road, 96067
(916) 926-3870; (916) 926-6882 (FAX)

The inn is situated in a rural setting with a majestic view of Mt. Shasta and features a main lodge, carriage house, and cottage. Group accommodations are available. Our breakfast room is ideally suited for seminars and retreats with large seating capacity. The game room includes piano, Ping-Pong, pool table, and board games. Guests also enjoy an outdoor jacuzzi. Nearby recreational facilities include alpine and Nordic skiing, fishing, hiking, mountain bike rentals, surrey rides, and museums. Call for pastor's discount.

Hosts: Bill and Mary Larsen
Rooms: 9 (4PB; 5SB) $55-75
Cabin: 1
Full Breakfast
Credit Cards: A, B, C
Notes: 2, 5, 7, 8, 9, 10, 11, 12

NAPA

Hennessey House Bed and Breakfast

1727 Main Street, 94559
(707) 226-3774; (707) 226-2975 (FAX)

Hennessey House, a beautiful Eastlake-style Queen Anne Victorian located in downtown Napa, is listed in the National Register of Historic Places. It features antique furnishings, fireplaces, whirlpools, patios, and a sauna. The dining room, where a sumptuous breakfast is served,

features one of the finest examples of a hand-painted stamped tin ceiling in California. Just a short walk to the Wine Train!

Hostesses: Lauriann and Andrea
Rooms: 10 (PB) $80-155
Full Breakfast
Credit Cards: A, B, C
Notes: 2, 5, 7, 10, 12

La Belle Epoque

1386 Calistoga Avenue, 94559
(707) 257-2161; (800) 238-8070

Elaborate Queen Anne architecture and extensive use of stained glass are complemented by elegant period furnishings. This century-old Victorian boasts six tastefully decorated guest rooms, each with private bath, two with fireplace. A generous, gourmet breakfast is offered each morning, either by fireside in the formal dining room or in the more relaxed atmosphere of the inn's plant-filled sunroom. Walk to Old Town, Wine Train, Opera House.

Hosts: Merlin and Claudia Wedepohl (owners)
Rooms: 6 (PB) $110-150
Full Gourmet Breakfast
Credit Cards: A, B, C, D
Notes: 2, 5, 8, 9, 10, 12

OAKHURST

Ople's Guest House

41118 Highway 41, 93644
(209) 683-4317

Set on a hill and half hidden by trees is the rambling style house where Yosemite travelers make a stop for the night. The easy-going atmosphere, the clean and pleasant accommodations, and affordable rates make Ople's Guest House a favorite

welcome; 7 Children welcome; 8 Tennis nearby; 9 Swimming nearby; 10 Golf nearby; 11 Skiing nearby; 12 May be booked through travel agent

in Oakhurst. Families are welcome, and guests may enjoy a fireplace and TV in the living room. You will appreciate the guest house that offers off-street parking and wheelchair access.

Host: Ople Smith
Rooms: 3 (SB) $40
Continental Breakfast
Credit Cards: A, B, D, F
Notes: 2, 5, 7, 8, 9, 10, 11, 12

PALM SPRINGS

Casa Cody Bed and Breakfast Country Inn

175 South Cahuilla Road, 92262
(619) 320-9346; (619) 325-8610 (FAX)

A romantic, historic hideaway is nestled against the spectacular San Jacinto mountains in the heart of Palm Springs Village. Completely redecorated in Santa Fe decor, it has 17 ground-level units consisting of hotel rooms, studio suites, and one- and two-bedroom suites with private patios, fireplaces, fully equipped, tiled kitchens. Cable TV and private phones; two pools; secluded, tree-shaded whirlpool spa.

Hosts: Therese Hayes and Frank Tysen
Rooms: 17 (PB) $35 summer midweek; $175 winter weekend
Continental Breakfast
Credit Cards: A, B, C
Notes: 2, 5, 6 (limited), 7 (limited), 8, 9, 10, 11

PALO ALTO

Adella Villa

122 Atherton Ave., 94027-4021
(415) 321-5195; (415) 325-5121 (FAX)

Luxurious 20's Italian villa on one acre of lovely manicured gardens with pool, foun-

tains, antiques and music room featuring Steinway grand piano. Four-thousand-square-foot inn with all the amenities! Pamper yourself in one of our jacuzzi tubs. Enjoy a full breakfast. Refreshments available throughout the day. Thirty minutes from San Francisco.

Hostess: Tricia Young
Rooms: 5 (PB) $99
Full Breakfast
Credit Cards: A, B, C, E
Notes: 2, 5, 8, 10, 12

PLACERVILLE

Combellack-Blair House

3059 Cedar Ravine, 95667
(916) 622-3764

This gracious Queen Anne Victorian home has stood as a landmark to travelers and Placerville alike for nearly a century. When you enter the front door you will enjoy the magnificent sight of the spiral staircase, which is a work of art. The front parlor is a collection of period furnishings recalling the 1890's. The house is located in quaint and historical Placerville. One block away is Main Street with many interesting antique shops, restaurants, and specialty boutiques.

Hosts: Al and Rosalie McConnell
Rooms: 2 (PB) $89-99
Full Breakfast
Credit Cards: A, B
Notes: 5, 10, 11

River Rock Inn

1756 Georgetown Drive, 95661
(916) 622-7640

Innkeeper Dorothy Irvin welcomes you to the gold country's River Rock Inn. Its

---

NOTES: Credit cards accepted: A MasterCard; B Visa; C American Express; D Discover Card; E Diners Club; F Other; 2 Personal checks accepted; 3 Lunch available; 4 Dinner available; 5 Open all year; 6 Pets

comfortable rooms tastefully furnished with antiques front on the spacious deck with uninterrupted view of the river. The large living room encourages you to relax with TV, conversation or listening to the sounds of the river. Gold Mine tours, Marshall State Park, fishing, hiking, white-water rafting are all available nearby. Hot tub on premises to relax in after activities.

Hostess: Dorothy Irvin
Rooms: 4 (2PB; 2(half baths)) $80-95
Full Breakfast
Credit Cards: None
Notes: 2, 5, 7, 8, 9, 10, 11, 12

POINT REYES STATION

Jasmine Cottage

P.O. Box 56, 94956
(415) 663-1166

The secluded privacy of these two country cottages is the ideal arrangement in a B&B: All amenities of a bed and breakfast with the seclusion of a vacation home, set in its own charming garden behind the owner's schoolhouse home. Jasmine Cottage is a complete home-away-from-home with a fully equipped kitchen, woodstove, garden room, naturalist's library, oak desk, queen beds and two twins, romantic alcove, and beautiful views of sunsets. Only one hour north of San Francisco and just five minutes from Pt. Reyes National Seashore on the California Coast! A secluded hot tub in a garden setting is ready for your relaxation. A full breakfast is included.

Hostess: Karen Gray
Rooms: 2 cottages (PB) $115
Full Breakfast
Credit Cards: A, B
Notes: 2, 5, 6, 7, 9, 12

Jasmine Cottage

Carriage House Bed and Breakfast

325 Mesa Road, P.O. Box 1239, 94956
(415) 663-8627; (415) 663-8431 (FAX)

Adjacent to the Point Reyes National Seashore, one hour north of San Francisco. Built in the 1920's and recently remodeled into two peaceful spacious suites. Bedrooms have queen beds, living room with fireplaces, queen sleeping couch, single daybed, and antiques. Full baths, complete kitchens, TV, outdoor BBQs. Families welcome, childcare available with advance notice. Over 100 miles of nearby trails for hiking, bicycling, horsback riding, bird watching, beach combing and whale-watching. Suite can accommodate 5.

Hostess: Felicity Kirsch
Rooms: 2 (PB) $100-120
Choice of Continental or Full Breakfast
Credit Cards: None
Notes: 2, 5, 7, 8, 10, 12

RUTHERFORD

Rancho Caymus

1140 Rutherford Rd., P.O. Box 78, 94573
(707) 963-1777; (707) 963-5387 (FAX)

This Spanish hacienda-style inn was designed to capture the rustic spirit of early California, with 26 suites encircling an

welcome; 7 Children welcome; 8 Tennis nearby; 9 Swimming nearby; 10 Golf nearby; 11 Skiing nearby; 12 May be booked through travel agent

award-winning garden courtyard. Rancho Caymus is located in the heart of Napa Valley, California's premier wine-growing region, within minutes of the area's top wineries. The inn is a unique blending of modern comforts (jacuzzi tubs in five of the suites), classic crafts (hand-carved Ecuadorian furnishings), and romantic atmosphere (fireplaces in all but four of the suites). Facilities are also available for meetings, retreats, and receptions.

Host: Otto Komes
Rooms: 26 (PB) $100-275
Continental Breakfast
Credit Cards: A, B, C
Notes: 3, 5, 12

Rancho Caymus

ST. HELENA

Bartels Ranch and Country Inn

1200 Conn Valley Road, 94574
(707) 963-4001; (707) 963-5100 (FAX)

Situated in the heart of the world-famous Napa Valley wine country is this secluded, romantic, elegant country estate overlooking a "100-acre valley with a 10,000-acre view." Honeymoon "Heart of the Valley" suite has sunken jacuzzi, sauna, shower, stone fireplace, and private deck with

vineyard view. Romantic, award-winning accommodations, expansive entertainment room, poolside lounging, personalized itineraries, afternoon refreshments, pool table, fireplace, library and terraces overlooking the vineyard. Bicycle to nearby wineries, lake, golf, tennis, fishing, boating, mineral spas, and bird watching.

Hostess: Jami Bartels
Rooms: 4 (PB) $99-275
Expanded Continental Breakfast
Credit Cards: A, B, C, D
Notes: 2, 3, 4, 5, 8, 9, 10, 12

Cinnamon Bear Bed and Breakfast

1407 Kearney Street, 94574
(707) 963-4653

Cinnamon Bear is furnished in the style of the 1920s with many fine antiques. Gleaming hardwood floors and Oriental carpets add to its unique elegance. Relax in front of the fireplace in the living room, or watch the world go by on the spacious front porch. Puzzles, games, and books are available in the parlor for your enjoyment, or peruse a selection of local menus.

Hostess: Genny Jenkins
Rooms: 4 (PB) $105-155 (midweek discount rates)
Full Breakfast
Credit Cards: A, B
Notes: 2, 5, 8, 9, 10

Cinnamon Bear Bed and Breakfast

Erika's Hillside

285 Fawn Park, 94574
(707) 963-2887

You will be welcomed with warm European hospitality when you arrive at this hillside chalet that is more than 100 years old. Just two miles from St. Helena, you will find a peaceful and romantic, wooded country setting with a view of vineyards and wineries. The spacious, airy rooms have private entrances and baths, fireplaces, and hot tubs. Continental breakfast and German specialties are served on the patio or in the garden room.

Hostess: Erika Cunningham
Rooms: 3 (PB) $65-165
Continental Breakfast
Credit Cards: A, B, C, E
Notes: 2, 5, 7, 8, 9, 10, 12

SAN FRANCISCO

Amsterdam Hotel

749 Taylor Street, 94108
(415) 673-3277; (800) 637-3444;
(415) 673-0453 (FAX)

Originally built in 1909, the hotel reflects the charm of a small European hotel. It is situated on Nob Hill, just two blocks from the cable car.

Hostess: Orisa
Rooms: 31 (26PB; 5SB) $49-70
Continental Breakfast
Credit Cards: A, B, C
Notes: 5, 8, 9, 11

Casa Arquello

225 Arguello Blvd., 94118
(415) 752-9482

Comfortable rooms in this cheerful, elegant flat are only 15 minutes from the center of town in a desirable residential neighborhood convenient to Golden Gate Park, the Presidio, Golden Gate Bridge, restaurants, and shops. Public transportation is at the corner.

Hostess: Emma Baires and Marina McKenzie
Rooms: % (2PB; 3SB) $40-67
Expanded Continental Breakfast
Credit Cards: None
Notes: 2, 5, 7, 8, 9, 10

The Chateau Tivoli Bed and Breakfast Inn

1057 Steiner Street, 94115
(415) 776-5462; (800) 228-1647;
(415) 776-0505 (FAX)

The Chateau is a landmark mansion built in 1892. Guests experience a time travel journey back to San Francisco's golden age of opulence. Choose from five rooms, two with fireplaces, and two suites; all with phones. Breakfast is served in guest rooms or in the dining room. Near shops, restaurants, opera, and symphony. Reservation deposit required.

Hosts: Rodney, Willard, and Shiobhan
Rooms: 7 (5PB; 2SB) $80-200
Full Breakfast; Continental breakfast weekdays
Credit Cards: A, B, C
Notes: 2, 5, 7, 8, 9, 10, 12

The Monte Cristo

600 Presidio Avenue, 94115
(415) 931-1875

The Monte Cristo has been a part of San Francisco since 1875, located two blocks from the elegantly restored Victorian shops, restaurants, and antique stores on Sacramento Street. There is convenient trans-

welcome; 7 Children welcome; 8 Tennis nearby; 9 Swimming nearby; 10 Golf nearby; 11 Skiing nearby; 12 May be booked through travel agent

portation to downtown San Francisco and to the financial district. Each room is elegantly furnished with authentic period pieces.

Host: George Yuan
Rooms: 14 (11PB; 3 SB) $63-108
Full Buffet Breakfast
Credit Cards: A, B, C, D, E
Notes: 5, 7, 12

SAN GREGORIO

Rancho San Gregorio

Route 1, Box 54, 94074 (hwy 84)
(415) 747-0810; (415) 747-0184 (FAX)

Five miles inland from the Pacific Ocean is an idyllic rural valley where Rancho San Gregorio welcomes travelers to share relaxed hospitality. Picnic, hike, or bike in wooded parks or on ocean beaches. Our country breakfast features local specialties. Located 45 minutes from San Francisco, Santa Cruz, and the Bay area.

Hosts: Bud and Lee Raynor
Rooms: 4 (PB) $65-135
Full Breakfast
Credit Cards: A, B, C
Notes: 2, 5, 7, 10

SANTA BARBARA

Long's Seaview Bed and Breakfast

317 Piedmont Road, 93105
(805) 687-2947

This ranch-style home overlooking Santa Barbara has views of the ocean and Channel Islands. The guest room with private entrance is furnished with antiques and

king bed. A huge patio and gardens are available. Near all attractions, beach, and Solvang. Your friendly host will be happy to provide you with maps and information about the area.

Host: La Verne Long
Room: 1 (PB) $75-79
Full Breakfast
Credit Cards: None
Notes: 2, 8, 9, 10

The Old Yacht Club Inn

431 Corona Del Mar Drive, 93103
(805) 962-1277; (800) 549-1676 California;
(800) 676-1676 U.S.A. (reservation only);
(805) 962-3989 (FAX)

The inn at the beach! These 1912 California craftsman and 1925 early California-style homes house nine individually decorated guest rooms furnished with antiques. Bicycles, beach chairs, and towels are included, and an evening social hour is provided. Gourmet dinner is available on Saturdays.

Hostesses: Nancy, Sandy, and Lu
Rooms: 9 (PB) $75-150
Full Breakfast
Credit Cards: A, B, C, D, E
Notes: 2, 3 (picnic), 4 (Saturdays), 5, 7, 8, 9, 10, 12

Simpson House Inn

121 East Arrellaga, 93101
(805) 963-7067; (800) 676-1280

This landmark Victorian jewel is secluded in an acre of formally landscaped gardens with magnificent shade trees. Intimate arbors, teak benches and fountains yet just a five-minute walk to fine restaurants, shops and historic Santa Barbara. The garden cottages, old barn suites, and guest rooms are elegantly appointed with antiques, Oriental carpets and fine art. They feature private decks overlooking the gardens, wood-burning fireplaces, jacuzzi tubs. A full gourmet breakfast can be enjoyed on your private deck, the spacious veranda, or fountain patio. Rates include afternoon beverages, hors d'oeuvres, bicycles, English croquet, and beach equipment.

Hostesses: Gillean Wilson, Linda, and Glyn Davies
Rooms: 13 (PB) $85-250
Full Breakfast
Credit Cards: A, B, C, D
Notes: 2, 5, 8, 9

Summerland Inn

2161 Ortega Hill Road, P. O. Box 1209, 93067
(805) 969-5225

Located minutes from beautiful Santa Barbara, this newly built New England-style bed and breakfast is a must for southern California travelers. Enjoy ocean views, fireplace rooms, brass and four-poster beds, country folk art, biblical quotations, and Christian motifs. Christian reading material is available. All rooms include cable TV and free local calls.

Host: James Farned
Rooms: 11 (PB) $65-140 (10% discount to *Christian Bed and Breakfast Directory* patrons)
Continental Breakfast
Credit Cards: A, B, C, E
Notes: 2, 5, 7, 8, 9, 10

The Upham Hotel and Garden Cottages

1404 De La Vina Street, 93101
(805) 962-0058; (805) 963 2825 (FAX)

The Upham is a charming hotel located in the heart of Santa Barbara, with 49 guest rooms, some with fireplace, cottages, private patios or porches. One of Santa Barbara's finest establishments and the oldest operating hotel in Southern California. We know you and your guests will be delighted with Upham as so many others have been.

Rooms: 49 (PB) $100-170
Continental Breakfast
Credit Cards: A, B, C, D, E
Notes: 3, 4, 5, 7, 8, 9, 10, 12

Valli's View

340 N. Sierra Vista Rd., 93108
(805) 969-1272

You'll love this beautiful home, its gardens, sunny patios, shady deck, and ever-changing mountain views. The charming guest room has color TV and private bath. The spacious back patios offer lounges for sunning and porch swings for relaxing. A shady fern garden surrounds the deck that overlooks mountains and valley. In the evening relax in the living room around grand piano and fireplace. This is a place God has blessed us with, and we enjoy sharing it with others.

Hosts: Valli and Larry Stevens
Rooms: 1 (PB) $75
Full Breakfast
Credit Cards: None
Notes: 2, 5, 6 (outside), 7, 8, 9, 10, 12

SANTA CRUZ

Babbling Brook Inn

1025 Laurel Street, 95060
(408) 427-2437; (800) 866-1131;
(408) 427-2457 (FAX)

The foundations of the inn date back to the 1790's when padres from the local mis-

welcome; 7 Children welcome; 8 Tennis nearby; 9 Swimming nearby; 10 Golf nearby; 11 Skiing nearby; 12 May be booked through travel agent

sion built a grist mill to take advantage of the stream to grind corn. In the 19th century, a water wheel generated power for a tannery. Then a few years later, a rustic log cabin was built, which remains as the heart of the inn. Most of the rooms are chalets in the garden, surrounded by pines and redwoods, cascading waterfalls, and gardens.

Hostess: Helen King
Rooms: 12 (PB) $85-150
Full Breakfast
Credit Cards: A, B, C, D, E, F
Notes: 2, 5, 7 (with restrictions), 8, 9, 10, 12

Valley View

P.O. Box 66593, 95067
(415) 321-5195; (415) 325-5121 (FAX)

Secluded, self-catering, Frank Lloyd Wright style glass/wood house on a cliff in the forest overlooking 20,000 acres of redwoods. Hot tub on large-view deck. Piano, stereo, cable TV, plush furnishings, one bedroom, one bath, 1,600-square-foot home ten minutes from Santa Cruz Beach. Two night minimum. Entire house is yours.

Hosts: Scott and Trisha Young
Rooms: 1 (PB) $125
Continental Breakfast
Credit Cards: A, B, E
Notes: 2, 5, 9, 10, 12

SANTA ROSA

Pygmalion House

331 Orange Street, 95407
(707) 526-3407

Pygmalion House, one of Santa Rosa's historical landmarks, is a fine example of Victorian Queen Anne architecture. This charming home was built in the 1880's on land owned by one of the city's leading developers, Mr. Thomas Ludwig. This house withstood the great earthquake and fire of 1906 that devastated much of Santa Rosa's heritage. Pygmalion House is a member of the Bed and Breakfast Innkeepers of Northern California.

Hostess: Lola L. Wright
Rooms: 5 (PB) $50-70
Full Breakfast
Credit Cards: A, B, C
Notes: 2, 5, 8, 9, 10, 12

SEAL BEACH

The Seal Beach Inn and Gardens

212 Fifth Street, 90740
(310) 493-2416; (310) 779-0483 (FAX)

Just outside Los Angeles and 20 miles from Disneyland, nestled in a charming beachside community is The Seal Beach Inn, French Mediterranean in style. Our Old World inn is surrounded by wrought iron balconies and lush gardens. The rooms vary, but all are furnished with antiques, hand-painted tiles, and lace comforters. Sit by the fireplace in our library, or listen to the fountains. Suites and all the services of a fine hotel are available.

Hosts: Marjorie Bettenhausen and Harty Schmaehl
Rooms: 23 (PB) $108-175
Full Breakfast
Credit Cards: A, B, C, D, F
Notes: 3, 4, 5, 8, 9, 10, 12

NOTES: Credit cards accepted: A MasterCard; B Visa; C American Express; D Discover Card; E Diners Club; F Other; 2 Personal checks accepted; 3 Lunch available; 4 Dinner available; 5 Open all year; 6 Pets

SONOMA

Sparrow's Nest Inn
424 Denmark St., 95476
(707) 996-3750

Sparrow's Nest Inn is a charming country cottage in the historic town of Sonoma. It is near the lovely town square and 45 minutes from the glorious Golden Gate Bridge. Surrounded by private flower gardens and patio, the one-bedroom cottage includes a small kitchen, breakfast nook, living room with phone and cable television, and bathroom. The decor is light, pleasing, and comfortable English country style. We hope to make your visit enjoyable and memorable!

Hosts: Thomas and Kathleen Anderson
Rooms: 1 (single cottage) (PB) $85-105
Both Full and Continental Breakfast available
Credit Cards: A, B, C
Notes: 2, 5, 6 (by special arrangement), 7 (over 10 yrs old), 8, 10

SUTTER CREEK

Gold Quartz Inn
15 Bryson Drive, 95685
(209) 267-9155, (800) 752-8738;
(209) 267-9170 (FAX)

An elegant getaway in Queen Anne style, located in the heart of the California Mother Lode Gold Country. Gold Quartz Inn blends the warmth and romance of a bed and breakfast with the comfort and luxury of an elegant hotel. Sleeping rooms are individually decorated with antiques. Each room has large private bath, telephone, TV, sitting porches. Entire inn handicap accessible and is a no smoking facility. One hour drive from Sacramento. King size beds available.

Hostess: Wendy Woolrich
Rooms: 24 (PB) $70-125
Full Breakfast
Credit Cards: A, B, C, D
Notes: 2, 5, 10, 11, 12

Gold Quartz Inn

Sutter Creek Inn
75 Main Street, P.O. Box 385, 95685
(209) 267-5606; (209) 267-0642

The inn is known for its fireplaces, hanging beds, and private patios. All rooms have private baths and electric blankets. All guests gather 'round the kitchen fireplace to enjoy a hot breakfast. A large library in the living room invites guests to while away the time before afternoon refreshments.

Hostess: Jane Way
Rooms: 19 (PB) $45-135
Full Breakfast
Credit Cards: None
Notes: 2, 5, 7, 8, 9, 10, 11, 12

---

welcome; 7 Children welcome; 8 Tennis nearby; 9 Swimming nearby; 10 Golf nearby; 11 Skiing nearby; 12 May be booked through travel agent

TRINIDAD

Trinidad Bed and Breakfast

560 Edwards Street, P. O. Box 849, 95570
(707) 677-0840

Our Cape Cod-style home overlooks beautiful Trinidad Bay and offers spectacular views of the rugged coastline and fishing harbor below. Two suites, one with fireplace, and two upstairs bedrooms are available. We are surrounded by dozens of beaches, trails, and Redwood National Parks; within walking distance of restaurants and shops. Breakfast delivered to guests staying in suites, while a family-style breakfast is served to guests in rooms.

Hosts: Paul and Carol Kirk
Rooms: 4 (PB) $105-145
Expanded Continental Breakfast
Credit Cards: A, B
Closed Monday and Tuesday, November 1 to February 28.
Notes: 2, 8, 10

UKIAH

Vichy Hot Springs Resort and Inn

2605 Vichy Springs Road, 95482
(707) 462-9515

Vichy Springs is a delightful two-hour drive north of San Francisco. Historic cottages and rooms await with delightful vistas from all locations. Vichy Springs features naturally sparkling 90-degree mineral baths, a communal 104-degree pool, and Olympic-size pool, along with 700 private acres with trails and roads for hiking, jogging, picnicking, and mountain bicycling. Vichy's idyllic setting is a quiet, healing environment.

Hosts: Gilbert and Marjorie Ashoff
Rooms: 14 (PB) $115-160
Full Breakfast
Credit Cards: A, B, C, D, E, F
Notes: 2, 5, 7, 8, 9, 10, 12

VENTURA

La Mer

411 Poli Street, 93001
(805) 643-3600

Built in 1890, this is a romantic European getaway in a Victorian Cape Cod home. A historic landmark nestled on a green hillside overlooking the spectacular California coastline. The distinctive guest rooms, all with private entrances, are each a European adventure, furnished in European antiques to capture the feeling of a specific country. Bavarian buffet-style breakfast and complimentary refreshments; midweek packages; horse carriage rides. AAA and Mobil approved.

Hostess: Gisela Flender Baida
Rooms: 5 (PB) $80-155
Full Breakfast
Credit Cards: A, B
Notes: 2, 5, 8, 9, 10, 12

WESTPORT

Howard Creek Ranch

P. O. Box 121, 95488
(707) 964-6725

Howard Creek Ranch is a historic 1867 oceanfront farm bordered by miles of beach and mountains in a wilderness area. Flower gardens, antiques, fireplaces, redwoods, a

---

NOTES: Credit cards accepted: A Master Card; B Visa; C American Express; D Discover Card; E Diners Club; F Other; 2 Personal checks accepted; 3 Lunch available; 4 Dinner available; 5 Open all year; 6 Pets

75-foot swinging footbridge over Howard Creek, cabins, hot tub, sauna, cold pool, and nearby horseback riding are combined with comfort, hospitality, and good food.

Hosts: Charles and Sally Grigg
Rooms: 9 (8PB; 1 SB) $55-125
Full Breakfast
Credit Cards: A, B
Notes: 2, 5, 6 (by arrangement), 7 (by arrangement)

WHITTIER

Coleen's California Casa

P. O. Box 9302, 90608
(310) 699-8427

Come to the top of the hill and find paradise. This home is less than five minutes from the #605 freeway, yet seems rural. The peacefulness is enhanced by the luxuriant patio where you will enjoy a full breakfast prepared by your home economist hostess. Near Disneyland, Knott's Berry Farm, and the beach, you will enjoy a king-sized electric adjustable bed or extra long twin beds, private bath, private entrance, off-street parking and a restful stay amid beautiful flowers and plants. The magnificent view of the city will enhance your leisurely enjoyment.

Hostess: Coleen Davis
Rooms: 3 and 2 suites (4PB; 1SB)) $60-65
Full Breakfast
Credit Cards: None
Notes: 2, 3, 4, 5, 7, 8, 9, 10

Howard Creek Ranch

welcome; 7 Children welcome; 8 Tennis nearby; 9 Swimming nearby; 10 Golf nearby; 11 Skiing nearby; 12 May be booked through travel agent

Colorado

ALLENSPARK

Allenspark Lodge

184 Main, 80510
(303) 747-2552

A classic high mountain bed an breakfast, nestled in a flower-starred village. Comfortable rooms, warm hospitality and magnificent surroundings make our historic, cozy, beautifully remodeled lodge the ideal place for that vacation weekend, reception, reunion, or retreat. Let the magic begin! Hot tub, continental breakfast, hospitality, and game room, near Rocky Mountain National Park.

Hosts: Mike and Becky Osmun
Rooms: 14 (5PB; 9SB) $39.95-74.95
Continental Breakfast
Credit Cards: A, B, D
Notes: 2, 3, 4, 5, 7, 11, 12

ASPEN

Cresta Haus Lodge

1301 E. Cooper Avenue, 81611
(303) 925-7081; (800) 344-3853; (303) 925-1610 (FAX)

European charm and ambience in 31 distinctive rooms featuring private baths, color cable TV and telephones. Complimentary buffet breakfast and apres-ski, daily housekeeping, laundry facilities, airport transportation, ample parking. Located one-quarter mile from downtown Aspen. Perfect peaceful setting for reunions, retreats, and families. Enjoy mountain views, outdoor hot tub and pool area, sauna, and mountain bike rentals. Catering available for special occasions. Informal meeting space for up to 30 people.

Hostess: Melinda Goldrich
Rooms: 31 (PB) $50-115 (summer) $75-175 (winter)
Deluxe Continental Breakfast
Credit Cards: A, B
Notes: 2, 5, 6, 7, 8, 9, 10, 11, 12

Cresta Haus Lodge

Little Red Ski Haus

118 East Cooper, 81611
(303) 925-3333

We are a quaint historic lodge that has had only one owner for 30 years. The 100-year-old Victorian house has additional rooms for a total of 21 bedrooms. Christian hosts look forward to welcoming Christian groups to their lodge. Rates vary depending on number of guests and pri-

---

vate or shared baths.

Hosts: Marge Babcock Rily and Jeannene Babcock
Rooms: 21 (4PB; 17SB) $70-110
Continental Breakfast in summer/fall
Includes Full Breakfast
Credit Cards: A, B, C
Notes: 7, 8, 9, 10, 11

BOULDER

Briar Rose Bed and Breakfast

2151 Arapahoe Ave., 80302
(303) 442-3007

Elegant small inn close to University of Colorado and downtown. Unique rooms have period antiques, featherbed comforters, fresh flowers, and good books. Friendly, attentive service includes afternoon and evening tea with our own shortbread cookies. Big breakfast served in dining room or on sun porch.

Hosts: Margaret and Bob Weisenbach
Rooms: 9 (PB) $85-119
Expanded Continental Breakfast
Credit Cards: A, B, C, E
Notes: 2, 5, 7, 8, 10, 11, 12

BRECKENRIDGE

Allaire Timbers Inn

9511 Hwy #9, South Main St., PO Box 4653, 80424
(303) 453-7530; (800) 624-4904; (303) 453-8699 (FAX)

Breckenridge's distinctive new mountain inn. Nestled in the trees at the south end of Main Street, this log house offers uniquely decorated guest rooms. Two suites boast private fireplace and hot tub. Relax by a crackling fire in the log and beam Greatroom. Unwind in the outdoor spa overlooking spectacular views of Breckenridge and Ten Mile Range. Gourmet breakfasts. Wheelchair accessible.

Hosts: Jack and Kathy Gumph
Rooms: 10 (PB) $105-225
Full Breakfast in ski season; Extended Continental Breakfast in summer
Credit Cards: A, B, C, D
Notes: 2, 5, 10, 11, 12

COLORADO SPRINGS

Holden House—1902 Bed and Breakfast Inn

1102 West Pikes Peak Avenue, 80904
(719) 471-3980

Historic 1902 storybook Victorian and carriage house filled with antiques and family treasures. Guest rooms boast feather pillows, individual decor, period furnishings and queen beds. Suites include fireplaces, "tubs for two," and more! Centrally located in residential area near historic Old Colorado City, shopping, restaurants and attractions. "The Romance of the Past with the Comforts of Today." Two friendly resident cats—Muffin and Mingtoy. AAA/Mobil approved. Full gourmet breakfast.

Hosts: Sallie and Welling Clark
Rooms: 5 (PB) $65-95
Full Breakfast
Credit Cards: A, B, C, D, E
Notes: 2, 5, 8, 9, 10, 12

Holden House

---

year; 6 Pets welcome; 7 Children welcome; 8 Tennis nearby; 9 Swimming nearby; 10 Golf nearby; 11 Skiing nearby; 12 May be booked through travel agent

DENVER

Castle Marne—A Luxury Urban Inn

1572 Race Street, 80203
(303) 331-0621

Come fall under the spell of one of Denver's grandest historic mansions. Your stay at the Castle Marne combines Old World elegance with modern day convenience and comfort. Each guest room is a unique experience in pampered luxury. All rooms have private baths. Afternoon tea and a full gourmet breakfast are served in the cherry-paneled dining room. Castle Marne is a certified Denver Landmark and on the National Register of Historic Structures.

Hosts: The Paiker Family
Rooms: 9 (PB) $85-165
Full Breakfast
Credit Cards: A, B, C, D, E, F
Notes: 2, 3, 4, 5, 8, 9, 10, 11, 12

Queen Anne Inn

2147 Tremont Place, 80205
(303) 296-6666 (Voice and FAX); (800) 432-4667

Two side-by-side Queen Anne Victorians (1879-1886) face Benedict Fountain Park in Downtown Denver. Fourteen rooms include four "Gallery suites" dedicated to well-known artists Remington, Rockwell, Audubon, and Calder. All have private baths, phones, fresh flowers, chamber music. Some have special tubs, fireplaces; one has a hot tub. The most honored B&B in Colorado; it was recently named best of the ten most romantic B&Bs in the nation and one of seven most romantic destinations in Colorado.

Host: Tom King
Rooms: 14 (PB) $75-150
Full Breakfast
Credit Cards: A, B, C, D, E
Notes: 2, 5, 8, 9, 10, 11, 12

DURANGO

Country Sunshine Bed and Breakfast

35130 Highway 550 North, 81301
(303) 247-2853; (800) 383-2853

This spacious ranch home on the Animas River has Ponderosa pines, quilts, and an informal atmosphere. It is a safe place for children and adults. A spacious hot springs spa is available to relax in, and there are plenty of common areas. The friendly hosts are in their sixth season.

Hosts: Jim and Jill Anderson
Rooms: 6 (PB) $70-80
Full Breakfast
Credit Cards: A, B
Notes: 2, 7, 9, 10, 11, 12

Country Sunshine

Logwood Bed and Breakfast—The Verheyden Inn
35060 U. S. Highway 550, 81301
(303) 259-4396

Built in 1988, this 4800-square-foot red, cedar log home sits on 15 acres amid the beautiful San Juan Mountains and beside the Animas River. Guest rooms are decorated with a southwestern flair. Homemade country quilts adorn the country-made queen-size beds. Private baths in all guest rooms. A large, river rock fireplace warms the elegant living and dining areas in the winter season. Award-winning desserts are served in the evening. Pamper yourselves. Come home to LOGWOOD.

Hosts: Debby and Greg Verheyden
Rooms: 5 (PB) $65-75
Full Breakfast
Credit Cards: A, B
Notes: 2, 5, 7 (over eight), 9, 10, 11, 12

EATON

The Victorian Vernada
515 Cheyenne Avenue, P.O. Box 361, 80615
(303) 454-3890

Beautiful Queen Anne 100-year-old home that features baby grand player piano, bicycles-built-for-two, hand-carved oak staircase, fireplaces, balcony with a mountain view, large wrap around porch, an enclosed back yard for guests to cook lunch or dinner, and a whirlpool bath. We are within one hour's drive to Denver, Estes Park, and Cheyenne, Wyoming.

Hosts: Dick and Nadine White
Rooms: 3 (1PB; 2SB) $45-60
Full Breakfast
Credit Cards: None
Notes: 2, 5, 7, 10, 11, 12

ESTES PARK

RiverSong Inn
P.O. Box 1910, 80517
(303) 586-4666; (303) 586-6185

RiverSong, a romantic nine-room country inn, is nestled at the end of a winding country lane on 30 wooded acres. There are trout streams and ponds, hiking trails, and porch swings. Many of the rooms have breath-taking views of the snow-capped peaks and nearby Rocky Mountain National Park; most have fireplaces and spacious whirlpool tubs for two. At RiverSong, you'll be lulled to sleep by the melody of our mountain stream.

Hosts: Gary and Sue Mansfield
Rooms: 9 (PB) $85-165
Full Gourmet Breakfast
Credit Cards: A, B
Notes: None

River Song Inn

FAIRPLAY

Hand Hotel Bed and Breakfast
P.O. Box 459, 531 Front St., 80440
(719) 836-3595

The Hand Hotel, built in the 1930's, overlooks the north fork of the South Platte River and Mosquito Range at an elevation of 9,950 feet. The hotel was totally reno-

year; 6 Pets welcome; 7 Children welcome; 8 Tennis nearby; 9 Swimming nearby; 10 Golf nearby; 11 Skiing nearby; 12 May be booked through travel agent

vated in 1987 to a turn-of-the-century Western/Victorian motif. The South Park area offers excellent hiking, jeeping, fishing, and South Park City Museum in the summer and a Nordic Center in Fairplay or downhill skiing in Breckenridge just 23 miles away. We're on the quiet side of the divide. Come see for yourself and enjoy.

Host: Pat Pocius
Rooms: 11 (PB) $60 (summer) $48 (off-season)
Extended Continental Breakfast
Credit Cards: A, B
Notes: 2, 5, 6 (with restrictions), 7 (with restrictions), 8, 11, 12

GEORGETOWN

The Hardy House

605 Brownell, P. O. Box 0156, 80444
(303) 569-3388

The Hardy House with its late-19th-century charm invites you to relax in the parlor by the pot-bellied stove, sleep under feather comforters, and enjoy a savory breakfast. Georgetown is only 55 minutes from Denver and the airport. Surrounded by mountains, it boasts unique shopping, wonderful restaurants, and close proximity to seven ski areas.

Hostess: Sarah Schmidt
Rooms: 4 (PB) $58-72
Full Breakfast
Credit Cards: A, B
Notes: 2, 5, 7 (over 7), 11

GOLDEN

The Royal Scot B & B

30500 US Hwy 40, 80401
(303) 526-2411

Our mountain retreat is a contemporary

home offering all the conveniences of modern day living, while at the same time giving you a taste of Scotland and a time gone past. Open all year round, it is located within an easy 30-minute drive of metro Denver. Our nine-acre property is nestled on a mountainside with breath-taking views across to the distant Rocky Mountain peaks. The local area offers fishing, hiking, horseback riding, golfing, shopping, and skiing.

Hosts: Jackie and William Thompson
Rooms: 5 (PB) $69-79
Continental Plus Breakfast
Credit Cards: A, B, C
Notes: 5, 7, 8, 9, 10, 11, 12

GREEN MOUNTAIN FALLS

Outlook Lodge

Box 5, 6975 Howard St., 80819
(719) 684-2303

A quaint lodge nestled at the foot of Pike's Peak. Built in 1889 as the parsonage for the Church of the Wildwood. Features stained-glass windows and hand-carved balustrades. Rooms furnished with brass beds and other antiques. Nearby swimming, hiking, tennis, fishing, horseback riding, restaurants, and shopping. Outlook Lodge provides nostalgia with a relaxing atmosphere.

Hosts: Hayley and Patrick Moran
Rooms: 8 (6PB; 2SB) $45-70
Continental Plus Breakfast
Credit Cards: A, B
Notes: 2, 5, 8, 9, 10, 12 (October-May)

LEADVILLE

Wood Haven Manor

P.O. Box 1291, 807/809 Spruce, 80461
(719) 486-0210; (800) 748-2570

Enjoy the taste and style of Victorian
Leadville by stepping back 100 years in
this beautiful home located on the presti-
gious "Banker's Row." Each room is
distinctively decorated in Victorian style
with private bath. One suite with whirlpool
tub. Spacious dining room, comfortable
living room with fireplace. Historic city
with a backdrop of Colorado's highest
mountains.

Hostess: Jolene Wood
Rooms: 8 (7PB; 1SB) $60
Full Breakfast
Credit Cards: A, B, C, D
Notes: 2, 5, 7, 8, 9, 10, 11, 12

OURAY

The Damn Yankee Bed and Breakfast

P.O. Box 709, 100 Sixth Avenue, 81427
(303) 325-4219; (800) 845-7512

Relax your body. Eight uniquely appointed
rooms await, each with a private bath and
entrance. Drift off to the soothing music of
a mountain stream from your luxurious
queen-sized bed. Snuggle under a plush
down comforter. Sit back and watch your
favorite film on cable television. Drink in
the fresh mountain air. Relax in our hot tub.
Or, gather around the parlor with friends
and sing along to music from a baby grand
piano. Feast your senses. You'll receive
complimentary fresh fruit upon arrival.
Enjoy afternoon snacks in our towering

observatory. And savor a hearty breakfast, as you watch the sun glint over the
mountaintops.

Rooms: 8 (PB) $58-145
Full Breakfast
Credit Cards: A, B, C, D
Notes: 2, 5, 8, 9, 10, 11, 12

Ouray 1898 House

322 Main Street, P. O. Box 641, 81427
(303) 325-4871

This 90-year-old house has been completely renovated and combines the elegance of the 19th century with the comfortable amenities of the 20th century.
Each room features a TV and a spectacular view of the San Juan Mountains from its
deck. Eat a health-conscious, full breakfast on antique china. Jeep rides, horseback riding, and the city's hot spring pool
are a few of the local diversions.

Hosts: Lee and Kathy Bates
Rooms: 4 (PB) $58-78
Full Breakfast
Credit Cards: A, B
Notes: 2, 7, 8, 9, 10

year; 6 Pets welcome; 7 Children welcome; 8 Tennis nearby; 9 Swimming nearby; 10 Golf nearby;
11 Skiing nearby; 12 May be booked through travel agent

PAGOSA SPRINGS

Davidson's Country Inn

Box 87, 81147
(303) 264-5863

Davidson's Country Inn is a three-story log house located at the foot of the Rocky Mountains on 32 acres. The inn provides a library, a playroom, a game room, and some outdoor activities. A two-bedroom cabin is also available. The inn is tastefully decorated with family heirlooms and antiques, with a warm country touch to make you feel at home. Two miles east of Highway 160.

Hosts: Gilbert and Evelyn Davidson
Rooms: 7 (4PB; 3SB) $38-62
Full Breakfast
Credit Cards: A, B
Notes: 2, 5, 7, 8, 9, 10, 11, 12

PUEBLO

Abriendo Inn

300 West Abriendo Avenue, 81004
(719) 544-2703

Experience the comfort, style, and luxury of the past in rooms delightfully furnished with antiques, crocheted bedspreads, and brass and four-poster beds. Breakfast is always hearty, home-baked, and served in the oak wainscoted dining room or one of the picturesque porches. Located within walking distance of restaurants, shops, and galleries...all in the heart of Pueblo. A classic bed and breakfast inn listed with the National Register of Historic Places.

Hosts: Kerrelyn and Chuck Trent
Rooms: 7 (PB) $54-85
Full Breakfast
Credit Cards: A, B, C, E
Notes: 2, 5, 7 (over 7), 8, 10, 11, 12

SALIDA

Gazebo Country Inn

507 E. 3rd., 81201
(719) 539-7806

A 1901, restored Victorian home with magnificent deck and porch views. Gourmet breakfast and private baths. Located in the heart of the Rockies. Whitewater rafting on the Arkansas River and skiing at the Monarch Mountain Lodge are a few of the amenities. We are committed to your comfort and relaxation.

Hosts: Don and Bonnie Johannsen
Rooms: 3 (PB) $45-55
Full Breakfast
Credit Cards: None
Notes: 2, 5, 8, 9, 10, 11, 12

SILVERTON

Christopher House

821 Empire Street, P. O. Box 241, 81433
(303) 387-5857 June-September;
(904) 567-7549 October-May

This charming 1894 Victorian home has the original, golden oak woodwork, parlor fireplace, and antiques throughout. All bedrooms offer comfortable mattresses, wall-to-wall carpeting, and a mountain view. Guests are warmly welcomed with mints and fresh wildflowers. A full breakfast is served to Christian and Irish music. Conveniently located only four blocks from the town's narrow-gauge train depot, Old

---

NOTES: Credit cards accepted: A Master Card; B Visa; C American Express; D Discover Card; E Diners Club; F Other; 2 Personal checks accepted; 3 Lunch available; 4 Dinner available; 5 Open all

West shops, restaurants, and riding stables. Guest transportation to and from the train depot is available.

Hosts: Howard and Eileen Swonger
Rooms: 4 (1PB; 3SB) $42-52
Full Breakfast
Credit Cards: None
Notes: 2, 7, 8, 10, 12

VAIL

Bed and Breakfast Vail / Ski Areas

P.O. Box 491, 81658
(303)949-1212 (voice and FAX)

Welcome to Bed and Breakfast Vail /Ski Areas. We would like to make your stay with us a most pleasurable one. We personally inspect all our host homes/inns to insure the high standard of quality that makes bed and breakfast special. All our hosts are gracious and caring with an interest in people. We hope that you will be considerate of their homes. So come enjoy the warmth and charm of Colorado Ski Country and the Vail Valley! Kathy Westerberg, coordinator.

WINTER PARK

Mulligan's Mountain Inn

P.O. Box 397, 80482
(303) 887-2877

Nestled in the beautiful Rocky Mountains, this cozy home is a quiet get-away. We are surrounded by year round activity with skiing in the winter and golfing and hiking in the summer. On the premises is an outdoor hot tub and recreation room with pool table, darts, and Nintendo. A full home-cooked breakfast is served each morning. You can expect quiet surroundings, a beautiful view, and friendly hospitality.

Hosts: Fred and Shirley Mulligan
Rooms: 4 (SB) $45-70
Full Breakfast
Credit Cards: None
Notes: 2, 5, 9, 10, 11

year; 6 Pets welcome; 7 Children welcome; 8 Tennis nearby; 9 Swimming nearby; 10 Golf nearby; 11 Skiing nearby; 12 May be booked through travel agent

Connecticut

CLINTON

Captain Dibbell House

21 Commerce Street, 06413
(203) 669-1646

Our 1886 Victorian, just two blocks from
the shore, features a wisteria-covered,
century-old footbridge and gazebo on our
half-acre of lawn and gardens. Spacious
living room and bedrooms are comfortably furnished with antiques and family
heirlooms, fresh flowers, fruit baskets,
home-baked treats. There are bicycles,
nearby beaches, and marinas to enjoy.

Hosts: Helen and Ellis Adams
Rooms: 4 (PB) $65-85
Full Breakfast
Credit Cards: A, B, C, D
Notes: 2, 8, 9, 10, 12

ESSEX

The Griswold Inn

36 Main Street, 06426
(203) 767-1776; (203) 767-0481 (FAX)

More than a country hotel. More than a
comfortable bed, an extraordinary meal...
The "Gris" is what Essex is all about. It
embodies a spirit understood perhaps only
as one warms up to its potbelly stove or is
hypnotized by the magic of a crackling log
in one of its many fireplaces. It is a
kaleidoscope of nostalgic images: A lovely
country place. An historic collection of
Antonio Jacobsen marine art. A gentle
smile and a helping hand from a waitress.
A cuisine unmatched for its genuineness
and purity.

Hosts: Vicky and Walian Wintuer
Rooms: 25 (PB) $90-175
Continental Breakfast
Credit Cards: A, B, C
Notes: None

FARMINGTON

The Farmington Inn

827 Farmington Avenue, 06032
(203) 677-2821; (203) 677-8332 (FAX)

The Farmington Inn is a 72-room luxury
inn located in the center of historical and
scenic Farmington, Connecticut. Complimentary eye-opening breakfast served
daily, top 40 movie rental, fitness passes to
large gym, discount tickets to local attractions. Only 100 miles from Boston or New
York City. Just minutes from downtown
Hartford. The best hospitality found in
New England. Warm and attentive personal service in a homey atmosphere.

NOTES: Credit cards accepted: A Master Card; B Visa; C American Express; D Discover Card; E
Diners Club; F Other; 2 Personal checks accepted; 3 Lunch available; 4 Dinner available; 5 Open all

Complimentary parking.

Hostess: Elise Aiello
Rooms: 72 (PB) $79-109
Continental Breakfast
Credit Cards: A, B, C, D, E, F
Notes: 2, 3, 4, 5, 6, 7, 8, 9, 10, 11, 12

GLASTONBURY

Butternut Farm

1654 Main Street, 06033
(203) 633-7197; (203) 633-7197 (FAX)

This 18th-century architectural jewel is furnished in period antiques. Prize-winning dairy goats, pigeons, and chickens roam in an estate setting with trees and herb gardens. The farm is located ten minutes from Hartford by expressway; one and one-half hours to any place in Connecticut.

Host: Don Reid
Rooms: 3 (PB); Suite (PB); Apartment (PB)
$65-85
Full Breakfast
Credit Cards: A, B, C
Notes: 2, 5, 7, 8, 9, 10, 11

The Adams House

MYSTIC

The Adams House

382 Cow Hill Road, 06355
(203) 572-9551; (800) 321-0433

The Adams House is located 15 miles from downtown Mystic and Mystic Seaport. This quaint country Colonial is surrounded by gardens and offers a colonial atmosphere. Built in 1740, the main house features six guest rooms, all with private baths, two with fireplaces; the carriage house features two guest rooms, one with kitchenette and sauna. Continental breakfast is served in our dining room with fireplace.

Hosts: Mary Lou and Gregory Peck
Rooms: 8 (PB) $75-155
Continental Breakfast
Credit Cards: A, B, C, D
Notes: 2, 5, 7 (limited), 9, 10

Harbour Inne and Cottage

Edgemont Street, 06355
(203) 572-9253

Harbour Inn and Cottage is located in downtown Mystic, overlooking the Mystic River. The Inne has several rooms each containing a double size bed, color cable TV, air conditioning, and a private bathroom. The Inne also has a kitchen that is open to all guests, and a common room with a fireplace. The cottage can sleep up to six people. It has a bedroom with two beds, and a fireplace. There is also a sofabed in the kitchen/livingroom for two more people. The cottage also has a private bath and its own parking. Hot tub spa on deck of cottage. Pets welcome.

Host: Charley Lecouras, Jr.
Rooms: 4 (PB) $45-95; Cottage (PB) $125-200
No meals provided, but guests have full use of kitchen to prepare own meals.
Credit Cards: None
Notes: 5, 6, 7, 8, 9, 10

---

year; 6 Pets welcome; 7 Children welcome; 8 Tennis nearby; 9 Swimming nearby; 10 Golf nearby; 11 Skiing nearby; 12 May be booked through travel agent

Harbour Inne and Cottage

Steamboat Inn

73 Steamboat Wharf, 06355
(800) 364-6100; (203) 572-1250 (FAX)

"Intimate and elegant," all of our rooms are directly on the Mystic River in the heart of downtown Mystic's historic district. Most rooms have fireplaces; all have whirlpool baths, TV's, telephones, and individual AC and heat. Visitors to Mystic usually visit the Seaport Museum, Mystic Aquarium, and Old Mystic Village. There's lots to do.

Hostess: Kitty Saletnik
Rooms: 10 (PB) $95-120
Continental Breakfast
Credit Cards: A, B, C
Notes: 2, 5, 8, 9, 10, 12

NEW HAVEN

Bed and Breakfast, Ltd.

P.O. Box 216, 06513
(203) 469-3260

Bed and Breakfast, Ltd. offers 125+ listings of B&B private homes throughout Connecticut—from elegantly simple to simply elegant. A quick call enables us to find the perfect accommodation to fit your needs and budget. We offer personalized service, variety, and congenial hosts ready to extend their hospitality. (New B&B listings nationwide welcome to join our service.) Jack M. Argenio, Director.

NORTH STONINGTON

Antiques and Accommodations

32 Main Street, 06359
(203) 535-1736

Stroll through our well-tended gardens filled with edible flowers and herbs. Relax on our porches and patios. Our country retreat is located 2.5 miles from I-95, minutes from Mystic Seaport, Aquarium, and superb beaches. Gracious hospitality awaits you at our lovingly restored homes: antiques, canopy beds, fireplace, private baths, air conditioned rooms, cable TV. Greet the day with our acclaimed four-course candlelight breakfast. Always an abundance of fresh flowers. We welcome children who appreciate antiques.

Hosts: Thomas and Ann Gray
Rooms: 3 and 2 cottages (PB) $95-195
Full Breakfast
Credit Cards: A, B
Notes: 2, 5, 7, 8, 9, 10, 12

OLD LYME

Old Lyme Inn

85 Lyme Street, 06371
(203) 434-2600

This 1850's Victorian country inn has 13 guest rooms all with private baths, telephones, clock radios, air-conditioning, and a complimentary continental breakfast. Located in the historic district of this art colony, The Old Lyme Inn is known nationally and internationally for its romantic setting and outstanding food. Near Mys-

NOTES: Credit cards accepted: A Master Card; B Visa; C American Express; D Discover Card; E Diners Club; F Other;   2 Personal checks accepted; 3 Lunch available; 4 Dinner available; 5 Open all

tic, Essex, and the Connecticut shoreline.

Hostess: Diana Field Atwood
Rooms: 13 (PB) $95-140
Continental Breakfast
Credit Cards: A, B, C, D, E
Notes: 2, 3, 4, 5, 6, 7, 8, 9, 10, 12

OLD MYSTIC

Red Brook Inn

P. O. Box 237, 06372
(203) 572-0349

Nestled on seven acres of old New England wooded countryside, bed and breakfast lodging is provided in two historic buildings: the Haley Tavern, circa 1740, is a restored center-chimney colonial tavern. The Crary Homestead, circa 1770, is a Colonial built by sea captain Nathaniel Crary. Each room is appointed with period furnishings, including canopy beds, and there are many working fireplaces throughout the inn. A hearty breakfast is served family style in the ancient keeping room. Enjoy a quiet, colonial atmosphere near Mystic Seaport Museum, antique shops, and Aquarium. Colonial dinner weekends are also available November and December. No smoking.

Hostess: Ruth Keyes
Rooms: 11(PB) $95-169
Full Breakfast
Credit Cards: A, B
Notes: 5, 7, 8, 9, 10

THOMPSON

A Taste of Ireland

47 Quaddick Road, 06277
(203) 923-2883

Charming country cottage c. 1780 on

National Historic Registry. Fireplaced sitting room. Home library of Irish literature and Celtic music. Hosts well-versed in assisting guests in geneology research and travel planning to "the old sod." Authentic imported foods and beverages complete the full breakfast served in atrium room overlooking gardens and lovely stone walls. Home is located in quiet corner of N.E. Connecticut—a nature lover's retreat area.

Hosts: Elaine Chicoine and husband Jean
Rooms: 2 (1PB; 1SB) $50-65
Full Irish Breakfast
Credit Cards: None
Notes: 2, 5, 7, 9, 10, 11, 12

WETHERSFIELD

Chester Bulkley House Bed and Breakfast

184 Main Street, 06109
(203) 563-4236

Nestled in the historic village of Old Wethersfield, this classic Greek Revival house has been lovingly restored by innkeepers Frank and Sophie Bottaro to provide a warm and gracious New England welcome to the vacationer, traveler, or businessperson. Built in 1830, the house boasts five delightfully airy guest rooms, each with a unique character and decorated with period antiques and vintage design details.

Hosts: Frank and Sophie Bottaro
Rooms: 5 (3PB; 2SB) $65-75
Full Breakfast
Credit Cards: A, B, C
Notes: 2, 5, 8, 9, 10, 11, 12

year; 6 Pets welcome; 7 Children welcome; 8 Tennis nearby; 9 Swimming nearby; 10 Golf nearby; 11 Skiing nearby; 12 May be booked through travel agent

Delaware

LEWES

The New Devon Inn

Second and Market Streets, 19958
(800) 824-8754; (302) 645-7196 (FAX)

In the heart of quaint historic Lewes, the New Devon Inn boasts 26 antique-filled rooms—all with private bath, air conditioning, phones, expanded continental breakfast and turndown service. Steps to dining, sightseeing, beaches, quality shops. Mobil three-star rated. Conferences, packages available including biking inn-to-inn. "…reminiscent of the small hotels in Europe…" *Washington Magazine*.

Hostesses: Barbara, Julie, Judith, Suzanne
Rooms: 26 (PB) $70-145
Continental Expanded Breakfast
Credit Cards: A, B, C, E
Notes: 2, 5, 8, 9, 10, 12

NEW CASTLE

William Penn Guest House

206 Delaware Street, 19720
(302) 328-7736

Visit historic New Castle and stay in a charmingly restored home, circa 1692, close to museums and major highways.

Hosts: Richard and Irma Burwell
Rooms: 4 (1 PB; 2 SB) $45-70
Continental Breakfast
Credit Cards: None
Notes: 2, 7 (over twelve), 8

REHOBOTH BEACH

Lord and Hamilton Seaside Inn

20 Brooklyn Avenue, 19971
(302) 227-6960

Founded in 1872 by the Methodists as a campground, Rehoboth has maintained a family emphasis and atmosphere even to the present time. Rehoboth has been known for years as "The Nation's Sum-

---

mer Capital." The Lord and Hamilton Seaside sits on the original plot of land purchased by the Reverend R.W. Todd, founder of Rehoboth Methodist Campground. Each room in the inn has its own distinctive personality although a rose motif is evident throughout the house. The bedrooms are comfortably furnished, clean, cheerful, and inviting with designer sheets and towels and accented with handcrafted quilts that Marge has been collecting for years. We are looking forward to your stay with us.

Hosts: Marge and Dick Hamilton
Rooms: 7 (3PB; 4SB) $50-100
Expanded Continental Breakfast
Credit Cards: None
Notes: 2, 8, 9, 10

Tembo Bed and Breakfast
100 Laurel St., 19971
(302) 227-3360

Tembo, named after Gerry's elephant collection, is a white frame beach cottage set among old shade trees in a quiet residential area just one block from the beach. Furnished with antique, comfortable furniture, hand-braided rugs, paintings, and carvings by Delaware artists. A cozy ambience pervades the casual, hospitable atmosphere.

Hosts: Don and Gerry Cooper
Rooms: 6 (1PB; 5SB)
Continental Breakfast
Credit Cards: None
Notes: 2, 6 (off-season), 8, 9, 10

year; 6 Pets welcome; 7 Children welcome; 8 Tennis nearby; 9 Swimming nearby; 10 Golf nearby; 11 Skiing nearby; 12 May be booked through travel agent

District of Columbia

Adams Inn

1744 Lanier Place NW, 20009
(202) 745-3600; (800) 578-6807

This turn-of-the-century town house is in the Adams-Morgan neighborhood with over 40 ethnic restaurants. It has clean, comfortable home-style furnishings.

Adams Inn, located north of the White House near the National Zoo, is convenient to transportation (Woodley Park-Zoo Metro), convention sites, government buildings, and tourist attractions.

Hosts: Gene and Nancy Thompson
Rooms: 25 (12 PB; 13 SB) $45-90
Expanded Continental Breakfast
Credit cards: A, B, C, D, E
Notes: 2, 5, 7, 12

The Reeds

P. O. Box 12011, 20005
(202) 328-3510

Built in the late 1800's, this large Victorian home features original wood panelng, including a unique oak staircase, stained glass, chandeliers, Victorian-style lattice porch, and art nouveau and Victorian antiques and decorations. The house has been featured in the *Washington Post* and the *Philadelphia Inquirer* and as part of "Christmas at the Smithsonian." It is located ten blocks from the White House at historic Logan Circle.

Hosts: Charles and Jackie Reed
Rooms: 6 (1 PB; 5 SB) $55-85
Continental Plus Breakfast
Credit Cards: A, B, C, E
Notes: 2 (two weeks in advance only), 5, 7, 8, 9

Adams Inn

NOTES: Credit cards accepted: A Master Card; B Visa; C American Express; D Discover Card; E Diners Club; F Other; 2 Personal checks accepted; 3 Lunch available; 4 Dinner available; 5 Open all

Florida

AMELIA ISLAND

Elizabeth Pointe Lodge

98 South Fletcher, 32034
(904) 277-4851; (904) 277-6500 (FAX)

The main house of the lodge is constructed in an 1890's Nantucket shingle style with a strong maritime theme, broad porches, rockers, sunshine, and lemonade. Located prominently by the Atlantic Ocean, the inn is only steps from often deserted beaches. Suites are available for families. A newspaper is delivered to your room in the morning, and breakfast is served overlooking the ocean.

Hosts: David and Susan Caples
Rooms: 20 (PB) $95-125
Full Breakfast
Credit Cards: A, B, C
Notes: 2, 3, 4, 5, 7, 8, 9, 10, 12

Florida House Inn

22 S. 3rd Street, P.O. Box 688, 32034
(904) 261-3300; (800) 258-3301

Located in the heart of our Victorian seaport village, Florida's oldest hotel dates from 1857. Recently restored, our award-winning inn is the perfect combination of historic charm and modern convenience. Each room is a comfortable blend of antiques and reproductions, vintage quilts, hand-made rugs, and polished pine floors. Deluxe rooms offer fireplaces, jacuzzis, or original clawfoot tubs. We serve a full breakfast each morning. A cozy English-style pub, original boarding house restaurant, and brick courtyard with gazebo are all a part of the Florida House experience.

Hosts: Bob and Karen Warner
Rooms: 11 (PB) $65-125
Full Breakfast
Credit Cards: A, B, C, E
Notes: 2, 3, 4, 5, 7, 8, 9, 10, 12

Florida House Inn

COLEMAN

The Son's Shady Brook Bed and Breakfast

P. O. Box 551, 33521
(904) PIT-STOP (748-7867)

Offering a refreshing change. Modern home, beautifully decorated rooms with comfortable beds and private baths. Overlooks spring-fed creek on 21 secluded, wooded acres. A relaxing retreat for elderly, handicapped, newlyweds, and others. Central air, heat, and sound system. Enjoy piano, library, fireplace, and more. Solitude and tranquility with therapeutic, scenic, picturesque surroundings. Easy to find, rural setting within 50 miles from Central Florida attractions, Orlando, and Tampa.

Hostess: Jean Lake Martin
Rooms: 4 (PB) $50-60
Full Breakfast
Credit Cards: A, B, C
Notes: 2, 3 (by arrangement), 4 (by arrangement), 5, 8, 9, 10

DAYTONA BEACH

Captain's Quarters Inn

3711 South Atlantic Avenue, 32127
(904) 767-3119; (800) 332-3119

Daytona's first bed and breakfast directly on the Atlantic Ocean has oceanfront suites in a quiet section of Daytona. "Your home away from home" is our motto. Enjoy private balconies, complete kitchens, guest laundry, daily newspapers, unique gift shop, pool heated to 80 degrees, fishing pier next door, and all new decorated rooms. Close to shopping. VCR's and TV's.

Hosts: Becky Sue Morgan and family
Rooms: 26 (PB) $75-195
Full Breakfast
Credit Cards: A, B, C, D
Notes: 2, 3, 5, 7, 8, 9, 10, 12

FORT MYERS

Embe's Place and Art Gallery

5570-4 Woodrose Ct., 33907
(813) 936-6378

This town house-type home is designed to be your home away from home. The spacious accommodation includes a bright and cheery suite with a large, private bath and dressing area. Located 15 minutes from the beaches, Sanibel and Captiva Islands, fine shopping, good restaurants, and the University of Florida. Resident cat.

Hostess: Embe Burdick
Rooms: 1 (PB) $55
Continental Breakfast
Credit Cards: None
Notes: 2, 5, 8, 9, 10

HOLMES BEACH

Harrington House

5626 Gulf Drive, 34217
(813) 778-5444; (813) 778-6303 (FAX)

Centrally located on the Anna Maria Island, in the small city of Holmes Beach directly overlooking the Gulf of Mexico, Harrington House awaits your visit. The largest three-story home on the island was constructed in 1925 and was owned by the first mayor of Holmes Beach. Flower gardens, inground pool, and beachfront swimming are attractive features you'll find at Harrington House. Our great room lends itself to reading, watching TV, listening to music, or just sitting and talking creating new friends or getting acquainted with old ones. Christmastime is especially

---

NOTES: Credit cards accepted: A Master Card; B Visa; C American Express; D Discover Card; E Diners Club; F Other; 2 Personal checks accepted; 3 Lunch available; 4 Dinner available; 5 Open all

festive at Harrington House. Rooms are gorgeously decorated each with its own atmosphere. Breakfast is served on the porch overlooking the sea or in the formal dining room.

Hosts: Jo and Frank Davis
Rooms: 11 (PB) $59-149
Credit Cards: A, B
Notes: 2, 5, 8, 9, 12

KISSIMMEE
Unicorn Inn
8 S. Orlando Ave., 34741
(407) 846-1200

The Unicorn is located in Historic Downtown Kissimmee off the Broadway, opposite the new Police station. It is also only 300 yards from the famous bass fishing of Lake Toldo, close to golf courses, and near to all the main attractions like Disney World and Sea World. We are an old Colonial-style home with 7 rooms or suites. British owned and run by Don and Fran of Yorkshire, England. Our room rate does not vary in season rates and the longer you stay—the less you pay!

Hosts: Don and Fran Williamson
Rooms: 7 (PB) $55
Full English Breakfast
Credit Cards: A, B
Notes: 2, 3 (packed for an outing), 5, 7, 8, 9, 10

LAKELAND
Sunset Motel & R.V. Park
2301 New Tampa Highway, 33801
(813) 683-6464

This resort motel with pool and clubhouse is central to Cypress Gardens, Disneyworld, Sea World, Universal Studios,

Busch Gardens, and more. Walk to banks and shopping. TV, telephone, and refrigerator in all rooms; microwaves and grills available; kitchenettes, apartments, suites.

Hosts: Eunice, Clifton, Will, and Bill
Rooms: 14 (PB) $38-89
Continental Breakfast (on request)
Credit Cards: A, B
Notes: 5, 7, 9, 12

LAKE WALES
Chalet Suzanne Country Inn and Restaurant
3800 Chalet Suzanne Dr., 33853
(813) 676-6011; (800) 433-6011; (813) 676-1814 (FAX)

Listed on the National Register of Historic Places, Chalet Suzanne has been family owned and operated since 1931. It is on 100 acres in a fairy tale setting. Thirty guest rooms have all the amenities. Our four-star restaurant serves breakfast, lunch, and dinner. We also have gift shops, a ceramic studio, swimming pool, soup cannery, and lighted airstrip. We are proud to say that our soups accompanied Jim Irwin on Apollo 15 to the moon. Ask about our mini vacation special.

Hosts: Carl and Vita Hinshaw
Rooms: 30 (PB) $125-185
Full Breakfast
Credit Cards: A, B, C, D, E, F
Notes: 2, 3, 4, 5, 6, 7, 8, 9, 10, 12

MARATHON
Hopp-Inn Guest House
500 Sombrero Beach Rd., 33050
(305) 743-4118

Established in 1981, this guest house is

year; 6 Pets welcome; 7 Children welcome; 8 Tennis nearby; 9 Swimming nearby; 10 Golf nearby; 11 Skiing nearby; 12 May be booked through travel agent

located in the heart of the Florida Keys and looks out on the ocean. Breakfast often includes home-made muffins or banana bread. We are convenient to Key West, Dolphin Research Center, and all water activities. We also have charter fishing packages available aboard the *Sea Wolf*. Also 1 and 2 bedroom villas.

Hosts: Joe and Joan Hopp
Rooms: 5 (PB) $55-75
Full Breakfast
Credit Cards: A, B
Notes: 8, 9, 10, 12

MIAMI

Miami River Inn

118 SW South River Drive, 33130
(305) 325-0045; (305) 325-9227

Enjoy a turn-of-the-century environment overlooking Miami's vibrant riverfront and downtown. Our forty-one rooms (thirty-eight with private bath), are each individually decorated and furnished with antiques, include touch-tone telephones, TV, and central air conditioning and heat. Our pool and jacuzzi are surrounded by lush tropical gardens. Complimentary breakfast and afternoon tea are served daily. The lobby contains a library of historical publications about Miami and menus from restaurants in the river district.

Hostess: Sallye Jude
Rooms: 41(38PB; 3SB) $75
Continental Breakfast
Credit Cards: A, B, C, D, E
Notes: 5, 7, 12

Peaceful Acres Ranch / Agency of Bed and Breakfast Hosts

P.O. Box 160, 7436 SW 117 Avenue, 33183
(305) 271-5422

Private, five-acre, equestrian estate. Safe, clean, beautiful. Three guest rooms; two apartments, all private whirlpool baths. Wraparound decks. Jacuzzi, treehouse. Breakfast under giant orchid tree. Romantic. Five minutes to restaurants, great shopping, movies. Fifteen minutes to zoo, Parrot Jungle, Monkey Jungle, Orchid Jungle. Twenty-five minutes to Miami Beach and Art Deco Center. Thirty minutes to Florida Keys for snorkeling, scuba diving, glass-bottom boats, deep sea fishing. Twenty minutes to Everglades National Park, etc. Call for brochure.

Hostess: Ms. Beck
Rooms: 3 and 2 apartments (PB) $45-65
Continental Breakfast
Credit Cards: None
Notes: 5, 9, 10, 12

NEW SMYRNA BEACH

Night Swan Intracoastal Bed and Breakfast

512 South Riverside Drive, 32168
(904) 423-4940

Come watch the pelicans, dolphins, sailboats, and yachts along the Atlantic Intracoastal Waterway from our beautiful front room, our wrap-around porch, or your room. Our spacious three-story home has kept its character and charm of 1906 in the Historic District of New Smyrna Beach, with its central fireplace and its intricate, natural wood in every room. We

---

NOTES: Credit cards accepted: A Master Card; B Visa; C American Express; D Discover Card; E Diners Club; F Other; 2 Personal checks accepted; 3 Lunch available; 4 Dinner available; 5 Open all

are located between Daytona Beach and Kennedy Space Center, on the Indian River, just two miles from the beach. AAA approved.

Hosts: Chuck and Martha Nighswonger
Rooms: 5 (PB) $49-89
Expanded Continental Breakfast
Credit Cards: A, B, C
Notes: 2, 5, 8, 10, 12

ORLANDO

The Courtyard at Lake Lucerne

211 North Lucerne Circle, East, 32801
(407) 648-5188; (800) 444-5289; (407) 246-1368 (FAX)

A unique property made up of three historic buildings furnished with antiques and surrounding a tropically landscaped brick courtyard, this establishment is located in the historic district on the southern edge of downtown Orlando, convenient to everything central Florida has to offer. Rooms have phones and cable TV; two suites have double jacuzzis and steam showers. Selected by *Country Inns Magazine* as one of 1992's "Best Inn Buys" and by Herb Hillier for *The Miami Herald* as one of the ten best inns in Florida for 1992.

Hosts: Charles Meiner and Paula S. Bowers
Rooms: 22 (PB) $65-150
Expanded Continental Breakfast
Credit Cards: A, B, C
Notes: 2, 5, 7, 8, 12

Perri House B & B

10417 State Road 535, 32836
(407) 876-4830; (800) 780-4830; (407) 876-0241 (FAX)

Perri House is a quiet, private, and se-

cluded country estate home conveniently nestled in 20 acres in the back yard of the Walt Disney World Resort area of Orlando! Because of its outstanding location, Perri House provides easy access to all that Disney and Orlando have to offer. Each guest room has its own private bath and private outside entrance, TV, telephone, and ceiling fan. After a day or evening of activities, arrive home to a relaxing pool and spa. An upscale continental breakfast awaits you each morning and features giant sweet muffins, breads, cereals, and fruit. After ten years of owning and operating their own restaurant and nightclub, Nick and Angi know how to offer a unique blend of cordial hospitality, comfort, and friendship!

Hosts: Nick and Angi Perretti
Rooms: 4 (PB) $65-75
Continental Breakfast
Credit Cards: A, B, C, D
Notes: 2, 5, 7, 8, 9, 10, 12

The Rio Pinar House

532 Pinar Drive, 32825
(407) 277-4903

Located in the quiet Rio Pinar golf community 30 minutes from Disney World, Sea World, and Universal Studios, the Rio Pinar House features comfortable rooms. A full breakfast is served in the formal dining room or on the screened-in porch overlooking the yard.

Hosts: Victor and Delores Freudenburg
Rooms: 3 (PB) $45-55
Full Breakfast
Credit Cards: None
Notes: 2, 5, 7, 8, 10,

---

year; 6 Pets welcome; 7 Children welcome; 8 Tennis nearby; 9 Swimming nearby; 10 Golf nearby; 11 Skiing nearby; 12 May be booked through travel agent

PALM BEACH

Palm Beach Historic Inn

365 So. County Road, 33480
(407) 832-4009; (407) 832-6255 (FAX)

Palm Beach Historic Inn is a charming, beautifully restored landmark building. All rooms have private baths, A/C and cable TV. We are perfectly located—one block from the beach, 2 blocks from world famous Worth Avenue, minutes from the airport and water sports of every kind, cruises, golf, tennis, jai alai, croquet, polo, comedy clubs, supper clubs, exciting nightlife, cultural events and performing arts of every kind. Walking distance from fabulous galleries, spectacular shopping, and exquisite dining.

Hosts: Barbara and Harry Kehr
Rooms: 13 (PB) $60-120
Continental Breakfast
Credit Cards: A, B, C
Notes: 5, 7, 8, 9, 10, 12

ST. AUGUSTINE

Carriage Way Bed and Breakfast

70 Cuna Street, 32084
(904) 829-2467

Built in 1883, a Victorian home located in the heart of the historic district amid unique and charming shops, museums, and historic sites. The atmosphere is leisurely and casual, in keeping with the general attitude and feeling of Old St. Augustine. All guest rooms have a private bath with a claw foot tub or shower. Rooms are furnished with antiques and reproductions including brass, canopy, or four poster beds. A full home-baked breakfast is served.

Hosts: Bill and Diane Johnson
Rooms: 9 (PB) $49-105
Full Breakfast
Credit Cards: A, B, D
Notes: 2, 3 & 4 (picnic), 5, 7 (over 8), 8, 9, 10, 12

Carriage Way Bed and Breakfast

Castle Garden Bed and Breakfast

15 Shenandoah Street, 32084
(904) 829-3839

Stay at a Castle and be treated like royalty! Relax and enjoy the peace and quiet of "royal treatment" at our newly restored 100-year-old Castle of Moorish Revival design where the only sound you'll hear is the occasional roar of a cannon shot from the old fort 200 yards to the south, or the creak of solid wood floors. Awaken to the aroma of freshly baked goodies as we prepare a full, mouth-watering, country breakfast just like "Mom used to make." The unusual coquina stone exterior remains virtually untouched while the interior of this former Castle Garden Carriage House boasts two magnificent bridal suites complete with soothing in-room jacuzzi, sunken bedrooms, and all of life's little pleasures! Amenities: complimentary wine, chocolates, bikes, and private parking.

Host: Bruce L. Kloeckner
Rooms: 6 (PB) $49-150
Full Breakfast
Credit Cards: A, B, C, D
Notes: 5, 7, 10, 12

Old Powder House Inn

38 Cordova Street, 32084
(800) 447-4149; (904) 824-4149

Towering pecan and oak trees shade verandas with large rockers to watch the passing horse and buggies. An introduction to a romantic escape in the charming turn-of-the-century Victorian inn. Amenities include high tea, hors d'oeuvres, jacuzzi, cable TV, parking, bicycles, family hospitality, picnics, special honeymoon packages, anniversaries, and birthdays.

Hosts: Al and Eunice Howes
Rooms: 9 (PB) $59-109
Full Breakfast
Credit Cards: A, B
Notes: 2, 5, 7, 8, 9, 10, 12

SAINT PETERSBURG

Mansion House

105 5th Ave. NE, 33701
(813) 821-9391; (813) 821-9754 (FAX)

Proprietors Alan and Suzanne left Wales in February of 1991 to embark on a remodeling venture of a turn-of-the-century southern home in St. Petersburg. Alan, interested in water color painting, woodwork, and design, used his skills to the full whilst Suzanne cleverly coordinated the interiors to achieve a Floridian-style B&B with an English flair. Located

within walking distance of marina, pier, museums, sunken gardens. Excellent shopping and superb beaches.

Hosts: Suzanne and Alan Lucas
Rooms: 6 (PB) $55-60
Full English Breakfast
Credit Cards: A, B
Notes: 2, 5, 7, 8, 9, 10, 12

Mansion House

SAINT PETERSBURG BEACH

Island's End Resort

1 Pass-A-Grille Way, 33706
(813) 360-5023; (813) 367-7890 (FAX)

The compelling appeal of all that paradise can offer abounds at Island's End. Deep blue sky, turquoise waters, exotic sunrise, and sweets all work in concert to relax and entertain you. Island's End features six unique, well-appointed guest homes including a fantastic three-bedroom house with atrium and private pool. Try your hand at fishing day or night from one of the best docks on Florida's west coast.

Hosts: Jone and Willard Gamble
Rooms: 3 (PB) call for prices
Continental Breakfast on Tuesdays, Thursdays, and Saturdays
Credit Cards: A, B
Notes: 2, 5, 7, 8, 9, 10

---

year; 6 Pets welcome; 7 Children welcome; 8 Tennis nearby; 9 Swimming nearby; 10 Golf nearby; 11 Skiing nearby; 12 May be booked through travel agent

SANFORD

The Higgins House
420 S. Oak Avenue, 32771
(407) 324-9238

Enjoy the romantic ambience this magnificent turn-of-the-century Queen Anne home has to offer. Built in 1894, it has been restored and is decorated in a dramatic Victorian manner. Sit in the large Victorian parlor and relive a time past. Breakfast in the elegant dining room, relax in the cozy pub room, or meander outside and enjoy beautiful Centennial Park from our porch swings. Victorian garden featuring both vegetables and flowers, and a hot tub outside overlooking the gardens is also available.

Hosts: Walter and Roberta Padgett
Rooms: 3 and cottage (1PB; 2SB) $75-100
Expanded Continental Breakfast
Credit Cards: A, B, C, D
Notes: 2, 5, 8, 10, 12

VENICE

The Banyan House
519 South Harbor Drive, 34285
(813) 484-1385

Experience the Old World charm of one of Venice's historic Mediterranean homes, circa 1926, on the Gulf coast. Relax in the peaceful atmosphere of our lovely courtyard dominated by a huge banyan tree. This provides an unusual setting for the garden patio, pool, and jacuzzi. Central to shopping, beaches, restaurants, and golf. Complimentary bicycles. No smoking. Minimum two night stay.

Hosts: Chuck and Susan McCormick
Rooms: 9 (7 PB; 2 SB) $49-89
Continental Breakfast
Credit Cards: None
Notes: 2, 5, 7 (over 12), 8, 9, 10

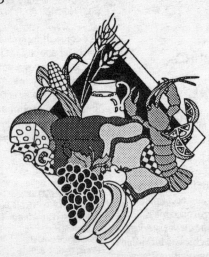

Georgia

ATLANTA

Beverly Hills Inn

65 Sheridan Drive, Northeast, 30305
(404) 233-8520 (voice and FAX); (800) 331-8520

A charming European-style hotel with 18 suites uniquely decorated with period furnishings offers fresh flowers, continental breakfast, and the little things that count. We're a morning star, not a constellation; a solitary path, not a highway. Only some will understand, but then, we don't have room for everybody!

Hosts: Bonnie and Lyle Klienhans
Rooms: 18 (PB) $74-120
Continental Breakfast
Credit Cards: A, B, C, E
Notes: 2, 5, 6, 7, 8, 9, 10, 12

Oakwood House B&B

951 Edgewood Ave. NE, 30307
(404) 521-9320; (404) 521-9320

Just two miles from Downtown Atlanta, in the city's first suburbs, Oakwood welcomes you with four guest rooms—each with a new private bath, and each furnished to complement the house's 1911 post-Victorian style, including original woodwork and hundreds of books. On mild days, breakfast is served on the deck overlooking a huge backyard oak tree that predates the neighborhood. The hosts live next door, offering attentive service and privacy. It's a short walk to Little 5 Points, Atlanta's Soho. Nearby are the Carter Presidential Library, Martin Luther King, Jr., grave site, stadium, Omni, World Congress Center, and Underground Atlanta. No smoking indoors.

Hosts: Judy and Robert Hotchkiss
Rooms: 4 (PB) $65-85
Expanded Continental Breakfast
Credit Cards: A, B
Notes: 2, 5, 7, 12

Shellmont Bed and Breakfast Lodge

821 Piedmont Avenue, Northeast, 30308
(404) 872-9290

Built in 1891, Shellmont is on the National Register of Historic Places and is a City of Atlanta Landmark Building. A true Victorian treasure of carved woodwork, stained and leaded glass, and unique architecture located in Midtown—Atlanta's restaurant, theater, and cultural district, one mile from downtown. It is furnished entirely with antiques.

Hosts: Ed and Debbie McCord
Rooms: 5 (PB) $65-90
Continental Breakfast
Credit Cards: A, B, C
Notes: 2, 5, 7 (limited), 8, 10

---

year; 6 Pets welcome; 7 Children welcome; 8 Tennis nearby; 9 Swimming nearby; 10 Golf nearby; 11 Skiing nearby; 12 May be booked through travel agent

The Woodruff Bed and Breakfast Inn

223 Ponce de Leon Avenue, 30308
(404) 875-9449; (800) 473-9449; (404) 875-2882
(FAX)

Prepare yourself for Southern charm, hospitality, and a full Southern breakfast. The Woodruff Bed and Breakfast Inn is conveniently located in Midtown Atlanta. It is a 1906 Victorian home built by a prominent Atlanta family and fully restored by the current owners. Each room has been meticulously decorated with antiques. The Woodruff has a very colorful past which lends to the charm and history of the building and the city. Close to everything. Ya'll come!

Hosts: Joan and Douglas Jones
Rooms: 10 (8PB; 2SB) $75-125
Full Breakfast
Credit Cards: A, B, D
Notes: 2, 5, 7, 8, 12

AUGUSTA

The Perrin Guest House Inn

208 LaFayette Drive, 30909
(706) 731-0920; (706) 731-9009 (FAX)

The Perrin Place is an old cotton plantation home established in 1863. The plantation has long since become the Augusta National Home of the Masters, while the three acres of the homeplace remain a little spot of magnolia heaven surrounded by shopping, golfing, and fine dining. Our guest house has beautifully redecorated bedrooms that feature fireplaces, jacuzzis, antiques, and comforters. Enjoy the privacy of your own fireplace in spacious accommodations; or share the pleasure of a front porch rocker, the comfort of a cozy parlor, or the cool of a scuppernong arbor with our other guests. Weddings, receptions, and other social functions become treasured events when held at the Perrin. Inn available by reservation only.

Hosts: Ed and Audrey Peel
Rooms: 10 (PB) $70-120
Continental Breakfast
Credit Cards: A, B, C
Notes: 5, 8, 10, 12

COMMERCE

The Pittman House

81 Homer Road, 30529
(706) 335-3823

A gracious, white Colonial built around 1890 is completely furnished with period antiques. If our furnishings are inspiring, visit our antique shop next door. Also, you may enjoy one of Tom's hand-carved Old World Santas. A discount shopping mall is only five minutes away.

Hosts: Tom and Dot Tomberlin
Rooms: 4 (2PB; 2SB) $45-65
Full Breakfast
Credit Cards: A, B
Notes: 2, 5, 7, 8, 9, 10, 12

DAHLONEGA

Worley Homestead Inn

410 West Main Street, 30533
(706) 864-7002

Worley Homestead has seven bedrooms, each with a private bath. Three guest rooms have fireplaces, as do the parlor

---

NOTES: Credit cards accepted: A Master Card; B Visa; C American Express; D Discover Card; E Diners Club; F Other; 2 Personal checks accepted; 3 Lunch available; 4 Dinner available; 5 Open all

and dining room. The home is furnished with antiques, and old photographs adorn the walls. Every effort is made for guests to have the feeling of going back in time but with modern conveniences. A hearty country breakfast is served each morning in the dining room.

Hosts: Bill and Mary Scott
Rooms: 7 (PB) $49-69
Full Breakfast
Credit Cards: A, B
Notes: 2, 5, 12

FLOWERY BRANCH

Whitworth Inn

6593 McEver Road, 30542
(404) 967-2386

Contemporary country inn on five wooded acres offers relaxing atmosphere. Ten uniquely decorated guest rooms with own baths. Two guest living rooms. Full country breakfast served in large sunlit dining room. Meeting/party space available. Thirty minutes northeast of Atlanta at Lake Lanier. Nearby attractions and activities include boating, golf, beaches and water parks. Close to Road Atlanta and Chateau Elan Winery/Golf Course. Easily accessible from major interstates. Three-diamond AAA rating.

Hosts: Ken and Chris Jonick
Rooms: 10 (PB) $55-65
Full Breakfast
Credit Cards: A, B
Notes: 2, 5, 7, 8, 9, 10, 12

Whitworth Inn

HAMILTON

Wedgwood B & B

P. O. Box 115, Highway 27 and Mobley, 31811
(706) 628-5659

Wedgwood is located five and a half miles south of world-famous Callaway Gardens, 20 miles from Roosevelt's Little White House in Warm Springs, and 18 miles from Columbus. This 1850 home radiates the warmth, friendliness, and enthusiasm of your hostess. The inside is Wedgwood blue with white stenciling. Spacious rooms are comfortably furnished with period antiques. Personalized service and complimentary refreshments. No smoking.

Hostess: Janice Neuffer
Rooms: 3 (PB) $65-75
Full Breakfast
Credit Cards: None
Notes: 2, 5, 7, 8, 9, 10, 12

HELEN

Chattahoochee Ridge Lodge

P.O. Box 175, 30545
(800) 476-8331 or (706) 878-3144

Alone on a woodsy mountain above a

---

year; 6 Pets welcome; 7 Children welcome; 8 Tennis nearby; 9 Swimming nearby; 10 Golf nearby; 11 Skiing nearby; 12 May be booked through travel agent

waterfall, a mile from downtown, the lodge has five new rooms and suites (kitchens and fireplaces) with private entrances, TV, AC, free phones, and jacuzzi; plus double insulation and back-up solar for stewards of the earth. Decor includes wide-board knotty pine, brass beds, wall-to-wall carpet, and paddle fans. You'll like the quiet seclusion, large windows, and deep-rock water. We'll help you plan great vacation days, including Bob's oom-pah band at a German restaurant.

Hosts: Mary and Bob Swift
Rooms: 5 (PB) $40-70
Continental Breakfast
Credit Cards: A, B, C, D
Notes: 2, 5, 7, 8, 9, 10, 12

Dutch Cottage B & B

P.O. Box 757, 30545
(706) 878-3135

Located in a beautiful alpine village in the mountains of north Georgia, a tranquil waterfall and ivy-covered hillside lead to this European-style bed and breakfast located in an idyllic wooded setting. Choose from 3 comfortable rooms, each with private bath, AC, and TV, or a charming hilltop honeymoon chalet. Full breakfast buffet. Walk to town. Open May through October.

Hosts: Bill and Jane Vander Werf
Rooms: 3 (4) (3PB; 1SB) $55-75
Credit Cards: None
Notes: 2, 7, 9, 10

Habersham Hollow Country Inn and Cabins

Route 6, Box 6208, 30523
(404) 754-5147; after May (706) 754-5147

Nestled in the northeast Georgia mountains, this elegant country B&B features

king beds, fireplace, private baths, and TV's in each room. Nearby on the secluded wooded grounds are cozy fireplace cabins with fully equipped kitchens, TV, and deck with BBQ grills where well-mannered pets are welcome.

Hosts: C. J. and Maryann Gibbons
Rooms: 4 (PB) $75-95
Full Breakfast
Credit Cards: A, B
Notes: 2, 5, 6, 7, 8, 9, 10, 11

MOUNTAIN CITY

York House, Inc.

P.O. Box 126, 30562
(800) 231-YORK (9675)

This lovely 1896 bed and breakfast inn has a country flair and is listed on the National Register of Historic Places. It is nestled among the beautiful north Georgia mountains and is close to recreational activities. Completely renovated, the 13 guest rooms are decorated with period antiques and offer cable color TV. Guests begin their day with a continental breakfast served on a silver tray. The York House is located between Clayton and Dillard, Georgia, a quarter-mile off Hwy 441.

Hosts: Angela and Joe Smith
Rooms: 13 (PB) $64-79
Continental Breakfast
Credit Cards: A, B, C, D
Notes: 2, 5, 7, 8, 9, 10, 11, 12

NOTES: Credit cards accepted: A Master Card; B Visa; C American Express; D Discover Card; E Diners Club; F Other; 2 Personal checks accepted; 3 Lunch available; 4 Dinner available; 5 Open all

SAUTEE

The Stovall House
Hwy. 225 North, 30571
(706) 878-3355

Our 1837 Victorian farmhouse, restored in 1983, is listed on the National Register of Historic Places. Located on 26 acres in the historic Sautee Valley, the Inn has views of the mountains in all directions. The recipient of several awards for its attentive restorations, the Inn is furnished with family antiques and decorated with hand-stenciling. The restaurant, open to the public, features regional cuisine prepared with a fresh difference and served in an intimate yet informal setting. It's a country experience!

Host: Ham Schwartz
Rooms: 5 (PB) $63-70
Continental Breakfast
Credit Cards: A, B
Notes: 2, 4, 5, 7, 8, 9, 10

The Stovall House

WoodHaven Chalet
Rt. #1 Box 1086, Covered Bridge Road, 30571
(706) 878-2580

Located in a secluded mountain setting on Covered Bridge Road, this charming chalet is only a few minutes drive from the Alpine village of Helen, Georgia. You can choose an upper bedroom with an antique double bed located near an inside balcony where there is a grand piano for sing-a-longs. Also a lower single unit with a private deck, entrance, and bath, including a color TV, fireplace, and cooking facilities. A deluxe continental breakfast is served for guests in the dining area and includes fruit in season, choice of juice, cereal, home-made breads, and hot beverages. No smoking allowed inside the house.

Hosts: Van and Ginger Wunderlich
Rooms: 3 (1PB; 2SB) $55-65
Expanded Continental Breakfast
Credit Cards: None
Notes: 2, 5, 10

SAVANNAH

Foley House Inn
14 West Hull Street, 31401
(912) 232-6622; (800) 647-3708; (912) 231-1218 (FAX)

The Foley House epitomizes the warmth and traditional hospitality that is embedded in the roots of the Old South. Built in the 1800's, this Victorian townhouse is located in the very heart of the historic district on Chippewa Square. Each of the 20 rooms displays its own unique character, filled with antiques, Persian rugs, hand-carved fireplaces and over-sized jacuzzi rooms. Evening reception with cordials, tea, and sweet breads.

Hostess: Susan Steinhauser
Rooms: 20 (PB) $85-185
Continental Plus Breakfast
Credit Cards: A, B, C
Notes: 2, 5, 7, 8, 9, 10, 12

year; 6 Pets welcome; 7 Children welcome; 8 Tennis nearby; 9 Swimming nearby; 10 Golf nearby; 11 Skiing nearby; 12 May be booked through travel agent

Jesse Mount House

209 West Jones Street, 31401
(912) 236-1774; (800) 347-1774; (912) 236-1774
(FAX)

Two, 3-bedroom suites featured in an elegant 1854 townhouse. Each suite accommodates from one to six people in a party. The garden suite has a full kitchen and access to the brick-walled rose garden. The upper suite has high, four-poster beds with canopies. Both suites have gas log fireplaces, complimentary candy, coffee or tea. The house has many rare antiques, a grand piano, and gilded harps. Bicycles and a super spa. A full breakfast is available upon request.

Host: Howard Crawford
Rooms: 1-3 bedroom suite (PB) $135(2)-225(8)
Continental Breakfast
Credit Cards: None
Notes: 2, 5, 6, 7, 8, 10, 12

Joan's on Jones

17 West Jones Street, 31401
(912) 234-3863; (912) 234-1455 (FAX)

In the heart of the historic district, two charming bed and breakfast suites grace the garden level of this three-story Victorian private home. Each suite has a private entry, off-street parking, bedroom, sitting room, kitchen, bath, private phone, and cable TV. Note the original heart-pine floors, period furnishings, and Savannah grey brick walls. Innkeepers Joan and Gary Levy, restaurateurs, live upstairs and invite you for a tour of their home if you're staying two nights or more.

Hosts: Joan and Gary Levy
Rooms: 2 suites (PB) $85-95
Continental Breakfast
Credit Cards: None
Notes: 2, 5, 6 (dogs in garden suite only), 7, 8, 9, 10, 12

Joan's on Jones

WARM SPRINGS

Hotel Warm Springs Bed and Breakfast Inn

17 Broad Street, P.O. Box 351, 31830
(706) 655-2114

Relive history and the Roosevelt Era in our 1907 hotel, restaurant, ice cream parlor, and gift shops. Authentically restored and beautifully decorated with Roosevelt furniture and family antiques. Our large living and dining room with Queen Anne furniture, Oriental rugs, and crystal teardrop chandelier is ideal for group meetings. Nestled in quaint Warm Springs Village—a shopper's paradise, home of FDR's Little White House, 14 miles from Callaway Gardens, and one hour from Atlanta.

Hosts: Lee and Geraldine (Gerrie) Thompson
Rooms: 14 (PB) $60-160
Southern Breakfast Feast
Credit Cards: A, B, C, D
Notes: 2, 3, 4, 5, 7, 8, 9, 10, 12

NOTES: Credit cards accepted: A Master Card; B Visa; C American Express; D Discover Card; E Diners Club; F Other; 2 Personal checks accepted; 3 Lunch available; 4 Dinner available; 5 Open all

Hawaii

HAWAII-KAMUELA

Kamuela Inn

P.O. Box 1994, 96743
(808) 885-4243; (808) 885-8857 (FAX)

Comfortable, cozy rooms and suites with private baths, with or without kitchenettes, all with cable color television. Complimentary continental breakfast served in our coffee lanai every morning. Situated in a quiet, peaceful setting just off Highway 19. Conveniently located near shops, retail outlets, banks, theatres, parks, tennis courts, museums, restaurants, and post office. The big island's famous white sand beaches, golf courses, horseback rides, valley and mountain tours are only minutes away.

Hostess: Carolyn Cascavilla
Rooms: 31 (PB) $54-165
Continental Breakfast
Credit Cards: A, B, C, D, E
Notes: 2, 5, 7, 8, 9, 10, 11, 12

HAWAII-LAHAINA

Blue Horizons

P.O. Box 10578, 96761
(808) 669-1965; (808) 661-1896 (FAX)

Want to mingle with the "locals" over breakfast, yet have all the privacy of your own one-bedroom suite complete with private bath and kitchen? Well, this spacious B&B offers it all! Just minutes north of Lahaina and with great views of Lanai and Molokai, choose one of our two guest rooms with private baths or one of the three honeymoon suites. Come and feel right at home at poolside or while viewing spectacular ocean sunsets!

Hosts: Jim and Beverly Spence
Rooms: 5 (PB) $75-95
Continental Breakfast
Credit Cards: A, B, C
Notes: 2, 5, 7 (over 12), 8, 9, 10, 12

The Walkus

c/o Trinity Tours, 1620 Ainakea Road, 96761
(808) 661-8085; (800) 621-8942; (808) 661-1896
(FAX)

Visit Maui...from home to home...Have the privacy of this entirely new four-bedroom, three bath home (the den can be used as a fifth bedroom). Sunbathe at poolside, relax in the jacuzzi, or take a short stroll to "Baby Beach" right in Lahaina. With central air-conditioning, modern laundry facilities, and a kitchen that lacks nothing, you'll be right at home. Great for families or small groups.

Rooms: 4 + den (1PB; 4SB) $400
Self-serve Breakfast
Credit Cards: A, B, C
Notes: 2, 5, 7, 8, 9, 10, 12

year; 6 Pets welcome; 7 Children welcome; 8 Tennis nearby; 9 Swimming nearby; 10 Golf nearby; 11 Skiing nearby; 12 May be booked through travel agent

KAILUA-KONA

Hale Maluhia B & B

76-770 Hualalai Road, 96740
(808) 329-5773; (800) 559-6627; (808) 326-5487

Only ten minutes from the Kailua Village
and resort area, you will find the large
rambling home of Hale Maluhia. Constructed in a rustic Hawaiian style with
green roofs and shingled exterior walls, the
interiors are finished with koa cabinets,
open beam ceiling, and lots of natural
woods. Nearby activities include snorkling,
horseback riding, dinner cruises, scuba
diving, hunting, and biking.

Hosts: Ken and Ann Smith
Rooms: 5 (SB) (private baths can be arranged)
$65-75
Continental Breakfast
Credit Cards: A, B, C
Notes: 2, 5, 7, 8, 9, 10, 12

KAUAI-PIOPU BEACH

Poipu Bed and Breakfast Inn and Vacation Rentals

2720 Hoonani Road, 96756
(800) 22-POIPU; (808) 742-1146; (808) 742-6843
(FAX)

This award-winning renovated historic
1933 Plantation Inn is in a tropical garden
setting one block from the water. Just a
few doors away, our new annex offers
spectacular ocean views and whale-
watching from the lanai. Rooms or suites
have TV, VCR, ceiling fans, wicker and
pine antiques. Most have whirlpool tubs
and king beds; some have kitchenettes.
One is air-conditioned and handicapped
accessible. Vacation rental cottages,
homes, and oceanfront condos with kitchens are also available from budget to
luxurious. Amenities include afternoon
tea, free videos and popcorn, barbeque,
laundry facilities, free tennis and pool at
nearby club. Walk to shops, restaurants,
and beaches. Car rental discounts, honeymoon packages, and weekly discounts
available.

Hostess: Dotti Cichon
Rooms: 9 (PB) $60-175
Tropical Continental Breakfast
Credit Cards: A, B, C, D, E, F
Notes: 2, 5, 7, 8, 9, 10, 12

KAUAI—PRINCEVILLE

Hale 'Aha
"House of Gathering"

P.O. Box 3370, 3875 Kamehameha Drive, 96722
(800) 826-6733; (808) 826-9052

"Where the East meets the West." The
Garden Island of the Pacific. Lovely new
guest house. Enjoy this beautiful home on
the golf course overlooking the ocean.
Send for colored brochure or call toll free.
Christian hosts.

Hosts: Herb and Ruth Bockelman
Rooms: 4 (PB) & $80; Suites: $110 to 190
Continental Breakfast
Credit Cards: None
Notes: 2, 5, 8, 9, 10, 12

MAUI-HAIKU

Haikuleana B & B

555 Haiku Road, 96708
(808) 575-2890

Experience the real feeling of "Aloha" in

NOTES: Credit cards accepted: A Master Card; B Visa; C American Express; D Discover Card; E
Diners Club; F Other; 2 Personal checks accepted; 3 Lunch available; 4 Dinner available; 5 Open all

an 1850's plantation home. Set in the agricultural district close to waterfalls and secluded beaches. Haikuleana is a convenient waystation for visitors headed to Hana and the Haleakala Crater. Swimming ponds, the world's best windsurfing, and golf course are all nearby. Fred completely renovated the house. You'll admire its high ceilings, plank floors, porch, and lush tropical gardens. The cool Hawaiian rooms are furnished with drapes, ticking comforters, wicker, and antiques.

Host: Frederick J. Fox
Rooms: 4 (PB) $80-85
Full Breakfast
Credit Cards: None
Notes: 2, 5, 7 (over 6), 8, 9, 10, 12

MAUI-KULA

Elaine's Up Country Guest Rooms

2112 Noalae Rd., 96790
(808) 878-6623

Quiet country setting. Splendid ocean and mountain views. All rooms have private baths, full kitchens, and sitting room privileges. Guests are welcome to cook breakfast or whatever meals they like. Next to our main house is a delightful cottage made to order for a family. One bedroom with queen-size bed and twin beds in the loft. Large kitchen. We ask that our guests do not smoke or drink.

Hosts: Elaine and Murray Gildersleeve
Rooms: 3 plus one cottage (PB) $90-110 +tax
Full Self-serve Breakfast
Credit Cards: F
Notes: 2, 5, 7, 9, 10, 12

MAUI-LAHAINA

The Guesthouse

1620 Ainakea Road, 96761
(808) 661-8085; (800) 621-8942

Conveniently located between the historic whaling town of Lahaina and the beach resort of Kaanapali, The Guesthouse offers a choice of five guest rooms, each with a different touch of Aloha. All have air-conditioning, TV, refrigerators, and a private jacuzzi has been added to our honeymoon suites. Enjoy the conveniences of home with our modern kitchen and laundry facilities. Relax at poolside or take a short stroll to the beach. We know your visit will be special, so expect outstanding accommodations at a moderate price.

Hosts: Fred and Tanna Branum
Rooms: 5 (PB) $60-95
Full Breakfast
Credit Cards: A, B, C,
Notes: 2, 5, 7 (over 12), 8, 9, 10, 12

OAHU-AIEA

Pearl Harbor View Bed and Breakfast

99-442 Kekoa Place, 96701
(808) 487-1228; (808) 487-1228 (FAX)

Lush tropical garden. Two bedrooms, bath, living room, complete kitchen. Upstairs apartment in two-story private home. Sleeps up to 5 guests. Antique oriental furniture.

Hostess: Doris Reichert
Rooms: 1 apartment (2 bedrooms) (PB) $65-75
Continental Breakfast
Credit Cards: A, B
Notes: 2, 5, 7, 12

year; 6 Pets welcome; 7 Children welcome; 8 Tennis nearby; 9 Swimming nearby; 10 Golf nearby; 11 Skiing nearby; 12 May be booked through travel agent

Idaho

COEUR D'ALENE

Cricket on the Hearth

1521 Lakeside Avenue, 83814
(208) 664-6926

Cricket on the Hearth, Coeur d'Alene's first bed and breakfast inn, has a touch of country that gives the inn a "down home" aura. Each of the five guest rooms is furnished in theme, from romantic to unique. After a relaxing weekend around the inn with its two cozy fireplaces and delicious full breakfast, guests are sure to find staying at Cricket on the Hearth habit forming.

Hosts: Al and Karen Hutson
Rooms: 5 (3PB; 2SB) $45-75
Full Breakfast
Credit Cards: None
Notes: 2, 5, 8, 9, 10, 11

Katie's Wild Rose Inn

5150 Couer d'Alene, 83814
(208) 765-9474; (800) 328-WISH (9474)

Looking through the pine trees to Lake Coeur d'Alene, Katie's Wild Rose Inn is a haven for the weary traveler. Only 600 feet from the public dock and beach road, the inn has four cozy rooms, one with its own jacuzzi. Guests can relax in the family room beside the fireplace or enjoy a game of pool. A full breakfast is served on the deck or in the dining room where you can admire the view.

Hosts: Joisse and Lee Knowles
Rooms: 4 (2PB; 2SB) $65-85
Full Breakfast
Credit Cards: A, B
Notes: 2, 5, 8, 9, 10, 11

Katie's Wild Rose Inn

LEWISTON

Shiloh Rose Bed and Breakfast

3414 Selway Dr., 83501
(208) 743-2482

The Shiloh Rose, decorated in a warm, country-Victorian style, offers a spacious three-room suite as your home away from home. Lace curtains, fragrant potpourri, and fresh roses in season invite you to linger. Have your morning coffee in the sitting room with a real wood-burning stove. Browse through the overflowing bookshelves, enjoy the TV/VCR...or the grand piano. A complete breakfast is served in the dining room or on the deck overlooking the valley. The views are fantastic. Join us, you'll love it!

Hostess: Dorothy A. Mader
Rooms: 1 (PB) $65-70
Full Breakfast
Credit Cards: A, B
Notes: 2, 5, 7 (over 10), 8, 9, 10, 11

SHOUP

Smith House Bed and Breakfast

49 Salmon River Road, 88469
(208) 394-2121; (800) 238-5915

Since opening in 1987, Smith House has achieved a relaxed sense of informality and cozy comfort. Lovely split-level log home plus guest house offers fine, distinctively different rooms. Hot tub, orchard, library, covered decks, kitchen, laundry, plus breathtaking view of the Salmon River. Complimentary beverages. Gift shop features local handcrafts. Weekly rates. Honeymoon/anniversary package. Open March 15 through November 30.

Hosts: Aubrey and Marsha Smith
Rooms: 5 (1SB; 4PB) $35-54
Continental Plus Breakfast
Credit Cards: A, B, D
Notes: 2, 6, 7, 9, 11, 12

year; 6 Pets welcome; 7 Children welcome; 8 Tennis nearby; 9 Swimming nearby; 10 Golf nearby; 11 Skiing nearby; 12 May be booked through travel agent

Illinois

CARLYLE

Country Haus

1191 Franklin, 62231
(618) 594-8313; (800) 279-4486

An 1890's Eastlake-style home decorated in cordial country comfort. Settle into the library with a good book or snuggle up to watch TV. Relax in the hot tub on the back deck gazebo, or visit Carlyle Lake for fishing, swimming, sailing, or hiking. A museum and golf courses are nearby. Pamper yourself with homey hospitality at Country Haus Bed and Breakfast.

Hosts: Ron and Vickie Cook
Rooms: 5 (PB) $45-65
Full Breakfast
Credit Cards: A, B, C
Notes: 2, 5, 8, 9, 10, 11

COLLINSVILLE

Maggie's Bed and Breakfast

2102 N. Keebler, 62234
(618) 344-8283

Beautiful, quiet, country setting just minutes from downtown St. Louis. Near hospital, restaurants, and shopping. Cooking with natural ingredients. Antiques and art objects collected in world-wide travels. Games, cable TV, and hot tub with terrycloth robes and house slippers.

Hostess: Maggie Leyda
Rooms: 5 (4PB; 1SB) $35-65
Full Breakfast
Credit Cards: A, B
Notes: 2, 5, 6, 7, 8, 9, 10, 12

EVANSTON

The Margarita European Inn

1566 Oak Avenue, 60201
(708) 869-2273; (708) 869-2353 (FAX)

The romantic at heart will truly enjoy this modest and charming European-style inn in Evanston, the home of Northwestern University. Relax in the grand parlor with the morning paper or in the roof garden at sunset. Explore the numerous antique and specialty shops nearby. On rainy days, curl up with a novel from our wood-paneled English library, or indulge in a culinary creation from our critically acclaimed northern Italian restaurant, Va Pensiero.

Hosts: Barbara and Tim Gorham
Rooms: 49 (15PB; 34SB) $40-80
Continental Breakfast
Credit Cards: A, B, C
Notes: 2, 3, 4, 5, 7, 8, 9, 10, 12

NOTES: Credit cards accepted: A Master Card; B Visa; C American Express; D Discover Card; E Diners Club; F Other; 2 Personal checks accepted; 3 Lunch available; 4 Dinner available; 5 Open all

GALENA

Avery Guest House

606 South Prospect Street, 61036
(815) 777-3883

This pre-Civil War home located near Galena's main shopping and historic buildings is a homey refuge after a day of exploring. Enjoy the view from our porch swing, feel free to play the piano, watch TV, or join a table game. Sleep soundly on comfortable queen beds, then enjoy our hearty continental breakfast in the sunny dining room with bay window. Mississippi river boats nearby.

Hosts: Flo and Roger Jensen
Rooms: 4 (2SB) $45-60
Expanded Continental Breakfast
Credit Cards: A, B
Notes: 2, 5, 7, 8, 9, 10, 11, 12

Belle Aire Mansion

11410 Route 20 West, 61036
(815) 777-0893

Belle Aire Mansion guest house is a pre-Civil War Federal home surrounded by 11 well-groomed acres that include extensive lawns, flowers, and a block-long, tree-lined driveway. We do our best to make our guests feel they are special friends.

Hosts: Jan and Lorraine Svec
Rooms: 5 (PB) $65-140
Full Breakfast
Credit Cards: A, B, D
Notes: 2, 7, 8, 10, 11

Brierwreath Manor Bed and Breakfast

216 North Bench Street, 61036
(815) 777-0608

Brierwreath Manor, circa 1884, is just one block from Galena's Main Street and has a dramatic and inviting wrap-around porch that beckons to you after a hard day. The house is furnished in an eclectic blend of antique and early American. You'll not only relax but feel right at home. Central air conditioning, ceiling fans, and cable TV add to your enjoyment.

Hosts: Mike and Lyn Cook
Rooms: 3 (PB) $70-80
Full Breakfast
Credit Cards: None
Notes: 2, 5, 8, 9, 10, 11

Colonial Guest House

1004 Park Avenue, 61036
(815) 777-0336

Built in 1826, this twenty-one-room mansion has eight outside doors, five large porches, one four-room penthouse that overlooks the city, and three suites with two to three rooms in each including a kitchen. It is two blocks off Main Street. This house is loaded with antiques and has operated as a guest house for thirty-three years.

Hostess: Mary Keller
Rooms: 6 (PB) $65-85
Continental Breakfast
Credit Cards: None
Notes: 2, 5, 7 (small), 8, 9, 10, 11, 12

Cottage at Amber Creek

P.O. Box 5, 61036 ·
(815) 777-9320; (815) 777-9432 (FAX)

Guest cottage on country estate of 300 secluded acres. Tastefully furnished with country antiques. Living room with fireplace, king bed under skylight. Full bath with double whirlpool, mini-kitchen, deck with beautiful view. Firewood, towels,

year; 6 Pets welcome; 7 Children welcome; 8 Tennis nearby; 9 Swimming nearby; 10 Golf nearby; 11 Skiing nearby; 12 May be booked through travel agent

linens provided; extra quilts and pillows. Abundant wildlife and hiking trails make Amber Creek a nature-lover's paradise. Ideal for a honeymoon, anniversary or romantic getaway.

Hostess: Kate Freeman
Rooms: 1 (PB) $85-145
Continental Breakfast
Credit Cards: A, B, C, D
Notes: 2, 5, 6, 7, 8, 9, 10, 11, 12

Country Gardens Guest House

1000 Third Street, 61036
(815) 777-3062

This 1858 home retains the charm of that bygone era and is furnished in a Victorian country manner. We have three guest rooms, private baths, central air conditioning, and a large wicker-filled porch. Guests breakfast in formal dining room and then have the beautiful town of Galena in which to shop, browse and dine—just four blocks away. Limited smoking permitted.

Hosts: Sandy and Dave Miller
Rooms: 3 (PB) $60-90
Hearty Continental Breakfast
Credit Cards: A, B
Notes: 2, 5, 8, 9, 10, 11

Park Avenue Guest House

208 Park Avenue, 61036
(815) 777-1075

1893 Queen Anne Painted Lady. Wraparound screened porch, gardens, and gazebo for summer. Fireplace, opulent Victorian Christmas in winter. One suite sleeps three, and there are three antique-filled guest rooms, all with queen size beds. Located in quiet residential area, it is only a short walk to Grant Park or across footbridge to Main Street shopping and restaurants.

Rooms: 4 (PB) $65-95
Hearty Continental Breakfast
Credit Cards: A, B, D
Notes: 2, 5, 9, 10, 11

Pine Hollow Inn

4700 N. Council Hill Rd., 61036
(815) 777-2975

Pine Hollow is located on a secluded 110-acre Christmas tree farm just one mile from Main Street Galena. Roam around the grounds and enjoy the wildlife or simply put your feet up, lean back and enjoy the country from our front porch. We provide all the comforts of home in a beautiful country setting. Each of our rooms is decorated in a country style with four poster queen size beds, fireplaces, and private bath. Whirlpool bath suites are available.

Hosts: Sally and Larry Priske
Rooms: 5 (PB) $75-100
Continental Breakfast
Credit Cards: A, B, D
Notes: 2, 5, 8, 9, 10, 11, 12

Pine Hollow Inn

NOTES: Credit cards accepted: A Master Card; B Visa; C American Express; D Discover Card; E Diners Club; F Other; 2 Personal checks accepted; 3 Lunch available; 4 Dinner available; 5 Open all

HIGHLAND

Phyllis' B & B

801 9th St., 62249
(618) 654-4619

Highland, known as "Neu-Schweizer-land," is located just 30 miles east of St. Louis. The inn was built around the turn of the century and is close to town square, stores, shops, and restaurants. In the square is a gazebo where festivals and music concerts are held in the summer. At Christmastime, the square and gazebo are decorated for the season. Points of interests include Latzer Homestead, Lindendale Park/Fairgrounds, Wicks Organ Company, and other fascinating landmarks. Each room is uniquely decorated. No smoking or alcoholic beverages permitted.

Hosts: Bob and Phyllis Bible
Rooms: 3 (PB) $40-55
Hearty Continental Breakfast
Credit Cards: A, B
Notes: 2, 5, 8, 9, 10

METROPOLIS

Park Street House Bed and Breakfast

310 Park Street, 62960
(618) 524-5966

Graced with original oak woodwork, antiques, and private collections, each room has unique character. This circa 1920 home is ideally located in a small river town within walking distance to shops, restaurants, and riverfront. Minutes away from Fort Massac State Park and Museum, the American Quilt Museum, numerous antique shops, and many scenic parks with hiking trails. Full breakfast served in dining room or patio overlooking the garden pond. Resident bent willow craftsman and gift shop on premises.

Hosts: Ron and Melodee Thomas
Rooms: 4 (PB) $45-75
Full Breakfast
Credit Cards: A, B
Notes: 2, 5, 7, 12

NAPERVILLE

Harrison House Bed and Breakfast

26 North Eagle Street, 60540
(708) 420-1117; (800) 842-7968 (out of state)

Harrison House Bed and Breakfast, circa 1911, is a warm and friendly guest house 25 miles west of Chicago. Four antique-filled air-conditioned guest rooms, one with a jacuzzi. Walk to the train, great shops, wonderful restaurants, and historic sites. Home-made chocolate chip cookies, fresh flowers, gourmet coffee, and a scrumptious breakfast. Gift certificates available. Prepare to be pampered!

Hosts: Neal and Lynn Harrison; Bette Coulter
Rooms: 4 (PB) $78-138 (midweek discounts available)
Full Breakfast on weekends; continental breakfast on weekdays
Credit Cards: A, B, C
Notes: 2, 5, 8, 9, 10, 11, 12

Harrison House

OAKLAND

Johnson's Country Home

109 E. Main Street, 61943
(217) 346-3274

This two-story brick Italiante style home, built in 1874 has had many uses in its years of history. During the Great Depression it was a multi-family dwelling. Later it was used for a VFW post—a restaurant known as the Old House. It was a storage building for farm equipment prior to the Johnson's ownership. Today it is again a lovely home, listed in the Coles County Register of Historic Places.

Hosts: Reece and June Johnson
Rooms: 2 (SB) $40
Continental Breakfast
Credit Cards: None
Notes: 2, 7, 8, 9, 10

QUINCY

The Kaufmann House Bed and Breakfast

1641 Hampshire, 62301
(217) 223-2502

Heart-warming hospitality, that's what you feel as you are welcomed into the genuine Midwest charm and hospitality of Quincy, the twice-acclaimed "All-American City." Imagine yourself sleeping in an intimate Victorian bed chamber, freshly treated with flowers and light, or slumbering on a painted iron bed among brightly pieced quilts in the simplicity of early American atmosphere…then waking to the delicious aroma of piping hot, home-made rolls, coffee and tea, complemented by chilled, fresh fruit—served to you on the stone terraced patio or the antique-filled Ancestor Room. Come, indulge and pamper yourself.

Hosts: Emery and Bettie Kaufmann
Rooms: 3 (1PB; 2SB) $45-65
Gourmet Continental Breakfast
Credit Cards: None
Notes: 2, 5, 7, 12

WHEATON

The Wheaton Inn

301 W. Roosevelt Road, 60187
(708) 690-2600; (800) 447-4667; (708) 690-2623 (FAX)

Get lost in the luxury of large, elegant rooms. Select from sixteen rooms that vary from the Wheaton Room, a Traditional Williamsburg elegance underscored by the room's chandeliers and fireplace, to the Mayor's Room patterned after an English gentleman's library with its rich leather furniture and corner fireplace. Special arrangements may be made for groups of 30 or more.

Hostess: Linda Matzen
Rooms: 16 (PB) $99-195
Full Breakfast
Credit Cards: A, B, C, D, E, F
Notes: 2, 5, 7, 8, 10, 12

NOTES: Credit cards accepted: A Master Card; B Visa; C American Express; D Discover Card; E Diners Club; F Other; 2 Personal checks accepted; 3 Lunch available; 4 Dinner available; 5 Open all

Indiana

BEVERLY SHORES

Dunes Shores Inn

33 Lakeshore County Road., 46301
(219) 879-9029

A bed and breakfast in the Gasthof tradition. Dunes Shores Inn is quiet and informal. It is located one mile from Lake Michigan and its national and state park beaches and is a four season oasis for those who wish to relax in the natural beauty of the Indiana Dunes. An ideal inn for stopping off to explore this unique area.

Hosts: Rosemary and Fred Brown
Rooms: 10 (SB) $50-60
Full Breakfast
Credit Cards: A, B
Notes: 2, 5, 7, 8, 9, 10, 11

BRISTOL

Tyler's Place

19562 St. Rd. 120, 46507
(219) 848-7145

Tyler's Place is located in the heart of Amish country. On a 27-hole golf course, with five rooms available, you can relax on the deck enjoying the outdoor water garden, and the warm Hoosier hospitality. Full breakfast. Three miles from I80-90 toll road.

Hostess: Esther Tyler
Rooms: 5 (1PB; 4SB) $45-65
Full Breakfast
Credit Cards: A, B
Notes: 2, 5, 7, 8, 9, 10, 11

CORYDON

The Kintner House Inn

101 South Capitol Street, 47112
(812) 738-2020

AAA rated, this completely restored inn, circa 1873, is on the National Register of Historic Places and is furnished with Victorian and country antiques. It features five fireplaces and serves a full breakfast in the dining room. The staff prides itself on personal attention and guests' comfort. Private baths.

Hostess: Mary Jane Bridgwater
Rooms: 15 (PB) $39-89
Full Breakfast
Credit Cards: A, B, C, D, E
Notes: 2, 5, 8, 9, 10, 11

CRAWFORDSVILLE

Davis House

1010 W. Wabash Ave., 47933
(317) 364-0461

You'll enjoy the unique colonial atmosphere of this 1870 country mansion. Located in a quiet neighborhood, conve-

---

year; 6 Pets welcome; 7 Children welcome; 8 Tennis nearby; 9 Swimming nearby; 10 Golf nearby; 11 Skiing nearby; 12 May be booked through travel agent

nient to Wabash College and several local museums. Renovated in 1940, this historic home combines the original grace with the modern guest conveniences. Common rooms available for group meetings. Limited smoking.

Hosts: Jan and Dave Stearns
Rooms: 5 (PB) $49-65
Full Breakfast
Credit Cards: A, B, C, D
Notes: 2, 5, 7, 12

Sugar Creek Queen Anne Bed and Breakfast
901 W. Market, Box 726, 47933
(217) 362-4095

Sugar Creek's decor is Victorian with a French Provincial touch. The turn-of-the-century home has two guest rooms with private baths and a honeymoon suite complete with a private sitting room and private bath. Behind the house is a beautiful rose garden and a fourth guest room with private bath, and a jacuzzi and fitness center. House has been newly remodeled with originality and creativity. Sugar Creek Bed and Breakfast is a member of the Indiana Bed and Breakfast Association. No smoking or alcohol permitted in the building.

Hostess: Mary Alice Barbee
Rooms: 4 (PB) $55
Full Breakfast
Credit Cards: A, B
Notes: 2, 5, 7, 8, 9, 10, 12

EVANSVILLE

Brigadoon Inn
1201 S.E. Second Street, 47713
(812) 422-9635

Built for a railroad executive in 1892, Brigadoon is situated in the historic area near the Ohio River. This sunny, peaceful Queen Anne invites you to relax with its parquet floors, four fireplaces, and stained-glass windows. Books abound in the library with Katelin's *Gone with the Wind* collection. The full breakfast includes home-made breads. The large guest rooms, Scottish, Irish, English, and Welsh, all have antique furnishings to enjoy.

Hostess: Katelin Forbes
Rooms: 4 (2PB; 2SB) $55
Full Breakfast
Credit Cards: C, D, E, F
Notes: 2, 5, 6, 7, 8, 9, 10

GOSHEN

Timberidge Bed and Breakfast
16801 SR 4, 46526
(219) 533-7133

The Austrian chalet, white pine log home is nestled in the beauty of the quiet woods, just two miles from Goshen and near many local points of interest. Our guests enjoy the privacy of a master suite. A path through the woods is frequented by birds, squirrels, deer. Nearby are Amish farms where field work is done by horse-drawn equipment. Timberidge offers the best of city and country—close to town, yet removed to the majestic beauty of the woods that evokes a love of nature and a reverence for God's creation. AC and TV.

Hosts: Edward and Donita Brookmyer
Rooms: 1 (PB) $60
Full and Continental Breakfast Available
Credit Cards: None
Notes: 2

NOTES: Credit cards accepted: A Master Card; B Visa; C American Express; D Discover Card; E Diners Club; F Other; 2 Personal checks accepted; 3 Lunch available; 4 Dinner available; 5 Open all

GREENCASTLE

The Walden Inn

2 Seminary Square, P.O. Box 490, 46135
(317) 635-2761; (317) 653-4833 (FAX)

Gracious hospitality reminiscent of a simpler time is the experience of guests at Walden Inn. It's a philosophy that envelops you the moment you arrive. You'll discover an atmosphere that is warm and unpretentious where guests feel comfortable with our special amentities, distinctive cuisine, and personal service. Because Walden Inn has just 55 guest rooms, our staff can provide the individual attention to detail that cannot be found in larger facilities.

Host: Matt O'Neal
Rooms: 55 (PB) $49-80
Full and Continental Breakfast Available
Credit Cards: A, B, C, D, E, F
Notes: 2, 3, 4, 5, 6, 7, 8, 9, 10, 12

FRANKLIN

Oak Haven Bed and Breakfast

Route #2, Box 57, 46131
(317) 535-9491

Our 1913 home is nestled among large trees that give a feeling of tranquility to our country setting. Enjoy the beautifully decorated rooms, antiques, and oak woodwork and floors throughout our home. Come play our player piano or relax on the porch swing. A full country breakfast is served in our formal dining room. We are conveniently located 25 minutes south of Indianapolis and close to golf courses and shopping centers. Come experience our country hospitality!

Hosts: Alan and Brenda Smith and Chris Hague
Rooms: 4 (2PB; 2SB) $42-63
Full Country Breakfast
Credit Cards: A, B
Notes: 2, 5, 7, 10

Oak Haven Bed and Breakfast

HARTFORD CITY

De'Coys' Bed and Breakfast

1546 W 100N, 47348
(317) 348-2164

Located just west of Hartford City, Indiana, De'Coys' Bed and Breakfast offers its clients extraordinary, attractive guest rooms with many special "Hoosier" touches. Guests enjoy a relaxed rural atmosphere in an old restored country home enriched with many amenities not customary to the typical hotel or motel setting. Each room demonstrates its own character, featuring antique furnishings and comfortable arrangements. An overnight stay includes a complimentary breakfast consisting of home-made specialties served from the thrasher kitchen.

Hosts: Chris and Tiann Coy
Rooms: 5 (1PB; 4SB) $44-50
Full Breakfast
Credit Cards: None
Notes: 2, 5, 7

year; 6 Pets welcome; 7 Children welcome; 8 Tennis nearby; 9 Swimming nearby; 10 Golf nearby; 11 Skiing nearby; 12 May be booked through travel agent

HUNTINGTON

Purviance House

326 South Jefferson, 46750
(219) 356-4218; (219) 356-9215

Built in 1859, this beautiful home is on the National Register of Historic Places. It features a winding cherry staircase, ornate ceilings, unique fireplaces, and parquet floors and has been lovingly restored and decorated with antiques and period furnishings to create a warm, inviting atmosphere. Amenities include TV in rooms, snacks, beverages, kitchen privileges, and library. Near recreational areas with swimming, boating, hiking, and bicycling. Historic tours available. One-half hour from Fort Wayne; two hours from Indianapolis.

Hosts: Bob and Jean Gernand
Rooms: 4 (2PB; 2SB) $40-65
Full Breakfast
Credit Cards: A, B, C, D
Notes: 2, 5, 7, 8, 9, 10

KNIGHTSTOWN

Old Hoosier House

7601 S. Greensboro Pike, 46148
(317) 845-2969; (800) 775-5315

Hosts: Jean and Tom Lewis
Rooms: 4 (PB) $57-67
Full Breakfast
Credit Cards: None
Notes: 2, 5, 7, 8, 10, 12

KOONTZ LAKE

Koontz House B & B

7514 North State Road 23, 46574
(219) 586-7090

Come enjoy the beautiful home Sam Koontz built, circa 1880, on the west edge of 387-acre Koontz Lake with swimming area and boat dock. The house features large, airy bedrooms with color TV. A lakeside restaurant, marina, boat rental, and antique shops are all within walking distance. Potato Creek State Park is 12 miles away; Christmas shop and paraplanes are 60 miles away.

Hosts: Les and Jan Davison
Rooms: 4 (SB) $40-60
Full Breakfast
Credit Cards: A, B
Notes: 2, 5, 7, 8, 9, 10, 11, 12

LAGRANGE

The 1886 Inn

P. O. Box 5, 46761
(219) 463-4227

The 1886 Inn bed and breakfast is filled with historic charm and elegance. Every room is aglow with old-fashioned beauty. It is the finest lodging in the area, yet affordable. Ten minutes from Shipshewana flea market.

Hosts: Duane and Gloria Billman
Rooms: 4 (PB) $89
Expanded Continental Breakfast
Credit Cards: A, B
Notes: 2, 8, 10

LEAVENWORTH

Ye Olde Scotts Inn

RR #1, Box 5, 47137-9701
(812) 739-4747

A severe flood in 1937 destroyed most of the old homes and businesses of Leavenworth and caused the rest of the

---

NOTES: Credit cards accepted: A Master Card; B Visa; C American Express; D Discover Card; E Diners Club; F Other; 2 Personal checks accepted; 3 Lunch available; 4 Dinner available; 5 Open all

town to move up on top of a bluff. Some
of the homes there were reconstructed
from lumber from the homes in the old
town after the flood waters receded and
thus Ye Olde Scotts Inn was constructed.
First as a boarding house, then as an
overnight lodging for traveling salesmen,
itinerant preachers, and workers from the
locks. Allimae and Jack Ramshaw purchased the home some years later and
restored it, trying to capture the mood of
the 1930's. Lots of things to do and see in
the area. After a day of activity, return to
the inn and enjoy watching the spectacular
sunset from the beautiful veranda.

The Thorpe House

Hosts: Jack and Allimae Ramshaw
Rooms: 4 (SB) $30-33
Continental Breakfast
Credit Cards: None
Notes: 2, 5, 9, 10, 11

METAMORA

The Thorpe House Country Inn

Clayborne Street, P.O. Box 36, 47030
(317) 932-2365; (317) 647-5425

Visit the Thorpe House in historic
Metamora where the steam engine still
brings passenger cars and the grist mill still
grinds cornmeal. Spend a relaxing evening
in this 1840 canal town home. Rooms are
tastefully furnished with antiques and country accessories. Enjoy a hearty breakfast
before visiting more than 100 shops in this
quaint village. Our family-style dining room
is also open to the public.

Hosts: Mike and Jean Owens
Rooms: 4 + two-room suite (PB) $60-100
Full Breakfast
Credit Cards: A, B, D
Notes: 2, 3, 4, 6, 7, 10, 12

MIDDLEBURY

Bee Hive Bed and Breakfast

Box 1191, 46540
(219) 825-5023

Come visit Amish country and enjoy Hoosier hospitality. The Bee Hive is a two-story,
open floor plan with exposed hand-sawed
red oak beams and a loft. Enjoy our
collection of antique farm machinery and
other collectibles. Snuggle under hand-
made quilts and wake to the smell of
freshly baked muffins.

Hosts: Herb and Treva Swarm
Rooms: 4 (1PB; 3SB) $52-68
Full Breakfast
Credit Cards: A, B
Notes: 2, 5, 7, 8, 10, 11

Bee Hive B & B

A Laber of Love—A Bed and Breakfast by Lori

11030 CR 10, 46540
(219) 825-7877

New Cape Cod home located in northern Indiana Amish farm country on three acres—two of which are wooded. Screened-in gazebo in woods ideal for quiet time or just relaxing. Queen size beds and private baths. (Guests rooms are located upstairs.) Close to large flea market open from May to October on Tuesdays and Wednesdays. Lots of shopping in Middlebury and Shipshewana. Home-baked cinnamon rolls highlight continental breakfast.

Hostess: Lori Laber
Rooms: 2 (PB) $55
Continental Breakfast
Credit Cards: None
Notes: 2, 5, 10

Look Out Bed and Breakfast

14544 CR 12, 46540
(219) 825-9809

Located in the Amish country of northeast Indiana. Near the Menno-Hof (Amish-Mennonite Information Center); Shipshewana auction and flea market; antique, craft, and gift shops; famous restaurants; and the 1832 Bonneyville mill. Enjoy the spectacular view with a country-style breakfast in the sunroom. Swim in the private pool, or walk the wooded trails.

Hosts: Mary-Lou and Jim Wolfe
Rooms: 5 (3PB; 2SB) $50-70
Full Breakfast
Credit Cards: A, B
Notes: 2, 5, 7, 9, 10, 11

Patchwork Quilt Country Inn

11748 CR 2, 46540
(219) 825-2417; (219) 825-5172 (FAX)

Relax and enjoy the simple grace and charm of our 100-year-old farmhouse. Sample our country cooking with home-made breads and desserts. Tour our back roads, and meet our Amish friends. Buy hand-made articles, then return to the inn and rest in our quaint guest rooms.

Hostesses: Maxine Zook and Susan Thomas
Rooms: 9 (SB) $50.95-95
Full Breakfast
Credit Cards: A, B
Closed first two weeks of January, holidays, Sundays
Notes: 2, 3, 4, 8, 10, 11

Yoder's Zimmer mit Frühstück Haus

P.O. Box 1396, 46540
(219) 825-2378

We enjoy sharing our Amish-Mennonite heritage in our spacious Crystal Valley home. The rooms feature hand-made quilts and antiques. Antiques and collectibles can be seen throughout the home. Three of our rooms can accommodate families. There are several common rooms available for relaxing, reading, TV, games, or socializing. Facilities are also available for pastor-elder retreats. Air conditioned, playground, swimming pool.

Hosts: Wilbur E. and Evelyn Yoder
Rooms: 5 (5 rooms to 2.5SB) $52.50
Full Breakfast
Credit Cards: A, B
Notes: 2, 5, 7, 8, 9, 10, 11, 12

NOTES: Credit cards accepted: A Master Card; B Visa; C American Express; D Discover Card; E Diners Club; F Other; 2 Personal checks accepted; 3 Lunch available; 4 Dinner available; 5 Open all

NAPPANEE

Market St. Guesthouse

253 E. Market Street, 46550
(800) 497-3791

Three-story brick Colonial home completely restored. On National Register of Historical Places. Private baths, full breakfast. Near Shipshewana and Notre Dame.

Hostess: Jean Janc
Rooms: 5 (3PB; 2SB) $50-60
Full Breakfast
Credit Cards: A, B
Notes: 2, 4, 5, 8, 9, 10, 11

NASHVILLE

Wraylyn Knoll Bed and Breakfast

2008 Greasy Ck. Rd., P.O. Box 481, 47448
(812) 988-0733

Wraylyn Knoll B&B is a family-owned and operated large main house with four guest rooms, small cottage with two guest rooms, and lots of common areas. Inground swimming pool, fishing pond, hiking trails over 12 acres. On a high hill, great view. Crochet on porch swings. Awesome view of the stars. Help yourself to refreshments in the evening. Cool breezes and warm welcomes! We welcome small groups, too.

Hosts: Marcia and Larry Wray
Rooms: 6 (PB)
Full Breakfast on Weekends (Continental on Weekdays)
Credit Cards: A, B
Notes: 2, 5, 7, 8, 9, 10, 11, 12

SHIPSHEWANA

Morton Street Bed and Breakfast

140 Morton Street, P. O. Box 775, 46565
(219) 768-4391; (800) 447-6475

Located in the heart of Amish country in Shipshewana you will find yourself within walking distance of all kinds of shops and the famous Shipshewana flea market. Special winter and weekend rates available.

Hosts: Joel and Kim Mishler and Esther Mishler
Rooms: 10 (PB) (call for rates)
Full Breakfast
Credit Cards: A, B, D
Notes: 2, 5, 10, 11, 12

SOUTH BEND

Queen Anne Inn

420 W. Washington, 46601
(219) 234-5959; (219) 234-4324 (FAX)

This Queen Anne Neo-Classical home built in 1893 was moved in order to preserve the historical structure. Frank Lloyd Wright bookcases, original hand-painted wallpaper, and an ornately carved tiger oak staircase are classics for the house. Guests can relax in the music room, the library, or the wrap-around porch. The inn is located near Notre Dame, the Studebaker Museum, and many other historic places. A great place to relax and reflect.

Hosts: Pauline and Bob Medhurst
Rooms: 5 (PB) $65-89
Full Breakfast
Credit Cards: A, B, C
Notes: 2, 5, 7, 8, 9, 10, 11 (cross country)

year; 6 Pets welcome; 7 Children welcome; 8 Tennis nearby; 9 Swimming nearby; 10 Golf nearby; 11 Skiing nearby; 12 May be booked through travel agent

TIPPECANOE

Bessinger's Hillfarm Wildlife Refuge Bed and Breakfast

4588 State Road 110, 46570
(219) 223-3288

This cozy log home overlooks 265 acres of rolling hills, woods, pasture fields, and marsh with 41 islands. It is ideal for geese and deer year-round. This farm features hiking trails with beautiful views, picnic areas, and benches tucked away in a quiet area. Varied seasons make it possible to canoe, swim, fish, bird-watch, hike, and cross-country ski. Start with a country breakfast and be ready for an unforgettable experience.

Hosts: Wayne and Betty Bessinger
Rooms: 3 (PB) $55-65
Full Breakfast
Credit Cards: None
Notes: 2, 4, 5, 9

Iowa

AMANA COLONIES

Die Heimat Country Inn

Main Street, Homestead, 52236
(319) 622-3937

Die Heimat Country Inn is located in the historic Amana Colonies. It was built in 1854 and is listed on the National Register of Historic Places. The inn is decorated with locally hand-crafted walnut and cherry furniture, with many home-made quilts and antiques throughout.

Hosts: Warren and Jacki Lock
Rooms: 19 (PB) $36-65
Full Breakfast
Credit Cards: A, B, D
Notes: 2, 5, 6, 7, 9, 10

BURLINGTON

Lakeview Bed and Breakfast

RR#5, Box 734, 52601
(319) 752-8735; (800) 753-8735

Built from the ruins of the county's third oldest home, the elegant country home stands where stagecoach passengers once slept. Now your retreat to Lakeview is a mix of the old and the new on 30 acres of magnificent country charm. The house features crystal chandeliers, antiques, collectibles, and a circular staircase. Outdoors you can enjoy a swim in our pool; fishing in our three-acre lake stocked with catfish, bass, crappie, and bluegill; or just spend time making friends with our family of miniature horses. Guests can also take advantage of our large video library of noted Christian speakers. A video studio is available for recording and small conferences.

Hosts: Jack and Linda Rowley
Rooms: 4 (PB) $45-60
Expanded Continental Breakfast
Credit Cards: A, B
Notes: 2, 5, 8, 9, 10, 12

CALMAR

Calmar Guesthouse

Rural Route 1, Box 206, 52132
(319) 562-3851

Newly remodeled, this century-old Victorian home was built by attorney John B. Kaye and has stained glass, antiques, and upstairs and downstairs sitting rooms with cable TV. It is located close to Bily Clocks in Spillville, the smallest church, Spook Cave, Niagara Cave, Lake Meyer, bike trails, golf courses, a community college, Norwegian museum, and Luther College in Decorah. Breakfast is served in the formal dining room. Bicycle trails

year; 6 Pets welcome; 7 Children welcome; 8 Tennis nearby; 9 Swimming nearby; 10 Golf nearby; 11 Skiing nearby; 12 May be booked through travel agent

are nearby.

Hosts: Art and Lucille Kruse
Rooms: 5 (SB) $35-45
Full Breakfast
Credit Cards: A, B
Notes: 2, 5, 7, 8, 9, 10, 11

CENTERVILLE

One of a Kind
314 West State, 52544
(515) 437-4540 (voice and FAX)

One of a Kind is a stately three-story brick home built in 1867. Situated in one of Iowa's delightful small communities. You will be within walking distance of antique shops, the town square, city park with tennis courts, swimming pool, etc. Twelve-minute drive to Iowa's largest lake.

Hosts: Jack and Joyce Stufflebeem
Rooms: 5 (2PB; 3SB) $35-60
Full Breakfast
Credit Cards: A, B
Notes: 2, 3, 4, 5, 8, 9, 10, 11, 12

One of a Kind

CLERMONT

Mill Street Bed and Breakfast
505 Mill Street, P. O. Box 34, 52135
(319) 423-5531

Mill Street Bed and Breakfast is a ranch-style home with central air conditioning. Near excellent restaurant and gift shops. Enjoy Montauk, canoeing, and fishing.

Hosts: Roger and Lois Amundson
Rooms: 2 (PB) $35
Full Breakfast
Credit Cards: None
Notes: 2, 5, 7, 8, 9, 10

DUBUQUE

The Hancock House
1105 Grove Terrace, 52001
(319) 557-8989

Located in Dubuque's Wealth Street Historic District, this gracious Queen Anne creates a timeless romantic atmosphere. Fireplaces, antique-filled guest quarters, whirlpool baths, and an outstanding panoramic view combine to make your stay unforgettable. Featured in *Victorian Sampler* for its "warm hospitality, cloud-like featherbeds, and a breakfast to ooh and ahh over."

Rooms: 9 (PB) $75-150
Full Breakfast
Credit Cards: A, B, C, D
Notes: 2, 5, 7, 8, 9, 10, 11, 12

ELK HORN

Joy's Morning Glory
4308 Main St., Box 12, 51531
(712) 764-5631

Be special guests in our beautiful refurbished 1912 home. As our guest, you will be greeted by an abundant array of flowers that line our walkways. Inside, your choice of floral decorated bedrooms awaits you

---

NOTES: Credit cards accepted: A Master Card; B Visa; C American Express; D Discover Card; E Diners Club; F Other; 2 Personal checks accepted; 3 Lunch available; 4 Dinner available; 5 Open all

as well. Breakfast is prepared on Joy's antique cookstove and served in the dining room, front porch, or flower filled backyard. Elk Horn community is home to the largest rural Danish settlement in the United States. The town has a working windmill and is home to the National Danish Immigrant Museum and the Tivoli Festival.

Hosts: Joy and Merle Petersen
Rooms: 3 (SB) $45
Full Breakfast
Credit Cards: None
Notes: 2, 7 (over 10), 8, 9, 10, 12
Closed January

FOREST CITY

The 1897 Victorian House

306 South Clark St., 50436
(515) 582-3613

Offering you hospitality in this turn-of-the-century Queen Anne Victorian home. As a guest at The 1897 Victorian House, you may choose from four beautifully decorated bedrooms, each with a private bath. Breakfast, included in your room rate, is served every morning in our dining room, and we specialize in home-made food. An antique shop is located on premises, and tours of various local interests are available. Gift certificates are available. Come relax in Forest City, a quiet yet progressive rural community.

Hosts: Richard and Doris Johnson
Rooms: 4 (PB) $50-70
Full Breakfast
Credit Cards: A, B
Notes: 2, 3&4 (by reservation), 5, 7 (by arrangement), 9, 10, 12

FORT MADISON

Kingsley Inn

707 Avenue H, 52627
(319) 372-7074; (800) 441-2327; (319) 372-7096 (FAX)

Experience complete relaxation in 1860's Victorian luxury. Fourteen spacious rooms are furnished in period antiques with today's modern comforts. Awaken to the aroma of "Kingsley Blend" coffee and enjoy the specialty breakfast in the elegant morning room. Private baths (some whirlpools), CATV, AC, and telephone. Stroll to replica of 1808 Fort, museum, parks, shops, and antique malls. Fifteen minutes from historic Nauvoo, Illinois. Treat yourself to a relaxing lunch or dinner at our unique restaurant, Alpha's on the Riverfront.

Hosts: Myrna M. Reinhard
Rooms: 14(PB) $65-105 (off season rates)
Continental Plus Breakfast
Credit Cards: A, B, C, D, E
Notes: 2, 3, 4, 5, 7(limited), 9, 12

GRINNELL

Clayton Farms Bed and Breakfast

621 Newburg Rd., 50112
(515) 236-3011

Extra nice contemporary farm home on 320-acre livestock, grain operation. Swimming, fishing area with screened shelter house in season on three-acre farm pond. Family room with fireplace, TV, VCR, library of movies, kitchenette, and central air. Family-style breakfast, home-made breads, rolls, jams, jellies. Ideal accommodations for pheasant hunters. Packages for groups of hunters. Seven miles from Grinnell College. One hour from Des Moines and Iowa City. No smoking. Member of Iowa Bed and Breakfast Innkeepers Association.

Hosts: Ron and Judie Clayton
Rooms: 3 (1 PB; 2 SB) $45 (special hunter's rate)
Full Breakfast
Credit Cards: A, B
Notes: 2 (for deposit only), 6 (hunting dogs), 7 (over five), 8, 9, 10, 11

IOWA CITY

Haverkamp's Linn St. Homestay B&B

619 N. Linn St., 52245
(319) 337-4363

Enjoy the warmth and hospitality in our 1908 Edwardian home filled with heirlooms and collectibles. Only a short walk to downtown Iowa City and the University of Iowa main campus, and a short drive to the Hoover Library in West Branch, to the Amish in Kalona, and to the seven Amana Colonies.

Hosts: Dorothy and Clarence Haverkamp
Rooms: 3 (SB) $30-40
Credit Cards: None
Notes: 2, 5, 7, 8, 9, 12

LANSING

Lansing House

291 Front Street, 52151
(319) 538-4263

Lansing House is a handsome riverfront home, situated next to the picturesque Blackhawk Bridge, offering its guests an atmosphere of comfort and elegance, along with a picture-window view of the great Mississippi River. Guests have a full breakfast with home-made muffins or breads and can take a pleasant walk along the river into town or just amble along the river.

Hosts: Chris and Margaret Fitzgerald
Rooms: 2 (SB) $63
Full Breakfast
Credit Cards: None
Notes: 2, 5, 8, 9, 10

MAQUOKETA

Squiers Manor Bed and Breakfast

418 West Pleasant Street, 52060
(319) 652-6961

Squiers Manor Bed and Breakfast is located in the West Pleasant Street Historic District. This 1892 Queen Anne mansion features walnut, cherry, and butternut woods throughout. Enjoy period furnishings, queen-size beds, in-room phone and television, private baths, single and double jacuzzis. Come hungry and enjoy delicious, candlelight evening desserts and breakfast (more like brunch) served in the elegant diningroom. Virl and Kathy's goal is to make your stay as pleasant and enjoyable as possible. Give us a call today!

Hosts: Virl and Kathy Banowetz
Rooms: 6 (PB) $65-95
Full Breakfast
Credit Cards: A, B, C
Notes: 2, 5, 7, 8, 9, 10, 11

NOTES: Credit cards accepted: A Master Card; B Visa; C American Express; D Discover Card; E Diners Club; F Other; 2 Personal checks accepted; 3 Lunch available; 4 Dinner available; 5 Open all

MARENGO

Loy's Farm Bed and Breakfast

Rural Route 1, Box 82, 52301
(319) 642-7787

This beautiful, modern home is on a working grain and hog farm with quiet and pleasant views of rolling countryside. A farm tour is offered with friendly hospitality. The large recreation room includes a pool table, table tennis, and shuffleboard. Swing set and sand pile are in the large yard. Close to the Amana Colonies, Tanger Mall, Kalona, Iowa City, West Branch, and Cedar Rapids. I-80, Exit 216 north, one mile.

Hosts: Loy and Robert Walker
Rooms: 3 (1PB; 2SB) $50-60
Full Breakfast
Credit Cards: None
Notes: 2, 4 (by arrangement), 5, 6 (caged), 7, 8, 9, 10, 12

PELLA

Avondgloren (Sunset View)

R.R. #3, P.O. Box 65, 50219-0065
(515) 628-1578

Our charming brick home is ideally situated 1 1/2 miles southwest of Pella and 1 1/2 miles northwest of Red Rock Dam. It is on an acreage with a view of both sunset and sunrise. It has decorating accents of live plants inside for your year-round enjoyment, as well as flower gardens outside, true to the Dutch heritage. Also, a family room with a TV and fireplace is available for your use. Central air conditioning. A back deck with a lovely country view can also be used for your leisure time enjoyment. Credit cards are only used to hold your room. Payment for stay paid with cash or check in order to keep room rates low.

Hosts: Henry and Luella M. Bandstra
Rooms: 3 (SB) $45-55
Full Breakfast
Credit Cards: None
Notes: 2, 5, 8, 10

Sunset View

Heritage House B & B

1345 Highway 163, 50143
(515) 626-3092

In business since 1983, this lovely 1918 farm home has TV's and central air conditioning. Rooms were redecorated and newly carpeted in 1993. The Victorian room is filled with antique furniture and an old pump organ. Located near Pella, Iowa, famous for Tulip Time the second week of May. Historical tours are available year-around to experience a touch of Holland. Dutch shops and gourmet restaurants. Many antique shops are nearby. Near Knoxville, Iowa—the sprint car racing capital. Enjoy a gourmet breakfast served in the formal dining room with crystal and lace. Member IBBIA.

Hostess: Iola Vander Wilt
Rooms: 2 (PB) $45-50
Full Breakfast
Credit Cards: None
Closed January
Notes: 2, 6, 7 (with restrictions), 8, 9, 10, 11, 12

year; 6 Pets welcome; 7 Children welcome; 8 Tennis nearby; 9 Swimming nearby; 10 Golf nearby; 11 Skiing nearby; 12 May be booked through travel agent

SAINT ANSGAR

Blue Belle Inn
513 W. 4th Street, 50472
(515) 736-2225

Rediscover the romance of the 1890's while enjoying the comfort and convenience of the 1990's in one of six distinctively decorated guest rooms at the Blue Belle Inn. The festive Victorian Painted Lady features air conditioning, fireplaces, and jacuzzis. Lofty tin ceilings, gleaming maple woodwork, stained glass, and crystal chandeliers set in bay and curved window pockets create a shimmering interplay of light and color. Enjoy breakfast on the balcony or gourmet dining by candlelight.

Hostess: Sherri C. Hansen
Rooms: 6 (5PB; 1SB) Call for rates
Full Breakfast
Credit Cards: A, B
Notes: 2, 3, 4, 5, 7, 9, 10, 12

SCOTCH GROVE

The Grove Bed and Breakfast
110th Avenue RR, 52331
(319) 465-3858

Have a mini-vacation or an overnite at this peaceful rural location. Home is surrounded by many lovely flower beds. Located on a hard-surfaced road, close to famous Grant Wood Country in Jones County and within 35 miles of Dubuque or Cedar Rapids. Big country breakfast featuring delicious home-made cinnamon rolls. Private wing and bath. Great antique shops within ten miles.

Hosts: Robert and Ruth Zirkelbach
Rooms: 1 (PB) $35+tax
Full Breakfast
Credit Cards: None
Notes: 2, 5, 7, 9, 10

SHELDON

A Touch of Murray
802 4th Avenue, 51201
(712) 324-3292

Visit the home of the three Murray sisters. Restored 1900's Victorian home, complete with original furnishings. Evening refreshments and hearty full breakfast in the morning. Central air, gift shop, gourmet teas and coffees. Luncheons, brunches, and teas served to the public. Located in a clean, quiet town in the Midwest. Surrounded by rich, fertile farmland. Join us in a state that celebrates four beautiful seasons of the year.

Hosts: Galen and Shirley Elgersma
Rooms: 3 (PB) $50-60
Full Breakfast
Credit Cards: None
Notes: 2, 3, 4, 5, 7, 8, 9, 10

TIPTON

Victorian House of Tipton
508 E. 4th St., 52772
(319) 886-2633

Iowa's oldest B&B, a "painted lady" "storybook" (6 pastel colors) Victorian on National Historical Registry and one of Iowa's rare treasures. Conveniently located near all S.E. Iowa activities, abundantly furnished with antiques making it a private museum. Visit us, step back a century, relax on our beautiful porch, enjoy the peace, let joys never cease, and just watch the rest of the world go by. Call for reservations. Gift certificates available. Ask for *Christian Bed and Breakfast Directory* discount.

Hosts: Lowell and Dee
Rooms: 4 (PB) $65 (weekends) - $60 (weekday)
2nd nite $10 off
Closed Jan and Feb
Full Breakfast
Credit Cards: A, B
Notes: 2, 4, 7, 8, 9, 10, 12

WALNUT

Clark's Country Inn

701 Walnut Street, Box 533, 51577
(712) 784-3010

Iowa's antique capital, one mile south of I-80 between Omaha and Des Moines. Six malls, individual shops, over 200 dealers, open all year. 1912 two-story home, oak interior, antiques. Newly remodeled guest rooms, private baths, king/queen beds, central air, full breakfast. MC/Visa deposit required. No smoking.

Hosts: Ron and Mary Lou Clark
Rooms: 3 (PB) $49
Full Breakfast
Credit Cards: A, B
Notes: 2, 5, 7(over 12), 8, 9, 10, 12

WEBSTER CITY

Centennial Farm B & B

1091 220th Street, 50595
(515) 832-3050

Centennial Farm is a bed and breakfast homestay located on a farm that has been in the family since 1869. Tom was born in the house. Guests may take a ride in a 1929 Model A pickup truck, if desired. In a quiet location near several good antique shops. Member of Iowa Bed and Breakfast Innkeepers Association, Inc. Air conditioned. Twenty-two miles west of I-35 at Exit 142 or Exit 144.

Hosts: Tom and Shirley Yungclas
Rooms: 2 (SB) $35
Full Breakfast
Credit Cards: None
Notes: 2, 5, 7, 8, 9, 10

WILLIAMSBURG

Lucille's Bett und Breakfast

R.R. 2, Box 55, 52361
(319) 668-1185

Experience Gemütlichkeit (German hospitality) in our country home. Family-style country breakfast with home-made breads, apfel kuchen, kolaches, etc. graciously served. The peaceful, quiet atmosphere lends itself to the perfect getaway retreat. Take I-80 to exit 225, Little Amena.

Hosts: Dale and Lucille Bell
Rooms: 2 (plus queen size sofa sleeper)(SB)
$55-60
Full Breakfast
Credit Cards: None
Notes: 2, 3, 4, 5, 7, 9, 10, 12

Lucille's Bett und Breakfast

year; 6 Pets welcome; 7 Children welcome; 8 Tennis nearby; 9 Swimming nearby; 10 Golf nearby; 11 Skiing nearby; 12 May be booked through travel agent

Kansas

FORT SCOTT

Huntington House Bed and Breakfast

324 S. Main, 66701
(316) 223-3644

Arrive as a guest, leave as a friend. Charming historic 1906 home on lovely tree-shaded brick street. Adjacent to uniquely restored downtown. Only five minutes from Fort Scott National Historic Site. Four sunny, imaginatively decorated bedrooms. Attractive 18' x 36' outdoor pool. Beautiful leaded and beveled windows. Air conditioning for your comfort. Fresh bread baked daily and served with a cup of gourmet coffee or tea.

Hostess: Jeannie Volker
Rooms: 4 (2PB; 2SB) $55-65
Full Breakfast
Credit Cards: A, B
Notes: 2, 5, 7, 8, 9, 10, 12

Huntington House

GREAT BEND

Peaceful Acres Bed and Breakfast

Rt. 5, Box 153, 67530
(316) 793-7527

Enjoy a mini-farm, sprawling, tree-shaded, old farmhouse furnished with some antiques. If you like quiet and peace, chickens, goats, guineas, kittens in the spring, and old-fashioned hospitality, you need to come and visit us. Breakfast will be fixed from home-grown products. We are near historical areas, Sante Fe Trail, Ft. Larned, Cheyenne Bottoms, zoo, and tennis courts. Member of the Kansas Bed and Breakfast Association.

Hosts: R. Dale and Doris J. Nitzel
Rooms: 3 (SB) $30
Full Breakfast
Credit Cards: None
Notes: 2, 5, 6, 8, 12

LENEXA

Bed and Breakfast Kansas City

P. O. Box 14781, 66285
(913) 888-3636

This reservation service can arrange your

NOTES: Credit cards accepted: A Master Card; B Visa; C American Express; D Discover Card; E Diners Club; F Other; 2 Personal checks accepted; 3 Lunch available; 4 Dinner available; 5 Open all

accommodations in Kansas City or the St. Louis, Missouri, area. From an 1857 plantation mansion on the river to a geodesic dome in the woods with hot tub, there is a price and style for everyone. Victorian, turn-of-the-century, English Tudor, and contemporary are available. Double, queen, or king beds, most with private baths. The service represents 35 inns and homes. $40-125.

LINDSBORG

Swedish Country Inn

112 West Lincoln, 67456
(913) 227-2985; out of state (800) 231-0266

The Swedish Country Inn is an authentic Swedish bed and breakfast. There are 19 rooms furnished with Swedish-pine imported furniture and hand-made quilts. Each room has a TV and phone. A full buffet Scandinavian breakfast is served. Use of sauna and bicycles is included. We have a small gift shop just off the lobby and are only one-half block off Main Street where there are wonderful shops and art galleries.

Hosts: Nick and Joan Wilson
Rooms: 19 (PB) $45-75
Full Breakfast
Credit Cards: A, B
Notes: 2, 5, 7, 8, 9, 10

NEWTON

Hawk House Bed and Breakfast

307 W. Broadway, 67114
(316) 283-2045

1914 turn-of-the-century elegance. Origi-

nal light fixtures, wallpaper from Europe, oak woodwork, and a large stained glass window await your arrival. Three blocks from downtown where quaint shops and antique stores can be found. Guests may use the common area to read, watch TV, play games, or visit. All guest rooms offer queen-size beds and antique furnishings. Facility is available for meetings, retreats, weddings, and receptions.

Hosts: Lon and Carol Buller
Rooms: 4 (1 PB; 3 SB) $50-60
Full Breakfast
Credit Cards: A, B
Notes: 2, 5, 7, 8, 9, 10

VALLEY FALLS

The Barn Bed and Breakfast Inn

Rural Route 2, Box 87, 66088
(913) 945-3225

In the rolling hills of northeast Kansas, this 100-year-old barn has been converted into a bed and breakfast. Sitting high on a hill with a beautiful view, it has a large indoor heated pool, fitness room, three living rooms, king or queen beds in all rooms. We serve you supper, as well as a full breakfast, and have three large meeting rooms available.

Hosts: Tom and Marcella Ryan
Rooms: 20 (PB) $63-76
Full Breakfast and Supper
Credit Cards: A, B, C, D
Notes: 2, 3, 4, 5, 7, 8, 9, 10, 12

year; 6 Pets welcome; 7 Children welcome; 8 Tennis nearby; 9 Swimming nearby; 10 Golf nearby; 11 Skiing nearby; 12 May be booked through travel agent

WAKEFIELD

Wakefield's Country Bed and Breakfast

RR #1, Box 212, 197 Sunflower Rd., 67487
(913) 461-5533

A touch of country living awaits you at our home. We are the third generation of our family living on our diversified grain and livestock farm. We offer quiet country hospitality. A short drive from Milford Lake, Abilene, Junction City and Manhattan.

Hosts: Vernon and Kathy Yenni
Rooms: 2 (PB) $45
Full Breakfast
Credit Cards: None
Notes: 2, 5, 6, 7

Kentucky

BARDSTOWN

Kenmore Farms

1050 Bloomfield Rd., US 62E, 40004
(502) 348-8023

Our 1860's Victorian-Italianate home on 165 acres features antique furnishings, oriental rugs, poplar floors, and a gleaming cherry stairway. Four gracious rooms are decorated with four-poster or Victorian-style beds and beautiful vintage linens. Private baths. Full country breakfast. Enjoy Southern hospitality, a tranquil farm setting, and the convenience of being near tourist attractions of historical Bardstown.

Hosts: Dorothy and Bernie Keene
Rooms: 3 (PB) $70
Full Breakfast
Credit Cards: None
Notes: 2, 5, 7 (over 12), 8, 9, 10

BOWLING GREEN

Alpine Lodge

5310 Morgantown Road, 42101-8201
(502) 843-4846

We are a Swiss Chalet located on nine and one-half acres of beautiful gardens, flowers, shrubs, and nature trails where you can watch our deer from five deer stands. The lodge has 6,000-square-feet and is decorated in antiques. We have a screened-in porch in which breakfast is usually served in season. Breakfast is a Southern menu of biscuits, gravy, grits, fried apples, eggs, sausage or ham, with fresh fruit in season from our orchard, coffee or tea. We have a deck, gazebo, and pool.

Hosts: Dr. and Mrs. David Livingston
Rooms: 5 and guest house (3PB; 2SB) $45-65
Full Breakfast
Credit Cards: None
Notes: 2, 3, 4, 5, 6 (dogs), 7, 9, 10, 12

GEORGETOWN

Pineapple Inn

645 S. Broadway, 40324
(502) 868-5453

Located in beautiful Georgetown, Kentucky, our beautiful home, built in 1876, is on The National Historic Register. Country French dining room, large living room. Three bedrooms with private baths upstairs. Grandma's room full bed, Victorian Room full bed, American room twin beds, Main floor room queen size bed with canopy. Shared bath. Home is furnished with antiques. Very beautifully decorated. Full breakfast served.

Hosts: Muriel and Les
Rooms: 4 (3PB; 1SB) $60
Full Breakfast
Credit Cards: None
Notes: 2, 5, 8, 9, 10

year; 6 Pets welcome; 7 Children welcome; 8 Tennis nearby; 9 Swimming nearby; 10 Golf nearby; 11 Skiing nearby; 12 May be booked through travel agent

HARRODSBURG

Canaan Land Farm B&B

4355 Lexington Rd., 40330
(606) 734-3984

Step back in time to a house nearly 200 years old. Canaan Land B&B is an historic home, c1795. Rooms feature antiques, collectibles, and feather beds. Full breakfast and true Southern hospitality. This is a working sheep farm with lambing. Your host is a shepherd/attorney, and your hostess is a handspinner/artist. Farm is secluded and peaceful. Close to Shaker Village. This is a non-smoking B&B.

Hosts: Fred and Theo Bee
Rooms: 3 (PB) $65-75
Full Breakfast
Credit Cards: None
Notes: 2, 3 and 4 (Picnic), 5, 7 (strictly supervised by parents), 10

LOUISVILLE

The Victorian Secret Bed and Breakfast

1132 South First Street, 40203
(502) 581-1914

"Step inside and step back 100 years in time" describes this three-story, Victorian brick mansion in historic Louisville. Recently restored to its former elegance, the 110-year-old structure offers spacious accommodations, high ceilings, and original woodwork. The Louisville area, rich in historic homes, will also tempt railbirds and would-be jockeys to make a pilgrimage to the famous track at Churchill Downs, Home of the Kentucky Derby.

Hosts: Nan and Steve Roosa
Rooms: 6 (2PB; 4SB) $48-68
Continental Breakfast
Credit Cards: None
Notes: 5, 7, 8, 9, 10, 11, 12

MIDDLESBORO

The Ridge Runner B & B

208 Arthur Heights, 40965
(606) 248-4299

This 1891 Victorian home is furnished with authentic antiques and nestled in the Cumberland Gap Mountains. A picturesque view is enjoyed from a 60-foot front porch. You are treated like a special person in a relaxed, peaceful atmosphere. Five minutes from Cumberland Gap National Historic Park, 12 miles from Pine Mountain State Park, 50 miles from Knoxville, Tennessee.

Hostess: Susan Richards
Rooms: 5 (2PB; 3SB) $45-50
Full Breakfast
Credit Cards: A, B
Notes: 2, 5

The Ridge Runner

NICHOLASVILLE

Sandusky House

1626 Delaney Ferry Road, 40356
(606) 223-4730

A tree-lined drive to the Sandusky House is just a prelude to a wonderful visit to the

Bluegrass. A quiet ten-acre country setting amid horse farms yet close to downtown Lexington, KY, horse park and Shakertown. The Greek Revival Sandusky House was built circa 1850 from bricks fired on the farm. A 1780 one-thousand-acre land grant from Patrick Henry, Governor of Virginia, given to Revolutionary War soldier, Jacob Sandusky.

Hosts: Jim and Linda Humphrey
Rooms: 3(PB) $69
Full Breakfast
Credit Cards: A, B
Notes: 2, 5, 7

PADUCAH

1857's Bed and Breakfast

127 Market House Square, P.O. Box 7771, 42002
(502) 444-3960

The 1857's Bed and Breakfast is in the center of Paducah's historic downtown on Market House Square. The three-story building was built in 1857 and is on the National Register of Historic Places. The first floor is a cafe. The second floor guest rooms have been renovated in Victorian Era style and period furnishings abound. Also available for guest enjoyment third floor game room with a view of the Ohio River. The game room features an elegant mahogany billiards table. Advance reservations advised.

Hosts: Steve and Deborah Bohnert
Rooms: 2(SB) $55-65
Continental Plus Breakfast
Credit Cards: A, B
Notes: 2, 5, 12

Ehrhardt's Bed and Breakfast

285 Springwell Lane, 42001
(502) 554-0644

Our brick Colonial ranch home is located just one mile off I-24, which is noted for its lovely scenery. We hope to make you feel at home in antique-filled bedrooms and a cozy den with a fireplace. Nearby are the beautiful Kentucky and Barkley lakes and the famous Land Between the Lakes area.

Hosts: Eileen and Phil Ehrhardt
Rooms: 2(SB) $35
Full Breakfast
Credit Cards: None
Notes: 2, 7 (over 6), 8, 9, 10

WILMORE

Scott Station Inn Bed and Breakfast

305 East Main St., 40390
(606) 858-0121

The Scott Station Inn is located in downtown, historic Wilmore, Kentucky, just three blocks from famous Asbury College, Asbury Seminary, and only minutes from Shakertown, Fort Harrod, and Lexington, Kentucky. Beautifully refurbished in 1990, this 100-year-old farmhouse has kept the charm of an old Kentucky home. Our inn has six rental rooms; three with shared baths ($39) and three with private baths ($49). We welcome pastor-staff and Sunday school retreats.

Hosts: Sandy and Mike Jansen
Rooms: 6 (3SB; 3PB) $39-49
Full Breakfast
Credit Cards: A, B
Notes: None

year; 6 Pets welcome; 7 Children welcome; 8 Tennis nearby; 9 Swimming nearby; 10 Golf nearby; 11 Skiing nearby; 12 May be booked through travel agent

Louisiana

CARENCRO/LAFAYETTE

La Maison de Campagne, Lafayette B & B

825 Kidder Road, 70520
(318) 896-6529; (800) 368-7308

The "Country House" is a turn-of-the-century country Victorian nestled on nine acres of old live oak and pecan trees fifteen minutes from downtown Lafayette. All guest rooms are individually decorated with antiques and private baths. Experience the joie de vive, the joy of life of the Cajun culture in the music, food, and festivals all within a 30-mile radius. Full complimentary cajun country gourmet breakfast included. Enjoy the pool in season.

Hosts: Fred and Joeann McLemore
Rooms: 3 (PB) $80
Full Breakfast
Credit Cards: A, B
Notes: 2, 5, 9

JACKSON

Milbank Historic House

P.O. Box 1204, 3045 Bank Street, 70748
(504) 634-5901

Located in the beautiful Felicianas of Louisiana, Milbank is a massive romantic antebellum mansion. It has a varied and interesting history. Rooms are furnished with authentic antique furniture of the late 1800's. Persian rugs, ormolu clocks, carved settees, poster beds, armoires, and much more. Upstairs galleries to stand on and enjoy scenic backyard—large backyard. Delicious breakfast, friendly hosts. Owners are Mr. and Mrs. M.L. Harvey.

Hosts: Paul and Margurite Carter
Rooms: 3 (PB) $65-75
Full Breakfast (Continental available on request)
Credit Cards: A, B
Notes: 5 (except holidays), 7 (12 and up), 10

Milbank Historic House

NEW ORLEANS

623 Ursulines
623 Ursulines Street, 70116
(504) 529-5489

Seven clean and quiet accommodations
with modern comforts in the Old World
charm of the historic Vieux Carre. Located within a short walking distance of all
the famous sights and sounds of Old New
Orleans, the world renowned restaurants,
Jackson Square with the magnificent St.
Louis Cathedral, Cabildo, Presbytere, and
sidewalk artists—the French Market for
coffee and beignets, the busy Mississippi
River, the many treasure-filled antique
shops along Royal Street, and of course,
the night life of Bourbon Street. Just
around the corner is the historic home of
General Beauregard and the first convent
of the Ursuline Nuns built in 1734.

Host: Don Heil
Rooms: 7(PB) $65-80
No Breakfast
Credit Cards: None
Notes: 2, 10

Fairchild House
1518 Prytania Street, 70130
(504) 524-0154; (800) 256-8096

Designed circa 1841, this Greek Revival
residence is rich with the history of the 19th
century. Situated among the picturesque
oaks of the Lower Garden District, the
house is located seventeen blocks from the
French Quarter and eight blocks from the
Convention Center. The eight rooms,
each with private bath/shower, are decorated in a refined antique setting. In addition, the house features hardwood floors.
Complimentary refreshments served upon
arrival. Tea is served from 3:30 to 5:00

pm, except on holidays and Sundays.

Hostess: Beatriz O. Aprigliano
Rooms: 8(PB) $65-95
Continental Breakfast
Credit Cards: A, B, C
Notes: 2, 5, 7, 10, 12

New Orleans Bed and Breakfast and Accommodations
P.O. Box 8163, 70182
(504) 838-0071; (504) 838-0140 (FAX)

New Orleans Bed and Breakfast and
Accommodations is a reservation service
with approximately one hundred units
throughout New Orleans. We have accommodations in historic sections like The
Garden District as well as the new condo-
miniums of the Riverfront in the Ware-
house District (these units are very convenient to the Convention Center). NOB&B
is celebrating its fifteenth year. Owner
Sarah Margaret Brown is always pleased
to assist guests. Prices range from $40 to
$200.

St. Charles Guest House
1748 Prytania Street, 70130
(504) 523-6556

A simple, cozy, and affordable pension in
the Lower Garden District on the streetcar
line is 10 minutes to downtown and the
French Quarter. Continental breakfast is
served overlooking a charming pool and
patio complete with banana trees. Tours
are available from our lobby.

Hosts: Joanne and Dennis Hilton
Rooms: 30 (26 PB; 4 SB) $30-75
Continental Breakfast
Credit Cards: A, B
Notes: 2 (in advance), 5, 7, 8, 9

year; 6 Pets welcome; 7 Children welcome; 8 Tennis nearby; 9 Swimming nearby; 10 Golf nearby;
11 Skiing nearby; 12 May be booked through travel agent

PONCHATOULA

The Bella Rose Mansion
255 North Eight Street, 70454
(504) 386-3857

"When only the best will do" Bella Rose is on the National Historical Register in the heart of America's Antique City and Plantations. Thirty-five minutes from New Orleans Airport and 45 minutes from Baton Rouge. Romantic heart-shaped jacuzzi, suites and unique rooms, exquisite spiral staircase crowned with a stained glass dome, the finest in the South. Marble walls, indoor tennazzo shuffleboard court, heated pool, solarium with a fountain of Bacchus and a European-style casino on premises are only a few of the magnificent features that await you at the Bella Rose Mansion Country Club. Now doing weddings and parties.

Hostess: Rose James
Rooms: 2 jacuzzi suites and 4 rooms (PB)
Full Breakfast
Credit Cards: A, B
Notes: 5, 8, 9, 10

The Bella Rose Mansion

PORT VINCENT

Tree House in the Park
Mailing address: 16520 Airport Road, Prairieville, 70769
(800) Le Cabin (800) 532-2246)

A Cajun cabin in the swamp on "stilts" with two B&B rooms and a bridal suite, all fully air conditioned. Each room has a private entrance, private bath, TV, VCR, queen-size waterbed, hot tub on a private deck under the stars, and steps down to the pool and sun deck. Bridal suite has double jacuzzi bath inside also. Boat slip and fishing dock. Four ponds, an island with a gazebo, foot bridges, swings, and benches. Two piroques and a double kayak for float trip included. Very private, peaceful, and beautiful four acres of cypress and Spanish moss.

Hostess: Fran Schmieder
Rooms: 3 (PB) $110-150
Full Breakfast and Supper
Credit Cards: A, B
Notes: 2, 5, 9, 12

SAINT FRANCISVILLE

Hemingbough
P.O. Box 1640, 70775
(504) 635-6617

Hemingbough was rebuilt from original plans of Uncle Sam's Plantation in Convent, Louisiana. All rooms have private baths, four poster rice beds, TVs, phones and include a continental breakfast. Two hundred and thirty-eight acre complex. One mile south of historical

---

NOTES: Credit cards accepted: A Master Card; B Visa; C American Express; D Discover Card; E Diners Club; F Other; 2 Personal checks accepted; 3 Lunch available; 4 Dinner available; 5 Open all

Rosedown Plantation.

Rooms: 10 (PB) $85-105
Continental Breakfast
Credit Cards: A, B, C
Notes: 2, 4, 5, 7, 10, 12

WHITE CASTLE

Nottoway Plantation Inn and Restaurant

Louisiana Highway 1, P.O. Box 160, 70788
(504) 545-2730; (504) 545-9167; (504) 545-8632
(FAX)

Built in 1859 by John Randolph, a wealthy sugar cane planter, Nottoway is a blend of Italianate and Greek Revival styles. Nottoway is the largest remaining plantation home in the South. Its guest rooms are individually decorated with period furnishings.

Hostesses: Cindy Hidalgo and Faye Russell
Rooms: 13 (10 rooms, 3 suites) (PB) $125-250
Full Breakfast
Credit Cards: A, B, C, D
Closed Christmas Day
Notes: 2, 3, 4, 5, 8, 9, 10, 12

year; 6 Pets welcome; 7 Children welcome; 8 Tennis nearby; 9 Swimming nearby; 10 Golf nearby; 11 Skiing nearby; 12 May be booked through travel agent

Maine

ANDOVER

Andover Arms Family Style Bed and Breakfast

28 Newton Street, P.O. Box 387, 04216-0387
(207) 392-4251

Discover Maine the way it used to be. Stay in this comfortable 1800's farmhouse in the village and feel right at home with the warm hospitality, country breakfasts, and cozy guest rooms with oil lamps for added charm. Relax by the wood stove or play the piano. Snowmobiling and cross country skiing from the door, 20 minutes to alpine skiing, including Sunday River. Excellent hunting, fishing, biking, foliage. Lawn games and bikes available. No smoking.

Host: Pat Wyman
Rooms: 4 (1PB; 3SB) $50
Full Breakfast
Credit Cards: A, B, C, D
Notes: 2, 4, 5, 6, 7, 8, 9, 11, 12

BAR HARBOR

The Atlantic Oakes—The Willows

P.O. Box 3, 04609
(207) 288-5801; (207) 288-5801 ext. 29 (FAX)

We have restored the Sir Harry Oakes mansion/summer cottage on our grounds.

This charming home was named *The Willows* after the willow trees on the entrance drive. About 200 summer cottages were built in Bar Harbour from 1880 to 1890. *The Willows* was built in 1913, one of the last estates built. The large wooden hotels (now gone) were built from 1865 to 1885. No matter how large and ostentatious the summer homes were, they were always called "cottages."

Rooms: 8 (PB) Call for prices
Continental Breakfast
Credit Cards: A, B, E
Notes: 2, 7, 8, 9, 10, 12

Black Friar Inn

10 Summer Street, 04609
(207) 288-5091

Black Friar Inn is a completely rebuilt and restored inn incorporating beautiful woodwork, mantels, windows, and bookcases from old mansions and churches on Mount

---

Desert Island. Gourmet breakfast includes home-made breads, pastry, and muffins, fresh fruit, eggs du jour, waffles, etc. Afternoon refreshments are provided. All rooms have queen beds. Within easy walking distance of the waterfront, restaurants, and shops, with ample parking available. Short drive to Acadia National Park.

Hosts: Barbara and Jim Kelly
Rooms: 6 (PB) $85-105
Full Breakfast
Credit Cards: A, B
Closed winter months
Notes: 2, 7(over 11), 8, 9, 10

Hearthside Bed and Breakfast

7 High Street, 04609
(207) 288-4533

Built in 1907 as a private residence, the inn features a blend of country and Victorian furnishings. All rooms have queen beds, some have a private porch or fireplace. We serve a home-made full breakfast, afternoon tea and home-made cookies, and evening refreshments. Located on a quiet side street in town, we are five minutes from Acadia National Park.

Hosts: Susan and Barry Schwartz
Rooms: 9 (PB) $55-75 in winter; $75-115 in season
Full Breakfast
Credit Cards: A, B
Notes: 2, 5, 8, 9, 10, 11

Long Pond Inn

Box 361, Mt. Desert, 04660
(207) 244-5854

Centrally located on the shore of beautiful Long Pond near the quaint village of Somesville, our Inn offers one of the quietest choices of country lodging on Mount Desert Island. The Inn is our year-round home built with vintage materials recovered from dismantled estates, summer cottages, country stores, and hotels. Long Pond Inn's four guest bedrooms are charmingly appointed featuring queen-size beds and private baths; one with a jacuzzi tub. Your stay includes a hearty continental breakfast of fresh seasonal fruits and home-made muffins. After breakfast, stroll the Inn's lavish vegetable, herb, and flower gardens or enjoy a swim or paddle on the Long Pond in one of our rental canoes. Within 15 minutes of Long Pond Inn in any direction is all that Mount Desert Island has to offer: Bar Harbor, Northeast Harbor, Southwest Harbor, and breath-taking Acadia National Park. Since our family includes two Springer Spaniels, other pets are not permitted. We at Long Pond look forward to hosting you soon and in years to come.

Hosts: Bob and Pam Mensick
Rooms: 4 (PB) $75-90
Full Breakfast
Credit Cards: A, B
Notes: 2, 9, 10

Wayside Inn

11 Atlantic Ave., 04609
(207) 288-5703 (voice and FAX); (800) 722-6671

A beautiful English Tudor building decorated in early Victorian offering private and semi-private rooms with fireplaces. Full gourmet breakfast served. Located on a quiet side street in historic district within walking distance to all in-town activities. Open all year. Lower rates off season.

Hosts: Steve and Sandi Straubel
Rooms: 8 (6PB; 2SB) 70-140 (seasonal rates available)
Full Breakfast
Credit Cards: A, B
Notes: 2, 5, 7, 8, 9, 10, 11

year; 6 Pets welcome; 7 Children welcome; 8 Tennis nearby; 9 Swimming nearby; 10 Golf nearby; 11 Skiing nearby; 12 May be booked through travel agent

BATH

Fairhaven Inn

Rural Route 2, North Bath Road, Box 85, 04530
(207) 443-4391

A 1790 Colonial nestled on the hillside
overlooking the Kennebec River on 20
acres of country sights and sounds.
Beaches, golf, and maritime museum
nearby, plus cross-country ski trails, wood
fires. Gourmet breakfast is served
year-round. Candlelight dinners available
in winter.

Hosts: Sallie and George Pollard
Rooms: 8 (7PB; 2SB) $60-80
Full Breakfast
Credit Cards: A, B, C
Notes: 2, 3 (box), 4 (weekend package), 5, 6 (by
arrangement), 7 (by arrangement), 8, 9, 10, 11

BELFAST

The Jeweled Turret Inn

16 Pearl Street, 04915
(207) 338-2304; (800) 696-2304 (in state)

This grand lady of the Victorian era, circa
1898, offers many unique architectural
features and is on the National Register of
Historic Places. The inn is named for the
grand staircase that winds up the turret,
lighted by stained- and leaded-glass pan-
els with jewel-like embellishments. Each
guest room is filled with Victoriana and has
its own bath. A gourmet breakfast is served.
Shops, restaurants, and waterfront are a
stroll away.

Hosts: Carl and Cathy Heffentrager
Rooms: 7 (PB) $65-85
Full Breakfast
Credit Cards: None
Notes: 2, 5, 8, 9, 10, 11, 12

BETHEL

Sunday River Inn and Cross Country Ski Center

RFD 2, Box 1688, 04217
(207) 824-2410; (207) 824-3181 (FAX)

A ski lodge and mountain home for family-
oriented outdoor enthusiasts, the Inn features cross-country skiing on professionally groomed trails from the doorstep and
world-class downhill skiing one-half mile
away. Breakfast and dinner are served
buffet style from the big open kitchen, and
guests relax in the traditional Finnish sauna
or curl up by the open fire to read or play
games. Individuals, families, and groups
enjoy the comfortable "old shoe" ambience.

Hosts: Steve and Peggy Wright
Rooms: 22 (1PB; 21SB) $78-146
Full Breakfast and Dinner
Credit Cards: A, B, C, D
Notes: 2, 4, 7, 8, 9, 10, 11, 12

BOOTHBAY HARBOR

Anchor Watch B&B

3 Eames Rd., 04538
(207) 633-7565

Our seaside captain's house welcomes
you to Boothbay Region. It's a pleasant
walk to unique shops, fine dining, and
scenic boat trips. A delicious homemade
breakfast is served in the sunny breakfast
nook looking out to the sea. Quilts, stenciling, and nautical decor make our four
bedrooms comfortable and cozy. Enjoy
your afternoon tea in the attractive sitting
room facing the ocean. Your host captains

NOTES: Credit cards accepted: A Master Card; B Visa; C American Express; D Discover Card; E
Diners Club; F Other; 2 Personal checks accepted; 3 Lunch available; 4 Dinner available; 5 Open all

the Monhegan and Squirrel Island ferries from nearby Pier 8.

Hostess: Diane Campbell
Rooms: 4(PB) $70-95
Full Breakfast
Credit Cards: A, B
Notes: 2, 5, 8, 9, 10, 12

The Howard House

Townsend Avenue, 04538
(207) 633-3933; (207) 633-6244

Located on 20 wooded acres away from the crowds but only one mile from beautiful Boothbay Harbor. Unique chalet design featuring high beamed cathedral ceilings, glass patio doors, private balconies, sparkling clean private baths, cable TV, and luxurious wall-to-wall carpeting. Early American style furnishings and appointments combine with natural wood walls to provide luxurious accommodations with a decidedly country-like feeling. Buffet breakfast featuring home-made cakes and bread.

Hosts: Jim and Ginny Farrin
Rooms: 15(PB) $48-79
Full Breakfast
Credit Cards: None
Notes: 2, 5, 7, 8, 9, 10, 12

The Howard House

BRUNSWICK

Harborgate Bed and Breakfast

Rural Delivery 2, #2260, 04011
(207) 725-5894

This contemporary redwood home is 40 feet from the ocean. Flower gardens and wooded landscape provide gracious relaxation. Two ocean-facing, first-floor bedrooms are separated by a guest living room with patio. Dock for swimming and sunbathing. Close to Bowdoin College, L. L. Bean, and sandy beaches. Wide selection of stores, gift shops, and steak and seafood restaurants. Summer theater, college art museum, Perry McMillan Museum, and historical society buildings and events.

Hostess: Carolyn Bolles
Rooms: 2 (SB) $60
Continental Breakfast
Credit Cards: None
Closed November - April
Notes: 2, 9

CAMDEN

Blackberry Inn

82 Elm St., 04843
(207) 236-6060; (800) 833-6674

A vintage 1840 Victorian featuring spacious rooms and scrumptious breakfasts, only a stroll from the village's harbor, shops, and restaurants. Rooms with fireplaces, televisions, and jacuzzis available, and a Carriage House suite with a queen size bed, bunk beds, kitchen, and television is perfect for families. Relax in the inn's parlors or sunny courtyard. Complimentary social hour and real Down East

year; 6 Pets welcome; 7 Children welcome; 8 Tennis nearby; 9 Swimming nearby; 10 Golf nearby; 11 Skiing nearby; 12 May be booked through travel agent

hospitality. See why the *Miami Herald* calls us "A delightful B&B." No smoking.

Rooms: 10(PB) $50-135
Full Breakfast
Credit Cards: A, B
Notes: 2, 4, 5, 7, 8, 9, 10, 11

CLARK ISLAND

Craignair Inn

Clark Island Road, 04859
(207) 594-7644; (800) 524-ROOM; (207) 596-7124 (FAX)

Located on the water, the inn is near great hiking trails along the shore or through the forests. The inn was formerly a boarding house for stonecutters from the nearby quarries that provide great swimming. The annex was once the village chapel. A peaceful and secluded setting.

Host: Terry Smith
Rooms: 22 (8 PB; 14 SB) $57-87
Full Breakfast
Credit Cards: A, B, C
Notes: 2, 4, 6, 7, 8, 9, 10, 11, 12

DAMARISCOTTA

Brannon-Bunker Inn

HCR 64, Box 045B, 04543
(207) 563-5941

Brannon-Bunker Inn is an intimate and relaxed country bed and breakfast situated minutes from sandy beach, lighthouse, and historic fort in Maine's mid-coastal region. Located in a 1920's Cape, converted barn, and carriage house, the guest rooms are furnished in themes reflecting the charm of yesterday and the comforts of today. Antique shops, too!

Hosts: Jeanne and Joe Hovance
Rooms: 7 (5PB; 2SB) $55-65
Expanded Continental Breakfast
Credit Cards: A, B, C
Closed Christmas week
Notes: 2, 5, 7, 8, 9, 10, 12

Down Easter Inn at Damariscotta

Bristol Road, Routes 129 and 130, 04543
(207) 563-5332; (201) 540-0500 winter

The Down Easter Inn, one mile from downtown Damariscotta, is in the heart of the rocky coast of Maine. On the National Register of Historic Places, it features a two-story porch framed by Corinthian columns. Minutes from golfing, lakes, and the ocean. Nearby are lobster wharfs for local fare and boat trips around Muscongus Bay and to Monhegan Island. The inn features 22 lovely rooms with TV's.

Hosts: Mary and Robert Colquhoun
Rooms: 22 (PB) $70-80
Continental Breakfast
Credit Cards: A, B
Notes: 2, 9, 10

EASTPORT

Todd House

Todd's Head, 04631
(207) 853-2328

Large, center-chimney Cape, circa 1775, overlooking Passamadoddy Bay. Barbecue facilities, deck, library with items of local history. In 1801, men formed a Masonic order in what is now a guest room. Beautiful sunrises and sunsets!

Hostess: Ruth M. McInnis
Rooms: 5 (2PB; 3SB) $45-80
Expanded Continental Breakfast
Credit Cards: None
Notes: 2, 5, 6, 7

NOTES: Credit cards accepted: A Master Card; B Visa; C American Express; D Discover Card; E Diners Club; F Other; 2 Personal checks accepted; 3 Lunch available; 4 Dinner available; 5 Open all

ELIOT

The Farmstead

379 Goodwin Rd., 03903
(207) 748-3145; (207) 439-4279

Lovely country inn on three acres. Warm friendly atmosphere exemplifies farm life late 1800's. Guest rooms are Victorian in style. Each has mini refrigerator and microwave for late evening snacks or special diet. Full breakfast may include blueberry pancakes or french toast, home-made syrup, fruit, and juice. Handicap accessible. Minutes from Kittery Factory Outlets, York Beaches, and Portsmouth, NH, historic sites. 1 hour from Boston.

Hosts: Meb and John Lippincott
Rooms: 6 (PB) $48
Full Breakfast
Credit Cards: A, B, C
Notes: None

FREEPORT

Captain Josiah Mitchell House

188 Main Street, 04032
(207) 865-3289

Two blocks from L. L. Bean, this house is a five-minute walk past centuries-old sea captains' homes and shady trees to all shops in town. After exploring, relax on our beautiful, peaceful veranda with antique wicker furniture and "remember when" porch swing. State inspected and approved. Family owned and operated.

Hosts: Loretta and Alan Bradley
Rooms: 6 (PB) $68-85 (winter rates are reduced)
Full Breakfast
Credit Cards: A, B
Notes: 2, 5, 9, 10, 11, 12

Country at Heart Bed and Breakfast

37 Bow Street, 04032
(207) 865-0512

Our cozy 1870 home is located off Main Street and only two blocks from L. L. Bean. Park your car and walk to the restaurants and many outlet stores. Stay in one of three country-decorated rooms: the Shaker room, Quilt room, or the Teddy bear room. Our rooms have hand-stenciled borders, hand-made crafts, and either antique or reproduction furnishings. There is also a gift shop for guests.

Hosts: Roger and Kim Dubay
Rooms: 3 (PB) $65-75
Full Breakfast
Credit Cards: None
Notes: 2, 5, 7, 9, 10, 11, 12

GREENVILLE

Greenville Inn

Norris Street, P.O. Box 1194, 04441
(207) 695-2206 (voice and FAX)

Restored 1895 lumber baron's mansion on a hillside overlooking Moosehead Lake and the Squaw Mountains. A large leaded-glass window decorated with a painted spruce tree, gas lights, embossed wallcoverings, and carved fireplace mantles grace the inn. A sumptuous continental breakfast buffet is included with the room. In the evening our restaurant is open to the public. Open year-round.

Hosts: Elfi, Susie, and Michael Schnetzer
Rooms: 9 (7PB; 2SB) $55-90
Full Breakfast
Credit Cards: A, B, D
Notes: 2, 4, 7, 8, 9, 10, 11, 12

year; 6 Pets welcome; 7 Children welcome; 8 Tennis nearby; 9 Swimming nearby; 10 Golf nearby; 11 Skiing nearby; 12 May be booked through travel agent

Hillside Gardens

Blairs Hill, Box 1189, 04441
(207) 695-3386

High on a hilltop overlooking miles of beautiful Moosehead Lake is a 100-year-old Victorian mansion with spacious rooms and private baths. The quietness and beauty of the estate makes you think you have slipped back in time to a more peaceful era. Over 70 acres of land and trails for you to explore. Come up with us to Hillside Gardens for your getaway vacation.

Hosts: Mary and Marty Hughes
Rooms: 5 (4PB; 2SB) $65-95
Full Breakfast
Credit Cards: A, B
Notes: 2, 3, 4, 5, 7 (over 12), 8, 9, 10, 11, 12

GUILFORD

The Guilford Bed and Breakfast

Elm and Prospect Street, 04443
(207) 876-3477

A lovely 1905 Post-Victorian with a half-wrap porch and situated high on a knoll within walking distance of the town and shops. Enjoy a hearty breakfast of home-made pastries or muffins, hash with poached egg, or buttermilk pancakes. In the winter, enjoy tea by the fireplace in our library. In the summer, have gourmet lunch on our lovely screen porch. Fish Moosehead Lake, hike the Appalachian Trail, ski Squaw Mountain.

Hosts: Pat and John Selicious
Rooms: 5(2PB; 3SB) $50
Full Breakfast
Credit Cards: A, B
Notes: 2, 5, 9, 10, 11

KENNEBUNK

Sundial Inn

P.O. Box 1147, 48 Beach Ave., 04043
(207) 967-3850

Unique oceanfront inn furnished with turn-of-the-century Victorian antiques. Each of the 34 guest rooms has a private bath, phone, color TV, and air conditioning. Several rooms also offer ocean views and whirlpool baths. Visit Kennebunkport's art galleries and studios, museums, and gift shops. Go whale-watching, deep-sea fishing, or hiking at the nearby wildlife refuge and estuary. Golf and tennis are nearby. Continental breakfast features muffins and coffee cakes. Wheelchair accessible.

Hosts: Larry and Pat Kenny
Rooms: 34 (PB) $65-151
Continental Breakfast
Credit Cards: A, B, C, E
Notes: 5, 8, 9, 10

KENNEBUNKPORT

The Captain Lord Mansion

P. O. Box 800, 04046
(207) 967-3141; (800) 522-3141; (207) 967-3172 (FAX)

The Captain Lord Mansion is an intimate and stylish Maine coast inn. Built during the War of 1812 as an elegant, private residence, it is now listed on the National Register of Historic Places. The large, luxurious guest rooms are furnished with rich antiques, yet have modern creature comforts. The gracious hosts and inn-keepers and their friendly staff are eager to make your visit enjoyable. Family-style

---

NOTES: Credit cards accepted: A Master Card; B Visa; C American Express; D Discover Card; E Diners Club; F Other; 2 Personal checks accepted; 3 Lunch available; 4 Dinner available; 5 Open all

breakfasts are served in an atmospheric country kitchen.

Hosts: Bev Davis and Rick Litchfield
Rooms: 16 (PB) $79-159 January-April; $149-199 May to December
Full Breakfast
Credit Cards: A, B, D
Notes: 2, 5, 8, 9, 10

The Captain Lord Mansion

The Green Heron Inn

Ocean Avenue, P.O. Box 2578, 04046
(207) 967-3315

Comfortable, clean, and cozy ten-room bed and breakfast. Each guest room has private bath, air conditioning, and color TV. A full breakfast from a menu is served. "Best breakfast in town."

Hosts: Charles and Elizabeth Reid
Rooms: 10 (PB) $68-120
Full Breakfast
Credit Cards: None
Notes: 2, 5, 6 (in advance), 7, 8, 9, 10

Maine Stay Inn and Cottages

34 Maine St., P.O. Box 500-A, 04046
(800) 950-2117; (207) 967-2117; (207) 967-8457 (FAX)

A grand Victorian Inn that exudes charm from its wrap-around porch to its perennial flower gardens and spacious lawns. The white clapboard house built in 1860 and listed on the National Historic Register and adjoining cottages sit grandly in Kennebunkport's Historic District. A variety of delightful accommodations from inn rooms, suites, and one-bedroom cottages (some with fireplaces) all with private baths and color TV's await you. A sumptuous full breakfast and afternoon tea are included. The Inn is an easy walk to Harbor, shops, galleries, and restaurants. AAA three diamond, Mobil Guide three star, and ABBA excellent rated.

Hosts: Carol and Lindsay Copeland
Rooms: 17 (PB) $75-185
Full Breakfast
Credit Cards: A, B, C, D
Notes: 2, 5, 7, 8, 9, 10, 12

KENT'S HILL

Home Nest Farm

Box 2350, 04349
(207) 897-4125

Off the beaten track, on a foothill of the Longfellow Mountains of West Central Maine's lake district, Home Nest Farm offers a 60-mile panoramic view to the White Mountains. A place for all seasons, it includes three historic homes, furnished with period antiques: the main house (1784); Lilac Cottage (c. 1800); and the Red Schoolhouse (c. 1830). Local activities include sheep tending, berry picking, Living History Farm Museum, exploring many trails (maintained for snowmobiling and skiing in the winter), swimming, fishing, boating (boats provided). Two day minimum stay.

Hosts: Arn and Leda Sturtevant
Rooms: 4 (PB) $50-95
Closed in March and April
Full Breakfast
Credit Cards: None
Notes: 2, 7, 9, 10, 11

year; 6 Pets welcome; 7 Children welcome; 8 Tennis nearby; 9 Swimming nearby; 10 Golf nearby; 11 Skiing nearby; 12 May be booked through travel agent

KITTERY

Enchanted Nights B & B

Rt. 103, 29 Wentworth Street, 03904
(207) 439-1489

Affordable luxury 75 minutes north of
Boston, Coastal Maine. Fanciful and
whimsical for the romantic at heart. French
and Victorian furnishings, with CATV's.
Three minutes to historic Portsmouth's
dining, dancing, concerts in the park, historic homes, theater, harbor cruises, cliff
walks, scenic ocean drives, beaches,
charming neighboring resorts, water park,
and outlet malls. Whirlpool tub for two.
Full breakfast or $12 less and enjoy a
Portsmouth cafe. Pets welcome. No
smoking indoors.

Hosts: Nancy Bogenberger and Peter Lamandia
Rooms: 6 (5PB; 2SB) $47-110
Full Breakfast
Credit Cards: A, B, C, D
Notes: 2, 5, 6, 7, 8, 9, 10, 12

Enchanted Nights

LINCOLNVILLE

The Youngstown Inn and Restaurant

RR 1, Box 4246, Rte. 52, 04849
(207) 763-4290

"A destination spot. A restaurant with
superior cuisine in a beautifully preserved
1810 farmhouse fitted as an inn." *Sunday
Telegram*, June, 1992. The Inn is located
four scenic miles north of Camden just
beyond Lake Olegunticook and Camden
Hills State Park. All rooms are well-
appointed with pumpkin pine floor, private
baths, balconies. The rate includes the
inn's full gourmet breakfast. Take a beautiful drive and discover the Youngstown
Inn year-round.

Hosts: Manuel and Mary Ann Mercier
Rooms: 6 (4PB; 2SB) $70-95
Full Breakfast
Credit Cards: A, B, C
Notes: 2, 4, 5, 7, 8, 9, 10, 11, 12

LUBEC

Breakers by the Bay

37 Washington Street, 04652
(207) 733-2487

Enjoy the breathtaking views of the sea
from your own private deck in this blue and
white New England home located close to
the international bridge leading to
Campobello and Roosevelt's house. Start
your day with a full breakfast in the dining
room. Then choose from the beautiful
vistas of Quoddy Head State Park and
Campobello, or just sit back and enjoy
relaxing. All rooms have 19-inch TV and
refrigerator.

Host: E. M. Elg
Rooms: 4 (3 PB [semi-private]; 1 SB) 1 suite
$40-60
Full Breakfast
Credit Cards: None
Closed November-April
Notes: 2, 10

NOTES: Credit cards accepted: A Master Card; B Visa; C American Express; D Discover Card; E
Diners Club; F Other; 2 Personal checks accepted; 3 Lunch available; 4 Dinner available; 5 Open all

MILLINOCKET

Katahdin Area Bed and Breakfast

94-96 Oxford Street, 04462
(207) 723-5220; (800) 275-5220

We are located 17 miles south of the entrance to Baxter State Park, the gateway to Katahdin, Maine's highest peak. With a population fewer than 8,000, Millinocket has small-town charm. The spectacular "Grand Canyon of the East" on Gulf Hagas is a short distance from here off Route 11 South. Appalachian Trail access; 156 miles of groomed trails; walking distance to Main Street, restaurants, shops, houses of worship. Cross-country skiing and white-water rafting opportunities available.

Hosts: Rodney and Mary Lou Corriveau
Rooms: 5 (1PB; 4SB) $40-50
Full Breakfast
Credit Cards: None
Notes: 2, 5, 7, 8, 9, 10, 11

PORTLAND

Inn on Carleton

46 Carleton St., 04102
(207) 775-1910 (voice and FAX); (800) 639-1779

The Inn on Carleton is a graciously restored 1869 Victorian townhouse located in Portland's historic West End. Situated on a quiet, tree-lined street in a unique residential neighborhood of Victorian architecture, the Inn on Carleton is close to the center of downtown Portland. It is a short walk to the Portland Museum of Art, Maine Medical Center, The Performing Arts Center and the city's business district. Close at hand are Casco Bay's Calendar Islands, the international ferry to Nova Scotia, and the Old Port area with its cobbled streets, colorful shops, and many fine restaurants.

Hosts: Phil and Sue Cox
Rooms: 7 (4PB; 3SB) $75-90 (seasonal rates available)
Full Breakfast
Credit Cards: A, B, D
Notes: 2, 5, 7, 8, 9, 10, 11, 12

RANGELEY

Northwoods Bed and Breakfast

Main Street, 04970
(407) 864-2440

An historic 1912 home of rare charm and easy elegance, Northwoods is centrally located in Rangeley Village. With spacious rooms, a lakefront porch, expansive grounds, and private boat dock, Northwoods provides superb accommodations. Golf, tennis, water sports, hiking, and skiing are a few of the many activities offered by the region.

Hosts: Carol and Robert Scofield
Rooms: 4 (3PB; 1SB) $60-75
Full Breakfast
Credit Cards: None
Notes: 2, 8, 9, 10, 11, 12

SACO

Crown 'n' Anchor Inn

P.O. Box 228, 121 North St., 04072-0228
(207) 282-3829

Located in the Thacher-Goudale House, a National Register Home in the state of Maine, the Crown 'n' Anchor Inn is a fully

---

year; **6** Pets welcome; **7** Children welcome; **8** Tennis nearby; **9** Swimming nearby; **10** Golf nearby; **11** Skiing nearby; **12** May be booked through travel agent

restored federal house in the Adamesque
style with Greek Revival temple front and
furnished throughout with period and country antiques. After a bountiful breakfast or
a busy day, socialize in the parlor or curl up
with a good book in the library.

Hosts: John Barclay and Martha Forester
Rooms: 6(PB) $60-85
Full Breakfast
Credit Cards: A, B
Notes: 2, 5, 7(by arrangement), 8, 9, 10, 11, 12

Crown 'n' Anchor Inn

SEARSPORT

Brass Lantern Inn

Rt. 1, P.O. Box 407, 04974
(207) 548-0150

Nestled at the edge of the woods, this
gracious Victorian inn, built in 1850 by a
sea captain, overlooks Penobscot Bay.
Each guest room has a private bath and is
designed for a comfortable stay. Enjoy a
sumptuous breakfast and friendly hospitality. Open all year, The Brass Lantern
will be lit to welcome you!

Hosts: Pat Gatto, Dan and Lee Anne Lee
Rooms: 4 (PB) $65-75
Full Breakfast
Credit Cards: A, B
Notes: 2, 5, 7, 8, 9, 10, 11, 12

Thurston House Bed and Breakfast Inn

8 Elm Street, P.O. Box 686, 04974
(207) 548-2213

This beautiful Colonial home, circa 1830,
with ell and carriage house was built as a
parsonage for Stephen Thurston, uncle of
Winslow Homer, who visited often. Now
you can visit in a casual environment. The
quiet village setting is steps away from
Penobscot Marine Museum, beach park
on Penobscot Bay, restaurants, churches,
galleries, antiques, and more. Relax in one
of four guest rooms, one with bay view,
two great for kids, and enjoy the "forget
about lunch" breakfasts.

Hosts: Carl and Beverly Eppig
Rooms: 4 (2PB; 2SB) $45-60
Full Breakfast
Credit Cards: A, B
Notes: 2, 5, 7, 8, 9, 10, 11, 12

SOUTHWEST HARBOR

The Island House

P.O. Box 1006, Clark Point Rd., 04679
(207) 244-5180

Relax in a gracious, restful seacoast home
on the quiet side of Mount Desert Island.
We serve such Island House favorites as
blueberry coffee cake and sausage-cheese
casserole. A charming private loft apartment is available. Acadia National Park is
only a five-minute drive away. Located
across the street from the harbor, near
swimming, sailing, biking, and hiking.

Hostess: Ann Gill
Rooms: 4 (SB) $50-95
Full Breakfast
Credit Cards: A, B
Notes: 2, 5, 7 (over 11), 9, 10

The Lamb's Ear Inn

P.O. Box 30, Clark Point Road, 04679
(207) 244-9828

Our old Maine house was built in 1857. It is comfortable and scenic, away from the hustle and bustle. Private baths, comfortable beds with crisp, fresh linens. Sparkling harbor views and a breakfast to remember. Come and be a part of this special village in the heart of Mount Desert Island surrounded by Acadia National Park.

Hosts: Elizabeth and George Hoke
Rooms: 6 (PB) $65-125
Full Breakfast
Credit Cards: A, B
Notes: 2 (restricted), 7 (limited), 8, 9, 10, 12

The Lamb's Ear Inn

THOMASTON

Cap'n Frost Bed and Breakfast

241 West Main (U.S. Route 1), 04861
(207) 354-8217

Our 1840 Cape is furnished with country antiques, some of which are for sale. If you are visiting our mid-coastal area, we are a comfortable overnight stay, close to Monhegan Island and a two-hour drive to Acadia National Park. Reservations are

helpful.

Hosts: Arlene and Harold Frost
Rooms: 3 (1PB; 2SB) $40-45
Full Breakfast
Credit Cards: A, B, D
Notes: 2, 5, 9, 11

WATERFORD

The Parsonage House Bed and Breakfast

Rice Road, P. O. Box 116, 04088
(207) 583-4115

Built in 1870 for the Waterford Church, this restored historic home overlooks Waterford Village, Keoka Lake, and Mt. Tirem. It is located in a four-season area providing a variety of opportunities for the outdoor enthusiast. The Parsonage is a haven of peace and quiet. Three double guest rooms are tastefully furnished. Weather permitting, we feature a full breakfast on the screened porch. Guests love our large New England farm kitchen and its glowing wood-burning stove.

Hosts: Joseph and Gail St-Hilaire
Rooms: 3 (1PB; 2SB) $45-75
Full Breakfast
Credit Cards: None
Notes: 2, 3, 5, 7, 9, 10, 11

WELD

Lake Webb House Bed and Breakfast

Church Street, P.O. Box 127, 04285
(207) 585-2479

Experience the beauty and solitude of the western Maine mountains from our 1870's home. Relax with porch rockers, hearty home-made breakfasts and country hospitality. Enjoy one of our three guest rooms with queen or twin beds, beautiful quilts, and ceiling fans. Many mountains to hike, and Mt. Blue State Park is close by. Snowmobiling and cross-country skiing in the winter.

Hosts: Fred and Cheryl England
Rooms: 3 (SB) $50+tax
Full Breakfast
Credit Cards: None
Notes: 2, 5, 7, 8, 9, 10, 11

YORK BEACH

Homestead Inn B&B

8 South Main St., Rt. 1A, 03910
(207) 363-8952

Friendly, quiet and homey—four rooms in an old (1905) boarding house; connected to our home in 1969. Panoramic view of ocean and shore hills. Walk to beaches (2), shops, and Nubble Lighthouse. Great for small, adult groups. Fireplace in living room. Breakfast served in barn board dining room and outside on private sun deck.

Hosts: Dan and Danielle Duffy
Rooms: 4 (SB) $59
Continental Breakfast
Credit Cards: None
Notes: 2, 8, 9, 10, 12

YORK HARBOR

Bell Buoy B & B

570 York Street, 03911
(207) 363-7264

At the Bell Buoy, there are no strangers, only friends who have never met. Located

minutes from I-95 and U.S. 1, minutes from Kittery outlet malls, and a short walk to the beach, enjoy afternoon tea served either on the large front porch or the living room. Fireplace and cable TV. Homemade breads or muffins are served with breakfast in the dining room each morning or on the porch.

Hosts: Wes and Kathie Cook
Rooms: 4 (1PB; 3SB) $55-80
Full Breakfast
Credit Cards: None
Notes: 2, 6, 7 (over six), 9, 10

York Harbor Inn

Route 1A, P.O. Box 573, 03911
(207) 363-5119; (800) 343-3869

For more than 100 years, the historic charm and hospitality of York Harbor Inn have welcomed those seeking distinctive lodging and dining experiences. A short walk takes you to a peaceful, protected beach. A stroll along Marginal Way reveals hidden coastal scenes and classic estates. Golf, tennis, biking, deep-sea fishing, and outlet shopping are close by. Air conditioning, antiques, phones, private baths, ocean views, and fireplaces. Full dining room and tavern with entertainment.

Hosts: Joe and Garry Dominguez
Rooms: 32 (28 PB; 4SB) $65-139
Continental Plus Breakfast
Credit Cards: A, B, C, E, F
Notes: 2, 3, 4, 5, 7, 8, 9, 10, 11, 12

Maryland

ANNAPOLIS

The Barn on Howard's Cove
500 Wilson Road, 21401
(410) 266-6840

The Barn on Howard's Cove welcomes you with warm hospitality to a restored 1850's horse barn overlooking a beautiful cove off the Severn River. You will be convenient to both Washington, D.C., and Baltimore and very close to historic Annapolis. Begin the day with choice of full country breakfast served on deck or in dining area overlooking river. Beautiful gardens, rural setting, antiques, quilts. Docking in deep water provided.

Hosts: Graham and Libbie Gutsche
Rooms: 2 (1/2PB; 1SB) $65 (plus $3.25 state lodging tax)
Full Breakfast (Continental if desired)
Credit Cards: None
Notes: 2, 5, 7, 8, 10, 12 (10%)

BALTIMORE

Government House
1125 North Calvert Street, 21201
(410) 539-0566; (410) 539-0567

Built in 1889 by noted architect Charles L. Carson, Government House stands in Baltimore's historic Mt. Vernon area recreated with all of the opulence that a prominent port city family home of the late 1800s would have to offer. Throughout the end of the 18th century, Government House first served as the private residence of famed Baltimore businessman John S. Gilman and later as the home of Victorian-era inventor William Painter, originator of the bottle cap. Along with lovely handcrafted wood interiors, stained glass windows and a grand staircase, the beauty of exquisite art, furnishings and antiques of Victorian, Edwardian and Oriental origin adorn the entirety of the house. Operated by Baltimore International Culinary College Hotels International.

Host: Marainna Palacios
Rooms: 20 (PB) call for prices
Continental Breakfast
Credit Cards: A, B, C, E
Notes: 2, 5, 7, 12

Government House

---

year; 6 Pets welcome; 7 Children welcome; 8 Tennis nearby; 9 Swimming nearby; 10 Golf nearby; 11 Skiing nearby; 12 May be booked through travel agent

Mulberry House

111 West Mulberry Street, 21201
(410) 576-0111

From this historic inn in the downtown area, walk to shopping, restaurants, and attractions. Four deluxe, double guest rooms feature antique armoires, four-poster or brass beds, and brass chandeliers. Grand piano, fireplace, and courtyard. Free parking, but a car is not necessary. Air conditioned.

Hosts: Charlotte and Curt Jeschke
Rooms: 4 (SB) $75
Full Breakfast
Credit Cards: None
Notes: 2, 5, 7(over 16), 12

BERLIN

Merry Sherwood Plantation

8909 Worcester Highway, 21811
(410) 641-2112; (800) 660-0358; (410) 641-3605
(FAX)

This 1859, pre-Civil War mansion allows the visitor to experience a glorious step back in time. Recently restored, this elegant and opulent home is furnished throughout with authentic Victorian antiques. Situated on 19 acres of beautiful 19th-century landscaping, upon entering the main gates, you definitely begin your very special getaway. Enjoy formal ballroom, stately dining room, warm fireplaces, and superb breakfast and loving hospitality.

Host: Kirk Burbage
Rooms: 8 (6PB; 2SB) $95-150
Full Gourmet Breakfast
Credit Cards: A, B
Notes: 2, 5, 8, 9, 10, 12

CHESTERTOWN

The River Inn at Rolph's Wharf

Rd. 1, Box 646, Rolph's Wharf Rd., 21620
(410) 778-6347

The River Inn at Rolph's Wharf is an 1830's Victorian Inn on 5 acres of the scenic Chester River, 3 miles south of Chestertown, Maryland. If you are looking for a quiet getaway, this is it. Enjoy beautiful sunsets on the deck, the beach, or the patio of the Sunset Grill Restaurant. Come by boat and stay at our marina or the inn. Swimming, crabbing, dining and relaxing...We have it all!

Hostess: Sandy Strouse
Rooms: 6 (PB) $65-115
Continental Breakfast
Credit Cards: A, B, C, D, E
Notes: 2, 3, 4, 5, 7, 9, 10

CUMBERLAND

Inn at Walnut Bottom

120 Green Street, 21502
(301) 777-0003; (800) 286-9718; (301) 777-1629
(FAX)

The Inn at Walnut Bottom is an established classic country inn bed and breakfast in the city of Cumberland. We offer our guests charming and comfortable accommodations in either the 1820 Cowden House or the 1890 Dent House. Rooms are furnished in antique and period reproduction furniture. The Inn at Walnut Bottom is within walking distance of the terminus of the Western Maryland Station and Museum, the Western Maryland Scenic Railroad, the Cumberland Theatre, Historic Downtown Cumberland, and the Washington Street historic district and History House Museum. Rocky Gap and New Germany State Parks, Frostburg State University, the Savage River, and Greenbridge Recreation areas are nearby. The Oxford House Restaurant at the inn serves country-inn food.

Hostess: Sharon Ennis Kazary
Rooms: 12 rooms and suites (8PB; 4SB) $65-85
Full Breakfast
Credit Cards: A, B, C, D
Notes: 3, 4, 5, 7, 9, 10, 11, 12

Inn at Walnut Bottom

ELKTON

Garden Cottage at Sinking Springs Herb Farm

234 Blair Shore Road, 21921
(410) 398-5566

With an early plantation house, including a 400-year-old sycamore, the garden cottage nestles at the edge of a meadow flanked by herb gardens and a historic barn with a gift shop. It has a sitting room with fireplace, bedroom, bath, air conditioning, and electric heat. Freshly ground coffee and herbal teas are offered with the country breakfast. Longwood Gardens and Winterthur Museum are 50 minutes away. Historic Chesapeake City is nearby

with excellent restaurants. Sleeps three in two rooms.

Hosts: Bill and Ann Stubbs
Room: 1 (PB) $85
Full Breakfast
Credit Cards: A, B
Notes: 2, 5, 8, 10, 12

FREDERICK

Middle Plantation Inn

9549 Liberty Road, 21701-3246
(301) 898-7128

From this rustic inn built of stone and log, drive through horse country to the village of Mount Pleasant. The inn is located several miles east of Frederick on 26 acres. Each room is furnished with antiques and has a private bath, air conditioning, and TV. The keeping room, a common room, has stained glass and a stone fireplace. Nearby are antique shops, museums, and many historic attractions. Located within 40 minutes of Gettysburg, Pennsylvania, Antietam Battlefield, and Harper's Ferry.

Hosts: Shirley and Dwight Mullican
Rooms: 4 (PB) $85-95
Continental Breakfast (optional)
Credit Cards: A, B
Notes: 2, 5, 8, 9, 10, 12

Middle Plantation Inn

year; 6 Pets welcome; 7 Children welcome; 8 Tennis nearby; 9 Swimming nearby; 10 Golf nearby; 11 Skiing nearby; 12 May be booked through travel agent

GAITHERSBURG

Gaithersburg Hospitality Bed and Breakfast

18908 Chimney Place, 20879
(301) 977-7377

This luxury host home just off I-270 with all amenities, including private parking, is located in the beautifully planned community of Montgomery Village, near churches, restaurants, and shops, and is five minutes from DC Metro Station or a convenient drive south to Washington, D.C., and north to historic Gettysburg, PA, and Harper's Ferry. This spacious bed and breakfast has two rooms with private baths; one has a queen bed. Also offered are a large, sunny third room with twin beds, and a fourth room with a single bed. Hosts delight in serving full, home-cooked breakfasts with your pleasure and comfort in mind.

Hosts: Suzanne and Joe Danilowiiz
Rooms: 4 (2PB; 2SB) $52
Full Breakfast
Credit Cards:
Notes: 2, 5, 7, 8, 9, 10, 12

HAGERSTOWN

Lewrene Farm B & B

9738 Downsville Pike, 21740
(301) 582-1735

Enjoy our quiet, Colonial country home on 125 acres near I-70 and I-81, a home away from home for tourists, business people, and families. We have room for family celebrations. Sit by the fireplace or enjoy the great outdoors. Antietam Battlefield and Harper's Ferry are nearby; Washington, D.C., and Baltimore are one and one-half hours away. Quilts for sale.

Hosts: Irene and Lewis Lehman
Rooms: 6 (3PB; 3SB) $50-85
Full Breakfast
Credit Cards: A, B
Notes: 2, 5, 7, 8, 9 10, 11

Sunday's Bed and Breakfast

39 Broadway, 21740
(800) 221-4828

This elegant 1890 Queen Anne Victorian home is situated in the historic north end of Hagerstown. Relax in any of the many public rooms and porches or explore the many historic attractions, antique shops, fishing areas, golf courses, museums, shopping outlets, and ski areas that are nearby. You'll experience special hospitality and many personal touches at Sunday's. A full breakfast, afternoon tea and desserts, evening refreshments, fruit baskets, fresh flowers, special toiletries, and late night cordial and chocolate are just some of the offerings at Sunday's. We are located less than 90 minutes from Baltimore and Washington, DC.

Host: Bob Forrino
Rooms: 3 (1PB; 2SB) $65-95
Full Breakfast
Credit Cards: None
Notes: 2, 4, 5, 6, 7, 8, 9, 10, 11, 12

Sunday's Bed and Breakfast

NOTES: Credit cards accepted: A Master Card; B Visa; C American Express; D Discover Card; E Diners Club; F Other; 2 Personal checks accepted; 3 Lunch available; 4 Dinner available; 5 Open all

NEW MARKET

National Pike Inn
9 W. Main St., P.O. Box 299, 21774
(301) 865-5055

Federal 1796-1804, offers four air conditioned guest rooms each decorated in different themes. Private baths are available. Our large Federal sitting room is open to our guests, and our private enclosed courtyard is perfect for a quiet retreat outdoors. A hearty breakfast will be provided each morning in our Colonial dining room. New Market, founded in 1793, has over 30 specialized antique shops all in historic homes along Main Street. An "old-fashioned general store" is everyone's favorite. Mealey's, well known for dining excellence, is a few steps away.

Hosts: Tom and Terry Rimel
Rooms: 5 (3PB; 2SB) $75-125
Full Breakfast
Credit Cards: A, B
Notes: 2, 5, 8, 9, 10, 11(cross country)

OAKLAND

The Oak and Apple Bed and Breakfast
208 N. Second Street, 21550
(301) 334-9265

Circa 1915, this restored Colonial Revival sits on a beautiful large lawn with mature trees and includes a large, columned front porch, enclosed sun porch, parlor with fireplace, and a cozy gathering room with television. Awaken to fresh continental breakfast served fireside in the dining room or on the sun porch. The quaint town of

Oakland offers a wonderful small-town atmosphere, and Deep Creek Lake, Wisp Ski Resort, and state parks with hiking, fishing, swimming, boating, and skiing are nearby.

Hosts: Ed and Jana Kight
Rooms: 4 (2PB; 2SB) $50-70
Expanded Continental Breakfast
Credit Cards: A, B
Notes: 2, 5, 8, 9, 10, 11, 12

ST. MICHAELS

Parsonage Inn
210 North Talbot Street, 21663
(800) 394-5519

This late Victorian, circa 1883, was lavishly restored in 1985 with seven guest rooms, private baths, and brass beds with Laura Ashley linens. Three rooms have working fireplaces. The parlor and dining room are in the European tradition. Striking architecture! Two blocks to the maritime museum, shops, and restaurants. Mobil three-star rated.

Hostess: Peggy Parsons
Rooms: 7 (PB) $82-114
Full Breakfast
Credit Cards: A, B
Notes: 2, 5, 7, 8

Parsonage Inn

Wades Point Inn on the Bay

P. O. Box 7, 21663
(410) 745-2500

For those seeking the serenity of the country and the splendor of the bay, we invite you to charming Wades Point Inn, just a few miles from St. Michaels. Complemented by the ever-changing view of boats, birds, and water lapping the shoreline, our 120 acres of fields and woodlands, with one mile walking or jogging trail, provide a peaceful setting for relaxation and recreation on Maryland's eastern shore.

Hosts: Betsy and John Feiler
Rooms: 15 winter, 25 summer (15PB; 10SB)
$69-169
Continental Breakfast
Credit Cards: A, B
Notes: 2, 5, 7, 8, 10

SALISBURY

White Oak Inn

804 Spring Hill Rd (Rt. 50), 21801
(410) 742-4887

Colonial home situated on five acres is one-half mile west of town. Choose from four lovely guest rooms. Architectural features of interest throughout the inn include crown moldings, high ceilings, wainscoting, and an elegant foyer. Relax by the fire in quiet living room overlooking a lake where you can fish and observe wildlife. Breakfast in the Florida Room among nature's best. Area attractions include Pemberton Hall, Salisbury State University, historic sites, shopping, antiques, and a riverboat cruise on the Wicomico River.

Ocean City beaches are only 30 miles away. Deluxe continental breakfast and complimentary afternoon tea served. Senior and Auto Club discounts.

Rooms: 4 (SB) $55-65
Deluxe Continental Breakfast
Credit Cards: A, B
Notes: None

SILVER SPRING

Varborg

2620 Briggs Chaney Road, 20905
(301) 384-2842

This suburban Colonial home in the countryside is convenient to Washington, D.C., and Baltimore, just off Route 29 and close to Route 95. Three guest rooms with a shared bath are available. This home has been inspected and given a two-star rating by the American Bed and Breakfast Association. No smoking.

Hosts: Robert and Patricia Johnson
Rooms: 3 (SB) $50
Full Breakfast (or continental if desired)
Credit Cards: None
Notes: 5, 7, 8

NOTES: Credit cards accepted: A Master Card; B Visa; C American Express; D Discover Card; E Diners Club; F Other; 2 Personal checks accepted; 3 Lunch available; 4 Dinner available; 5 Open all

Massachusetts

BOSTON

A B&B Agency of Boston
47 Commercial Wharf, 02110
(617) 720-3540; (800) 248-9262

Downtown Boston's largest selection of
guest rooms in historic bed and breakfast
homes including Federal and Victorian
townhouses and beautifully restored
1840's waterfront lofts. Available nightly,
weekly, monthly. Or choose from the
loveliest selection of fully furnished private
studios, one and two bedroom condo-
miniums, corporate suites, and lofts with all
the amenities including fully furnished kitchens, private baths (some with jacuzzis),
TV, and telephones. Available nightly,
weekly, monthly. Exclusive locations include waterfront, Faneuil Hall/Quincy
Market, North End, Back Bay, Beacon
Hill, Copley Square, and Cambridge.

Host: Ferne Mintz
Rooms: 120 (80PB; 40SB) $65-120
Continental Breakfast
Credit Cards: A, B
Notes: 2, 5, 7, 12

82 Chandler St. Bed and Breakfast
82 Chandler St., 02116
(617) 482-0408

This 1863 red-brick terrace townhouse is
located just off Copley Square on a tree-
lined street in historic residential neighborhood in downtown Boston. Around the
corner from John Hancock Tower, Back
Bay/South End, Amtrack Station. Short
walk to Hynes Convention Center, Free-
dom Trail, Newbury Street shops. Each
well-furnished bedroom has a private
bath, kitchenette, and telephone. You'll
receive a warm welcome, enjoy a tasty
American family-style breakfast in our
penthouse kitchen, and be within easy
walking distance of all the city's sights.
Mentioned in *Frommer's Guide* as one
of the best. This is a downtown Boston
B&B, enjoy the advantages of being in the
heart of the city. No smoking, please.

Hosts: Denis F. Noté and Dominic C. Beraldi
Rooms: 5 (PB) $95-125
Full Breakfast
Credit Cards: None
Notes: 5, 12

BREWSTER—CAPE COD

Captain Freeman Inn
15 Breakwater Road, 02631
(508) 896-7481; (800) 843-4664

A charming Victorian sea captain's mansion located on beautiful historic Cape
Cod. Outdoor pool, badminton, croquet,
fireplaces, whirlpool spas. Furnished in
antiques of the era. A short stroll down
beautiful Breakwater Road to the white

year; 6 Pets welcome; 7 Children welcome; 8 Tennis nearby; 9 Swimming nearby; 10 Golf nearby;
11 Skiing nearby; 12 May be booked through travel agent

sand beach on Cape Cod Bay. Full gourmet breakfast included. Antiquing, whale-watching, museums, parks, and much more to see and do.

Hostess: Carol Covitz
Rooms: 12 (9PB; 3SB)
Full Breakfast
Credit Cards: A, B, C
Notes: 2, 5, 7 (over 10), 8, 9, 10, 12

BROOKLINE

Beacon Inn

1750 and 1087 Beacon Street, 02146
(617) 566-0088

These turn-of-the-century townhouses have been converted into two of Brookline's most charming guesthouses. The original woodwork is reminiscent of their 19th-century construction, and the lobby fireplace offers a friendly welcome to travelers. Large, comfortably furnished, sunny rooms provide pleasant accommodations at a reasonable price. The Beacon Inn is minutes away from downtown Boston. The area offers a wide variety of restaurants, shops, museums, theater, and other tourist attractions.

Hosts: Megan Rockett and Maureen Keaney
Rooms: 24 (14PB; 10SB) $48-76
Continental Breakfast
Credit Cards: A, B, C
Notes: 5, 7, 12

CAMBRIDGE

A B & B in Cambridge

Cambridge St., 02138-4316
(617) 868-7082; (800) 795-7122; (617) 876-8991 (FAX)

A five-minute walk to Harvard Square, this bed and breakfast is in the heart of Cambridge and very near downtown Boston. Reservations and a 50% deposit are required. Two night minimum stay. Near the T, Boston's subway, and other conveniences.

Host: Doane Perry
Rooms: 3 (SB)
Continental Breakfast
Credit Cards: A, B, C
Notes: 2, 5, 7, 8, 9, 12

A Bed and Breakfast in Cambridge

CENTERVILLE

Long Dell Inn

436 South Main St., 02632
(508) 775-2750

An historic 1850's sea captain's home in the Greek Revival style. Furnished with antiques and oriental rugs. Fireplace in living room. Delightfully comfortable and romantic. Canopied beds and private decks. Full breakfast served. Everything homemade and home-baked. Five-minute walk to famous Craigville Beach. Shelter for bikes. Off-street parking. Shopping nearby. 10 minutes to ferries.

Hosts: Roy and Joy Swayze
Rooms: 6 (PB) $70-80; 1 efficiency apartment $90/night or $525/week.
Full Breakfast
Credit Cards: None
Notes: 2, 5, 7, 8, 9, 10, 12

NOTES: Credit cards accepted: A Master Card; B Visa; C American Express; D Discover Card; E Diners Club; F Other; 2 Personal checks accepted; 3 Lunch available; 4 Dinner available; 5 Open all

CHATHAM—CAPE COD

The Cranberry Inn at Chatham

359 Main Street, 02633
(508) 945-9232; (800) 332-4667 reservations;
(508) 945-3769 (FAX)

Welcoming Cape Cod visitors since 1830, The Cranberry Inn is ideally located in the heart of Chatham's picturesque historic district! Elegant yet relaxed, the inn offers eighteen delightful guest rooms each individually decoratred with antique and reproduction furnishing. Rooms feature four-poster, brass, or canopy beds, private bath, air conditioning, telephone, and television. Many rooms have fireplaces and balconies. Golfing, swimming, boating, and some of the finest shops and restaurants on the Cape are all nearby.

Hosts: Peggy DeHan and Richard Morris
Rooms: 18 (PB) $90-165
Expanded Continental Breakfast
Credit Cards: A, B, C
Notes: 2, 7 (over 8), 8, 9, 10, 12

CHELMSFORD

Westsview Landing

P. O. Box 4141, 01824
(508) 256-0074

This large, contemporary home overlooking Hart's Pond is located three miles from Routes 495 and 3, 30 miles north of Boston, and 15 minutes south of Nashua, New Hampshire. It is close to historic Lexington, Concord, and Lowell. Many recreational activities, including swimming, boating, fishing, and bicyling are nearby;

and there is a hot spa on the premises.

Hosts: Robert and Lorraine Pinette
Rooms: 3 (SB) $40-50
Full Breakfast
Credit Cards: None
Notes: 2, 6, 7, 8, 9, 10, 11

CONCORD

Hawthorne Inn

462 Lexington Road, 01742
(508) 369-5610

Fast by the ancient way, that the Minute Men trod to first face the British Regulars, rests this most colorful inn where history and literature gracefully entwine. On earth once claimed by Emerson, Hawthorne, and the Alcotts, the Hawthorne Inn beckons the traveler to refresh the spirit in a winsome atmosphere abounding with antique furnishings and delight the eye exploring rooms festooned with hand-made quilts, original artwork and archaic artifacts.

Host: G. Burch
Rooms: 7 (PB) $100-160
Continental Plus Breakfast
Credit Cards: None
Notes: 2, 5, 7, 8, 9, 11

Hawthorne Inn

year; 6 Pets welcome; 7 Children welcome; 8 Tennis nearby; 9 Swimming nearby; 10 Golf nearby; 11 Skiing nearby; 12 May be booked through travel agent

DANVERS

Cordwainer Bed and Breakfast at the Samuel Legro House

78 Center Street, 01923
(508) 774-1860

A circa 1854 home on the National Register of Historic Places, featuring beamed ceilings, canopy queen beds, fireplaces in the kitchen and the living room. The swimming pool is open from June to September for your enjoyment. Danvers is located twenty miles north of Boston and five miles west of Salem.

Hostess: Peggie Blais
Rooms: 4 (1PB; 3SB) $55-75
Expanded Continental Breakfast
Credit Cards: None
Notes: 5, 7, 8, 9, 10

Cordwainer B & B at the Samuel Legro House

DEERFIELD-SOUTH

Deerfield's Yellow Gabled House

307 North Main Street, 01373
(413) 665-4922

Located in Deerfield South, this country house is located in the heart of a historical and cultural area and is the site of the Bloody Brook Massacre of 1675. It is furnished with period antiques and promises a comfortable stay with the ambience of yesteryear. Enjoy the casual elegance and quiet charm of this vintage home. One mile from the crossroads of I-91 Route 116, and Routes 5 and 10, and close to historic Deerfield and five-college area. Air conditioned.

Hostess: Edna Julia Stahelek
Rooms: 3 (1PB; 2SB) $50-80
Full Breakfast
Credit Cards: None
Notes: 2, 5, 7 (over 10), 8, 9, 10, 11, 12

DENNIS

Isaiah Hall Bed and Breakfast Inn

152 Whig St., 02638
(508) 385-9928; (800) 736-0160

Enjoy country ambience and hospitality in the heart of Cape Cod. Tucked away on a quiet historic side-street, this lovely 1857 farmhouse is within walking distance of the beach, restaurants, shops, and playhouse. Delightful gardens surround the Inn with country antiques, Oriental rugs and quilts within. Most rooms have private baths and queen size beds. Some have balconies or fireplaces. Near biking, golf, and tennis. AAA three diamond rating and ABBA three crown award.

Hostess: Marie Brophy
Rooms: 11 (10PB; 1SB) $57-102
Expanded Continental Breakfast
Credit Cards: A, B, C
Notes: 2, 7(over 7), 8, 9, 10, 12

NOTES: Credit cards accepted: A Master Card; B Visa; C American Express; D Discover Card; E Diners Club; F Other; 2 Personal checks accepted; 3 Lunch available; 4 Dinner available; 5 Open all

DENNISPORT

The Rose Petal B & B

152 Sea St., P.O. Box 974, 02639
(508) 398-8470

Conveniently situated in the heart of Cape
Cod and a short walk past century-old
homes to a sandy beach. Inviting 1872
home, lovingly restored, beautifully landscaped yard, four attractive guest rooms
with queen size or twin beds. Home-
baked pastries highlight a superb full breakfast. Near all of the Cape's attractions:
shops, antiques, dining, golf, beaches, bike
trails, ferries to the Islands, whale-watching. ABBA approved.

Hosts: Dan and Gayle Kelly
Rooms: 4 (SB) $45-59
Full Breakfast
Credit Cards: A, B
Notes: 5, 7, 8, 9, 10, 12

EAST ORLEANS

Nauset House Inn

143 Beach Road, Box 774, 02643
(508) 255-2195

A real, old-fashioned, country inn farmhouse, circa 1810, is located on three
acres with an apple orchard, one-half mile
from Nauset Beach. A quiet romantic
getaway. Large common room with fireplace and a brick-floored dining room
where breakfast is served. Cozily furnished with antiques, eclectic—a true fan-
tasy.

Hosts: Diane and Al Johnson; John and Cindy
Vessella
Rooms: 14 (8 PB; 6 SB) $45-95
Full or Continental Breakfast
Credit Cards: A, B
Notes: 2, 8, 9, 10

Ship's Knees Inn

186 Beach Road, P. O. Box 756, 02643
(508) 255-1312; (508) 240-1351 (FAX)

This 170-year-old restored sea captain's
home is a three-minute walk to beautiful
sand-duned Nauset Beach. Inside the
warm, lantern-lit doorways are 19 rooms
individually appointed with special Colonial color schemes and authentic antiques.
Some rooms feature authentic ship's knees,
hand-painted trunks, old clipper ship mod-
els, braided rugs, and four-poster beds.
Tennis and swimming are available on the
premises. Three miles away overlooking
Orleans Cove, the Cove House property
offers three rooms, a one-bedroom efficiency apartment, and two cottages.

Hosts: Jean and Ken Pitchford
Rooms: 22, 1 apartment, 2 cottages (11 PB; 14
SB) $45-100
Continental Breakfast
Credit Cards: A, B
Notes: 2, 5, 7 (Cove House property), 10, 12

EDGARTOWN, MARTHA'S
VINEYARD

The Arbor

222 Upper Main Street, P.O. Box 1228, 02539
(508) 627-8137

Some say it was floated over on a barge
from Chappaquiddick at the turn of the
century. Others say it was pulled by oxen
on a sled of sorts across the icy narrows
of Katama Bay. History abounds at The
Arbor, but it cannot touch the warmth and
hospitality which exists today. Enjoy a
delicious continental breakfast with home-
baked bread by the fireplace in the dining
room or in the English tea garden. Join

year; 6 Pets welcome; 7 Children welcome; 8 Tennis nearby; 9 Swimming nearby; 10 Golf nearby;
11 Skiing nearby; 12 May be booked through travel agent

us at The Arbor.

Hostess: Peggy Hall
Rooms: 10 (8PB; 2SB) $85-135 (off season rates available)
Continental Breakfast
Credit Cards: A, B
Notes: 2, 7 (over 12), 8, 9, 10, 12

The Arbor

Colonial Inn of Martha's Vineyard

38 North Water Street, 02539
(508) 627-4711; (800) 627-4701; (508) 627-5904 (FAX)

The charm of Martha's Vineyard is echoed by the history and style of the Colonial Inn, overlooking the harbor in the heart of historic Edgartown. Affordable luxury awaits you. All rooms have heat, air-conditioning, color cable TV, and telephones. Continental breakfast is served in the sunroom with patio seating available.

Hostess: Linda Malcouronne
Rooms: 42 (PB) $60-175
Continental Breakfast
Credit Cards: A, B, C
Closed January-March
Notes: 2, 3, 4, 7, 8, 9, 10, 12

Governor Bradford Inn of Edgartown

128 Main Street, P.O. Box 239, 02539-0235
(508) 627-9510

Built in 1860, the Governor Bradford Inn was moved to its present location by horse-drawn wagons. In 1980 the Victorian Gothic home was expanded to its present size and converted to a bed and breakfast inn. The guest rooms are luxurious and comfortable with modern conveniences. Most have king-size beds! The many common rooms include a homey living room with fireplace and a modern conference room. The full breakfast includes such specialties as Belgian waffles and Eggs Benedict. All types of functions can be held at the inn.

Hosts: Ray and Brenda Raffurty
Rooms: 16 (PB) $60-195
Full Breakfast
Credit Cards: A, B, C
Notes: 2, 5, 7 (limited), 8, 9, 10, 12

Point Way Inn

104 Main Street, Box 5255, 02539
(508) 627-8633

One of Edgartown's finest inns, the Point Way Inn is a renovated 1830 sea captain's home, open all year. Enjoy our gardens, croquet, and lemonade in the gazebo. In cooler months, an afternoon tea is served before the fire in our library. All 15 rooms have private baths, many with fireplaces and balconies. Continental breakfast included. Use of our "inn" auto is available to our guests.

Hosts: Linda and Ben Smith
Rooms: 15 (PB) $65-225
Continental Breakfast Buffet
Credit Cards: A, B, C
Notes: 2, 5, 7, 8, 9, 10, 12

Point Way Inn

NOTES: Credit cards accepted: A Master Card; B Visa; C American Express; D Discover Card; E Diners Club; F Other; 2 Personal checks accepted; 3 Lunch available; 4 Dinner available; 5 Open all

The Shiretown Inn

North Water Street, P.O. Box 921, 02539
(508) 627-3353; (800) 541-0090; (508) 627-8478
(FAX)

Shiretown Inn on the island of Martha's
Vineyard, listed in the National Register of
Historic Places. In the center of Edgartown,
one block from the Chappaquiddick Ferry
and yacht harbor. 1700s whaling captain's
houses, carriage houses, cottage, all with
private baths. Some rooms have canopy
bed, harbor and garden views, deck, cable
color television, telephone, air conditioning. Lovely Garden Terrace Restaurant
and Pub. Complimentary breakfast. Call
us toll free.

Rooms: 33(PB) $49-259
Continental Breakfast
Credit Cards: A, B, C, D
Notes: 2, 3, 4, 7, 8, 9, 10, 12

ESSEX

George Fuller House

148 Main Street, 01929
(508) 768-7766

Built in 1830, this handsome Federalist-style home retains much of its 19th-century
charm, including Indian shutters and a
captain's staircase. Three of the guest
rooms have working fireplaces. Decoration includes hand-made quilts, braided
rugs, and caned Boston rockers. A full
breakfast may include such features as
Cindy's French toast drizzled with brandy
lemon butter. The inn's 30-foot sailboat is
available for day sailing or lessons.

Hosts: Cindy and Bob Cameron
Rooms: 6 (PB) $70-100
Full Breakfast
Credit Cards: A, B, C, D
Notes: 1, 5, 7, 8, 9, 10, 12

FALMOUTH

Captain Tom Lawrence House Inn

75 Locust Street, 02540
(508) 540-1445

1861 whaling Captain's residence in historic village close to beach, bikeway, ferries, bus station, shops, and restaurants.
Explore entire Cape, Vineyard, and Plymouth by day trips. Six beautiful guest
rooms have private baths, firm beds, some
with canopies. Antiques, a Steinway piano, and fireplace in sitting room. Homemade delicious breakfasts include specialties from organic grain. German spoken.
No Smoking!

Hostess: Barbara Sabo-Feller
Rooms: 6 (PB) $75-99
Full Breakfast
Credit Cards: A, B
Closed November-January
Notes: 2, 7 (over 12), 8, 9, 10

Captain Tom Lawrence House B & B

The Elms

495 W. Falmouth Highway (Rt. 28A), 02574
(508) 540-7832

Charming Victorian built in the early 1800's
features nine beautifully appointed bedrooms, seven with private baths, and antique decor throughout. A four-course

---

year; 6 Pets welcome; 7 Children welcome; 8 Tennis nearby; 9 Swimming nearby; 10 Golf nearby;
11 Skiing nearby; 12 May be booked through travel agent

gourmet breakfast is served each morning. Tour the manicured grounds to survey the flower and herb gardens or relax in the gazebo over the deck. One-half mile from the ocean. Walk to restaurants, tennis courts, and antique shops. Ten minutes to Woods Hole.

Hosts: Elizabeth and Joseph Mazzucchelli
Rooms: 9 (7PB; 2SB) $55-85+tax
Full Breakfast
Credit Cards: C
Notes: 2, 5, 8, 9, 10

Grafton Inn

261 Grand Ave. S., 02540
(508) 540-8688; (800) 642-4069; (508) 540-1861 (FAX)

Oceanfront Victorian. Miles of beach and breath-taking views of Martha's Vineyard. Sumptuous full breakfast served on enclosed porch overlooking Nantucket Sound. Tastefully decorated rooms with period antiques. Thoughtful amenities. Flowers, home-made chocolates. Complimentary bicycles. Late afternoon wine and cheese. Walk to restaurants, shops, and Island ferry. Open all year. No Smoking!

Hosts: Liz and Rudy Cvitan
Rooms: 11 (PB) $75-135
Full Breakfast
Credit Cards: A, B, C
Notes: 2, 5, 8, 9, 10

Grafton Inn

The Inn at One Main Street

One Main Street, 02540
(508) 540-7469

Escape the hustle and bustle of the real world and share a relaxing or romantic interlude in one of the inn's freshly and uniquely decorated rooms. Wake up to a full gourmet breakfast in the cheerful dining room with specialties such as gingerbread pancakes topped with fresh whipped cream, cheesy egg puffs, and Cape Cod cranberry pecan waffles.

Hostesses: Mari Zylinski and Karen Hart
Rooms: 6 (PB) $65-95
Full Breakfast
Credit Cards: A, B
Notes: 2, 5, 8, 9, 10, 12

The Palmer House Inn

81 Palmer Avenue, 02540
(508) 548-1230; (800) 472-2632; (508) 540-1878 (FAX)

Located in the historic district, this turn-of-the-century Victorian offers eight rooms, antique furnishings, and a gourmet breakfast. Enjoy *pain perdue* with orange cream or Finnish pancakes with strawberry soup. Walk to beaches, shops, restaurants. Bicycles are available. Reservations suggested.

Hosts: Ken and Joanne Baker
Rooms: 8 (PB) $65-115
Full Breakfast
Credit Cards: A, B, C, D, E, F
Notes: 5, 8, 9, 10, 12

NOTES: Credit cards accepted: A Master Card; B Visa; C American Express; D Discover Card; E Diners Club; F Other; 2 Personal checks accepted; 3 Lunch available; 4 Dinner available; 5 Open all

Peacock's Inn on the Sound

P. O. Box 201, 02541
(508) 457-9666

This oceanfront bed and breakfast offers ten spacious guest rooms, fireplaces, country charm, and comfort. Enjoy the breathtaking view, sample our deluxe full breakfast, then spend your day touring year-round attractions. We are within walking distance of the island ferry, shops, and restaurants. Reservations suggested. Two-night minimum stay.

Hosts: Bud and Phyllis Peacock
Rooms: 10 (PB) $85-125
Full Breakfast
Credit Cards: A, B, C, D, E
Notes: 2, 5, 8, 9, 10

Village Green Inn

40 W. Main Street, 02540
(508) 548-5621

Gracious, old, 1804 Colonial-Victorian is ideally located on Falmouth's historic village green. Walk to fine shops and restaurants, bike to beaches and picturesque Woods Hole along the Shining Ski Bike Path. Enjoy 19th-century charm and warm hospitality amidst elegant surroundings. Four lovely guest rooms and one romantic suite all have private baths and unique fireplaces (two are working). A full gourmet breakfast is served featuring delicious house specialties. Many thoughtful amenities are included.

Hosts: Linda and Don Long
Rooms: 5 (PB) $80-110
Full Breakfast
Credit Cards: A, B, C
Notes: 2, 8, 9, 10

Village Green Inn

FALMOUTH HEIGHTS

The Moorings Lodge

207 Grand Avenue South, 02540
(508) 540-2370

A Victorian sea captain's home is across from a sandy beach with lifeguard safety and within easy walking distance of restaurants and island ferry. The home-made breakfast buffet is served on the large, glassed-in porch overlooking Martha's Vineyard. Comfortable, airy rooms, most with private baths. Call us "home" while you tour Cape Cod.

Hosts: Ernie and Shirley Bernard
Rooms: 8 (6PB; 2SB) $60-85
Full Breakfast
Credit Cards: A, B
Notes: 2, 7 (over 6), 8, 9, 10

GREENFIELD

Hitchcock House

15 Congress St., 01301
(413) 774-7452

A lovely, old, Victorian house owned by Betty and Peter Gott. It was built in 1881 by Edward Hitchcock and designed by F.C. Currier, renowned Springfield archi-

---

year; 6 Pets welcome; 7 Children welcome; 8 Tennis nearby; 9 Swimming nearby; 10 Golf nearby; 11 Skiing nearby; 12 May be booked through travel agent

tect. Greenfield was formerly a part of historic Deerfield. Surrounded by well-known colleges and schools, it is a fine place to stop when headed for ski country, leaf peeping, school functions, or exploring the many nearby points of historic interest. Our rooms are complemented by antique furnishings, country quilts and accessories. Sit in our homey dining room and savor Betty's home-made muffins, fresh fruits and specialty of the day, after which you can relax on our front porch, sunporch, or patio. You can then embark on your own tour from our conveniently located inn, a few blocks from a woodland park and minutes from a shopping area. We will be happpy to assist you in tour planning and restaurant selection. Special rates for weekdays, off-season, and extended stays.

Hosts: Betty and Peter Gott
Rooms: 5 (2PB; 3SB) $50-75
Full Breakfast on weekends, Expanded Continental on weekday.
Credit Cards: A, B
Notes: 2, 5, 6, 7, 8, 9, 10, 11, 12 (10%)

HARWICH, WEST

Cape Cod Sunny Pines Claddagh Inn

77 Main St., P.O. Box 667, 02671
(508) 432-9628; (800)356-9628 (reservations)

"Irish hospitality in a Victorian ambience." All private suites beautifully decorated in comfortable Victorian charm. Unpretentious, fun-loving guests wanted to fill the house from April 1 to January 15. Authentic Irish pub, Irish art gallery and candle-light dining in the Blarney Room. Sponta-neous singalong with Irish music played on the instruments provided. A true Irish experience on Cape Cod.

Hosts: Jack and Eileen Connell
Rooms: 8(PB) $85-100
Gourmet Irish Family Style Breakfast
Credit Cards: A, B
Notes: 2, 3, 4, 8, 9, 10, 12 (15%)

HYANNIS

The Inn on Sea Street

358 Sea Street, 02601
(508) 775-8030

Elegant Victorian nine-room inn plus cottage just steps from the beach. Antiques, canopy beds, and Persian rugs abound in this friendly, relaxed atmosphere. Gourmet breakfast of fruit and home-baked delights is served with silver, crystal, china, and flowers at individual tables. One night stays welcome. Credit cards accepted.

Hosts: Lois Nelson and J. B. Whitehead
Rooms: 9 (plus 1 cottage) (8PB; 2SB) $70-95
Full Breakfast
Credit Cards: A, B, C, D
Notes: 2, 3, 4, 8, 9, 10

Sea Breeze Inn

397 Sea Street, 02601
(508) 771-7213

Sea Breeze is a 14-room quaint bed and breakfast. It is just a three-minute walk to the beach and 20 minutes to the island ferries. Restaurants, night life, shopping, golf, tennis are within a ten-minute drive. Some rooms have ocean views. An expanded continental breakfast is served between 7:30 and 9:30 each morning. All rooms are air conditioned.

Hosts: Patricia and Martin Battle
Rooms: 14 (PB) $45-85
Expanded Continental Breakfast
Credit Cards: A, B, C
Notes: 2, 5, 7, 8, 9, 10, 12 (10%)

Sea Breeze Inn

LENOX

Cornell Inn

197 Main St., 01240
(800) 637-0562

We are a cozy 1880 country inn with an intimate, fireplaced restaurant and pub. All rooms have private baths, phones, and air conditioning; some have fireplaces, whirlpool tubs, and TV. Our condominium-style suites have living room, kitchen, fireplace, jacuzzi tub, and TV. Our parlors offer fireplaces, TV's, VCR's, movies, board games, etc. Our health spa offers large whirlpool, sauna, steam and exercise equipment. Perfect for an anniversary, birthday, or just a relaxing getaway.

Host: Jack D'Elia
Rooms: 18 (PB) $49-199
Full Breakfast (Continental breakfast available)
Credit Cards: A, B, C, D, E
Notes: 2, 3, 4, 5, 7, 8, 9, 10, 11, 12

Cornell Inn

Garden Gables Inn

141 Main St., P.O. Box 52, 01240
(413) 637-0193;, (FAX) (413) 637-4554

220-year-old charming and quiet inn located in historic Lenox on five wooded acres dotted with gardens. 72-foot swimming pool. Some rooms have fireplaces, and sitting rooms are furnished with antiques and a Steinway grand piano. All rooms have private baths, and some also have whirlpool tubs and private porches. Breakfast is included. In-room phones are provided and the famous Tanglewood Festival is only one mile away. Restaurants are all within walking distance.

Hosts: Mario and Lynn Mekinda
Rooms: 14 (PB) $65-180
Full Breakfast
Credit Cards: A, B, C, D
Notes: 2, 5, 8, 10, 11, 12

Walker House Inn

64 Walker St., 01240
(413) 637-1271

Situated on three wooded acres near the center of a charming New England village,

Walker House, constructed in 1804, offers eight guest rooms named for composers, all with antiques, some with fireplaces. The large parlor has a grand piano; the library, hundreds of books and a seven-foot video screen on which guests may watch films, operas, and special events. Breakfast and afternoon tea are served in the dining room, and two verandas provide additional space for relaxation. Good restaurants, galleries, an arts center, churches, and shops are within walking distance. No smoking allowed in inn.

Hosts: Richard and Peggy Houdek
Rooms: 8 (PB) $50-160 (seasonal)
Generous Continental Breakfast
Credit Cards: None
Notes: 2, 5, 6 (by approval), 7 (over 12), 8, 9, 10, 11

MARBLEHEAD

Harborside House

23 Gregory Street, 01945
(617) 631-1032

An 1850 Colonial overlooks picturesque Marblehead Harbor, with water views from the paneled living room with a cozy fireplace, period dining room, sunny breakfast porch, and third-story deck. A generous breakfast includes juice, fresh fruit, home-baked goods, and cereals. Antique shops, gourmet restaurants, historic sites, and beaches are a pleasant stroll away. The owner is a professional dressmaker and a nationally-ranked competitive swimmer. No smoking.

Hostess: Susan Livingston
Rooms: 2 (SB) $60-75
Expanded Continental Breakfast
Credit Cards: None
Notes: 2, 5, 7 (over 10), 8, 9

Spray Cliff on the Ocean

25 Spray Avenue, 01945
(508) 744-8924; (800) 626-1530

Panoramic views stretch out in grand proportions from this English Tudor mansion, circa 1910, set high above the Atlantic. The inn provides a spacious and elegant atmosphere inside. The grounds include a brick terrace surrounded by lush flower gardens where eider ducks, black cormorants, and seagulls abound. Fifteen miles from Boston.

Hosts: Diane and Dick Pabich
Rooms: 7 (PB) $105-200
Continental Breakfast
Credit Cards: A, B, C, D, E
Notes: 5, 8, 9, 12

NANTUCKET

House of the Seven Gables

32 Cliff Road, 02554
(508) 228-4706

A 150-year-old Victorian, The House of Seven Gables is a quiet, informal guest house. There is a parlor with a television and a fireplace for your comfort and relaxation. A continental breakfast is served to your room. The rooms are bright and sunny and some have a view of the harbor. Museums, restaurants, tennis, and beaches are all within walking distance.

Hostess: Suzanne Walton
Rooms: 10 (8PB; 2SB) $40-140
Continental Breakfast
Credit Cards: A, B, C
Notes: 2, 5, 8, 9, 10

NOTES: Credit cards accepted: A Master Card; B Visa; C American Express; D Discover Card; E Diners Club; F Other; 2 Personal checks accepted; 3 Lunch available; 4 Dinner available; 5 Open all

The Woodbox Inn

29 Fair Street, 02554
(508) 228-0587

The Woodbox is Nantucket's oldest inn, built in 1709. It is one and one-half blocks from the center of town, serves "the best breakfast on the island," and offers gourmet dinners by candlelight. There are nine units, queen size beds, private baths, including 1- and 2-bedroom suites with working fireplaces.

Host: Dexter Tutein
Rooms: 9 (PB) $120-200
Full Breakfast Available
Credit Cards: None
Notes: 2, 4, 7, 8, 9, 10, 12

OAK BLUFFS

The Beach Rose, Martha's Vineyard

Box 2352, Columbian Ave., 02557
(508) 693-6135

This charming home, nestled in an oak and pine woodland on the beautiful island of Martha's Vineyard, is uniquely decorated in country antique style. Greet the morning with a continental plus breakfast of fresh fruits, a delicious entreé du jour, homemade muffins and jams, and freshly brewed beverages. Your hosts provide warm hospitality and personal attention. They can direct you to such places as the gingerbread cottages of the Methodist Campmeeting grounds, the Gay Head Cliffs and the historic whaling homes of Edgartown. The Vineyard has a myriad of sightseeing and other activities including unspoiled beaches, walking trails, sailing, fishing, biking, and much more. Courtesy transportation to and from ferry.

Hosts: Gloria and Russ Everett
Rooms: 3 (SB) (house has two baths) $80-90
Expanded Continental Breakfast
Credit Cards: None
Open May-October
Notes: 2, 7, 8, 9, 10

ONSET

The Onset Pointe Inn

9 Eagleway, P.O. Box 1450, 02558
(508) 295-8442

This elegant, award-winning, turn-of-the-century beachfront mansion with cottage and guest house caters to a discerning traveler. All accommodations enjoy water views. Many rooms with queen poster beds and sitting areas to take advantage of spectacular sunsets. Wide verandas, sun parlor and beachside gazebo provide all-day space to lull guests toward their favorite evening activity. A bayside breakfast is complimentary to mansion guests.

Hosts: Toni and Carl Larrabee
Rooms: 14 (14PB) $65-135
Both Full and Continental Breakfast (by season)
Credit Cards: A, B, C
Notes: 2, 5, 8, 9, 10, 12

REHOBOTH

Gilbert's Bed and Breakfast

30 Spring Street, 02769
(508) 252-6416

Our 150-year-old home is special in all seasons. The in-ground pool refreshes

---

year; 6 Pets welcome; 7 Children welcome; 8 Tennis nearby; 9 Swimming nearby; 10 Golf nearby; 11 Skiing nearby; 12 May be booked through travel agent

weary travelers, and the quiet walks through our 100 acres give food for the soul. Guests also enjoy the horses. We praise God for being allowed to enjoy the beauty of the earth and want to share this beauty with others. No smoking inside the house.

Hosts: Jeanne and Martin Gilbert
Rooms: 3 (SB) $45-50
Full Breakfast
Credit Cards: None
Notes: 2, 5, 6, 7, 8, 9 , 10, 12 (10%)

ROCKPORT

Lantana House

22 Broadway, 01966
(508) 546-3535

An intimate guest house in the heart of historic Rockport, Lantana House is close to Main Street, the T-Wharf, and the beaches. There is a large sun deck reserved for guests, as well as TV, games, magazines and books, a guest refrigerator, and ice service. Nearby you will find a golf course, tennis courts, picnic areas, rocky bays, and inlets. Boston is one hour away by car.

Hostess: Cynthia Sewell
Rooms: 7 (5PB; 2SB) $60-70
Continental Breakfast
Credit Cards: None
Notes: 2, 5, 7, 8, 9, 10

Morringstone for Non-smokers

12-14 Norwood Avenue, 01966-1715
(508) 546-2479

Mary and David added on to their home in 1987 to establish this contemporary smoke-free B&B. Each of the quiet, comfortable, ground-floor rooms has air conditioning, cable TV, refrigerator, microwave and toaster ovens, and parking. Walt Disney Productions named Rockport Harbor "one of the ten most scenic places in the country." Rockport is also an ideal base for day trips in New England. Ask for our special rates (without breakfast and housekeeping) five days to five months. AAA listed.

Hosts: David and Mary Knowlton
Rooms: 3 (PB) $76-84
Continental Plus Breakfast
Closed Mid-October to Mid-May
Credit Cards: A, B, C
Notes: 2, 8, 9, 10, 12

SALEM

Amelia Payson Guest House

16 Winter Street, 01970
(508) 744-8304

Built in 1845, 16 Winter Street is one of Salem's finest examples of Greek Revival architecture. Elegantly restored and beautifully decorated, each room is furnished with period antiques and warmed by a personal touch. Located in the heart of Salem's historic district, a five-minute stroll finds downtown shopping, historic houses, museums, and Pickering Wharf's waterfront dining. The seaside towns of Rockport and Gloucester are a short drive up the coast; downtown Boston is only 30 minutes away by car or easily reached by train or bus. Color brochure available. No smoking.

Hosts: Ada and Donald Roberts
Rooms: 4 (PB) $65-85
Continental Plus Breakfast
Credit Cards: A, B, C
Notes: 5, 9, 10

The Salem Inn

7 Summer Street, 01970
(508) 741-0680; (800) 446-2995

In the midst of the historical and beautifully restored city of Salem is The Salem Inn, originally three townhouses built in 1834 by Captain Nathaniel West. The captain would have approved of the spacious, comfortably appointed guest rooms with a blend of period detail and antique furnishings. Some have working fireplaces. Ideal for families are two-room suites complete with equipped kitchen. All rooms have air conditioning, phones, TV. Complimentary continental breakfast served in our two intimate dining rooms, rose garden, and brick terrace. Rail and bus transportation available to Boston, only 18 miles away. Jacuzzis available.

Hosts: Richard and Diane Pabich
Rooms: 22 (PB) $85-140
Continental Breakfast
Credit Cards: A, B, C, D, E
Notes: 2, 4, 5, 6, 7, 9, 10, 12

SANDWICH

Bay Beach Bed and Breakfast

1-3 Bay Beach Lane, Box 151, 02563
(508) 888-8813

Cape Cod is the pristine setting for Bay Beach, an extraordinary contemporary bed and breakfast. Bay Beach has spacious suites with private baths, some with jacuzzis, oceanfront decks, cable TV, telephones, refrigerators, air conditioning, compact disc player, and unparalleled amenities. Bicycles, exercise room, plus a full continental breakfast. A non-smoking property for adults only. Visit nearby museums, boardwalk, and fine restaurants within walking distance! Rated four diamonds from AAA.

Hosts: Emily and Reale J. Lemieux
Rooms: 3 (PB) $100-175
Continental Breakfast
Credit Cards: A, B
Notes: 2, 8, 9, 10, 12

Captain Ezra Nye House

152 Main Street, 02563
(508) 888-6142; (800) 388-2278

Whether you come to enjoy summer on Cape Cod, a fall foliage trip, or a quiet winter vacation, the Captain Ezra Nye House is the perfect place to start. Located 60 miles from Boston, 20 from Hyannis, and within walking distance of many noteworthy attractions, including Heritage Plantation, Sandwich Glass Museum, and the Cape Cod Canal.

Hosts: Elaine and Harry Dickson
Rooms: 7 (5PB; 2SB) $55-90
Full Breakfast
Credit Cards: A, B, C, D
Notes: 2, 5, 7 (over six), 8, 9, 10, 12

The Summer House

158 Main Street, 02563
(508) 888-4991

This exquisite 1835 Greek Revival home featured in *Country Living* magazine is located in the heart of historic Sandwich village and features antiques, working fireplaces, hand-stitched quilts, flowers, large sunny rooms, and English-style gardens. We are within strolling distance of dining, museums, shops, pond, and the boardwalk to the beach. Bountiful breakfasts

year; 6 Pets welcome; 7 Children welcome; 8 Tennis nearby; 9 Swimming nearby; 10 Golf nearby; 11 Skiing nearby; 12 May be booked through travel agent

and elegant afternoon tea in the garden.

Hosts: David and Kay Merrell
Rooms: 5 (1PB; 4SB) $55-75
Full Breakfast
Credit Cards: A, B, C, D
Notes: 2, 5, 7 (over 5), 8, 9, 10

SOUTH CHATHAM

Ye Olde Nantucket House

2647 Main St., 02659
(508) 432-5641

Originally built on Nantucket before its prosperous whaling business began to fail, this classic Greek Revival-style home was brought to its present South Chatham location around 1867. Today, Ye Olde Nantucket House is a delightfully restored bed and breakfast. The five rooms have stenciled walls, pine floors, antiques, and attractive window and wall coverings, and they all combine for a unique country Victorian style. You'll find the atmosphere friendly and informal at Ye Old Nantucket House.

Hosts: Steve and Ellen Londo
Rooms: 5 (PB) $68-78
Continental Breakfast
Credit Cards: A, B, C
Notes: 2, 5, 7 (over 8), 8, 9, 10

SOUTH DARTMOUTH

The Little Red House

631 Elm St., 02748
(508) 996-4554

A charming gambrel Colonial home located in the lovely coastal village of Padanaram. This home is beautifully furnished with country accents, antiques, lovely livingroom with fireplace, luxuriously comfortable four-poster or brass-and-iron beds. A full home-made breakfast in the romantic, candlelit dining room is a delectable treat. Close to the harbor, beaches, historic sites, and a short distance to Newport, Plymouth, Boston, Cape Cod. Martha Vineyard's ferry is just 10 minutes away.

Host: Meryl Zwirblis
Rooms: 2 (SB) $60-65
Full Breakfast
Credit Cards: None
Notes: 2, 5, 8, 9, 10, 12 (10%)

SOUTH LANCASTER

Deershorn Manor Bed and Breakfast and Conference Center

P.O. Box 805, 357 Sterling Rd., 01561
(508) 365-9002

Deershorn Manor, built circa 1886 for the Honorable Herbert Parker, Attorney General of the Commonwealth of Massachusetts, 1901-1905, rests within acres of formal gardens with gazebos and fountains, bordering wildlife sanctuary. Tranquil and historic, its large library with religious books and prayer corner, four-season solarium, and parlor with baby grand piano complement any getaway. Let the Manor's Doric pillars and formal circular staircase usher you into a bygone era of elegance. Non-smoking.

Host: S.P. Lamb
Rooms: 7 (2PB; 5SB) $45-95
Buffet Continental Breakfast
Credit Cards: None
Notes: 2, 5, 10, 11

NOTES: Credit cards accepted: A Master Card; B Visa; C American Express; D Discover Card; E Diners Club; F Other; 2 Personal checks accepted; 3 Lunch available; 4 Dinner available; 5 Open all

STOCKBRIDGE

Arbor Rose Bed and Breakfast

Box 114, 8 Yale Hill Rd., 01262
(413) 298-4744

Lovely, old, New England mill house with pond, gardens, and mountain view. Walk to Berkshire Theater and Stockbridge Center. Beautiful rooms, comfy, good beds, antiques, water colors, and sunshine. Fireplace and TV in common room. Home-baked mmm... breakfast.

Hosts: Christina M. Alsop and family
Rooms: 4 (2PB; 2SB) $55-150
Continental Breakfast on Mon-Sat; Full Breakfast on Sunday
Credit Cards: A, B, C
Notes: 2, 5, 7, 8, 9, 10, 11, 12

STURBRIDGE

Bethlehem Inn

72 Stallion Hill, P.O. Box 451, 01566
(508) 347-3013

Bethlehem Inn in Sturbridge is operated by Agnes Duquette to help defray the costs of operating Bethlehem in Sturbridge. They offer two rooms and a continental breakfast consisting of juice, coffee, and homemade blueberry muffins. The home is located just up Stallion Hill Road from the Old Sturbridge Village parking lot. Call for more informaiton.

Hostess: Agnes Duquette
Rooms: 2 (SB) $60-65
Continental Breakfast
Credit Cards: None
Notes: 2, 5, 8, 9, 10, 11

The Colonel Ebenezer Crafts Inn

Rt. 131, P.O. Box 187, 01566
(508) 347-3313

The Colonel Ebenezer Crafts Inn was built in 1786 by David Fiske, Esquire, on one of the highest points of land in Sturbridge, which offered him a commanding view of his cattle and farmland. The house has since been magnificently restored by the management of the Publick House. Accommodations at Crafts Inn are charming. There are two queen-size canopy beds, as well as some four-poster beds. Guests may relax by the pool or in the sunroom, take an afternoon tea, or enjoy sweeping views of the countryside. Breakfast includes freshly baked muffins and sweet rolls, fresh fruit and juices, and coffee and tea. Those seeking a heartier breakfast, lunch, or dinner can stroll down to the Publick House located just over a mile away.

Rooms: 2 plus cottage suite (PB) call for rates
Continental Breakfast
Credit Cards: None
Notes: 2, 5, 7, 9

Sturbridge Country Inn

530 Main Street, 01566
(508) 347-5503; (508) 347-5319 (FAX)

At this historic 1840's inn each room has a fireplace and private whirlpool tub. It is close to Old Sturbridge Village and within walking distance of restaurants, shops, antiques. Breakfast available in room.

Host: Mr. MacConnel
Rooms: 9 (PB) $69-149
Continental Breakfast
Credit Cards: A, B, C, D
Notes: 2, 5, 7, 8, 9, 10, 11, 12

year; 6 Pets welcome; 7 Children welcome; 8 Tennis nearby; 9 Swimming nearby; 10 Golf nearby; 11 Skiing nearby; 12 May be booked through travel agent

STURBRIDGE-WARE

The 1880 Country Bed and Breakfast

14 Pleasant Street, 01082
(413) 967-7847; (413) 967-3773

Built in 1876, this Colonial style has pumpkin and maple hardwood floors, beamed ceilings, six fireplaces, and antique furnishings. Afternoon tea is served by the fireplace; breakfast is served in the dining room or on the porch, weather permitting. It is a short, pretty country ride to historic Old Sturbridge Village and Old Deerfield Village; hiking and fishing are nearby. Midpoint between Boston and the Berkshires, this is a very comfortable bed and breakfast.

Hostess: Margaret Skutnik
Rooms: 5 (2PB; 3SB) $40-65
Full Breakfast
Credit Cards: None
Notes: 2, 5, 8, 9, 10, 11, 12

TYRINGHAM

The Golden Goose

Main Rd, Box 336, 01264
(413) 243-3008

Warm, friendly circa 1800 B&B nestled in secluded valley. Near to Tanglewood, Stockbridge, skiing, and hiking. All homemade jams, applesauce, and biscuits, fresh fruit in season, and hot and cold cereals. Open all year.

Hosts: Lilja and Joe Rizzo
Rooms: 7 (5PB; 2SB) $65-125
Semi-Full Breakfast
Credit Cards: A, B, C, D
Notes: 2, 5, 7, 8, 9, 10, 11, 12

VINEYARD HAVEN

Hanover House

10 Edgartown Road, P. O. Box 2107, 02568
(508) 693-1066

Located on the island of Martha's Vineyard, The Hanover House is a large, old inn that has been brought into the 20th century while still retaining the charm and personalized hospitality of the gracious, old inns of yesteryear. Decorated in a classic country style that typifies a New England inn, Hanover House is just a short walk from town and the ferry.

Hosts: Ron and Kay Nelson
Rooms: 15 (PB) $68-158
Continental Breakfast
Credit Cards: A, B, C
Notes: 2, 7, 8, 9, 10, 12

WEST BROOKFIELD

The Spy Room B & B

9 W. Main Street, 01585
(508) 867-2877 (voice and FAX)

The Spy Room Bed and Breakfast is a gracious Victorian home decorated with period antiques. Many guests comment that their stay is like a visit to Grandma's. Beautiful West Brookfield has summer concerts on the Common just down the street from the Spy Room. The town is in central Massachusetts just 10 miles north of historic Old Sturbridge Village, and amidst the lakes, woods, and rugged countryside of New England.

Hosts: Lynn and Dan Welaver
Rooms: 3 (1PB; 2SB) $55-65
Continental Breakfast
Credit Cards: None
Notes: 2, 5, 7, 9

NOTES: Credit cards accepted: A Master Card; B Visa; C American Express; D Discover Card; E Diners Club; F Other; 2 Personal checks accepted; 3 Lunch available; 4 Dinner available; 5 Open all

Michigan

ALMA

Saravilla B & B

633 N. State St., 48801
(517) 463-4078

Great location for travelers, right off highway in the center of the state. Enjoy the charm and original features of this 1894 10,000-square-foot Dutch Colonial home which has Victorian influences. On Michigan's Historical Register, this home has imported woodwork, wood carvings, hand-painted wall coverings, lead glass windows. Rooms are spacious and comfortable, several with fireplaces. A variety of common rooms available—TV, billiards, library, sunroom with hot tub. A full, home-made breakfast is served on antique china in the elegant turret dining room.

Hosts: Linda and Jon Darrow
Rooms: 6 (4PB; 2SB) $55-75
Full Breakfast
Credit Cards: A, B, D
Notes: 2, 5, 7, 8, 10, 12

BATTLE CREEK

Greencrest Manor

6174 Halbert Road, 49017
(616) 962-8633

To experience Greencrest is to step back in time to a way of life that is rare today. From the moment you enter the iron gates, you will be mesmerized. This French Normandy mansion situated on the highest elevation of St. Mary's Lake is constructed of sandstone, slate, and copper. Three levels of formal gardens include fountains, stone walls, iron rails, and cut sandstone urns. Air conditioned. Featured "Inn of the Month" in *Country Inns Magazine*, August 1992 edition, and chosen as one of their top twelve inns in the nation for 1992.

Hosts: Tom and Kathy Van Daff
Rooms: 5 (3PB; 2SB) $75-170
Expanded Continental Breakfast
Credit Cards: A, B, C
Notes: 2, 5, 7, 8, 10, 11

BAY CITY

Stonehedge Inn Bed and Breakfast

924 Center Avenue (M25), 48708
(517) 894-4342

With stained-glass windows and nine fireplaces, this 1889 English Tudor home is indeed an elegant journey into the past. The magnificent open foyer and staircase lead to large, beautiful bedrooms on the upper floors. Original features include speaking tubes, a warming oven, chandeliers, and a fireplace picturing Bible stories

---

year; 6 Pets welcome; 7 Children welcome; 8 Tennis nearby; 9 Swimming nearby; 10 Golf nearby;
11 Skiing nearby; 12 May be booked through travel agent

and passages on Blue Delft tiles. In the historic district, Frankenmuth is 20 miles away. Birch Run Manufacturer's Marketplace is 35 miles away.

Hostess: Ruth Koerber
Rooms: 7 (3SB) $65-85
Expanded Continental Breakfast
Credit Cards: A, B, C, D
Notes: 2, 5, 7, 8, 9, 10, 11, 12

BAY VIEW

Terrace Inn

P.O. Box 226, 216 Fairview, 49770
(616) 347-2410; (800) 530-9898

The Terrace Inn is set in the heart of the Christian summer community of Bay View, one mile north of Petroskey on US 31. The Chautauqua programs are still alive since being established in 1876. The ecumenical community offers religious, cultural, and family activities. The inn was built in 1910 and has been recently restored. All guest rooms have private baths, and the dining room serves wonderful food, including planked whitefish. You have not seen Michigan until you have stayed at the Terrace Inn.

Hosts: Patrick and Mary Lou Barbour
Rooms: 44 (PB) $48-91
Continental Breakfast
Credit Cards: A, B, C
Notes: 2, 4, 5, 7, 8, 9, 10, 11, 12
(313) 229-2673

Aaron's Windy Hill

CHARLEVOIX

Aaron's Windy Hill B & B

202 Michigan, 49720
(616) 547-2804; (616) 547-6100

Victorian-style home with huge riverstone porch where you can enjoy a homemade buffet-style breakfast. Each of the eight spacious rooms are individually decorated and each has its own bath. Three rooms can accommodate up to five guests. One block north of drawbridge, shops, and restaurants, and one block east of Lake Michigan's swimming and sunsets.

Hostess: Nancy DeHollanden
Rooms: 8 (PB) $65-95
Continental Plus Breakfast
Credit Cards: None
Open May 15 through October 30.
Notes: 2, 7, 8, 9, 10

CLIO

Chandelier Guest House

1567 Morgan Road, 48420
(810) 687-6061

Relax in our country home. Enjoy bed and breakfast comforts including choice of rooms with twin, full, or queen beds. You may wish to be served full breakfast in bed, or beneath the beautiful crystal chandelier, or on the sunporch with a view of surrounding woods. Located minutes from Clio Amphitheater, Flint Crossroad Village, Birch Run Manufacturer's Marketplace, Frankenmuth, and Chesaning. Senior citizen discount. Call for directions.

Hosts: Alfred and Clara Bielert
Rooms: 2 (1PB; 1SB) $49.95-54.95
Full Country Breakfast
Credit Cards: None
Notes: 2, 5, 7, 10, 12

NOTES: Credit cards accepted: A Master Card; B Visa; C American Express; D Discover Card; E Diners Club; F Other; 2 Personal checks accepted; 3 Lunch available; 4 Dinner available; 5 Open all

COLDWATER

Batavia Inn

1824 West Chicago Road, U.S. 12, 49036
(517) 278-5146

This 1872 Italianate country inn has original massive woodwork, high ceilings, and restful charm. Seasonal decorations are a specialty. Christmas festival of trees. Located near recreation and discount shopping. In-ground pool available in season. Guest pampering is the innkeepers' goal with treats, turn down, homemade breakfasts. Perfect for small retreats.

Hosts: E. Fred and Alma Marquardt
Rooms: 5(PB) $59-69
Full Breakfast
Credit Cards: None
Notes: 2, 5, 9, 10

Batavia Inn

DAVISON

Oakbrook Inn

7256 East Court Street, 48423
(313) 658-1744

Oakbrook is located on twenty acres of rolling landscape with woods and creek less than five minutes from Flint. Guest rooms are furnished with antiques, handicrafts, and handmade quilts. The indoor pool and hot tub are open year-round. An outdoor deck is available for enjoying the warm summer sun and the cool evening breezes.

Hosts: Jan and Bill Cooke
Rooms: 7 (PB) $46-98
Continental Breakfast
Credit Cards: A, B, C
Notes: 2, 5, 7, 8, 9, 10, 11, 12 (no commission)

ELK RAPIDS

Cairn House Bed and Breakfast

8160 Cairn Hwy., 49629
(616) 264-8994

Built in the style of an 1880's Colonial home and located 15 minutes north of Traverse City, two miles from Grand Traverse Bay and Port of Elk rapids. Rooms furnished to make you feel at home. Full breakfast served in the nook in the all-oak kitchen. Boat trailer parking available.

Rooms: 3 (PB) $60
Full Breakfast
Credit Cards: None
Notes: 2, 7, 8, 9, 10, 11, 12

FENNVILLE

The Kingsley House Bed and Breakfast

626 West Main Street, 49408
(616) 561-6425

This elegant Queen Anne Victorian was built by the prominent Kingsley family in 1886 and selected by *Inn Times* as one of 50 best bed and breakfasts in America. It was featured in *Innsider* magazine. Near

---

year; 6 Pets welcome; 7 Children welcome; 8 Tennis nearby; 9 Swimming nearby; 10 Golf nearby; 11 Skiing nearby; 12 May be booked through travel agent

Holland, Saugatuck, Allegan State Forest, sandy beaches, cross-country skiing. Bicycles available, whirlpool bath, getaway honeymoon suite. Enjoy the beautiful surroundings, family antiques. Breakfast is served in the formal dining room.

Hosts: David and Shirley Witt
Rooms: 7 (PB) $75-125
Full Breakfast
Credit Cards: A, B, C, D
Notes: 2, 5, 8, 9, 10, 11, 12

The Kingsley House

FRANKENMUTH

Bavarian Town Bed and Breakfast

206 Beyerlein St., 48734
(517) 652-8057

Beautifully redecorated Cape Cod dwelling with central air conditioning and private half-baths in a peaceful, residential district of Michigan's most popular tourist town, just three blocks from Main Street. Bilingual hosts are descendants of original German settlers. Will share knowledge of area including historic St. Lorenz Lutheran Church. Full breakfasts. Two rooms with color TV and soft chairs.

Hosts: Louie and Kathy Weiss
Rooms: 2 (P1/2B, shower is shared) $50-55
Full Breakfast
Credit Cards: None
Notes: 2, 5, 7, 8, 9, 10, 12

Bed and Breakfast at the Pines

327 Ardussi Street, 48734
(517) 652-9019

A friendly, ranch-style home with casual atmosphere in a quiet residential neighborhood. A secluded yard, surrounded by evergreens and many flowers. A leisurely walk to famous restaurants and main tourist areas. Bedrooms furnished with heirloom quilts, ceiling fans, cotton sheets, and fresh flowers; shared bathrooms; terry robes provided. A continental-plus breakfast of homemade breads and rolls, seasonal fruits, and beverages. Plus friendly conversation with other guests. Breakfast recipes to take home.

Hosts: Richard and Donna Hodge
Rooms: (SB)
Continental Breakfast
Credit Cards: None
Notes: 2, 5, 6, 7

GRAND HAVEN

Boyden House Inn B & B

301 South 5th, 49417
(616) 846-3538; (616) 847-3645 (FAX)

Built in 1874, our charming Victorian inn is decorated with treasures from faraway places, antiques, and original art. Enjoy the comfort of air conditioned rooms with private baths. Some rooms feature fireplaces or balconies. Relax in our common room and veranda surrounded by a beautiful perennial garden. Full, home-made breakfast served in our lovely dining room. Walking distance to boardwalk beaches, shopping, and restaurants.

Hosts: Carrie and Berend Snoeyer
Rooms: 5 (plus 1 apt.) (PB) $55-85
Full Breakfast
Credit Cards: A, B, C
Notes: 2, 5, 7, 8, 9, 10, 11, 12

Seascape Bed and Breakfast

20009 Breton, Spring Lake, 49456
(616) 842-8409

On private Lake Michigan beach. Relaxing lakefront rooms. Enjoy the warm hospitality and cozy "country living" ambience of our nautical lakeshore home. Full, home-made breakfast served in gathering room with fieldstone fireplace or on the sun deck. Either offers a panoramic view of Grand Haven Harbor. Open all year. Stroll or cross-country ski on Duneland nature trails. Special rates Sunday-Thursday reservations, stay five nights, pay for four.

Hostess: Susan Meyer
Rooms: 3 (PB) $65-90
Full Breakfast
Credit Cards: A, B
Notes: 2, 5, 8, 9, 10, 11, 12 (no commission)

HARBOR SPRINGS

Mottls Getaway

1021 Birchcrest Ct., 49740
(616) 526-9682

Mottls Getaway B&B apartment includes a kitchenette with stove and refrigerator, large stone fireplace in furnished living room, and a private outside entrance. It is close to the sandy beaches of beautiful Little Traverse Bay and other inland lakes, the ski resorts of Nubs Nob and Boyne Highlands, good golf courses, cross country ski trails, and the art galleries and boutiques of Harbor Springs and Petoskey.

Hostess: Carol Mottl
Rooms: 2 (PB) $50
Self-Serve, Full Breakfast
Credit Cards: None
Notes: 2, 5, 7, 8, 9, 10, 11

HOLLAND

Dutch Colonial Inn

560 Central Avenue, 49423
(616) 396-3664

Relax and enjoy a gracious 1928 Dutch Colonial. Your hosts have elegantly decorated their home with family heirloom antiques and furnishings from the 1930's. Guests enjoy the cheery sunporch, honeymoon suites, or rooms with whirlpool tubs for two. Special, festive touches are everywhere during the Christmas holiday season. Nearby are Windmill Island, wooden shoe factory, Delftware factory, tulip festival, Hope College, Michigan's finest beaches, bike paths, and cross-country ski trails. Corporate rates are available for business travelers.

Hosts: Bob and Pat Elenbaas, Diana Klungel
Rooms: 5 (PB) $65-100
Full Breakfast
Credit Cards: A, B, C, D
Notes: 2, 5, 8, 9, 10, 11, 12

---

year; **6** Pets welcome; **7** Children welcome; **8** Tennis nearby; **9** Swimming nearby; **10** Golf nearby; **11** Skiing nearby; **12** May be booked through travel agent

Reka's Bed and Breakfast

300 N. 152nd Avenue, 49424
(616) 399-0409

"True Dutch atmosphere" is found in this unique new bed and breakfast in Holland, MI. Close to bicycle paths, Lake Michigan beaches, Lake Macatawa, Manufacturers' Outlet Mall, downtown Holland, Hope College, theaters, restaurants, etc. The guest rooms offer king and queen size beds, air conditioning, and walkouts to the patio where at times you may spot a deer or other wildlife and where you are able to enjoy amazing sunsets in the most quiet setting. We serve a delicious full breakfast that will satisfy all. The B&B has been professionally designed and decorated with Blue Delft Vases and much more wonderful art for your enjoyment.

Hosts: Kay and Rein Wolfert
Rooms: 3 (PB) $80
Full Breakfast
Credit Cards: A, B, F
Notes: 2, 5, 7, 8, 9, 10, 11, 12

IONIA

Union Hill Inn Bed and Breakfast

306 Union Street, 48846
(616) 527-0955

Elegant 1868 Italiante home noted for its expansive veranda and panoramic view, yet only two blocks from downtown. Home built by Lucius Miles, Captain in the Civil War. He built bridges during the war. You can see his bridge-building capabilities in the porches. Breakfast is served on the porch when weather permits. Each room has TV and air conditioning. Love and peace abide here.

Hosts: Tom and Mary Kay Moular
Rooms: 5 (SB) $50-60
Full Breakfast
Credit Cards: None
Notes: 2, 5, 7, 10

JACKSON

Summit Place Bed and Breakfast

1682 W. Kimmel Rd., 49201
(517) 787-0468

Come and enjoy warmth and elegance where the past blends with the present in a beautiful, quiet countryside. Enjoy a full breakfast in our formal dining room overlooking a flower garden or served on the deck or in the privacy of your room. Snacks and desserts by the fireplace in winter. Relax in our comfortable living room with books, music, piano, or enjoy cable TV in your private room. Member of Lake to Lake Bed and Breakfast Association.

Hosts: Douglas and Marlene Laing
Rooms: 2 (SB) $60+tax
Full Breakfast
Credit Cards: A, B
Notes: 2, 5, 7, 9, 10, 11

Summit Place

NOTES: Credit cards accepted: A Master Card; B Visa; C American Express; D Discover Card; E Diners Club; F Other; 2 Personal checks accepted; 3 Lunch available; 4 Dinner available; 5 Open all

KEARSARGE

Belknap's Garnet House

238 County Road, 49942
(906) 337-5607

This century-old house, built for a mining captain during the copper rush in the Keewenaw Peninsula of Michigan's Upper Peninsula, features the original fireplaces, leaded/bevelled glass, pantries, fixtures, and woodworking. It is now a comfortable house with period antiques where guests are invited to enjoy the huge porch, three acres of grounds, or a tour of the house. Visit historic Calumet (designated a historic national park), local mines, lighthouses, or go fishing, hiking, or golfing.

Hosts: Howard and Debby Belknap
Rooms: 5 (1PB; 4SB) $45-65
Continental Plus Breakfast
Credit Cards: A, B
Notes: 2, 7 (over 8), 9, 10, 11

Belknap's Garnet House

LAMONT

The Stagecoach Stop Bed and Breakfast

0-4819 Leonard Road W., P.O. Box 18, 49430
(616) 677-5971

The quaint and charming Grand River village of Lamont is the setting of this restored 1850's Gothic Revival home, furnished with antiques and country primitives. Once an overnight stop for stagecoaches making the trip between Grand Rapids and Grand Haven, both cities are now only a twenty-minute drive. Just three minutes south of I-96, exit 19. Crib available.

Hosts: Marcia and Gene Ashby
Rooms: 3 (1PB; 2SB) $55-65
Full Breakfast
Credit Cards: A, B
Notes: 2, 5, 7, 9, 10

LUDINGTON

Bed and Breakfast at Ludington

2458 S. Beaune Road, 49431-9327
(616) 843-9768

State land, a horse farm, and apple orchards surround our 16 acres. We use all for trails, foot or ski. Snowshoes provided, also toboggans—great hill, creek and pond. Golf 1/2 mile; barn loft hideaway, hot tub, table tennis. Country Breakfast, crib, fireplaces.

Hosts: Grace Schneider and Robert Schneider
Rooms: 3 (2PB; 1SB) $35-55
Full Breakfast
Credit Cards: None
Notes: 2, 5, 6, 7, 8, 9, 10, 11, 12

Doll House Inn

709 E. Ludington Avenue, 49431
(616) 843-2286

Gracious 1900 American Foursquare, seven rooms including bridal suite with whirlpool tub for two. Enclosed porch, smoke- and pet-free, adult accommodations. Full heart-smart breakfast. Air conditioning, corporate rates, bicycles, cross-country skiing, walk to beach, town, special weekend packages—fall and winter. Transportation to and from car ferry-airport.

Hosts: Joe and Barb Gerovac
Rooms: 7(5PB; 2SB) $55-95
Full Breakfast
Credit Cards: A, B
Closed December 20 to January 3.
Notes: 2, 5, 8, 9, 10, 11

MACKINAC ISLAND

Haan's 1830 Inn
Huron Street, P. O. Box 123, 49757
(906) 847-6244; winter (414) 248-9244

The earliest Greek Revival home in the Northwest Territory, this inn is on the Michigan Historic Registry and is completely restored. It is in a quiet neighborhood three blocks around Haldiman Bay from bustling 1800's downtown and Old Fort Mackinac. It is also adjacent to historic St. Anne's Church and gardens. Guest rooms are furnished with antiques. Enjoy the island's 19th-century ambience of horse-drawn buggies and wagons. Winter address: 1134 Geneva Street, Lake Geneva, Wisconsin 53147.

Hosts: Nicholas and Nancy Haan; Vernon and Joy Haan
Rooms: 7 (5PB; 2SB) $75-109
Expanded Continental Breakfast
Credit Cards: None
Closed late October to mid-May
Notes: 2, 7, 8, 9, 10

Metivier Inn
Box 285, 49757
(906) 847-6234

The Metivier Inn is conveniently located on Market Street in the downtown historic district. Louis Metivier originally built the home as a private residence in 1877. In keeping with the French and English influence, the home has been completely renovated. This small lovely country inn offers bedrooms with private baths and efficiency apartments. Guests may also enjoy the cozy living room with its fireplace or the spacious, comfortable, wicker-furnished front porch. Deluxe continental breakfast served to all guests. The inn is perfect for small conferences, wedding parties, and reunions.

Hosts: Janice and Mike Graves
Rooms: 20 (PB) $98-165
Continental Breakfast
Credit Cards: A, B, D
Notes: 2, 7, 8, 9, 10, 12

Metivier Inn

MAPLE CITY/LELAND AREA

Leelanau Country Inn
149 E. Harbor Hwy, Maple City, 49664
(616) 228-5060

For over 100 years, the inn has stood

ready to be of service. We feature eight country-appointed guest rooms and a 150-seat award-winning restaurant specializing in fresh seafood flown directly to us from Boston, choice steaks, home-made pasta, and a large array of desserts. All items are made from scratch. Eight miles south of Leland on M-22. Surrounded by churches of all faiths.

Hosts: John and Linda Sisson
Rooms: 8 (SB) $30-40
Continental Breakfast
Credit Cards: A, B, C
Notes: 2, 4, 5, 6, 7, 8, 9, 10, 11

MENDON

Mendon Country Inn

440 W. Main, 49072
(616) 496-8132; (FAX) (616) 496-8403

Overlooking the St. Joseph River, this romantic country inn has antique guest rooms with private baths. Free canoeing, bicycles built for two, fifteen acres of woods and water, restaurants, and Amish tour guide. Featured in *Country Living* and *Country Home* magazines. Nine jacuzzi suites with fireplaces.

Hosts: Dick and Dolly Bueckle
Rooms: 18 (PB) $50-150
Expanded Continental Breakfast
Credit Cards: A, B, C, D
Notes: 2, 5, 7, 8, 9, 10, 11, 12

OMENA

Frieda's Bed and Breakfast

3141 Omena Point Road, 49674
(616) 386-7274; (210) 659-4041 (out of season)

Full Breakfast in dining room or on deck.

Within walking distance to the village of Omena. Only a 30-minute drive from Traverse City. Turn east and go one mile on Omena Point Road. A quaint, modern cottage atmosphere nestled along the shore of Traverse Bay. Private beach for your enjoyment. Many local activites are nearby. Reservations in advance with deposit, please.

Hostess: Frieda Putnam
Rooms: 3 (PB) $75-85
Full Breakfast
Credit Cards: None
Notes: 2, 8, 9, 10, 11, 12

ONEKAMA

Lake Breeze House

5089 Main Street, 49675-0301
(616) 889-4969

Our two-story frame house on Portage Lake is yours with a shared bath, living room, and breakfast room. Each room has its own special charm with family antiques. Come relax and enjoy our back porch and the sounds of the babbling creek. By reservation only. Boating and charter service available.

Hosts: Bill and Donna Erickson
Rooms: 3 (SB) $55
Full Breakfast
Credit Cards: None
Notes: 2, 5, 8, 9, 10, 11

OWOSSO

Rossman's R & R Ranch

308 East Hibbard Road, 48867
(517) 723-3232 day; (517) 723-2553 evening

A newly remodeled farmhouse from the early 1900's, the ranch sits on 130 acres overlooking the Maple River valley. A large concrete circle drive with whiteboard fences leads to stables of horses and cattle. The area's wildlife includes deer, fox, rabbits, pheasant, quail, and songbirds. Observe and explore from the farm lane, river walk, or outside deck. Country-like accents adorn the interior of the farmhouse, and guests are welcome to use the family parlor, garden, game room, and fireplace.

Hosts: Carl and Jeanne Rossman
Rooms: 2 (SB) $40-45
Continental Breakfast
Credit Cards: None
Notes: 2, 5, 6, 7, 10

PENTWATER

Historic Nickerson Inn

P.O. Box 109, 262 Lowell St., 49449
(616) 869-6731; (616) 869-6151 (FAX)

The Historic Nickerson Inn has been serving guests with "special hospitality" since 1914. Our inn was totally renovated in 1991. All our rooms have private baths, with air-conditioning. We have two jacuzzi suites with fireplaces and balconies overlooking Lake Michigan. Two short blocks to Lake Michigan beach, and three blocks to shopping district. New ownership. Open all year. Casual fine dining in our 80-seat restaurant. Excellent for retreats, workshops, year-round recreation.

Hosts: Gretchen and Harry Shiparski
Rooms: 10 rooms, 2 suites - 12 total (PB) $75-95 (rooms), $160 (suites)
Full Breakfast
Credit Cards: A, B,
Notes: 2, 3, 4, 5, 8, 9, 10, 11

Historic Nickerson Inn

PLAINWELL

The 1882 John Crispe House

404 East Bridge Street, 49080
(616) 685-1293

Enjoy museum-quality Victorian elegance on the Kalamazoo River. Situated between Grand Rapids and Kalamazoo just off US 131 on Michigan 89, the John Crispe House is close to some of western Michigan's finest gourmet dining, golf, skiing, and antique shops. Air conditioned. No smoking or alcohol. Gift certificates are available.

Hosts: Ormand J. and Nancy E. Lefever
Rooms: 5 (3PB; 2SB) $55-95
Full Breakfast
Credit Cards: A, B
Notes: 2, 5, 7, 8, 10, 11

PORT AUSTIN

Lake Street Manor Bed and Breakfast

8569 Lake Street, 48467
(517) 738-7720

Lake Street Manor was built in 1875. Large bays and high-peaked roof with its gingerbread trim set off this brick manor

NOTES: Credit cards accepted: A Master Card; B Visa; C American Express; D Discover Card; E Diners Club; F Other; 2 Personal checks accepted; 3 Lunch available; 4 Dinner available; 5 Open all

house. Fenced yard, pavilion with tables and chairs, yard sports, brick barbeque, and bikes for guests' use. Hot tub, in-room movies, and continental breakfast are all included. Two-night weekend stay, seasonal rates.

Hosts: Carolyn Greenqod and my dog Libbie
Rooms: 5(3PB;2SB) $35-55
Continental Breakfast
Credit Cards: None
Open from May to end of October.
Notes: 2, 7 (over 12), 8, 9, 10, 11

PORT HURON

The Victorian Inn
1229 Seventh Street, 48060
(313) 984-1437

The Victorian Inn features fine dining and guest rooms in authentically restored Victorian elegance. One hour north of metropolitan Detroit, it is located in the heart of the church district and one-half block from the museum. All food and beverages are prepared with the utmost attention to detail, which was the order of the day in a bygone era.

Hostess: Kelly Lozano
Rooms: 4 (2PB; 2SB) $55-65
Continental Breakfast
Credit Cards: A, B, C, D, E, F
Notes: 2, 3, 4, 5, 7, 8, 9, 10

SAUGATUCK

"The Porches" Bed and Breakfast
2297 Lakeshore Drive, Fennville 49408
(616) 543-4162

Built in 1897, "The Porches" offers five

guest rooms each with private bath. Located three miles south of Saugatuck, we have a private beach and hiking trails. The large common room has a TV. We overlook Lake Michigan with beautiful sunsets from the front porch.

Hosts: Bob and Ellen Johnson
Rooms: 5 (PB) $59-69
Full or Expanded Continental Breakfast
Credit Cards: A, B
Open May 1 to November 1.
Notes: 2, 7(Sunday-Thursday), 8, 9, 10

Sherwood Forest Bed and Breakfast
938 Center St., P.O. Box 315, 49406
(616) 857-1246

Surrounded by woods, this beautiful Victorian home was built in the 1890's. Amenities include wrap-around porch, traditional furnishings, large guest rooms with private baths, jacuzzi, and heated swimming pool. There is also a separate cottage that sleeps seven. The Eastern Shore of Lake Michigan and the public beach are 1/2 block away. The area's wide, white sandy beaches are the perfect place for strolling, swimming, or watching spectacular sunsets. We're also located just minutes from the charming shops of Saugatuck.

Rooms: 5 (PB) $70-130
Expanded Continental Breakfast
Credit Cards: A, B
Notes: 2, 5, 8, 9, 10, 11, 12

Twin Gables Country Inn
P.O. Box 881, 900 Lake Street, 94953
(616) 857-4346

Overlooking Kalamazoo Lake, The State

year; 6 Pets welcome; 7 Children welcome; 8 Tennis nearby; 9 Swimming nearby; 10 Golf nearby; 11 Skiing nearby; 12 May be booked through travel agent

Historic Inn, central air-conditioned throughout, features 14 charming guest rooms with private baths, furnished in antiques and country. Wintertime cross-country skiers relax in indoor hot tub and cozy up to a warm crackling fireplace, whilst summer guests may take a refreshing dip in the outdoor pool and enjoy glorious sunsets on the front veranda overlooking the lake. Three separate two- and one-bedroom cottages are also available. Open all year.

Hosts: Denise and Michael Simcik
Rooms: 14(PB) $54-94
Expanded Continental Breakfast
Credit Cards: A, B
Notes: 2, 5, 7(prior arrangements), 8, 9, 10, 11, 12

SHELBY

The Shepherd's Place Bed and Breakast

2200 32nd Avenue, 49455
(616) 861-4298

Enjoy a peaceful retreat on 20 acres of apple orchards and woodland. Choose between a cozy queen size bed or twin beds with private baths. Enjoy a full breakfast in the comfort of our woodstoved dining area on chilly mornings. Beach activities, golf, fishing, and horseback riding nearby.

Hosts: Hans and Diane Oehring
Rooms: 2(PB) $55
Full Breakfast
Open May 15 until October
Credit Cards: None
Notes: 2, 9, 10

WEST BRANCH

The Rose Brick Inn

124 East Houghton Avenue, 48661
(517) 345-3702

A 1906 Queen Anne-style home with a graceful veranda, white picket fence, and cranberry canopy, the Rose Brick Inn is tucked in the center two floors of the Frank Sebastian Smith house listed in Michigan's Register of Historic Sites. It is located on downtown Main Street in Victorian West Branch. Golfing, hiking, biking, cross-country skiing, snowmobiling, hunting, shopping, and special holiday events await you year-round. Jacuzzi.

Host: Leon Swartz
Rooms: 4 (PB) $48-58
Continental Breakfast
Credit Cards: A, B
Notes: 2, 5, 7, 8, 9, 10, 11

The Shepherd's Place

NOTES: Credit cards accepted: A Master Card; B Visa; C American Express; D Discover Card; E Diners Club; F Other; 2 Personal checks accepted; 3 Lunch available; 4 Dinner available; 5 Open all

Minnesota

ALBERT LEA

Victorian Rose Inn

609 W. Fountain, 56007
(507) 373-7602; (800) 252-6558

Queen Anne Victorian home (1898) in virtually original condition, with fine woodwork, stained glass, gingerbread, and antique light fixtures. Antique furnishings, down comforters. Spacious rooms, one with fireplace. Air-conditioned. Full breakfast. Business/extended-stay rates; gift certificates. Children by arrangement; no pets; no smoking.

Hosts: Darrel and Linda Roemmich
Rooms: 4 (2PB; 2SB) $50-65
Full Breakfast
Credit Cards: A, B
Notes: 2, 5, 7, 8, 10, 12

Victorian Rose Inn

BAGLEY

El Shaddai

Rt. 2, Box 97, 56621
(218) 694-6431

Experience the tranquil peace of life in northern Minnesota at El Shaddai. El Shaddai reflects the warmth of the community with country style furnishings, fireplaces, large back yard with gardens, wooded walkways, outdoor eating and fishing available in nearby area lakes.

Hosts: Josh and Leota Dahl
Room: 3 (SB) call for rates
Full Breakfast
Credit Cards: None
Notes: 2, 5, 7, 8, 9, 10, 11

CHATFIELD

Lunds' Guest Houses

218 Southeast Winona Street, 55923
(507) 867-4003

These charming 1920's homes are decorated in the 1920's and 1930's style and located only 20 minutes from Rochester, at the gateway to beautiful Bluff country. Personalized service includes kitchens, living and dining rooms, two screened porches, TV, piano, and organ.

year; 6 Pets welcome; 7 Children welcome; 8 Tennis nearby; 9 Swimming nearby; 10 Golf nearby; 11 Skiing nearby; 12 May be booked through travel agent

Hosts: Shelby and Marion Lund
Rooms: 4 (2PB; 2S1.5B) $50-65
Continental Breakfast
Credit Cards: None
Notes: 2, 6 (restricted), 7 (restricted), 8, 9, 10, 11

CROOKSTON

Elm Street Inn

422 Elm Street, 56716
(218) 281-2343; (800) 568-4476; (218) 281-1756

Georgian Revival (1910) home with antiques, hardwood floors, stained and beveled glass. Wicker-filled sun porch. Old-fashioned beds, quilts, terry robes, fresh flowers. Memorable candlelight full breakfast; intimate dinners available. Bicycles. Limo to casino; community pool next door. Murder mystery and quilting weekends. Special anniversary and honeymoon packages. Children welcome, no pets, no smoking.

Hosts: John and Sheryl Winters
Rooms: 4 (2PB; 2SB) $55-65
Full Breakfast
Credit Cards: A, B
Notes: 2, 3, 4, 5, 7, 8, 9, 10, 12

Elm Street Inn

DULUTH

The Mansion

3600 London Rd., 55804
(218) 724-0739

This magnificent home was built in 1929 and was opened in 1983 as Duluth's first bed and breakfast. The seven-acre estate is nestled on 525 feet of Lake Superior beach with manicured lawns, woods, and gardens. Overnight guests are encouraged to make themselves at home on the grounds and inside the mansion. The common rooms include the library, living room, summer room, gallery, dining room, and trophy room. Come and let us share our home with you!

Rooms: 11 (7PB; 4SB) $95-125
Full Breakfast
Credit Cards: A, B
Notes: 2, 10, 11

FERGUS FALLS

Bakketopp Hus

Rural Route 2, Box 187 A, Long Lake, 56537
(218) 739-2915

Quiet, spacious lake home with vaulted ceilings, fireplace, private spa, flower garden patio and lakeside decks. Antique furnishings from family homestead, four-poster, draped, French canopy bed, waterbed, private or shared bath. Here you can listen as loons call to each other across the lake in the still of dusk, witness the fall foliage splendor, relax by a crackling fire, or sink into the warmth of the hot tub after a day of hiking or skiing. Near antique shops, Maplewood State Park.

NOTES: Credit cards accepted: A Master Card; B Visa; C American Express; D Discover Card; E Diners Club; F Other; 2 Personal checks accepted; 3 Lunch available; 4 Dinner available; 5 Open all

Ten minutes off I-94. Gift certificates available. Reservation with deposit.

Hosts: Dennis and Judy Nims
Rooms: 3 (PB) $55-90
Full Breakfast
Credit Cards: None
Notes: 2, 5, 7, 8, 9, 10, 11

HOUSTON

Addie's Attic Bed and Breakfast

P.O. Box 677, 117 S. Jackson St., 55943
(507) 896-3010

Beautiful turn-of-the-century home, circa 1903; cozy front parlor with curved glass window. Games, TV, player piano available. Guest rooms decorated and furnished with "attic finds." Hearty country breakfast served in dining room. Near hiking, biking, and cross-country skiing trails, canoeing, and antique shops. Weekday rates. No credit cards.

Hosts: Fred and Marilyn Huhn
Rooms: 4 (SB) $45-50
Full Breakfast
Credit Cards: None
Notes: 2, 5, 8, 10, 11

LANESBORO

Historic Scanlan House Bed and Breakfast

708 Parkway Avenue South, 55949
(507) 467-2158; (800) 944-2158

Visit the Victorian elegance and charm of a wealthy banker's mansion. This gingerbread-style home was built in 1889 by Michael Scanlan (known as the founder of Lanesboro) and is Lanesboro's largest and oldest operating bed and breakfast. We have fireplaces, whirlpool tubs for two, unique gifts, and, of course, our famous five-course breakfast. The interior is adorned throughout with elegant woodwork, stained glass, and the ornate built-in furnishings typical of a fine and exquisite turn-of-the-century residence.

Hosts: Kristen, Mary and Gene Mensing
Rooms: 5 (3PB; 2SB) $55-125
Full Breakfast
Credit Cards: A, B, C, D
Notes: 2, 5, 8, 9, 10, 11, 12

OWATONNA

The Northrop-Oftedahl House

358 East Main Street, 55060
(507) 451-4040

This 1898 Victorian with stained glass is three blocks from downtown. It has pleasant porches, grand piano, six-foot footed bathtub, souvenirs (antiques and collectibles from the estate). Northrop family-owned and operated, it is one of 12 historical homes in the area, rich in local history with an extensive reading library, backgammon, croquet, badminton, bocce, and more. Near hiking, biking trails, golf, tennis, parks, and 35 miles to Mayo Clinic. Special group rates for retreats.

Hosts: Jean and Darrell Stewart
Rooms: 5 (SB) $39-56
Continental Breakfast; Full breakfast on request
Credit Cards: None
Notes: 2, 3 (by arrangement), 4 (by arrangement), 5, 6 (by arrangement), 7, 8, 9, 10, 11

year; 6 Pets welcome; 7 Children welcome; 8 Tennis nearby; 9 Swimming nearby; 10 Golf nearby; 11 Skiing nearby; 12 May be booked through travel agent

The Northrop-Oftedahl House

ST. CHARLES

Thoreson's Carriage House Bed and Breakfast

606 Wabasha Avenue, 55972
(507) 932-3479

Located at the edge of beautiful Whitewater State Park with its swimming, trails, and demonstrations by the park naturalist, we are also in Amish territory and minutes from the world-famous Mayo Clinic. Piano and organ are available for added enjoyment. Please write for free brochure.

Hostess: Moneta Thoreson
Rooms: 2 (SB) $30-35
Full Breakfast
Credit Cards: None
Notes: 2, 5, 7, 8, 9, 10

SPRING LAKE

Anchor Lake

Highway 4, 56680
(218) 798-2718

Lodge in the Chippewa National Forest on the Bigfork Canoe Trail; built in the early 1920's and originally used by duck hunters. Decorated with antique furniture and memorabilia. Shared bath. Delicious breakfast. State parks, historic sites, and restaurants nearby. Boats and motors available. Reservations. Open May through October.

Hosts: Charles and Virginia Kitterman
Rooms: 4 (SB) $30-55
Full Breakfast
Credit Cards: A, B
Notes: 2, 7

Anchor Lake

STILLWATER

Lowell Inn

102 North Second Street, 55082
(612) 439-1100

The Williamsburg-style, red-brick building fronts 13 white pillars to represent the 13 original colonies. The inn's remodeled guest rooms create intimate boudoirs with state-of-the-art bathing facilities. The inn is located in the heart of one of Minnesota's earliest settlements on a hillside two blocks from the St. Croix River.

NOTES: Credit cards accepted: A Master Card; B Visa; C American Express; D Discover Card; E Diners Club; F Other; 2 Personal checks accepted; 3 Lunch available; 4 Dinner available; 5 Open all

We offer American Plan rates that include dinner and breakfast on weekends; European Plan on Sunday through Thursday. Lunch and dinner served daily.

Hosts: Arthur and Maureen Palmer
Rooms: 21 (PB) $109-189
Full Breakfast
Credit Cards: A, B
Notes: 2, 3, 4, 5

TYLER

Babette's Inn

308 S. Tyler Street, 56178
(507) 247-3962

Privacy, luxury and small town peace await you at Babette's inn. Located in the Danish-American village of Tyler, Minnesota, the inn features European cuisine, antiques, gift shop, free use of vintage bicycles, books and foreign films. Open all year, the inn also hosts gourmet evenings in a relaxed, comfortable style. Close to Pipestone National Monument, Laura Ingalls Wilder pageant and several state parks with hiking and cross country skiing.

Hosts: Jim and Alicia Johnson
Rooms: 3 (PB) $55-65
Full Breakfast
Credit Cards: None
Notes: 5, 11

year; 6 Pets welcome; 7 Children welcome; 8 Tennis nearby; 9 Swimming nearby; 10 Golf nearby; 11 Skiing nearby; 12 May be booked through travel agent

Mississippi

FRENCH CAMP

French Camp Bed and Breakfast Inn
Box 120, 39745
(601) 547-6835

The inn is located on the historic Natchez Trace National Parkway halfway between Jackson and Tupelo, Mississippi. It has been constructed from two restored, authentic hand-hewn log cabins, each more than 100 years old. Indulge in Southern cooking at its finest: sorghum-soaked "scratch" muffins, creamy grits, skillet-fried apples, fresh cheese, scrambled eggs, crisp slab bacon, and lean sausage, with two kinds of homemade bread and three homemade jellies. Life doesn't get any better!

Hosts: Ed and Sallie Williford
Rooms: 4 (PB) $60
Full Breakfast
Credit Cards: None
Notes: 2, 3, 4, 5, 6, 7, 8, 9, 12

French Camp

LONG BEACH

Red Creek Colonial Inn
7416 Red Creek Rd., 39560
(601) 452-3080

This circa 1899 three-story raised French cottage with 64-foot porch is situated on 11 acres of live oaks and fragrant magnolias and is just one and one-half miles south of Interstate 10, Long Beach exit 28. Just five miles north of gulf beaches, this tranquil inn is furnished in Victorian, French, English, and country antiques, including an organ, victrola, and wooden radios. Golf packages are available. Ministerial discount of 10%.

Hosts: Dave and Christina Smith
Rooms: 5 (3PB; 2SB) $49-69
Continental Plus Breakfast
Credit Cards: None
Notes: 2, 5, 7, 8, 9, 12

MERIDIAN

Lincoln, Ltd. Bed and Breakfast Mississippi Reservation Service
P.O. Box 3479, 2303 23rd Avenue, 39303
(601) 482-5483; (601) 693-7447 (FAX, call first)

Service offers B&B accommodations in historic homes and inns in the whole state

---

NOTES: Credit cards accepted: A Master Card; B Visa; C American Express; D Discover Card; E Diners Club; F Other; 2 Personal checks accepted; 3 Lunch available; 4 Dinner available; 5 Open all

of Mississippi, also SE Louisiana, Western Tennessee, and Southern Alabama. One phone call convenience for your B&B reservations and trip planning through Mississippi. Experience history; we offer antebellum mansions, historic log houses, and contemporary homes. Also, there is a B&B suite on the premises. Call for details and brochure. Barbara Lincoln Hall, co-ordinator.

NATCHEZ TRACE

Natchez Trace Bed and Breakfast Reservation Service

P.O. Box 193, Hampshire, TN, 38461
(800) 377-2770

This reservation service is unusual in that all the homes listed are close to the Natchez Trace, the delightful National Parkway running from Nashville, Tennessee, to Natchez, Mississippi. Kay can help you plan your trip along the Trace, with homestays in interesting and historic homes along the way. Locations of homes include Nashville, Franklin, Hampshire, Lawrenceburg, Tennessee; Florence, Alabama; and Corinth, French Camp, Kosciusko, Vicksburg, Lorman, and Natchez, Mississippi. Rates from $50-115.

PORT GIBSON

Oak Square Plantation

1207 Church Street, 39150
(601) 437-4350; (800) 729-0240; (601) 437-5768 (FAX)

This restored antebellum mansion of the Old South is in the town General U. S. Grant said was "too beautiful to burn." On the National Register of Historic Places, it has family heirloom antiques and canopied beds and is air conditioned. Your hosts' families have been in Mississippi for 200 years. Christ is the Lord of this house. "But as for me and my house, we will serve the Lord," Joshua 24:15. On U.S. Highway 61, adjacent to the Natchez Trace Parkway. Four-diamond rated by AAA.

Hosts: Mr. and Mrs. William Lum
Rooms: 12 (PB) $75-95; special family rates
Full Breakfast
Credit Cards: A, B, C, D
Notes: 2, 5, 7

Oak Square Plantation

Missouri

BRANSON

Cameron's Crag

P. O. Box 526, Point Lookout, 65726
(417) 335-8134; (800) 933-8529

Located high on a bluff overlooking Lake Taneycomo and the valley, three miles south of Branson, enjoy a spectacular view from a new three-room private suite with king bed, hot tub, kitchen, living area, and bedroom. A second room has a private entrance, queen bed, view of the lake, private hot tub on deck. The fourth room has twin or king beds.

Hosts: Glen and Kay Cameron
Rooms: 4 (PB) $60-95
Full Breakfast
Credit Cards: A, B, C
Notes: 2, 4

Ozark Mountain Country Bed and Breakfast Service

Box 295, 65616
(417) 334-4720; (800) 695-1546

Ozark Mountain Country has been arranging accommodations for guests in southwest Missouri and northwest Arkansas since 1982. In the current list of over 100 homes and small inns, some locations offer private entrances and fantastic views, guest sitting areas, swimming pools, jacuzzis, or fireplaces. Most locations are available all year. Personal checks accepted. Some homes welcome children; a few welcome pets (even horses). Write for complimentary host listing and discount coupon. Coordinator: Kay Cameron. $35-95.

CALIFORNIA

Memory Lane Bed and Breakfast

102 S. Oak, 65018
(314) 796-4233

This 1894 home has been carefully renovated to retain its Victorian character. The guest rooms feature antique furnishings while the remainder of the house is decorated with a blend of antique and new furniture. The Lake of the Ozarks, historic Arrow Rock, and Hermann, Missouri, are only a few of the many locations within easy driving distance.

Hosts: Joe and Mary Ellen LaPrise
Rooms: 3 (SB) $37
Full Breakfast
Credit Cards: None
Notes: 2, 5, 8, 9, 10, 12

NOTES: Credit cards accepted: A Master Card; B Visa; C American Express; D Discover Card; E Diners Club; F Other; 2 Personal checks accepted; 3 Lunch available; 4 Dinner available; 5 Open all

CARTHAGE

Brewer's Maple Lane Farm Bed and Breakfast

Rural Route 1, Box 203, 64836
(417) 358-6312

Listed on the National Register of Historic Places, this Victorian home has 20 rooms furnished mostly with family heirlooms, four guest rooms. Our 240-acre farm is ideal for family vacations and campers. We have a playground, picnic area, hunting, and fishing in our 22-acre lake. Nearby are artist Lowell Davis' farm and Sam Butcher's Precious Moments Chapel.

Hosts: Arch and Renee Brewer
Rooms: 4 (SB) $50
Expanded Continental Breakfast
Credit Cards: None
Notes: 2, 5, 7, 8, 10, 12

EUREKA

Windhaven

707 Eureka Road, 63025
(314) 938-9122

Windhaven sits on a hill, and you can relax on the patio overlooking a magnificent view of hills and lights from the Six Flags Park, I-44, and the lights of Eureka, known as the town full of antique stores and winter skiing. The surroundings of the 22 acres are very quiet.

Hosts: Audie and Candy Laubinger
Rooms: 2 (SB) $45-55
Full Breakfast
Credit Cards: None
Notes: 2, 7, 8, 10, 11

Fifth Street Mansion

HANNIBAL

Fifth Street Mansion Bed and Breakfast Inn

213 South Fifth Street, 63401
(314) 221-0445; for reservations only call
(800) 874-5661

Built in 1858 in Italianate style by friends of Mark Twain, antique furnishings complement the stained glass, ceramic fireplaces, and original gaslight fixtures of the house. Two parlors, dining room, and library with hand-grained walnut paneling, plus wraparound porches provide space for conversation, reading, TV, games. Walk to Mark Twain historic district, shops, restaurants, riverfront. The mansion blends Victorian charm with plenty of old-fashioned hospitality. The whole house is available for reunions and weddings.

Hosts: Mike and Donalene Andreotti
Rooms: 7 (PB) $65-90
Full Breakfast
Credit Cards: A, B, C, D
Notes: 2, 5, 7, 8, 9, 10, 12

year; 6 Pets welcome; 7 Children welcome; 8 Tennis nearby; 9 Swimming nearby; 10 Golf nearby; 11 Skiing nearby; 12 May be booked through travel agent

HERMANN

Die Gillig Heimat

HCR 62, Box 30, 65041
(314) 943-6942

Capture the beauty of country living on this farm located on beautiful rolling hills. The original Gillig home was built as a log cabin in 1842 and has been enlarged several times. Awake in the morning to beautiful views in every direction, and enjoy a hearty breakfast in the large, country kitchen. Stroll the pastures and hills of the working cattle farm while watching nature at its best. Historic Hermann is nearby.

Hosts: Ann and Armin Gillig
Rooms: 2 (PB) $55-60
Full Breakfast
Credit Cards: None
Notes: 2, 5, 7 (by arrangement)

KANSAS CITY

Doanleigh Wallagh Inn

217 E. 37th St., 64111
(816) 753-2667; (816) 753-2408 (FAX)

Internationally known for its comfortable elegance, Doanleigh Wallagh Inn is a haven for people seeking the ultimate in bed and breakfast experience. All rooms have either a queen or king bed, telephone, television. The inn is in the center of things to do in Kansas City; five-minute drive to Hallmark Crown Center, Country Club Plaza, Westport, and Nelson-Atkins Museum of Art.

Hosts: Carolyn and Edward Litchfield
Rooms: 5 (PB) $80-110
Full Breakfast
Credit Cards: A, B, C
Notes: 2, 5, 7, 8, 12

Southmoreland on The Plaza

116 E. 46th St., 64112
(816) 531-7979

Two-time winner "Top B&B in the US," "Outstanding Achievement in Preservation" award winner, Association of American Historic Inns; "Most Romantic New Urban Inn" by Romantic Hideaways Newsletter. Classic New England Colonial mansion located between renowned Country Club Plaza (shopping/entertaining district) and Nelson-Atkins Museum of Art. Elegant B&B ambience with small hotel amenities. Many rooms with private decks or fireplaces. Special services for business travelers. Sport and dining privileges at nearby Historic Private Club. 1993 Mobil Travel Guide four star award. Reed Travel Group, Star Service "Superstar."

Hostesses: Penni Johnson, Susan Moehl
Rooms: 12 (PB) $105-135
Full Breakfast
Credit Cards: A, B, C
Notes: 2, 5, 8, 9, 10, 12

PLATTE CITY

Basswood Country Inn Resort

15880 Interurban Road, 64079-9185
(816) 431-5556

Come stay where the rich and famous relaxed and played in the 1940's and 1950's! These are the most beautiful, secluded, wooded, lakefront accommodations in the entire Kansas City area. Choose from two-bedroom, full kitchen suites, 1935 cottage, or king suites. Five miles

---

NOTES: Credit cards accepted: A Master Card; B Visa; C American Express; D Discover Card; E Diners Club; F Other; 2 Personal checks accepted; 3 Lunch available; 4 Dinner available; 5 Open all

from Kansas City International Airport.

Hosts: Don and Betty Soper
Rooms: 7 (PB) $63-125
Cottage: 1 (PB) $93
Continental Breakfast
Credit Cards: A, B, D
Notes: 2, 5, 7, 9, 10, 11, 12

ST. JOSEPH

Harding House Bed and Breakfast

219 N 20th St., 64501
(816) 232-7020

Gracious turn-of-the-century home. Elegant oak woodwork and pocket doors. Antiques and beveled leaded glass windows. Historic area near museums, churches, antique shops, and restaurants. Five unique guest rooms. Eastlake has romantic wood-burning fireplace and queen size bed; Blue Room has antique baby crib. Children welcome. Full breakfast with homemade pastry. Tea Room across the street serves dinner Wednesday thru Saturday from 5:30-8:30 pm, buffet on Sunday 11:30 am until 5:30 pm.

Hosts: Glen and Mary Harding
Rooms: 5 (1PB; 4SB) $40-55
Credit Cards: A, B, C, D
Notes: 2, 4 (Wed-Sat), 5, 7, 12

ST. LOUIS

Geandaugh House Bed and Breakfast

3835-37 South Broadway, 63118
(314) 771-5447

Built circa 1790, the limestone "Prairie

House" section of the Geandaugh House, located in South St. Louis, is one of the oldest structures in the state. A Federal-style brick addition was added in the 1800's. Antiques and collections fill the inn revealing Gea and Wayne's love for history. Irish lace curtains, hand-made quilts, and old pharmacy cupboard in the dining room are some of the unique furnishings. As a pastor and retired music teacher, Wayne and Gea are eager to share their home with travelers seeking lodging in a Christian atmosphere. They have two cats.

Hosts: Gea and Wayne Popp
Rooms: 4 (PB) $60
Full Breakfast
Credit Cards: A, B
Notes: 2, 5 (except Christmas), 7, 8, 10, 12

Lafayette House Bed and Breakfast

2156 Lafayette Avenue, 63104
(314) 772-4429

This 1876 Victorian mansion with modern amenities is in the center of things to do in St. Louis and on a direct bus line to downtown. It is air conditioned and furnished with antiques and traditional furniture. Many collectibles and large, varied library to enjoy. Families welcome. Resident cats and dog.

Hosts: Sarah and Jack Milligan
Rooms: 5 (2PB; 3SB) $50-75
Full Breakfast
Credit Cards: A, B
Notes: 2, 5, 7, 8, 9, 10, 12

year; 6 Pets welcome; 7 Children welcome; 8 Tennis nearby; 9 Swimming nearby; 10 Golf nearby; 11 Skiing nearby; 12 May be booked through travel agent

SPRINGFIELD

The Mansion at Elfindale Bed and Breakfast

1701 S. Fort, 65807
(417) 831-5400; (417) 831-2965 (FAX)

Welcome to the elegance of the magnificent gray stone structure. Built in the 1800's, The Mansion features ornate fireplaces, stained glass windows, and unique architecturally designed rooms. We invite you to choose from 13 private suites. Each is a color essay designed with maximum comfort in mind, and each luxuriate in all the splendor of the Victorian era. A hearty breakfast is served in our dining areas, featuring foods from around the world.

Host: Jef Wells
Rooms: 13 (PB) $60-95
Full Breakfast
Credit Cards: A, B, C, D
Notes: 2, 5, 12

NOTES: Credit cards accepted: A Master Card; B Visa; C American Express; D Discover Card; E Diners Club; F Other; 2 Personal checks accepted; 3 Lunch available; 4 Dinner available; 5 Open all

Montana

BOZEMAN

Bergfeld Bed and Breakfast

8515 Sypes Canyon Road, 59715
(406) 586-7778

Bergfeld (German for mountain field) sits on the edge of Bridger Mountain slope and sports 360 degree views. Amenities include hot tub, private bathrooms, queen beds, wildlife-watching. One room has a kitchenette. Only 10 minutes from town and airport. Close to two ski resorts. Quiet and relaxing, country, comfortable atmosphere. Built in 1992. Outstanding restaurants are close by.

Hosts: Mark and Laura DeGroot
Rooms: 4 (PB) $65-80
Full Breakfast
Credit Cards: A, B
Notes: 2, 5, 7, 8, 9, 10, 11, 12

BUTTE

Cooper King Mansion

219 West Granite, 59701
(406) 782-7580

Step back in time and experience Victorian elegance in this beautiful three-story, thirty-four room, red-brick mansion. Built in 1884, by multi-millionaire William Andrews Clark, the home cost approximately $250,000. It features stained glass windows, frescoed ceilings, hand-carved woodwork, and lavish antique furnishings. Spend an evening living like a king. It is located in historic Uptown Butte, one block west of Montana Street on Granite Street.

Hosts: Chris and Maria Wagner
Rooms: 4 (2PB; 2SB) $55-95
Full Breakfast
Credit Cards: A, B, C, D
Notes: 2, 5, 7, 10, 11

EUREKA

Huckleberry Hannah's Montana Bed & Breakfast

3100 Sophie Lake Road, 59917
(406) 889-3381

Nearly 6,000-square-feet of old-fashioned, country-sweet charm, the answer to vacationing in Montana. Sitting on 50 wooded acres, and bordering a fabulous trout-filled lake with glorious views of the Rockies. This bed and breakfast depicts a quieter time in our history when the true pleasures of life represented a walk in the woods or a moonlight swim. Or maybe just a little early morning relaxation in a porch swing, sipping a fresh cup of coffee,

---

year; 6 Pets welcome; 7 Children welcome; 8 Tennis nearby; 9 Swimming nearby; 10 Golf nearby; 11 Skiing nearby; 12 May be booked through travel agent

and watching a colorful sunrise. The surrounding area is 91% public lands, perfect for hiking, biking, hunting, fishing, and swimming. It's a cross-country skiier's dream in winter, also easy driving distance to downhill skiing in Whitefish. And don't forget those comfortable sunny rooms and all that wonderful home-cooked food. The B&B is owned and operated by the author of one of the Northwest's Best-Selling Cookbooks "Huckleberry Hannah's Country Cooking Sampler." Questions cheerfully answered. Ask about kids and pets and Senior Discounts! Local airport nearby. Free brochure.

Hosts: Jack and Deanna Doying
Rooms: 5 + Lake Cottage (PB) $50-75
Full Breakfast (Continental available upon request)
Credit Cards: A, B, D
Notes: 2, 3, 4, 5, 6 (some), 7 (over 12), 9, 11, 12

KALISPELL

Stillwater Inn
206 4th Avenue East, 59901
(406) 755-7080; (800) 398-7024

Relax in this lovely historic home built in 1900, decorated to fit the period, and furnished with turn-of-the-century antiques. Four guest bedrooms, two with private baths. Full gourmet breakfast. Walking distance to churches, shopping, dining, art galleries, antique shops, Woodland Park, and the Conrad Mansion. Short drive to Glacier National Park, Big Mountain skiing, six golf courses, excellent fishing and hunting. Please, no smoking in the house.

Hosts: Pat and Jane Morison
Rooms: 4 (2PB; 2SB) $70-85
Full Breakfast
Credit Cards: A, B
Notes: 2, 5, 7, 8, 9, 10, 11, 12

LAUREL

Riverside Bed and Breakfast
2231 Theil Rd., 59044
(800) 768-1580

Just off I-90, fifteen minutes from Billings, on a main route to skiing and Yellowstone National Park. Fly fish the Yellowstone from our back yard; soak away stress in the hot tub; linger and look at the loveable llamas; take a spin on our bicycle built for two; enjoy a peaceful sleep, a friendly visit, and a fantastic breakfast.

Hosts: Lynn and Nancy Perey
Rooms: 2 (PB) $50-60
Full Breakfast
Credit Cards: B
Notes: 2, 5, 7 (over 10), 10, 11, 12

VIRGINIA CITY

Stonehouse Inn B & B
306 East Idaho, 59755
(406) 843-5504

Located on a quiet street only blocks away from the historic section of Virginia City, this Victorian stone home is listed on the National Register of Historic Places. Brass beds and antiques in every room give the inn a romantic touch. Six bedrooms share two baths. Full breakfasts are served each morning, and smoking is allowed on our porches. Skiing, snowmobiling, golfing, hunting, and fly fishing nearby.

Hosts: John and Linda Hamilton
Rooms: 6 (SB) $50 + tax
Full Breakfast
Credit Cards: A, B
Notes: 2, 4, 5, 7, 8, 10, 12

NOTES: Credit cards accepted: A Master Card; B Visa; C American Express; D Discover Card; E Diners Club; F Other; 2 Personal checks accepted; 3 Lunch available; 4 Dinner available; 5 Open all

Nebraska

FREMONT

Bed & Breakfast of Fremont

1624 East 25th Street, 68025
(402) 727-9534

Hosts: Paul and Linda VonBehren
Rooms: 3 (1SB) $40-55
Full Breakfast
Credit Cards: None
Notes: 2, 5, 7, 8, 9, 10, 12

Kirschke House

GRAND ISLAND

Kirschke House Bed and Breakfast

1124 West 3rd St., 68801
(308) 381-6851

Very comfortable, romantic, 1902 Victorian home decorated with period furnishings, lace, and stained glass. Rustic wooden hot tub in the wash house. Homemade country gourmet breakfasts.

Hostess: Lois Ann Hank
Rooms: 4 (SB) $45-55
Full Breakfast
Credit Cards: A, B, C, D
Notes: 2, 5, 9, 12

OMAHA

The Jones'

1617 South 90th Street, 68124
(402) 397-0721

Large, private residence with large deck and gazebo in the back. Fresh cinnamon rolls are served for breakfast. Your hosts' interests include golf, travel, needlework, and meeting other people. Located five minutes from I-80.

Hosts: Theo and Don Jones
Rooms: 3 (1PB: 2SB) $25
Continental Breakfast
Credit Cards: None
Notes: 2, 5, 6, 7, 8, 10

year; 6 Pets welcome; 7 Children welcome; 8 Tennis nearby; 9 Swimming nearby; 10 Golf nearby; 11 Skiing nearby; 12 May be booked through travel agent

WILBER

Hotel Wilber

203 South Wilson, P.O. Box 641, 68465
(402) 821-2020

Whether you are in pursuit of business or
pleasure, need a room for an intimate
social gathering or business meeting, or
just desire a romantic, peaceful weekend
away, Hotel Wilber is an ideal retreat.
Upon entering our lobby, you will begin
your step back to the old country. Experience Old World charm in the dining
room, bar, garden, or one of our eleven
antique-filled rooms. Just thirty minutes
southwest of Lincoln. From I-80 exit 388,
head south on Nebraska Hwy 103 to
Junction of Hwy 103 and 41, then one
block west and one block north. Group
retreat rates available.

Hostess: Frances L. Erb
Rooms: 10 (SB) $42.95-69.95
Full Breakfast
Credit Cards: A, B
Notes: 2, 3, 4, 5, 7, 9

Nevada

INCLINE VILLAGE

Haus Bavaria

593 North Dyer Circle, P. O. Box 3308, 89450
(702) 831-6122

This European-style residence in the heart of the Sierra Nevadas, is within walking distance of Lake Tahoe. Each of the five guest rooms opens onto a balcony, offering lovely views of the mountains. Breakfast, prepared by your host Bick Hewitt, includes a selection of home-baked goods, fresh fruit, juices, freshly ground coffee, and teas. A private beach and swimming pool are available to guests. Ski at Diamond Peak, Mt. Rose, Heavenly Valley, and other nearby areas.

Host: Bick Hewitt
Rooms: 5 (PB) $90
Full Breakfast
Credit Cards: A, B, C, D
Notes: 2, 5, 8, 9, 10, 11, 12

New Hampshire

ALBANY

Kancamagus Swift River Inn

P.O. Box 1650, 03818
(603) 447-2332

This is a quality inn with that Old World flavor in a stress-free environment. Located in the White Mountains of New Hampshire in the Mt. Washington Valley on the most beautiful highway in the state, the Kancamagus Highway, one and one-half miles off route 16. We are only minutes from all factory outlets, attractions, and fine restaurants.

Hosts: Joseph and Janet Beckenbach
Rooms: 10 (PB) $40-90
Continental Breakfast
Credit Cards: None
Notes: 5, 7, 8, 9, 10, 11, 12

ANDOVER

The English House

P.O. Box 162, Main Street, 05216
(603) 735-5987

The English House is a 1906, shingled house that was fully restored by Ken and Gillian Smith in the late 1980's. It has been decorated and furnished by its British owners in the style of an English country home. A full breakfast and afternoon tea are served to guests. Queen and twin bedded rooms are available. Andover has many activities adjacent to suit all tastes, or guests can just enjoy the surrounding mountains and lakes.

Hosts: Ken and Gillian Smith
Rooms: 7 (PB) $75
Full Breakfast
Credit Cards: A, B
Notes: 2, 5, 8, 9, 10, 11, 12

ASHLAND

Glynn House Victorian Inn

43 Highland Street, 03217
(603) 968-3775; (800) 637-9599;
(603) 968-9338 (FAX)

A picture-perfect example of the Victorian era, guests marvel at the inn's cupola towers and gingerbread, wrap-around porch. Upon arrival, guests are greeted by a magnificent foyer accented with carved oak woodwork and pocket doors. The inn is beautifully furnished with Queen Anne furniture offering guests the warmth and hospitality of being "home" in the 1890's! Each bedroom has its own mood, distinguished by unique interior decor,

---

period furnishings, and amenities.

Hosts: Karol and Betsy Paterman
Rooms: 6 (4PB; 2SB) $65-95
Full Breakfast
Credit Cards: A, B
Notes: 2, 5, 7 (limited with restrictions), 8, 9, 10, 11, 12

BETHLEHEM

Adair - A Country Inn

Old Littleton Road, 03574
(603) 444-2600; (603) 444-4823 (FAX)

A 200-acre country estate with extensive gardens offering quiet elegance in the heart of the White Mountains. Huge bedrooms, terrific breakfasts, dramatic views, tennis, golf, skiing, walking, and hiking. Delightful bistros and great shopping nearby. AAA three diamond rating.

Hosts: Hardy, Pat, and Nancy Banfeld
Rooms: 8 (PB) $125-175
Full Breakfast
Credit Cards: A, B, C
Notes: 2, 4 (parties of six or more), 5, 8, 9, 10, 11, 12

BRADFORD

The Bradford Inn

Rural Route 1, Main Street, Box 40, 03221
(603) 938-5309; (800) 669-5309

The Bradford Inn was built as a small hotel in the 1890's. It has two parlors for guest use, one with a fireplace, one with a TV. J. Albert's Restaurant features turn-of-the-century ragtime and rhapsodies, "grandma gourmet" cuisine, and was the 1991-92 winner Best Apple Pie in New Hampshire, *Yankee* magazine. The area abounds in outdoor activities in all seasons and offers craft and antique shops, auc-

tions, summer theater, local fairs, and festivals. We can accommodate small groups (28-34) for retreats, family parties, or church outings.

Hosts: Tom and Connie Mazol
Rooms: 12 (PB) $59-79
Full Breakfast
Credit Cards: A, B, C, D, E, F
Notes: 2, 4, 5, 6, 7, 8, 9, 10, 11, 12

Candlelite Inn Bed and Breakfast

RR 1, Box 408, Old Center Road, 03221
(603) 938-5571

An 1897 country Victorian Inn nestled on three acres in the Lake Sunapee Region. All of our guest rooms are tastefully decorated and have queen beds, private baths, and mountain views. A gazebo porch is there for your enjoyment on a lazy summer day. And in the parlor is a corner fireplace for those chilly evenings. A full breakfast is served in our lovely dining room or in the sun room overlooking a babbling brook and pond. Within minutes to skiing, hiking, antiquing, and restaurants. We are a non-smoking inn.

Hosts: Les and Marilyn Gordon
Rooms: 6 (PB) $65-75
Full Breakfast
Credit Cards: A, B, D
Notes: 2, 5, 7, 8, 9, 10, 11

CLAREMONT

Goddard Mansion Bed and Breakfast

25 Hillstead Road, 03743-3399
(603) 543-0603; (800) 736-0603; (603) 543-0657 (FAX)

Located on seven acres with panoramic

---

year; 6 Pets welcome; 7 Children welcome; 8 Tennis nearby; 9 Swimming nearby; 10 Golf nearby; 11 Skiing nearby; 12 May be booked through travel agent

mountain views, this delightful, restored, early-1900's English Manor-style mansion has 18 rooms and expansive porches and tea house. Eight uniquely decorated guest rooms await, including an airy French-country room; step-back-in-time Victorian; whimsical cloud room; and romantic bridal suite. A full, natural breakfast starts each day. Four-season activities are nearby, national historic landmark, antique buff's adventureland. Smoke-free inside, clean air outside.

Hosts: Debbie and Frank Albee
Rooms: 8 (2PB; 6SB) $65-95
Expanded Continental Breakfast
Credit Cards: A, B, D, E, F
Notes: 2, 5, 7, 8, 9, 10, 11

COLEBROOK

Monadnock B & B

One Monadnock Street, 03576
(603) 237-8216; (800) 698-8216 (in New Hampshire only)

Located one block off Main Street, with easy access to shops and restaurants, in a quiet, picturesque, country community of 2,500 people, this 1916 house has a natural fieldstone porch, chimney, and foundation. Inside it has gorgeous, natural woodwork. Three guest bedrooms upstairs include two with double beds sharing facilities and one with a double and single bed with private half-bath. Common areas are available for relaxing or playing games and watching a large-screen TV. A roomy balcony is good for relaxing and soaking up the sun's rays.

Hosts: Barbara and Wendell Woodard
Rooms: 3 (SB) $43-54
Full Breakfast
Credit Cards: A, B
Notes: 2, 5, 6 (by prior arrangement), 7, 10, 11

EATON CENTER (NEAR CONWAY)

The Inn at Crystal Lake

Route 153, 03832
(603) 447-2120; (800) 343-7336

You deserve pampering! Unwind in our 1884 Victorian inn with balconies in a quiet, picture-perfect village. Enjoy our antiques and extraordinary four-course, multi-entree, eye-appealing dinner presented on china, crystal, and lace in our metal sculpture-enhanced dining room with fireplace. Begin the day with Irish soda bread and a full country breakfast. We have a Victorian parlor, a comfortable TV den/library, and a cozy lounge (the only room where smoking is permitted).

Hosts: Walter and Jacqueline Spink
Rooms: 11 (PB) $70-120 plus 15% service charge
Full Breakfast
Credit Cards: A, B, C, D
Notes: 2, 4 (by prior arrangement), 5, 7, 8, 9, 10, 11, 12

FREEDOM

Freedom House B & B

1 Maple Street, P.O. Box 478, 03836
(603) 539-4815

This Victorian home with six guest rooms is located 15 minutes from Conway. King Pine ski resort is five minutes away. Lake Ossipee and Loon Lake are great resort areas for enjoying an abundance of recreation. One church is located in the village; others are 15 minutes away. A smoke-free environment.

Hosts: Marjorie and Bob Daly
Rooms: 6 (SB) $50-60
Full Breakfast
Credit Cards: A, B
Notes: 2, 7, 8, 9, 10, 11

NOTES: Credit cards accepted: A Master Card; B Visa; C American Express; D Discover Card; E Diners Club; F Other; 2 Personal checks accepted; 3 Lunch available; 4 Dinner available; 5 Open all

GREENFIELD

The Greenfield Inn
Box 400, Forest Road, 03047
(603) 597-6327

Bob Hope and his wife, Dolores, have visited twice because it is romance in Victorian splendor. Breakfast with crystal, china, and Mozart. In quiet valley surrounded by mountains and big veranda views. Only 90 minutes from Boston or 40 minutes from Manchester airports.

Hosts: Barbara and Vic Mangini
Rooms: 9 (7PB; 2SB) $49-99
Full Breakfast
Credit Cards: A, B
Notes: 2, 5, 7 (restrictions), 8, 9, 10, 11, 12

HAMPSTEAD

Stillmeadow Bed and Breakfast at Hampstead
P.O. Box 565, 545 Main Street, 03841
(603) 329-8381

Historic home built in 1850 with five chimneys, three staircases, hardwood floors, oriental rugs, and woodstoves. Set on rolling meadow adjacent to professional croquet courts. Single, doubles, and suites all with private bath. Families are welcome, with amenities such as fenced-in playyard and children's playroom. Easy commute to Manchester, New Hampshire, and Boston, Massachusetts. Complimentary refreshments, and the cookie jar is always full. Formal dining and living rooms, expanded Continental breakfast.

Hosts: Lori and Randy Offord
Rooms: 4 (PB) $60-90
Full Breakfast, Expanded Continental
Credit Cards: C
Notes: 2, 5, 7, 8, 9, 10, 11, 12

Stillmeadow

HAMPTON BEACH

The Oceanside
365 Ocean Boulevard, 03842
(603) 926-3542; (603)-926-3549 (FAX)

This boutique hotel on the oceanfront has period furnishings, private baths, and is smoke-free. Within easy walking distance of activities and shops. Intimate breakfast cafe, decks, and sidewalk terrace, turn-down service. Beach towels and chairs are available.

Hosts: Skip and Debbie Windemiller
Rooms: 10 (PB) $86-110 (off season discounts available)
Expanded Continental Breakfast except July and August
Credit Cards: A, B, C, D
Notes: 8, 10, 12

HOLDERNESS

The Inn on Golden Pond
Route 3, P. O. Box 680, 03245-0680
(603) 968-7269

An 1879 Colonial home is nestled on 50 wooded acres offering guests a traditional New England setting where you can escape and enjoy warm hospitality and personal service of the resident hosts. Rooms

year; **6** Pets welcome; **7** Children welcome; **8** Tennis nearby; **9** Swimming nearby; **10** Golf nearby; **11** Skiing nearby; **12** May be booked through travel agent

are individually decorated with braided rugs and country curtains and bedspreads. Hearty, home-cooked breakfast features farm fresh eggs, muffins, homemade bread, and Bonnie's most requested rhubarb jam.

Hosts: Bonnie and Bill Webb
Rooms: 9 (PB) $85-135
Full Breakfast
Credit Cards: A, B, C
Notes: 2, 5, 8, 9, 10, 11, 12

KEARSARGE

Isaac E. Merrill House Inn

P.O. Box 8, 720 Kearsarge Street, 03847
(603) 356-9041; (800) 328-9041

Experience 150 years of hospitality in historic Kearsarge village. Located at the base of Mount Cranmore, this 220-year-old inn features a fireplaced dining room, three peaceful sitting rooms, views of Cathedral Ledge, and minutes to North Conway's discount shopping. Full country breakfast and tea with pastries daily.

Rooms: 22 (17PB; 5SB) $49-120
Full Breakfast
Credit Cards: A, B, C, D
Notes: 5, 6, 7, 8, 9, 10, 11, 12

JACKSON

Ellis River House

Route 16, P. O. Box 656, 03846
(603) 383-9339; (800) 233-8309

Enjoy a taste of old New England at our enchanting country inn overlooking our spectacular Ellis River. Antiques, whirlpool tubs, romantic fireplace rooms, two-room family suites, heated outdoor pool,

and scenic balconies. Minutes to golf and hiking in our White Mountains, located at the base of Mt. Washington. Cross-country skiing from our door.

Hosts: Barry and Barbara Lubao
Rooms: 18 (15PB; 3SB) $55-195
Full Country Breakfast
Credit Cards: A, B, C
Notes: 2, 4, 6, 7, 8, 9, 10, 11

JEFFERSON

Applebrook

Route 115A, 03583
(603) 586-7713; (800) 545-6504

Taste our mid-summer raspberries while enjoying spectacular mountain views. Applebrook is a comfortable, casual bed and breakfast in a large Victorian farmhouse with a peaceful, rural setting. After a restful night's sleep, you will enjoy a hearty breakfast before venturing out for a day of hiking, fishing, antique hunting, golfing, swimming, or skiing. Near Santa's Village and Six-Gun City. Dormitory available for groups. Brochures available. Hot tub under the stars.

Hostess: Sandra J. Conley
Rooms: 12 + dormitory (3PB; 8SB) $40-60
Full Breakfast
Credit Cards: A, B, D
Notes: 2, 5, 6, 7, 8, 9, 10, 11

Applebrook

The Jefferson Inn

Route 2, 03583
(603) 586-7998; (800) 729-7908

This charming, 1896 Victorian near Mt. Washington has a 360-degree mountain view. Summer activities include hiking from our door, a swimming pond, six golf courses nearby, summer theater, and excellent cycling. In the winter, enjoy Bretton Woods, cross-country skiing, and skating across the street. Afternoon tea is served daily. Three family suites are available. Discounted rates in spring, and midweek discounts in the summer and fall.

Hosts: Greg Brown and Bertie Koelewijn
Rooms: 13 (PB) $52-77
Full Breakfast
Credit Cards: A, B, C, D, E
Notes: 2, 7, 8, 9, 10, 11, 12

MOULTONBOROUGH

Olde Orchard Inn

RR 1, Box 256, 03254
(800) 598-5845

Circa 1790, Federal-style inn located in New Hampshire Lakes District within one hour of five major ski areas. Inn is furnished with antiques and oriental carpets collected by owners during their 25 years in the diplomatic service. Inn is situated on 12 acres with over 150 fruit trees, a pond, and a historic cemetery where the original occupants are buried. Bikes available for rent, or hike the beautiful nearby trails.

Hostess: Mary Senner
Rooms: 5 & Cottage (All PB) $70-90
Full Breakfast
Credit Cards: C
Notes: 5, 6, 7, 8, 9, 10, 11

NEW IPSWICH

The Inn at New Ipswich

Porter Hill Road, P. O. Box 208, 03071
(603) 878-3711

The inn is situated at the heart of New England in New Hampshire's Monadnock region. The 1790 Colonial, with classic red barn, set amid stone walls and fruit trees, heartily welcomes guests. Guest rooms feature firm beds and country antiques. Also featured are wide-pine floors and six original fireplaces. Downhill and cross-country skiing, hiking, antique shops, concerts, auctions are all nearby.

Hosts: Ginny and Steve Bankuti
Rooms: 6 (PB) $65
Full Breakfast
Credit Cards: A, B
Notes: 2, 5, 10, 11, 12

NEW LONDON

Pleasant Lake Inn

125 Pleasant Street, P. O. Box 1030, 03257
(603) 526-6271; (800) 626-4907

Our 1790 lakeside country inn is nestled on the shore of Pleasant Lake with Mt. Kearsarge as its backdrop. The panoramic location is only one of the many reasons to visit. All four seasons offer activities from our doorway: lake swimming, fishing, hiking, skiing, or just plain relaxing. Dinner is available. Call or write for a brochure.

Hosts: Margaret and Grant Rich
Rooms: 11 (PB) $75-90
Full Breakfast
Credit Cards: A, B
Notes: 2, 4, 5, 7 (over seven), 8, 9, 10, 11, 12

year; 6 Pets welcome; 7 Children welcome; 8 Tennis nearby; 9 Swimming nearby; 10 Golf nearby; 11 Skiing nearby; 12 May be booked through travel agent

NEWPORT

The Inn at Coit Mountain

523 North Main Street, 03773
(603) 863-3583; (800)-367-2364; (603) 863-7816
(FAX)

All four seasons provide nature's backdrop to this gracious, historic, Georgian home. Whether you prefer the greening spring, languid summer afternoons, colorful autumn foiliage, or winter-white mornings, you will delight in a stay at the inn. Available for small retreats of ten to fifteen people.

Hosts: Dick and Judi Tatem
Rooms: 5 (2PB; 3SB) $85-125
Full Breakfast
Credit Cards: A, B, C
Notes: 2, 4 (by arrangement), 7,8, 9, 10, 11

NORTH CONWAY

The 1785 Inn

3582 White Mtn Hwy, P.O. Box 1785, 03860-1785
(603) 356-9025; (800) 421-1785 (reservations for U.S. and Canada)

The 1785 Inn is a relaxing place to vacation at any time of the year. The 1785 Inn is famous for its views and food. Located at The Scenic Vista, popularized by the White Mountain School of Art, its famous scene of Mt. Washington is virtually unchanged from when the inn was built over 200 years ago. The inn's homey atmosphere will make you feel right at home, and the food and service will make you eagerly await your return.

Hosts: Becky and Charlie Mallar
Rooms: 17 (12PB; 5SB) $59-119
Full Breakfast
Credit Cards: A, B, C, D, E
Notes: 2, 4, 5, 7, 8, 9, 10, 11, 12

The Buttonwood Inn

The Buttonwood Inn

Mt. Surprise Road, P. O. Box 1817, 03860
(603) 356-2625; (800) 258-2625 outside New Hampshire; (603) 356-3140 (FAX)

The Buttonwood is tucked away on Mt. Surprise in the heart of the White Mountains. It is secluded and quiet, yet only two miles from excellent restaurants and factory outlet shopping. Built in 1820, this New England-style Cape Cod has antique-furnished guest rooms with wide-plank floors, a large outdoor pool, hiking, and cross-country skiing from the door. Alpine skiing is one mile away. A hearty dinner is served weekends during the winter. Two star Mobil Travel Guide rating, three crowns ABBA rating.

Hosts: Hugh and Ann Begley
Rooms: 9 (3PB; 6SB) $50-100
Full Breakfast
Credit Cards: A, B, C
Notes: 2, 5, 7, 8, 9, 10, 11, 12

The Center Chimney— 1787

River Road, P.O. Box 1220, 03860
(603) 356-6788

Cozy, affordable Cape in a quiet location

NOTES: Credit cards accepted: A Master Card; B Visa; C American Express; D Discover Card; E Diners Club; F Other; 2 Personal checks accepted; 3 Lunch available; 4 Dinner available; 5 Open all

just off Saco River with swimming, canoeing, and fishing. Near Main Street and North Conway village with summer theater, free cross-country skiing, ice skating, shops, and restaurants. Package plans available.

Host: Farley Whitley
Rooms: 4 (SB) $44-55
Continental Breakfast
Credit Cards: None
Notes: 2, 5, 7, 8, 9, 10, 11

Nereledge Inn

River Road, 03860
(603) 356-2831

Enjoy the charm, hospitality, and relaxation of a small 1787 bed and breakfast inn overlooking Cathedral Ledge. Walk to river or village. Close to all activities. Comfortable, casual atmosphere. Rates include delicious breakfast with warm apple pie.

Hosts: Valerie and Dave Halpin
Rooms: 9 (4PB; 5SB) $59-85
Full Breakfast
Credit Cards: A, B, C
Notes: 2, 5, 7, 8, 9, 10, 11

The Victorian Harvest Inn

P.O. Box 1763, 28 Locust Lane, 03860
(603) 356-3548; (800) 642-0749

Non-smokers delight in your comfortably elegant B&B home at the edge of quaint North Conway Village. Explore unique shoppes, outlets, and the AMC trails. Our 1850's multi-gabled Victorian find comes with six large comfy rooms, all with mountain views. Start your romantic adventure with a bounteous dining experience and classic New England hospitality. Relax by the fireplace or snuggle with a literary treasure in our elegant library. Private baths, lovely in-ground pool, and full A/C add to your comfort. AAA 3 diamond award. American Bed and Breakfast Association: rated "A" 3 crowns. Cross-country skiing from the door, and 3-10 minutes to downhill skiing.

Hosts: Linda and Robert Dahlberg
Rooms: 6 (4PB; 2SB) $65-100
Full Breakfast
Credit Cards: A, B, C, D
Notes: 2, 5, 7(over 6), 8, 9, 10, 11, 12

PLYMOUTH

Northway House

Rural Free Delivery 1, 03264
(603) 536-2838

Located in the heart of New Hampshire in the beautiful Pemigewasset River Valley, the Northway House is near Newfound, Squam, and Winnepesaukee Lakes, as well as the ski areas of Waterville Valley, Loon, and Cannon. Hospitality-plus awaits the traveler in this charming Colonial house that is homey, comfortable, and reasonably priced.

Hosts: Micheline and Norman McWilliams
Rooms: 3 (SB) $27-41
Full Breakfast
Credit Cards: None
Notes: 2, 5, 6, 7, 9, 10, 11

RYE

Rock Ledge Manor Bed and Breakfast

1413 Ocean Boulevard, Route 1-A, 03870
(603) 431-1413

A gracious, traditional, seaside, manor

year; 6 Pets welcome; 7 Children welcome; 8 Tennis nearby; 9 Swimming nearby; 10 Golf nearby; 11 Skiing nearby; 12 May be booked through travel agent

home with an excellent location offers an ocean view from all rooms. It is central to all New Hampshire and southern Maine seacoast activities; six minutes to historic Portsmouth and Hampton; 20 minutes to the University of New Hampshire; 15 minutes to Exeter Academy. Reservations are advised.

Hosts: Norman and Janice Marineau
Rooms: 4 (2PB; 2SB) $60-85
Full Breakfast
Credit Cards: None
Notes: 2, 5, 7 (over 10), 8, 9, 10, 11

SUTTON MILLS

The Village House at Sutton Mills

Box 151 Grist Mill Road, 03221
(603) 927-4765

This Village House is an 1857 country Victorian overlooking the quaint New England village of Sutton Mills. The location is quiet, yet convenient to New London, shopping, antiquing, and all summer and winter activities. The house is situated on four acres, and hikers, cross-country skiers, and snowmobilers enjoy starting out through our property. Guests enjoy the privacy of the guest house, tastefully decorated with antiques and old quilts. No smoking.

Hosts: Peggy and Norm Forand
Rooms: 3 (S2.5B) $50
Full Breakfast
Credit Cards: None
Notes: 2, 5, 8, 9, 10, 11, 12

THORNTON

Amber Lights Inn Bed and Breakfast

Route 3, 03223
(603) 726-4077

Amber Lights Inn B&B is a beautifully restored, 1815 Colonial in the heart of the White Mountains in Thornton, New Hampshire, in a quiet country setting. We have five meticulously clean guest rooms, all appointed with luxurious queen size beds, handmade quilts and antiques. In the early evening join in a conversation with the innkeepers over our nightly hors d'oeuvres and beverages. We are conveniently located between Loon Mountain and Waterville Valley, close to all White Mountain attractions.

Hosts: Paul Sears and Carola Warnsman
Rooms: 5 (1PB; 4SB) $60-75 (reduced rates available)
Full Breakfast
Credit Cards: A, B, C, D
Notes: 2, 5, 7, 8, 9, 10, 11, 12

Amber Lights Inn

WALPOLE

The 1801 House
Washington Square, 03608
(603) 756-9055

Set on historic New England Village Common, guests will enjoy comfort and convenience in our family home with private bath. The Blue Room is a master suite with a queen size bed and picture window looking west to the Vermont Mountains. The Swan room currently hosts a single bed and faces across the street to other Colonial homes. Local antiques, concerts on the Common, and other cultural and casual attractions and activities abound. There are three churches on the Common and one a block away. Welcome!

Hosts: Whit and Jean Aldrich
Rooms: 2 (PB) $40-50
Continental Breakfast
Credit Cards: None
Notes: 2, 5, 8, 9, 10, 11, 12

WARNER

Jacob's Ladder Bed and Breakfast
Main Street, Rural Free Delivery 1, Box 11, 03278
(603) 456-3494

Situated in the quaint village of Warner, Jacob's Ladder is conveniently located between exits 8 and 9 off I-89. The early-1800's home is furnished predominantly with antiques, creating a tasteful country atmosphere. Cross-country ski and snowmobile trail on site with three ski areas within 20 miles. Lakes, mountains, covered bridges, arts and crafts, and more nearby. No smoking.

Hosts: Deb and Marlon Baese
Rooms: 4 (SB) $40
Full Breakfast
Credit Cards: D
Notes: 2, 5, 7, 8, 9, 10, 11

WILTON CENTER

Stepping Stones Bed and Breakfast
208 Bennington Battle Trail, 03086
(603) 654-9048

Stepping Stone is owned by a garden designer and weaver. Display gardens surround the 19th-century house set in the quiet, rural Monadnock region. A scrumptious breakfast is served on the porch or terrace in summer, and in the solar garden room year-round. Enjoy good reading, stereo, TV in the cozy living room, or watch active weaver and gardener at work in a serene and civilized atmosphere.

Hostess: Ann Carlsmith
Rooms: 3 (1PB; 2SB) $35-50
Full Breakfast
Credit Cards: None
Notes: 2, 5, 6, 7, 10, 11, 12

---

year; 6 Pets welcome; 7 Children welcome; 8 Tennis nearby; 9 Swimming nearby; 10 Golf nearby; 11 Skiing nearby; 12 May be booked through travel agent

New Jersey

AVON-BY-THE-SEA

The Avon Manor Inn

109 Sylvania Avenue, 07717-1338
(908) 774-0110

The Avon Manor Inn is a gracious turn-of-the-century home (circa 1907) built in the Colonial Revival style. Enjoy breakfast in our sunny dining room, ocean breezes on our full wrap-around veranda, and the charm of this small seaside town. Eight air conditioned bedrooms and only one block to beach and boardwalk. The large living room has a cozy fireplace for winter nights. Many antiques, period pieces, and family heirlooms make this a special retreat to savor the serenity of yesteryear.

Hosts: Kathleen and Jim Curley
Rooms: 8 (4PB; 4SB) $60-100
Full and Continental Breakfast
Credit Cards: A, B, C
Notes: 5, 7, 8, 9, 10, 12

Cashelmara Inn

22 Lakeside Avenue, 07717
(908) 776-8727; (800) 821-2976

A tastefully restored turn-of-the-century inn rests on the bank of a swan lake and the Atlantic Ocean. This desirable beachfront location offers a unique opportunity to smell the fresh salt air, to feel the ocean breeze, and to hear the sounds of the surf and the sea gulls from the privacy of your seaside room. Hearty breakfasts are a tradition at Cashelmara Inn.

Host: Martin Mulligan
Rooms: 14 (PB) $60-157
Full Breakfast
Credit Cards: A, B, C, D
Notes: 2, 5, 7, 8, 9, 10

CAPE MAY

The Albert Stevens Inn

127 Myrtle Avenue, 08204
(609) 884-4717; (609) 884-2627

Built in 1898 by Dr. Albert G. Stevens as a wedding gift for his bride, Bessie, the inn is just a ten-minute walk to the beach and two blocks from Victorian shopping. The guest rooms are furnished with antiques, and have private baths and air conditioning. A 102-degree, six-person jacuzzi is privately scheduled for guests' comfort. Home of the original Cat's Garden Tea and Tour, the Inn is known for its comfort, privacy, and gourmet breakfasts. Dinner is served from January to April.

Hosts: Curt and Diane Rangen
Rooms: 8 (PB) $85-165
Full Breakfast
Credit Cards: A, B, D
Notes: 2, 4, 5, 8, 9, 10, 12

NOTES: Credit cards accepted: A Master Card; B Visa; C American Express; D Discover Card; E Diners Club; F Other; 2 Personal checks accepted; 3 Lunch available; 4 Dinner available; 5 Open all

New Jersey 191

Bedford Inn

805 Stockton Avenue, 08204
(609) 884-4158

The Bedford Inn is centrally located in Cape May, 300 feet from the ocean. Fully heated with a cozy fireplace in the parlor, the inn is completely Victorian and furnished with antiques. All rooms have air conditioning. On-site parking; mid-week discounts September to June. Many activities nearby.

Hosts: Cindy and Al Schmucker
Rooms: 11 (PB) $90-150
Full Breakfast
Credit Cards: A, B, C
Notes: 2, 7 (7 and older), 8, 9, 10, 11, 12

The Chalfonte Hotel

301 Howard Street, 08204
(609) 884-8409

Come home to gracious Southern hospitality. The Chalfonte Hotel, built in 1876, offers traditional Southern cooking, delightful architecture, breezy rooms, and long porches for rocking. Dinner and breakfast are included in the room rates. Families are always welcome, and children enjoy their own supervised children's dining room. Ideal location for retreats, reunions, rest, and relaxation.

Hostesses: Anne LeDuc and Judy Bartella
Rooms: 72 (11 PB; 61 SB) $53-154
Full Breakfast & Dinner
Credit Cards: A, B
Notes: 2, 4, 7, 8, 9, 10, 12

Duke of Windsor Inn

817 Washington Street, 08204
(609) 884-1355

This grande 1890 Victorian home offers gracious, relaxing accommodations furnished with period antiques, high-backed beds, and marble-topped tables and dressers. Two octagon rooms in our 40-foot turret are particularly fun and romantic. The dining room has five chandeliers and an elaborate plaster ceiling. We are within walking distance of the beach, historical attractions, tennis, and shopping.

Hosts: Bruce and Fran Prichard
Rooms: 9 (8PB; 1SB) $65-135
Full Breakfast
Credit Cards: A, B (for deposit only)
Open February to December.
Notes: 2, 8, 9, 10

The Mason Cottage

625 Columbia Avenue, 08204
(609) 8844-3358

Built in 1871 for a wealthy Philadelphia businessman, the inn is in the French Empire style. The Mason family purchased the house in 1945 and started welcoming guests in 1946. The curved wood-shingle mansard roof was built by the local shipyard carpenters, and restored original furniture remains in the house. The house endured the 1878 Cape May fire and several hurricanes. Honeymoon packages and gift certificates available.

Hostess: Joan E. Mason
Rooms: 9 $85-165
Full Breakfast
Credit Cards: A, B
Notes: 2, 7 (over 12), 8, 9, 10, 12

The Queen Victoria

102 Ocean Street, 08204
(609) 884-8702

The Queen Victoria includes three 1800's homes that have been restored and furnished with antiques. There are two par-

year; 6 Pets welcome; 7 Children welcome; 8 Tennis nearby; 9 Swimming nearby; 10 Golf nearby; 11 Skiing nearby; 12 May be booked through travel agent

lors, one with fireplace and one with TV and games. Two dining rooms serve a hearty country breakfast and afternoon tea. Special services include free bicycles, beach showers, and towels, and turned-down beds with a special chocolate on your pillow. All rooms are air conditioned, and have private baths—many with whirlpool tubs.

Hosts: Dane and Joan Wells
Rooms: 22 (PB) $65-235
Full Breakfast
Credit Cards: A, B
Notes: 2, 5, 7, 8, 9, 10

Windward House

24 Jackson Street, 08204
(609) 884-3368

An elegant, Edwardian seaside inn has an entry room and staircase that are perhaps the prettiest in town. Spacious, antique-filled guest rooms have queen beds and air conditioners. With three sun-and-shade porches, cozy parlor fireplace, and Christmas finery, the inn is located in the historic district, one-half block from the beach and shopping mall. Rates include homemade breakfast, beach passes, parking, and bicycles. Midweek discounts September to June; off season weekend packages.

Hosts: Owen and Sandy Miller
Rooms: 8 (PB) $75-140
Full Breakfast
Credit Cards: A, B (deposit only)
Notes: 2, 5, 7 (over 12), 8, 9, 10

The Wooden Rabbit Inn

609 Hughes Street, 08204
(609) 884-7293

Charming country inn in heart of Cape May, surrounded by Victorian cottages. Cool, shady street, the prettiest in Cape May. Two blocks to beautiful, sandy beaches, one block to shops and fine restaurants. Guest rooms are air conditioned, have private baths, TV, and comfortably sleep two - four. Decor is country, with relaxed family atmosphere. Delicious breakfasts and afternoon tea time. Two pet cats to fill your laps.

Hosts: Greg and Debby Burow
Rooms: 3 (PB) $65-165 (winter); $145-165 (summer)
Full Breakfast
Credit Cards: A, B
Notes: 2, 5, 7, 8, 9, 10, 12

The Wooden Rabbit Inn

EDGEWATER PARK, BEVERLY

Historic Whitebriar, Home of John Fitch, Steam Ship Inventory 1787

1029 Cooper Street, Whitebriar, 08010
(609) 871-3859

Historic Whitebriar is a German Salt Box Style home that has been added on to many times since it was the home of John Fitch, Steam Ship Inventory 1787. The latest addition is an English Conservatory, built in Beverly, England, from a 200-year-old design and shipped to Beverly, New Jersey, just a few years ago. The Conservatory is on the east side of the house, and breakfast is served here overlooking the season pool and spa. Whitebriar is a living history farm with animals to be tended, and guests are welcome to collect the eggs, brush the ponies, and pick the raspberries. Located just 30 minutes from historic Philadelphia, three hours from Washington, and one and one-half hours from The Big Apple, just off interstates.

Hosts: Carole and Bill Moore and their twin daughters Carrie and Lizzie
Rooms: 2 + apartments (SB) $50-85
Full Breakfast
Credit Cards: None
Notes: 2, 5, 6, 7 (additional charge), 9

Whitebriar

FRENCHTOWN

Hunterdon House
12 Bridge Street, 08825
(908) 996-3632; (800) 382-0375

Built in 1864, Hunterdon Houe is a true Victorian mansion notable for its distinctive Italianate style. We are one block from the Delaware River which offers sports enthusiasts fishing, boating, tubing,

canoeing. A biking/hiking trail follows the river also. We are deep in antiquing territory just minutes from Bucks Co, PA. Fine restaurants are plentiful. For modern tastes, there is a wealth of local artists and craftsmen in the many specialty shops on Bridge Street.

Hosts: Clark and Karen Johnson
Rooms: 7 (PB) $90-145
Full Breakfast
Credit Cards: A, B, C
Notes: 2, 5, 9, 12

MILFORD

Chestnut Hill on the Delaware
63 Church Street, Box N, 08848
(908) 995-9761

Perched high on the banks of the scenic Delaware River, Chestnut Hill offers guests a magnificent view while drawing them into the gracious living of a century past. Linda and Rob welcome you to share their home, offering the care and attention of a more gentle era. Enjoy a candlelit country breakfast, while dining in Victorian elegance. The bedrooms are old-fashioned and romantic, including Teddy's Place, a real favorite with honeymooners. Spend the afternoon rocking on the wrap-around veranda overlooking the river. No smoking.

Hosts: Linda and Rob Castagna
Rooms: 5 (3PB; 2SB) $75-100
Full Breakfast
Credit Cards: None
Notes: 2, 5, 8, 9

---

year; 6 Pets welcome; 7 Children welcome; 8 Tennis nearby; 9 Swimming nearby; 10 Golf nearby; 11 Skiing nearby; 12 May be booked through travel agent

OCEAN CITY

Barna Gate Bed and Breakfast Inn

637 Wesley Avenue, 08226
(609) 291-9366

Enjoy the small, intimate accommodations of our 1895 seashore Victorian. The cozy rooms are decorated in country style with quilts on the antique beds and paddle fans to keep you cool. All rooms are named for flowers. Guests use our common area or front porch under burgundy awnings with white wicker rockers. Near Cape May, Atlantic City, county zoo, and antique shops. We've got everything--beach, boardwalk, and ocean. Hospitality is our specialty. Open year-round.

Hosts: Frank and Lois Barna
Rooms: 5 (1PB; 4SB) $60-75
Full Breakfast; Continental in summer
Credit Cards: A, B
Notes: 2, 5, 7, 8, 9, 10

DeLancey Manor

869 DeLancey Place, 08226
(609) 398-9831

A turn-of-the-century summer house just 100 yards to a great beach and our 2.45 mile boardwalk. Summer fun for families and friends at "America's greatest family resort." Two breezy porches with ocean view. Walk to restaurants, boardwalk fun, and the Tabernacle with its renowned speakers. Located in a residential neighborhood in a dry town. Larger family rooms available. Breakfast optional for a small charge. Advance reservations recommended.

Hosts: Stewart and Pam Heisler
Rooms: 7 (3PB; 4SB) $40-60
Expanded Continental Breakfast
Credit Cards: None
Notes: 2, 7, 8, 9, 10

New Brighton Inn

519 Fifth Street, 08226
(609) 399-2829

This charming 1880 Queen Anne Victorian has been magnificently restored to its original beauty. All rooms and common areas (living room, library, sun porch) are elegantly and comfortably furnished with antiques. The front veranda is furnished with rockers and a large swing. Rates include beach tags and use of bicycles.

Hosts: Daniel and Donna Hand
Rooms: 6 (PB) $75-85
Full Breakfast
Credit Cards: A, B, C
Notes: 2, 5, 8, 9, 10

The Cordova

OCEAN GROVE

The Cordova

26 Webb Avenue, 07756
(908) 774-3084 in season; (212) 751-9577 winter

Ocean Grove was founded as a religious retreat center at the turn of the century. This flavor has lasted in the quiet, peaceful atmosphere. Constant religious programs for the family are arranged in the 7,000-seat Great Auditorium. The Cordova rooms are uniquely charming and Victorian. Friendliness, hospitality, cleanliness, and quiet one block from the magnificent white sand beach and boardwalk. The porches have a splendid ocean view. Midweek specials; also, seven nights for the price of five. Saturday night refreshments. The Cordova was selected by *New Jersey Magazine* as ". . .one of the seven best places to stay on the Jersey shore. Also featured in the travel guide, *O' New Jersey,* in 1992.

Hostess: Doris Chernik
Rooms: 14 (3 PB; 11 SB) $32-65
Cottages: 2 (PB) $95-105 (weekly rates available)
Continental Plus Breakfast
Credit Cards: None
Notes: 2, 7, 8, 9, 12

PRINCETON

Bed and Breakfast of Princeton
P.O. Box 571, 08542
(609) 924-3189; (609) 921-6271 (FAX)

Bed and Breakfast of Princeton is a reservation service offering a pleasant alternative to local hotel/motel lodging. The service represents several private residences and provides a variety of "homestay" accommodations. Rates reflect the accommodations and facilities provided. Availability and content of the complimentary breakfast varies from host to host but is usually continental style. Bathrooms may be shared. Some hosts do not permit smoking. Homes are recommended based on availability and infor-

mation provided by the guest. A listing of host homes is *not* available.

SPRING LAKE

The Hewitt Wellington Hotel
200 Monmouth Avenue, 07762
(908) 974-1212

"Spring Lake's landmark in luxury." AAA four-diamond award winner. Twelve beautifully appointed single rooms and 17 two-room suites on the lake overlooking the ocean have private balconies, wraparound porches, air-conditioning, ceiling fans, private marble baths, remote cable TV's, and phones. Heated pool and free beach passes. Refined dining in our intimate restaurant. Free brochure.

Rooms: 29 (PB) $70-210
Continental Breakfast
Credit Cards: A, B, C
Notes: 3, 4, 7, 8, 10

Sea Crest by the Sea
19 Tuttle Ave., 07762
(201) 449-9031

Escape to the romantic refuge of a luxury bed and breakfast inn by the sea. For a week or a weekend, we will pamper you with warmth and hospitality that is friendly yet unobtrusive. The Sea Crest is our lovingly restored 1885 Victorian inn for ladies and gentlemen on seaside holiday.

Hosts: John and Carol Kirby
Rooms: 12 (PB) $85-147
Expanded Continental Breakfast
Credit Cards: A, B
Notes: 2, 5, 8, 9, 10

---

year; 6 Pets welcome; 7 Children welcome; 8 Tennis nearby; 9 Swimming nearby; 10 Golf nearby; 11 Skiing nearby; 12 May be booked through travel agent

New Mexico

ALBUQUERQUE

Bottger Mansion·B & B

110 San Felipe N.W., 87104
(505) 243-3639

A historic landmark, built before New Mexico was granted statehood. Its Victorian style is unusual as compared to most of Old Town's architecture. The gracious tin ceilings, hand-painted wall murals, marble fireplaces, floor, and courtyards add elegance to the comfortable accommodations awaiting our guests. King- and queen-size beds, private baths, jet tub, full breakfast and daily refreshments and bizcichitos right in historic Old Town, just footsteps to museums, shops, and restaurants.

Hosts: Vince and Patsy Garcia
Rooms: 3 (PB) $59-99
Full Breakfast
Credit Cards: A, B, C
Notes: 2, 5, 7, 8, 9, 10, 11, 12

CEDAR CREST (ALBUQUERQUE)

Enchanted Vista B & B

10700 Del Rey NE, 87122
(505) 823-1301

A southwest villa on a one-acre estate, totally fenced for privacy with parking in rear by private entrance to all suites. Spacious suites with decks and verandas that offer spectacular views. Continental breakfast served at your convenience in your suite. Suites include micro-kitchens, perfect for extended stays. Just 20 minutes from airport and 45 minutes to Sante Fe. Just minutes from ski slopes, and only five minutes from the "tram."

Hosts: Tillie and Al Gonzales
Rooms: 2 (PB) $62-74
Continental Breakfast
Credit Cards: None
Notes: 2, 5, 7, 8, 9, 10, 11, 12

Le Pommier

12050 Highway 14 North, Box 287, 87008
(505) 281-6058, (505) 281-3092

Authentic adobe guest studio with rustic brick floors, log-beamed ceiling, kiva fireplace; sleeps one to four. Located streamside with mountain views in every direction; private entrance, bath, kitchen, antiques, CATV, phone, king bed, and queen hide-a-bed. Self-catered breakfast features homemade breads, waffles, French toast, fruit, juice, coffee and teas, jams, and cereals. Seven miles east of Albuquerque on the scenic Turquoise Trail; 1.5

NOTES: Credit cards accepted: A Master Card; B Visa; C American Express; D Discover Card; E Diners Club; F Other; 2 Personal checks accepted; 3 Lunch available; 4 Dinner available; 5 Open all

miles north of I-40.

Hosts: Garland and Norma Curry
Rooms: 1 (PB) $59-109
Full Breakfast (self-catered)
Credit Cards: None
Notes: 2, 5, 6, 7, 8, 9, 10, 11, 12

Maggie's Raspberry Ranch Bed and Breakfast

9817 Eldridge Rd., NW, 87114
(505) 897-1523

Lots of fruit trees and berry bushes, flowers, a fish-and-lily pond, geese-and-duck pond, and 20-by 40 foot swimming pool. Fresh-baked bread daily served with jams and jellies I make from fruit raised here. Tame roadrunners, lots of hummingbirds and more. Guests may feed the chickens, ducks, and geese, and gather the fresh eggs for their own omelet or pick fresh raspberries and grapes. Maggie helps you plan day trips in and around Albuquerque. This is an equestrian community.

Hosts: Maggie McKenzie
Rooms: 2 suites that sleep 6 (2PB; 1SB) $50-85
Full Breakfast
Credit Cards: None
Notes: 2, 5, 6, 7, 8, 9, 10, 11, 12

NOGAL

Hacienda de Nogal

P.O. Box 93, 88341
(505) 354-2826

1856 restored adobe ranch on seven acres in the Sacramento Mountains, surrounded by Lincoln National Forest and White Mountain Wilderness. Endless hiking and horse trails. Tennis court on premises. Tranquil courtyard for dining. Short drive to Ski Apache (Sierra Blanca 12,300 feet), historic Lincoln, and Ruidoso. Horseback riding available. Day excursions to old mining towns where you can pan for gold. Minimum stay of three days.

Hostess: Jane Ketchman
Rooms: 4 (2PB; 2SB) $70-100
Full Breakfast
Credit Cards: None
Notes: 2, 4, 5, 7, 8, 10, 11

Monjeau Shadows

H.C. 67, Box 87, 88341
(505) 336-4191

Four-level Victorian farm house located on 10 acres of beautiful, landscaped grounds. Picnic area, nature trails. King and queen beds. Furnished with antiques. Just minutes from Lincoln National Forest and White Mountain Wilderness. Cross-country skiing, fishing, horseback riding. For fun or just relaxing. Enjoy the year-round comfort of Monjeau Shadows.

Hosts: J.R. and Kay Newton
Rooms: 6 (4PB; 2SB) $65-75
Full Breakfast
Credit Cards: A, B
Notes: 2, 5, 7, 9, 10, 11

PILAR

The Plum Tree

Highway 68 at Highway 570, Box B-4, 87531
(505) 758-0090; 800-999-PLUM

The Plum Tree Hostel and Bed and Breakfast Inn offers lodging at $11, $24 and $35 dollars a night in private or dormitory accommodations. We are ideally located at a bend in the Rio Grande with opportunities for boating, fishing, hiking, and quiet

year; 6 Pets welcome; 7 Children welcome; 8 Tennis nearby; 9 Swimming nearby; 10 Golf nearby; 11 Skiing nearby; 12 May be booked through travel agent

reflection. In the surrounding hills of the Carson National Forest you can view petroglyphs as well as take advantage of many hiking trails and recreational opportunities for the naturalist. Tao's ski areas and Indian reservations are close destinations for day trips.

Hostess: Eva Behrens
Rooms: 5 (1PB; 4SB) $24-35
Continental Breakfast
Credit Cards: A, B
Notes: 2, 3, 4, 5, 7, 9, 11

SANTA FE

Alexander's Inn

529 E. Palace Ave., 87501
(505) 986-1431

For a cozy stay in Santa Fe, nestle into a bed and breakfast featuring the best of American country charm: Alexander's Inn. Quiet and romantic yet just minutes from the Plaza and Canyon Road, Alexander's Inn offers you a world of warmth and hospitality. Come share the Sante Fe experience with us.

Hostess: Carolyn Lee
Rooms: 7 (5PB; 2SB) $75-150 (off season rates available)
Full Breakfast
Credit Cards: A, B
Notes: 2, 5, 7 (6 and older), 8, 9, 10, 11, 12

Canyon Road Casitas

652 Canyon Road, 87501
(505) 988-5888; (800) 279-0755

Luxury accommodations are featured in this 100-year-old historic Territorial adobe within walking distance of distinctive art galleries, numerous museums, unique

shops, and historic landmarks. Both guest rooms have kitchenettes, down quilts and pillows, feather beds, separate entrances, and private patios. This is truly a four-season retreat.

Hostess: Trisha Ambrose
Rooms: 2 (PB) $85-165
Continental Breakfast
Credit Cards: A, B, C, D
Notes: 2, 5, 7, 11, 12

El Paradero

220 West Manhattan, 87501
(505) 988-1177

El Paradero is located on a quiet, downtown side street, ideal for exploring the heart of historic Santa Fe. The owners have turned the old, adobe, Spanish farmhouse into a warm and relaxing experience of true southwestern camaraderie and hospitality. The inn is furnished in the southwestern tradition with folk art and has an eccentric, rambling character typical of old adobes. Breakfasts are huge and special.

Hosts: Ouida MacGregor and Thom Allen
Rooms: 12 (8PB, 4SB) $50-130
Suites: 2
Full Breakfast
Credit Cards: None
Notes: 2, 5, 6, 7 (4 and older), 8, 9, 10, 11, 12

TAOS

Orinda Bed and Breakfast

P.O. Box 4451, 87571
(505) 758-8581

A 50-year-old adobe home, dramatic pastoral setting on two acres. View of

Taos Mountains, surrounded by elm and cottonwood trees. Decorated southwestern design. Original art presented in rooms and common areas. Kiva fireplaces in suites. Quiet, on private road, but only 15-minute walk to galleries, plaza, and restaurants.

Hosts: Cary and George Pratt
Rooms: 2 suites and 3 bedrooms (PB) $70-90
Full Breakfast
Credit Cards: A, B
Notes: 2, 5, 7, 8, 9, 10, 11, 12

Stewart House

P. O. Box 2326, 87571
(505) 776-2913

This Taos landmark was built over a 15-year period from what the artist/builder called reclaimed parts of history. The inn is an extraordinary mix of styles and textures, combining elements from Moorish to Mayan, Spanish to Scandinavian. The innkeepers have been in the fine art business for more than 20 years, so each room is filled with art and antiques. Gallery artists are frequent visitors. Enjoy mountain views, sunsets, outdoor hot tub, and hearty breakfasts only five minutes from Taos Plaza in a quiet, country setting. Featured on the Learning Channel's *Great Country Inn Series.*

Hosts: Mildred and Don Cheek
Rooms: 4 (PB) $75-120
Full Breakfast
Credit Cards: A, B
Notes: 2, 5, 7 (12+ years), 8, 9, 10, 11, 12

Orinda

New York

ALBANY

American Country Collection of Bed and Breakfasts and Country Inns Reservation Service

4 Greenwood Lane, Delmar, 12054-1606
(518) 439-7001 information and reservations;
(518) 439-4301 (FAX)

This reservation service provides reservations for eastern New York, western Massachusetts, all of Vermont, northern New Hampshire, and St. Thomas, U.S.V.I. Just one call does it all. Relax and unwind at any of our 115 immaculate, personally-inspected bed and breakfasts and country inns. Many include fireplace, Jacuzzi, and/or Modified American Plan. We cater to the budget-minded, yet also offer luxurious accommodations in older Colonial homes and inns. Urban, suburban, and rural locations available. $35-180. Arthur R. Copeland, coordinator.

Mansion Hill Inn

115 Philip Street at Park Avenue, 12202
(518) 465-2038

The urban inn is located around the corner from the New York state governor's executive mansion. The inn consists of 12 rooms and is in the mansion historic district in three separate buildings. It features an award-winning restaurant that serves regional American cuisine. Please write for a free brochure.

Hosts: Mary Ellen, Elizabeth, and Steve Stofelano
Rooms: 12 (PB) $105-145
Full Breakfast
Credit Cards: A, B, C, E
Notes: 2, 3, 4, 5, 6, 7, 8, 9, 10, 11, 12

Pine Haven Bed and Breakfast

531 Western Avenue, 12203
(518) 482-1574

A century-old Victorian home in Albany's finest neighborhood offers off-street parking and access to bus transportation to state capital offices, hospitals, colleges, and downtown. Restaurants, theater, and stores are within walking distance. Rooms are furnished with Victorian-era antiques, and beds have removable feather mattresses. Robes are provided for comfortable lounging, and there is a phone in each room. No smoking.

Host: Janice Tricarico
Rooms: 4 (S2B) $64
Continental Breakfast
Credit Cards: None
Notes: 2, 5, 7 (over 12), 12

NOTES: Credit cards accepted: A Master Card; B Visa; C American Express; D Discover Card; E Diners Club; F Other; 2 Personal checks accepted; 3 Lunch available; 4 Dinner available; 5 Open all

ALBION

Friendship Manor

349 South Main Street, 14411
(716) 589-7973

This historic house, dating back to 1880, is surrounded by lovely roses, an herb garden, and lots of shade trees. A swimming pool and tennis court are provided for your pleasure. The intimate interior is an artful blend of Victorian-style furnishings with antiques throughout. Enjoy a breakfast of muffins, breads, fruit, juice, coffee, or tea in the formal dining room served buffet style for your convenience. Friendship Manor is central to Niagara Falls, Buffalo, or Rochester. For traveling through or just a getaway.

Hosts: John and Marilyn Baker
Rooms: 4 (1PB; 2SB) $45+tax
Continental Breakfast
Credit Cards: None
Notes: 2, 5, 7, 8, 9, 10, 12

BAINBRIDGE

Berry Hill Farm Bed and Breakfast

Rural Delivery 1, Box 128, 13733
(607) 967-8745

This restored 1820's farmhouse on a hilltop is surrounded by vegetable and flower gardens and 180 acres where you can hike, swim, bird-watch, pick berries, skate, cross-country ski, or sit on the wraparound porch and watch the natural parade. Our rooms are furnished with comfortable antiques. A ten-minute drive takes you to restaurants, golf, tennis, auctions, and antique centers. Cooperstown and most local colleges are only 45 minutes away.

Hosts: Jean Fowler and Cecilio Rios
Rooms: 3 (SB) $55-65
Full Breakfast
Credit Cards: A, B, C
Notes: 2, 5, 7, 8, 9, 10, 11, 12

Berry Hill Farm

BOLTON LANDING

Hilltop Cottage Bed and Breakfast

Box 186, Lakeshore Drive, 12814
(518) 644-2492

A clean, comfortable, renovated farmhouse is near Lake George in the beautiful eastern Adirondack Mountains. Walk to beaches, restaurants, and marinas. Enjoy a quiet, home atmosphere with hearty breakfasts. In the summer, this is a busy resort area. Autumn offers fall foliage, hiking, skiing. There is a wood-burning stove for use in winter. A brochure is available.

Hosts: Anita and Charlie Richards
Rooms: 4 (2PB; 2SB) $45-65
Full Breakfast
Credit Cards: A, B
Notes: 2, 5

BURDETT

The Red House Country Inn

4586 Picnic Area Road, 14818
(607) 546-8566

The inn is located in the beautiful 13,000-acre Finger Lakes National Forest with 28 miles of maintained hiking and cross-country ski trails. Six award-winning wineries are within ten minutes from the completely restored 1840's farmstead on five acres of groomed lawns and flower gardens. Enjoy beautifully appointed rooms, country breakfasts, in-ground pool, fully equipped kitchen. Twelve minutes north of Watkins Glen, 20 minutes from Ithaca, 30 minutes from Corning.

Hostesses: Sandy Schmanke and Joan Martin
Rooms: 5 (SB) $60-85
Full Breakfast
Credit Cards: A, B, C, D
Notes: 2, 5, 9, 10, 11, 12

CAMBRIDGE

Battenkill Bed and Breakfast

Route 313, Rural Delivery 1, Box 143, 12816-9717
(518) 677-8868; (800) 676-8768

Relax in the beautiful Annaquassicoke Valley and enjoy our post-and-beam home. Veronica delights in creative cooking, and Walt is a jazz musician. In the winter, our bed and breakfast offers snow-shoeing on site and cross-country skiing nearby. Spring, summer, and fall offer you fishing, canoeing, tubing the beautiful Battenkill River, or biking through the valley. Equip-

ment for all these activities is available at our rental office.

Hosts: Veronica and Walter Piekarz
Rooms: 2 (SB) $60
Full Breakfast
Credit Cards: A, B, C, D
Notes: 2, 3 & 4 (by arrangement), 5, 10, 11

CAMILLUS

The Re Family Bed and Breakfast

4166 Split Rock Rd., 13031
(315) 468-2039

100-year-old early American farm house featuring lodge-style den, country kitchen, side deck utilized for fair weather breakfasts, 40' pool, lawns, 2 guest rooms with queen size brass beds and orthopedic mattresses, pedestal sink in each room. Next to garden-style bathroom with walk-in tile shower, vanity with double sinks, and full-mirrored back wall. Also one room with full bed and captain's bed for two singles or for children. Stress-free environment close to Syracuse.

Hosts: Joseph and Terry Re
Rooms: 3 (SB) $55-75
Full or Continental Breakfast
Credit Cards: None
Notes: 2, 5, 7, 8, 9, 10, 11, 12

CAMPBELL HALL

Point of View Bed and Breakfast

RR 2, Box 766H, Ridge Rd., 10916
(914) 294-6259

Enjoy peace and tranquility in a country setting with splendid views of rolling hills

---

NOTES: Credit cards accepted: A Master Card; B Visa; C American Express; D Discover Card; E Diners Club; F Other; 2 Personal checks accepted; 3 Lunch available; 4 Dinner available; 5 Open all

and farmland. Adjoins 250-acre horse farm with full equine facility. One hour from New York City, 20 minutes from the Stewart Airport, and three miles from historic village of Goshen. Spacious rooms, private baths, and guest-only sitting room.

Hosts: Rev. Bill Frankle and Elaine Frankle
Rooms: 2 (PB) $55-65
Full Breakfast
Credit Cards: A, B
Notes: 2, 5, 10, 11

CAZENOVIA

Brae Lock Inn

5 Albany Street (U.S. Route 20), 13035
(315) 655-3431; (800) 722-0674

Brae Loch stands today at corner of Albany Street (U.S. Route 20) and East Lake Road and is as close to a Scottish inn as you will find this far west of Edinburgh, Scotland. The atmosphere is very Scottish.

Hostess: Valerie Barr
Rooms: 15 (13PB; 2SB) $65-125
Continental Breakfast
Credit Cards: A, B, C
Notes: 2, 4, 5, 7, 8, 9, 10, 11, 12

Lincklaen House

79 Albany Street, Box 36, 13035
(315) 655-3461

To visit Lincklaen House is to return to an era of elegant hospitality. Lincklaen House is an extraordinary, four-season, country inn built in 1835 as a luxurious stopover for colonial travelers. Carefully renovated, the hotel provides the amenities that 20th-century travelers demand, while retaining a charm preserved since the 19th century.

Afternoon tea is served.

Host: Howard M. Kaler, GM
Rooms: 21 (PB) $70-130
Continental Breakfast
Credit Cards: A, B
Notes: 2, 3, 4, 5, 6, 7, 8, 9, 10, 11, 12

CLARENCE

Asa Ransom House

10529 Main Street, 14031
(716) 759-2315

Warmth, comfort, and hospitality are our main attractions. Nine guest rooms have antique and period furnishings, seven of these have fireplaces. We also have a library, gift shop, and herb garden on a two-acre lot in the village. The original building housing the library, gift shop and tap room dates back to 1853, built by Asa Ransom who received the land from the Holland Lace Company in 1799.

Hosts: Bob and Judy Lenz
Rooms: 4 (PB) $85-135
Full Breakfast
Credit Cards: A, B, D
Closed Fridays and January
Notes: 2, 4, 7, 8, 9, 10

CORNING

1865 White Birch Bed and Breakfast

69 East First Street, 14830
(607) 962-6355

The White Birch, Victorian in structure but decorated in country, has been refurbished to show off its winding staircase, hardwood floors, and wall window in the dining room that overlooks the back yard. We

year; 6 Pets welcome; 7 Children welcome; 8 Tennis nearby; 9 Swimming nearby; 10 Golf nearby; 11 Skiing nearby; 12 May be booked through travel agent

are located in a residential area two blocks from restored historic Market Street and six blocks from the Corning Museum of Glass. A warm fire during the colder months welcomes guests in the common room where TV and great conversation are available. A full gourmet breakfast is served each morning.

Hosts: Kathy and Joe Donahue
Rooms: 4 (2PB; 2SB) $50-70
Full Breakfast
Credit Cards: A, B, C
Notes: 2, 5, 7, 8, 9, 10, 11

Delevan House

188 Delevan Avenue, 14830
(607) 962-2347

This Southern Colonial house sits on a hill overlooking Corning. It is charming, graceful, and warm in quiet surroundings. Delicious breakfast. Check in time 3 pm, check out time 10:30 am. Breakfast served from 8:00-9:00 am. Free transportation to airport.

Hostess: Mary De Pumpo
Rooms: 3 (1PB; 2SB) $55-85
Full Breakfast
Credit Cards: None
Notes: 2, 5, 7 (over 10), 10, 11, 12

CROTON ON HUDSON

Alexander Hamilton House

49 Van Wyck St., 10520
(914) 271-6737; (914) 271-3927 (FAX)

An 1889 Victorian inn nestled on a cliff overlooking the Hudson River 28 miles north of New York City. The inn has six guest rooms, all with private bath and air-

conditioning, three are suites. Full breakfast is included. Non-smoking throughout. Walk to village of Croton on Hudson. We are convenient to many historic homes, West Point, lots of hiking, and climbing. Under an hour to New York City by train or car.

Hostess: Barbara Notarrs
Rooms: 6 (PB) $95-250
Full Breakfast
Credit Cards: A, B, C, D
Notes: 2, 5, 7, 9, 10, 11, 12

DOLGEVILLE

Adrianna B & B

44 Stewart Street, 13329
(315) 429-3249

Rural, Little Falls area near I-90 exit 29A. Cozy residence blending antique and contemporary furnishings. Convenient to Saratoga, Cooperstown, historic sites, and snowmobile, cross country and hiking trails. Four guest rooms, two with private bath, full breakfast. Smoking restricted. Air conditioning.

Hostess: Adrianna Naizby
Rooms: 4 (2PB; 2SB) $46.50-55+tax
Full Breakfast
Credit Cards: A, B
Notes: 2, 5, 6 (well-behaved), 7 (over 5), 10, 11, 12

DRYDEN

Margaret Thacher's Spruce Haven B & B

9 James Street, 13053
(607) 844-8052

This 1976 log home is warm and friendly

NOTES: Credit cards accepted: A Master Card; B Visa; C American Express; D Discover Card; E Diners Club; F Other; 2 Personal checks accepted; 3 Lunch available; 4 Dinner available; 5 Open all

and is surrounded by spruce trees that give the feeling of being in the woods, even though we are located in the village. Within 12 miles of Ithaca, Courtland, lakes, golf, skiing, colleges, museums, and restaurants.

Hostess: Margaret Thacher Brownell
Rooms: 2 (SB) Call for rates
Full Breakfast
Credit Cards: None
Notes: 2, 5, 6, 8, 9, 10, 11

EAST HAMPTON

Mill House Inn

33 North Main Street, 11937
(516) 324-9766

This 1790 Colonial is located in "America's most beautiful village." Enjoy lemonade while overlooking the old Hook windmill, or take a restful nap in our back-yard hammock. In the off-season, enjoy hot cider by the fireplace or a brisk walk to the ocean beach. Antiquing, golf, tennis, Long Island wineries, and whale-watching are nearby.

Hosts: Barbara and Kevin Flynn
Rooms: 8 (6PB; 2SB) $95-165
Full Breakfast
Credit Cards: A, B, C
Notes: 2, 5, 7; (over 11), 8, 9, 10

ELLINGTON

The Bonnie Dale Bed and Breakfast

846 Main Street, 14732
(716) 287-3312

Our late 1800's farmhouse was restored

in 1990. We are located 60 miles south of Buffalo, 15 miles north of Jamestown on the edge to the Allegheny Forest and the Amish country. Our area offers excellent skiing, snowmobiling, hunting, fishing, hiking, golfing, antiquing, and boating. Our house is furnished with comfortable antiques, offering a relaxed atmosphere for a quiet getaway. Family rates available.

Hosts: Jim and Bonnie Monk
Rooms: 3 (2PB; 1SB) $45-50
Full Breakfast
Credit Cards: None
Notes: 2, 5, 7 (over 6), 10, 11

The Bonnie Dale B & B

FAIR HAVEN

Frost Haven Resort, Inc.

West Bay Road, Box 241, 13064
(315) 947-5331

Located on Little Sodus Bay on the southern shores of Lake Ontario, the inn is surrounded with views of the waterfront and spacious, well-kept grounds. A full breakfast is served from 5:00 to 9:00 a.m. We make sure that fishermen are full as they try their luck with the famous trout and salmon fishing. All types of water sports

year; 6 Pets welcome; 7 Children welcome; 8 Tennis nearby; 9 Swimming nearby; 10 Golf nearby; 11 Skiing nearby; 12 May be booked through travel agent

are available with beaches and launch ramps nearby. July and August bring the Renaissance Faire. A full brochure is available upon request.

Hosts: Brad and Chris Frost
Rooms: 4 (SB) $66
Full Breakfast
Credit Cards: A, B
Notes: 2, 5, 7, 10, 11, 12

FOSTERDALE

Fosterdale Heights House

205 Mueller Road, 12726
(914) 482-3369

This historic, 1840, European-style, country estate in the Catskill Mountains is less than two hours from New York City. It is gentle and quiet, with a bountiful breakfast. Enjoy the mountain view overlooking the pond, acres of Christmas trees (cut your own in season), and natural forest. Informal evenings of chamber music and parlor games break out frequently.

Host: Roy Singer
Rooms: 11 (5PB; 6SB) $56-115
Full Breakfast
Credit Cards: A, B
Notes: 4, 5, 8, 9, 10, 11

Fosterdale Heights House

FRIENDSHIP

A Merry Maid Inn Bed and Breakfast

53 West Main Street, 14739-1301
(716) 973-7740; (716) 968-1301 (FAX)

Elegant Queen Anne stick-style built in 1883 and lovingly maintained for your comfort and enjoyment. Beautifully original carved woodwork, parquet floors, and stained, etched, and leaded glass make your stay one you'll remember. Four large guest rooms furnished in Victorian and country antiques collected by Moon from family treasures. Treat yourself from a wide selection of stress reduction therapies by Mark and Moon, a registered nurse. A haven for the weary traveler.

Hosts: Mark and Moon Beiferman-Haines
Rooms: 4 (1PB; 3SB) $55-65
Full Breakfast
Credit Cards: A, B, D, E, F
Notes: 2, 4, 5, 7, 8, 9, 10, 11, 12

FULTON

Battle Island Inn

RR 1, Box 176, 13069
(315) 593-3699

Battle Island Inn is a pre-Civil War farm estate that has been restored and furnished with period antiques. The inn is across the road from a golf course that also provides cross-country skiing. Guest rooms are elegantly furnished with imposing high-back beds, TVs, phones, and private baths.

Breakfast is always special in the 1840's dining room.

Hosts: Joyce and Richard Rice
Rooms: 5 (PB) $60-85
Full Breakfast
Credit Cards: A, B, C, D
Notes: 2, 5, 7, 10, 11

HAMBURG

Sharon's Lake House Bed and Breakfast

4862 Lakeshore Rd., 14075
(716) 627-7561

On the shore of Lake Erie, with a marvelous view of the Canadian shore and Buffalo skyline. Rooms are new and beautifully decorated with waterfront view. Hot tub room with widow's watch overlooking the lake is one of the amenities. All prepared food is gourmet quality style.

Hostess: Sharon DiMaria
Rooms: 2 (PB) Call for rates
Full Breakfast
Credit Cards: None
Notes: 2, 3, 4, 5, 9, 10, 11, 12

HAMMONDSPORT

Gone with the Wind on Keuka Lake

453 West Lake Road, 14418
(607) 868-4603

The name paints the picture of this 1887 stone Victorian on 14 acres on a slight rise that is adorned by an inviting gazebo overlooking a quiet lake cove. Feel the magic of total relaxation and peace of mind in the

solarium hot tub, nature trails, three fireplaces, delectable breakfasts, private beach, and dock. One hour south of Rochester in the Finger Lakes area of New York.

Hosts: Linda and Robert Lewis
Rooms: 6; $65-95
Full Breakfast
Credit Cards: None
Notes: 2, 5, 8, 9, 10, 11

Gone with the Wind on Keuka Lake

HAMPTON BAYS

House on the Water

Box 106, 11946
(516) 728-3560

Quiet waterfront residence in Hampton Bays surrounded by two acres of garden on Shinnecock Bay. A pleasant neighborhood on a peninsula, good for jogging and walking. Two miles to ocean beaches. Seven miles to Southampton. Kitchen facilities, bicycles, boats, lounges, and umbrellas. A full breakfast from 8:00 am to 12:00 pm is served on the terrace overlooking the water. Watch the boats and swans go by. Adults only. No pets. Rooms have water view, private baths and entrances. German, French, and Spanish spoken.
Hostess: Mrs. Ute

year; 6 Pets welcome; 7 Children welcome; 8 Tennis nearby; 9 Swimming nearby; 10 Golf nearby; 11 Skiing nearby; 12 May be booked through travel agent

Rooms: 2 (PB) $75-95
Full Breakfast
Credit Cards: None
Notes: 2, 8, 9, 10, 12

HEMPSTEAD

Country Life Bed and Breakfast

237 Cathedral Avenue, On the Garden City Line, 11550
(516) 292-9219

This charming Dutch Colonial on the Garden City line is near airports, trains to New York City, beaches, universities, and Nassau coliseum. It is furnished with antique reproductions, and rooms have air conditioning and color TV. We offer on-site parking and are near many tourist attractions. No smoking.

Hosts: Richard and Wendy Duvall
Rooms: 5 (3PB; 2SB) $60-95
Full Breakfast
Credit Cards: A, B
Notes: 2 (deposit only), 4,5, 7, 9, 10

HERKIMER

Bed and Breakfast Leatherstocking

P.O. Box 53, 13350
(315) 733-0040

Enjoy New York State's heartland at our 30-plus inspected host homes. Accommodations range from Adirondack foothills, Mohawk Valley, urban to country, all offering hospitality and amenities to suit your every need. Area attractions/sites include antiquing, National Baseball Hall of Fame in Cooperstown, Greater Utica area, Colgate University, and four-season recreation areas. Discover New York State's best kept secrets! Coordinator, Joe Martuscello.

HOBART

Breezy Acres Farm Bed and Breakfast

R.D. 1, Box 191, 13788
(607) 538-9338

You'll feel right at home in our circa 1830's rambling farm house. Remodeled with our guests' comfort in mind, each of our three rooms is individually decorated and has its own full bath. Relax on the huge leather sofa in the TV room or in front of the living room fireplace. Take a soak in our spa or hike through our 300 wooded acres. Wake up to a delightful breakfast—all homemade. Friendly, country hospitality.

Hosts: Joyce and David Barber
Rooms: 3 (PB) $50-60
Full Homemade Breakfast
Credit Cards: A, B
Notes: 2, 5, 7 (some restrictions), 8, 9, 10, 11, 12

Breezy Acres Farm

HORSEHEADS

Burch Hill Bed and Breakfast

2196 Burch Hil Road, 14845
(607) 739-2504

This modern country home is minutes from Elmira, Corning, Watkins Glen, Ithaca, Finger Lakes, wineries, six colleges, international auto race track, museums, Mark Twain's grave site. Each room has its own water closet plus use of the large bathrooms. Rooms can accommodate four people by use of a sofa bed. Make our home yours when in the south Finger Lakes area. No smoking.

Hosts: Bob and Doris Roller
Rooms: 2 (SB) $50
Full Breakfast
Credit Cards: None
Notes: 2, 3, 4, 5, 9, 10, 12

ITHACA

A Slice of Home

178 N. Main St., Spencer, 14883
(607) 589-6073

Newly remodeled 150-year-old farmhouse with 4 bedrooms and two baths. Country cooking with hearty weekend breakfasts and continental weekday breakfasts. Acreage to ski, hike, fish. 20 minutes to Ithaca, Elmira and Watkins Glen. No smoking, outside pets.

Hostess: Beatrice Brownell
Rooms: 4 (1PB; 2SB) $35-75
Both Full and Continental Breakfasts
Credit Cards: None
Notes: 2, 5, 7 (over 12), 12

Log Country Inn Bed and Breakfast of Ithaca

P.O. Box 581, 14851
(607) 589-4771; (800) 274-4771; (607) 589-6151 (FAX)

Rustic charm of a log house at the edge of 7,000 acres of state forest; 11 miles south from Ithaca, off 96B. Modern accommodations provided in the spirit of international hospitality. Home atmosphere. Sauna and afternoon tea. Full Eastern European breakfast. Convenient to Cornell, Ithaca College, Corning Glass Center, Watkins Glen, wineries, and antique stores. Open year round.

Hostess: Wanda Grunberg
Rooms: 3 (1PB; 2SB) $45-65
Full Breakfast
Credit Cards: A, B
Notes: 2, 5, 6, 7, 10, 11

JAMESVILLE

High Meadows Bed-N-Breakfast

3740 Eager Road, 13078
(315) 492-3517

You are invited to enjoy country hospitality nestled in the tranquil hills just 12 miles south of Syracuse. High Meadows offers two guest rooms, a shared bath, air conditioning, fireplace, plant-filled solarium, and a wrap-around deck with magnificent 40-mile view. One queen and one double room are available. Syracuse area offers restaurants, museums, theaters, concerts, and collegiate and professional sporting

year; 6 Pets welcome; 7 Children welcome; 8 Tennis nearby; 9 Swimming nearby; 10 Golf nearby; 11 Skiing nearby; 12 May be booked through travel agent

events. Corporate and weekly rates and seniors' discounts available.

Hosts: Alexander and Nancy Mentz
Rooms: 2 (SB) $35-55
Continental Breakfast
Credit Cards: None
Notes: 2, 5, 7, 10, 11

LAKE LUZERNE

The Lamplight Inn Bed and Breakfast

2129 Lake Avenue, P.O. Box 70, 12846
(518) 696-5294

This romantic 1890 Victorian has individually decorated bedrooms with fireplaces and features antiques, wicker, fluffy comforters, and air conditioning. A memorable breakfast is served on the spacious sun porch with a mountain view. The southern Adirondack Mountains are one block from Lake Luzerne. Ten miles south of Lake George, 18 miles north of Saratoga Springs. Nearby endless activities include horseback riding, outlet shopping, white water rafting, antiquing.

Hosts: Eugene and Linda Merlino
Rooms: 10 (PB) $70-140
Full Breakfast
Credit Cards: A, B, C, D
Notes: 2, 5, 7 (over 12), 8, 9, 10, 11, 12

LAKE PLACID

Highland House Inn

3 Highland Place, 12946
(518) 523-2377; (518) 523-1863 (FAX)

The Highland House Inn is centrally

located in a lovely residential setting just above Main Street in the village of Lake Placid. Seven tastefully decorated rooms are available, along with a darling, fully efficient, country cottage. A full breakfast is served with blueberry pancakes, a renowned specialty served in our year-round garden dining room. New additions include outdoor hot tub spa and televisions in all rooms.

Hosts: Teddy and Cathy Blazer
Rooms: 7 plus cottage (PB) $55-100
Full Breakfast
Credit Cards: A, B
Notes: 2, 5, 7, 8, 9, 10, 11, 12

LIMA

The Fonda House Bed and Breakfast

(716) 582-1040

National Register listed Italianate Village home circa 1853 situated on 2-acre, wooded lot. All rooms tastefully decorated with antiques. Be pampered in the Victorian style. Within walking distance to village services and Elim Bible Institute. Beautiful drive to Finger Lakes, Letchworth State Park, and Niagara Falls.

Hostess: Millie Fonda
Rooms: 3 (1PB; 2SB) $45-55
Full Breakfast
Credit Cards: A, B, D, E
Notes: 2, 5, 7, 9, 10, 11, 12

NOTES: Credit cards accepted: A Master Card; B Visa; C American Express; D Discover Card; E Diners Club; F Other; 2 Personal checks accepted; 3 Lunch available; 4 Dinner available; 5 Open all

MOHAWK

Country Hills B & B

Rural Delivery 1, Box 80, 13407
(315) 866-1306

All suites. All private. Smoke-free atmosphere. Spacious 1860's farm house amid rolling lawns and private woods overlooks Mohawk Valley. Queen and double suites have fully equipped kitchens, comfortably accommodate up to four, private bath, air-conditioning and TV. Separate entrance to suites assures privacy. Near I-90. A short, scenic drive to famed Cooperstown, Glimmerglass Opera, Oneida, Indian Nation Casino, Remington Arms museum, Herkimer Diamond digging, Jordanville, Russian Monastery, Revolutionary period historic sites, antique shops.

Hosts: Maryann and Jim Hill
Rooms: 2 (PB) $55-75
Full Breakfast
Credit Cards: A, B
Notes: 2, 5, 7, 8, 9, 10, 11,12

NEW YORK

. . .Aaah! Bed and Breakfast

P.O. Box 200, 10108-0200
(212) 246-4000; FAX (212) 265-4346

This reservation service offers 170 hosted or unhosted (self-catered) accommodations throughout Manhattan. It offers a very personal approach to matching people to accommodations by in and out dates, location, allergies, and smoking habits. No lists available; call to inquire. Studio and one- and two-bedroom apartments are also available. $60-80. William Salisbury, coordinator.

Urban Ventures

306 West 38th, 6th Floor, 10018
(212) 594-5650; (212) 947-9320

Bed and breakfast accommodations are large and well-furnished. They are less expensive, safer, and located all over the city. No tips, just friendly, achieving New Yorkers offering advice on what makes our city joyous! Urban Ventures was established in 1979, one of the first bed and breakfast reservation services in America. We've watched the bed and breakfast industry evolve into the fastest growing segment of the travel industry. New York is worth the effort. Urban Ventures is the agency that can let you see what we New Yorkers delight in.

OLIVEREA

Slide Mountain Forest House

Rd. 805, 12410
(914) 254-5365

Nestled in the Catskill Mountains State Park, our inn offers the flavor and charm of the old country. Come and enjoy our beautiful country setting, superb lodging, fine dining, and chalet rentals. Family-run for over 60 years, we strive to give you a pleasant and enjoyable stay. German and continental cuisine, lounge, pool, tennis, hiking, fishing, antiquing, and more available for your pleasure.

Hosts: Ralph and Ursula Combe
Rooms: 19 (17PB; 2SB) $50-70
Full Breakfast
Credit Cards: A, B, D
Notes: 2, 3, 4, 5 (chalets only), 7, 8, 9, 10, 11

---

year; 6 Pets welcome; 7 Children welcome; 8 Tennis nearby; 9 Swimming nearby; 10 Golf nearby; 11 Skiing nearby; 12 May be booked through travel agent

ONTARIO

The Tummonds House

5392 Walworth/Ontario Rd., 14519
(315) 524-5381

1897 Victorian home in a quiet, country setting. Guests enjoy private entrance, dining room, living room with TV and piano. Home is completely restored to original elegance, chestnut wood trim. Modern bath conveniences, and full sprinkler fitted for fire safety. Located 20 miles east of Rochester, N.Y.

Hosts: James and Judith Steensma
Rooms: 4 (2PB; 2SB) $40-50
Full Breakfast
Credit Cards: None
Notes: 2, 5, 10, 11

OXFORD

Whitegate Bed and Breakfast in the Country

P.O. Box 917, 13830
(607) 843-6965

This charming 1820 Greek Revival farmhouse is located on 196 acres of serene meadows and lush woodlands midway between Cooperstown and the Finger Lakes. Stroll on the hiking paths, relax by one of the ponds, come inside and sit by the fire, or enjoy the view from the solarium. Traditional furniture and antiques combine to make Whitegate a most welcoming place.

Hosts: Wanda and Pual Mitten
Rooms: 4 (2PB; 2SB) $45-65
Full Breakfast
Credit Cards: A, B
Notes: 2, 3 & 4 (reservations), 5, 8, 9, 10, 11, 12

PALENVILLE

Kaaterskill Creek Bed and Breakfast

H.C.R. 1, Box 14, Kaaterskill Avenue, 12463
(518) 678-9052

This lovely country Colonial bed and breakfast built in 1882 has four charming rooms dotted with antiques. Flannel sheets in winter and air conditioned in summer. Relax in front of ten-foot fireplace in sitting room or enjoy our glass-enclosed, wicker-furnished front porch. Area attractions include Hunter Mountain Ski Slope, Ski Windham, cross-country skiing, swimming, fishing, hiking, horseback riding, golfing, antiquing, country auctions, and The Catskill Game Farm. Country hospitality with a personal touch.

Hosts: JoAnn and Steve Murrin
Rooms: 4 (1PB; 3SB) $55-65+tax
Full Breakfast
Credit Cards: A, B
Notes: 2, 5, 7 (limited), 9, 10, 11

Kaaterskill Creek

The Kenmore Country Bed and Breakfast

HCR 1, Box 102 (Malden Ave), 12463
(518) 678-3494

A charming 1890's boarding house nestled

---

at the foot of Hunter Mountain. Full country breakfast. Near major ski areas and many summer attractions. Four-bedroom efficiency cottage also available, which is perfect for families. Stay with us and "rediscover" Greene County.

Hosts: John and Lauren Hanzl
Rooms: 3 (1PB; 2SB) $60-75
Full Breakfast
Credit Cards: A, B, D, E
Notes: 5, 7, 9, 10, 11

PALMYRA

Canaltown Bed and Breakfast

119 Canandaigua Street, 14522
(315) 597-5553

This 1850s historic village home of Greek Revival architecture is located near antique stores, Erie Coverlet Museum, country store museum, Erie Canal hiking trail, canoe rental. Rooms are furnished with iron and brass beds and antiques. Enjoy the livingroom fireplace.

Hosts: Robert and Barbara Leisten
Rooms: 2 (SB) $50-60
Full Breakfast
Credit Cards: C
Notes: 2, 5, 6, 8, 10, 11, 12

PENN YAN

The Wagener Estate Bed and Breakfast

351 Elm Street, 14527
(315) 536-4591

The Wagener Estate Bed and Breakfast is a 16 room historic house, furnished with antiques and country charm, located at the edge of the village on four scenic acres with shaded lawns, apple trees, and gentle breezes. The pillared veranda is a perfect spot for quiet reflection, conversation, and refreshments. Penn Yan is in Finger Lakes Wine Country and close to Corning Glass Museum and Watkins Glen.

Hosts: Norm and Evie Worth
Rooms: 5 (3PB; 2SB) $60-70
Full Breakfast
Credit Cards: A, B, C
Notes: 2, 8, 9, 10

The Wagener Estate

PORT JEFFERSON

Compass Rose Bed and Breakfast

415 W. Broadway (Rte. 25A), 11777
(516) 474-1111; (516) 928-9326

Hostess: Kathy Burk
Rooms: 4 (2PB; 2SB) $58-125
Continental Breakfast
Credit Cards: A, B, C, D
Notes: 2, 5, 7, 8, 9, 10, 12

year; 6 Pets welcome; 7 Children welcome; 8 Tennis nearby; 9 Swimming nearby; 10 Golf nearby; 11 Skiing nearby; 12 May be booked through travel agent

PURLING

Shepherd's Croft

HCR 263 Mountain Avenue, 12470
(518) 622-9504

Nestled in the northern Catskill Mountains approximately midway between the Hunter and Windham ski slopes, Shepherd's Croft has been an inn under various names and owners for more than 100 years. The entire property has undergone extensive renovations under the current owners during the last five years. Accommodations include six historic rooms in the main building, five motel rooms, and four suites with kitchen/living facilities. Children are welcome in the suites and motel rooms at no extra charge.

Hosts: Raimond and Linda Bang
Rooms: 15 (8 PB; 7 SB) $40-50
Full Breakfast; Continental weekdays
Credit Cards: A, B
Notes: 2, 5, 6, 7, 9, 10, 11, 12

QUEENSBURY

Crislip's B & B

Rural Delivery 1, Ridge Road, Box 57, 12804
(518) 793-6869

Located in the Adirondack area just minutes from Saratoga Springs and Lake George, this landmark Federal home provides spacious accommodations complete with period antiques, four-poster beds, and down comforters. The country breakfast menu features buttermilk pancakes, scrambled eggs, and sausages. Your hosts invite you to relax on the porches and enjoy the mountain view of Vermont.

Hosts: Ned and Joyce Crislip
Rooms: 3 (PB) $55-75
Full Breakfast
Credit Cards: A, B, C
Notes: 2, 5, 7, 8, 9, 10, 11

RICHFIELD SPRINGS

Country Spread Bed and Breakfast

23 Prospect Street, Route 28, P. O. Box 1863, 13439
(315) 858-1870

From our guest book. . . . "A refreshing night and fun conversation." Enjoy genuine hospitality in our 1893 country-decorated home. Located in the heart of central New York, we are close to the National Baseball Hall of Fame in Cooperstown, opera, antiquing, and four-season recreation. Delicious breakfasts (your choice) await. Member of local and national associations. Families welcome. Rated and approved by the American Bed and Breakfast Association.

Hosts: Karen and Bruce Watson
Rooms: 2 (PB) $45-65
Full Breakfast
Credit Cards: A, B
Notes: 2, 5, 7, 8, 9, 10, 11, 12

ROCHESTER

Dartmouth House Bed and Breakfast

215 Dartmouth St., 14607
(716) 271-7872; (716) 473-0778

Enjoy 1905 Edwardian charm, warm hospitality, antiques, cozy window seats, grand piano, fireplace, and private baths. Stroll through this quiet architecturally fascinating neighborhood to visit George Eastman Mansion and Museum of Photography. Walk to Rochester's largest collection of antique shops, bookstores, and trendy restaurants. Breakfast? Full, gourmet, and served by candlelight. Dress code? "Be comfy!" Children over 12 welcome. No pets. Smoking outside please. Cable TV, in-room phones. Beverages. Air conditioning.

Hosts: Ellie and Bill Klein
Rooms: 4 (2PB; 2SB) $65-80
Full Breakfast
Credit Cards: C
Notes: 2, 5, 8, 9, 10, 12

SARATOGA SPRINGS

The Inn on Bacon Hill Bed and Breakfast

P.O. Box 1462, 12866
(518) 695-3693

Relax in the peacefulness of elegant living in this spacious, recently restored, 1862 Victorian just 12 minutes from historic Saratoga Springs and its racetracks. Four air-conditioned bedrooms overlook fertile farmland. A baby grand piano adorns the Victorian Parlor Suite. Enjoy our lovely gardens, extensive library, comfortable guest parlor, and many architectural features unique to the Inn, an inn where you come as strangers and leave as friends! Off season, a comprehensive innkeeping course is offered.

Hostess: Andrea Collins-Breslin
Rooms: 4 (2PB; 2SB) $65-85 (seasonal rates)
Full Breakfast
Credit Cards: A, B
Notes: 2, 5, 7 (over 12), 8, 9, 10, 11, 12

The Inn on Bacon Hill

Six Sisters B & B

149 Union Ave., 12866
(518) 583-1173; (518) 587-2470 (FAX)

A uniquely styled 1880's Victorian beckons you with its relaxing veranda. Conveniently situated within walking distance of museums, city park, downtown specialty shops, antiques, and restaurants. Spacious rooms, each with private bath and luxurious bed, prepare you for a full home-cooked breakfast. Mineral bath and massage package available November-March.

Hosts: Kate Benton and Steve Ramirez
Rooms: 4 (PB) $65-105 (except racing and special weekends)
Full Breakfast
Credit Cards: None
Notes: 2, 5, 8, 9, 10, 11

SHELTER ISLAND

The Bayberry B & B

36 South Menantic Road, P.O. Box 538, 11964-0538
(516) 749-3375

Experience an island accessible only by ferry with a simple, peaceful, lifestyle and a third of it is a nature conservancy. Activities include hiking, birdwatching, biking, beaches, boating, fishing, winery tours,

year; **6** Pets welcome; **7** Children welcome; **8** Tennis nearby; **9** Swimming nearby; **10** Golf nearby; **11** Skiing nearby; **12** May be booked through travel agent

and antiquing. Our home is in a setting abounding with wildlife, furnished with antiques, has exceptionally large king size bedroom and a twin bedroom, cozy living room with piano and fireplace, hammocks, and swimming pool.

Hosts: Suzanne and Richard Boland
Rooms: 2 (PB) $95-115 (seasonal rates available)
Full Breakfast
Credit Cards: None
Notes: 2, 5, 7 (over 12), 8, 9, 10

SOUTHOLD

Goose Creek Guesthouse

1475 Waterview Drive, 11971
(516) 765-3356

Goose Creek Guesthouse is a Civil War-era farmhouse secluded on a creek by the woods. We are in a resort area with many beaches, golf, charter boat fishing, antique shops, and museums. Near ferries to Connecticut or Montauk and the south shore via Shelter Island.

Hostess: Mary Mooney-Getoff
Rooms: 4 (SB) $60-75
Full Country Breakfast
Credit Cards: None
Notes: 2 (for deposit), 7, 8, 9, 10, 12

STONE RIDGE

Hasbrouck House Bed Breakfast

P.O. Box 76, 12484
(914) 687-0151

This is a 25 room stone house built in 1757 and 1835. 35-acre estate—large outdoor swimming pool. Close to hiking and biking areas. Large living room for lounging. Period antiques in rooms.

Hosts: Staff of the Hasbrouck House
Rooms: 8 (SB) $85-100
Full Breakfast
Credit Cards: A, B, D
Notes: 2, 5, 8, 9, 10, 11

SYRACUSE—SEE ALSO JAMESVILLE

Elaine's Bed and Breakfast Reservation Service

4987 Kingston Rd., 13060
(315) 689-2082 (after 10 am)

This is a reservation service in Central New York handling Finger Lakes, the metro Syracuse area, including: Apulia, Auburn, Baldwinsville, Cayuga Lake, Cazenovia, Clay, Cleveland and Constantia (on Oneida Lake), Conquest, DeWitt, Durhamville, Elbridge, Edmeston (near Cooperstown), Fayetteville, Geneva, Glen Haven, Groton, Homer, Jamesville, Lafayette, Liverpool, Manlius, Marathon, Marcellus, Owasco Lake, Phoenix, Pompey, Port Ontario, Pulaski, Rome, Saranac Lake, Sheldrake-on-Cayuga, Skaneateles, Syracuse, Tully, Vernon, Vesper, Waterloo, and Watertown. Also in the Berkshires in Western Massachusetts: Alford, Great Barrington, Lenox, New Lebanon, NY, North Egremont, Otis, Sheffield, Stockbridge, and South Egremont. Elaine can match you up with just what you want. Rates per couple range from $45 to $125.

TRUMANSBURG

Westwind Bed and Breakfast

1662 Taughannock Boulevard, 14886
(607) 387-3377

Gracious hospitality and casual elegance await you in our 1870 Victorian farmhouse situated on the hillside above Cayuga Lake. Whether you are on vacation or a short getaway weekend, you will enjoy the country charm and convenience of Westwind. Located one-half mile south of Taughannock State Park and only 20 minutes from Cornell University and Ithaca College. Nearby is the Hangar Theatre, area golf courses, museums, antiques, and shopping.

Hostess: Sharon Scott
Rooms: 4 (S2B) $55-75
Full Breakfast
Credit Cards: A, B
Notes: 2, 5, 7 (over 10), 8, 9, 10, 11

WARRENSBURG

Bent Finial Manor

194 Main St., 12885
(518) 623-3308

Spacious Victorian manor that preserves the turn-of-the-century atmosphere with its cherry staircase and stained glass windows. Five bed chambers, queen beds, private baths, full candlelight breakfast with homemade maple syrup, strawberry jam amd apple cider. Enjoy coffee on our porch, in front of a crackling fireplace or in our conservatory. One mile to I-87, hiking, biking, riding, sleigh rides, skiing, swimming, boating and antiquing, too!

Hostess: Patricia Scully
Rooms: 5 (PB) $75-85
Full Breakfast
Credit Cards: None
Notes: 2, 3, 4, 5, 7 (limited), 8, 9, 10

The Merrill Magee House

2 Hudson St., 12885
(518) 623-2449

From the inviting wicker chairs on the porch to the elegant candlelit diningrooms, the inn offers the romance of a visit to an earlier more gracious era. Guest rooms feature hand-made quilts, fine linens, four-poster beds, and working fireplaces. Situated in the Adirondack Park, there are outdoor activities for everyone, plus outlet shopping and antiquing. Family suite, outdoor pool, meeting rooms. A warm, friendly staff.

Hosts: Ken and Florence Carrington
Rooms: 10 plus one 3-room family suite (PB)
$85-105
Full Breakfast
Credit Cards: A, B, C, D
Notes: 2, 3, 4, 5, 7, 8, 9, 10, 11, 12

White House Lodge

53 Main Street, 12885
(518) 623-3640

An 1847 Victorian home in the heart of the queen village of the Adirondacks, an antiquer's paradise. The home is furnished with many Victorian antiques which send you back in time. Five minutes to Lake George, Fort William Henry, and Great Escape. Walk to restaurants and shopping. Enjoy air-conditioned TV lounge for

---

year; 6 Pets welcome; 7 Children welcome; 8 Tennis nearby; 9 Swimming nearby; 10 Golf nearby; 11 Skiing nearby; 12 May be booked through travel agent

guests only. Wicker rockers and chairs on front porch. Window and casablanca fans.

Hosts: Jim and Ruth Gibson
Rooms: 3 (SB) $85
Continental Breakfast
Credit Cards: A, B
Notes: 5, 7 (over 8 years), 9, 10, 11

WARWICK

Willow Brook Inn
Warwick Turnpike, P. O. 375, 10990
(201) 853-7728

On the New York/New Jersey border, enjoy 120 acres of beauty with hiking trails, ponds with row boats, and outdoor party facilities. Inside we have clean and quiet sleeping rooms, TV lounge, pool table, and refrigerator and microwave for guest use. Indoor party facilities include a dining room that seats 60 people. We are less than a mile from the Appalachian Trail.

Host: Stan Streczyk
Rooms: 14 (4PB; 10SB) $44.50
Full Breakfast
Credit cards: None
Notes: 2, 3, 4, 5, 7, 8, 9, 10, 11

WATERTOWN

Starbuck House
253 Clinton Street, 13601
(315) 788-7324

In operation since 1988, the Starbuck House is the choice of business travelers and tourists alike. Built in 1863 for State Senator James F. Starbuck, this 16-room Italianate Mansion is situated in a historic neighborhood two blocks from downtown Watertown. Starbuck House has been included in the company of many distinguished inns. Owners Marsha and Gary Saal combine the warmth and hospitality of a bed and breakfast inn with the amenities of a small European hotel to make every guest feel welcome and every visit memorable. Watertown is 70 miles north of Syracuse off I-81 and is six miles from Lake Ontario and the gateway in the Adirondack Mountains, the Thousand Island Resort Region, and Canada. The area provides year-round recreation opportunities.

Hosts: Marsha and Garl Saal
Rooms: 4 (3PB; 1SB) $70
Full Gourmet Breakfast
Credit Cards: A, B, C
Notes: 2, 5, 7 (over 10), 8, 9, 10, 11, 12

WATERVILLE

B & B of Waterville
211 White Street, 13480
(315) 841-8295

This lovely Victorian home in Waterville's Historic Triangle District is near Hamilton College and Colgate University and many antique shops along U.S. Route 20. Cooperstown's museums and Glimmerglass Opera are a short distance away. Accommodations include a first floor room with private bath and two on the seond floor with a shared bath. A delicious full breakfast is served.

Hosts: Stanley and Carol Sambora
Rooms: 3 (1PB; 2SB) $40-50
Full Breakfast
Credit Cards: A, B
Notes: 2, 5, 7, 8, 10, 12

NOTES: Credit cards accepted: A Master Card; B Visa; C American Express; D Discover Card; E Diners Club; F Other; 2 Personal checks accepted; 3 Lunch available; 4 Dinner available; 5 Open all

WESTHAMPTON BEACH

1880 House

2 Seafield Lane, P. O. Box 648, 11978
(800) 346-3290

The Seafield House is a hidden, 100-year-old country retreat perfect for a romantic hideaway, a weekend of privacy, or just a change of pace from city life. Only 90 minutes from Manhattan, Seafield House is ideally situated on Westhampton Beach's exclusive Seafield Lane. The estate includes a swimming pool and tennis court and is a short, brisk walk to the ocean beach. The area offers outstanding restaurants, shops, and opportunities for antique hunting. Indoor tennis, Guerney's International Health Spa, and Montauk Point are nearby.

Hostess: Elsie Collins
Rooms: 3 (PB) $100-200 Suites
Full Breakfast
Credit Cards: A, B, C
Notes: 2, 5, 8, 9, 10, 12

1880 House

WINDSOR

Country Haven

66 Garrett Rd., 13865
(607) 655-1204

A restored 1800's farmhouse in a quiet country setting on 350 acres. A haven for today's weary traveler and a weekend hideaway where warm hospitality awaits you. Craft shops with 70 artisans. Located 1 mile from Rt. 17 East, Exit 78, 12 miles east of Binghamton and 7 miles from Rt. 81.

Hostess: Rita Saunders
Rooms: 4 (1PB; 2SB) $45-55
Full Breakfast
Credit Cards: None
Notes: 2, 5, 8, 9, 10

YOUNGSTOWN/NIAGARA FALLS

The Cameo Manor North

3881 Lower River Road, 14174
(716) 745-3034

Located just seven miles north of Niagara Falls, our English manor house is the perfect spot for that quiet getaway you have been dreaming about. Situated on three secluded acres, the manor offers a great room with fireplaces, solarium, library, and an outdoor terrace for your enjoyment. Our beautifully appointed guest rooms include suites with private sunrooms, cable TV. A breakfast buffet is served daily.

Hosts: Greg and Carolyn Fisher
Rooms: 5 (3PB; 2SB) $60-125
Full Breakfast
Credit Cards: A, B, D
Notes: 2, 5, 7, 8, 9, 10, 11, 12

year; 6 Pets welcome; 7 Children welcome; 8 Tennis nearby; 9 Swimming nearby; 10 Golf nearby; 11 Skiing nearby; 12 May be booked through travel agent

North Carolina

ASHEVILLE

Aberdeen Inn

64 Linden Avenue, 28801
(704) 254-9336

We invite you to share our 1909 Colonial-style home six blocks from downtown and six minutes from Biltmore Estate. Lovely gardens and old shade trees provide privacy. Enjoy a buffet breakfast or a wicker rocker on our huge wraparound porch. The parlor and four of the nine bedrooms feature wood-burning fireplaces. Comfortable antiques, and collectibles. Friendly hosts (plus four cats) welcome you.

Hosts: Linda and Ross Willard
Rooms: 9 (PB) $55-75
Full Breakfast
Credit Cards: A, B
Notes: 2, 5, 8, 9, 10, 11

Cairn Brae

217 Patton Mountain Road, 28804
(704) 252-9219

A mountain retreat on three secluded acres above Asheville features beautiful views, walking trails, and a large terrace overlooking Beaver Dam Valley. Homemade full breakfast. Quiet, away from traffic, only minutes from downtown.

Hosts: Edward and Millicent Adams
Rooms: 3 (PB) $80-95
Full Breakfast
Credit Cards: A, B
Open April-November
Notes: 2, 3, 7 (over 10), 8, 9, 10

Cedar Crest Victorian Inn

674 Biltmore Avenue, 28803
(704) 252-1389; (800) 252-0310

This 1890 Queen Anne mansion is listed on the National Register of Historic Places. One of the largest and most opulent residences surviving Asheville's 1890's boom period. A captain's walk, projecting turrets, and expansive verandas welcome guests to lavish interior woodwork and stained glass. All rooms are furnished with antiques, with satin and lace trappings.

Hosts: Jack and Barbara McEwan
Rooms: 13 (9PB; 4SB) $75-130
Expanded Continental Breakfast
Credit Cards: A, B, C, D
Notes: 2, 5, 7 (over 12), 8, 10, 12

Dry Ridge Inn

26 Brown Street, Weaverville, 28787
(704) 658-3899, (800) 839-3899

Part of this country-style inn was built in 1849 as a parsonage and was used as a hospital during the Civil War. The rest of the house was built in 1889. Large guest rooms have antiques and hand-made quilts. In a small-town setting, it is 10 minutes north of Asheville and all of its attractions.

Hosts: Paul and Mary Lou Gibson
Rooms: 7 (PB) $50-70
Full Breakfast
Credit Cards: A, B,
Notes: 2, 5, 7, 10, 11, 12

Reed House

119 Dodge Street, 28803
(704) 274-1604

This comfortable Queen Anne Victorian with rocking chairs and swings on the porch has a rocking chair and fireplace in every room. Breakfast features home-made muffins, rolls, and jams and is served on the porch. Listed on the National Register of Historic Places; near Biltmore Estate. Open May 1 through November 1.

Hostess: Marge Turcot
Rooms: 2 (SB) $50, 2BR Family Cottage $95
Suite: 1 (PB) $75
Continental Breakfast
Credit Cards: A, B
Open May 1 through November 1.
Notes: 2, 7, 8, 9, 10, 11

BREVARD

The Red House Inn

412 West Probart Street, 28712
(704) 884-9349

The Red House was built in 1851 and has served as a trading post, a railroad station, the county's first courthouse, and the first post office. It has been lovingly restored and is now open to the public. Charmingly furnished with turn-of-the-century antiques. Convenient to the Blue Ridge Parkway, Brevard Music Center, and Asheville's

Biltmore Estate.

Hostess: Mary Lynne MacGillycuddy
Rooms: 6 (2PB; 4SB) + one cottage (PB) $43-69
Full Breakfast
Credit Cards: A, B, C
Closed January-March
Notes: 2, 7, 8, 9, 10, 12

Womble Inn

301 W. Main Street, 28712
(704) 884-4770

The Womble Inn invites you to relax in a welcoming, comfortable atmosphere. Each of the six guest rooms is especially furnished in antiques and decorated to make you feel cared for. All of the guest rooms have private baths and air conditioning. Your breakfast will be served to you on a silver tray or you may prefer to be seated in the dining room. The Inn is one-half mile from the exciting Brevard Music Center.

Hosts: Beth and Steve Womble
Rooms: 6 (PB) $48-58
Continental Breakfast
Credit Cards: A
Notes: 2, 5, 7, 8, 10

BRYSON CITY

Randolph House Inn

P.O. Box 816, 28713
(704) 488-3472

The inn is located 60 miles southwest of Asheville in a quaint mountain town at the gateway to the Great Smoky Mountain National Park. It overlooks the town and is close to white-water activities, horseback riding, hiking, trout streams, Cherokee Indian Reservation, the Blue Ridge Parkway, Fontana Lake, and scenic trails and highways. Near depot and excursions on the Great Smoky Mountain railway. Listed on the National Register of Historic Places and recommended by *The New York Times*.

Hosts: Bill and Ruth Randolph Adams
Rooms: 6 (3 PB; 3 SB) $75
Full Breakfast
Credit Cards: A, B, C
Closed November-March
Notes: 2, 4, 8, 12

BURNSVILLE

NuWray Inn

Town Square, 28714
(704) 682-2329; (800) 368-9729

Historic country inn...since 1833. Nestled in the Blue Ridge Mountains in a quaint town-square setting. Thirty miles northeast of Asheville. Close to Mt. Mitchell, Blue Ridge Parkway, Grandfather Mountain, antiques, golf, crafts, hiking, fishing, or just relaxing on the porch. Room rates include a hearty country breakfast and afternoon refreshments, with our nationally famous family-style dinners also available.

Hosts: Chris and Pam Strickland
Rooms: 26 (PB) $70-110
Full Breakfast
Credit Cards: A, B, C
Notes: 2, 3, 4, 5, 7, 8, 9, 10, 11, 12

CHARLOTTE

The Homeplace B & B

5901 Sardis Road, 28270
(704) 365-1936

Restored 1902 country Victorian with

wrap-around porch and tin roof is nestled among two and one-half wooded acres. Secluded "cottage style" gardens with a gazebo, brick walkways, and a 1930's log barn further enhance this nostalgic oasis in southeast Charlotte. Experienced innkeepers offer four guest rooms, a full breakfast, and a Victorian Garden Room for small meetings and special occasions. Opened in 1984, the Homeplace is a "reflection of the true bed and breakfast."

Hosts: Peggy and Frank Dearien
Rooms: 4 (2PB; 2SB) $68-88
Full Breakfast
Credit Cards: A, B, C
Notes: 2, 5, 12 (10%)

The Homeplace

McElhinney House

10533 Fairway Ridge Road, 28277
(704) 846-0783

A two-story traditional home located in popular southeast Charlotte, 25 minutes from Charlotte-Douglas Airport. Close to fine restaurants, museums, Carowinds Park, and many golf courses. A lounge area with cable TV, a hot tub, laundry facilities, and barbeque are available. Families are welcome. A continental breakfast is served in the lounge or on the deck.

Hosts: Mary and Jim McElhinney
Rooms: 2(PB) $55-65
Continental Breakfast
Credit Cards: A, B
Notes: 2, 5, 7, 8, 9, 10

CLINTON

The Shield House

216 Sampson Street, 28328
(919) 592-2634; (800) 462-9817 (reservations only)

Reminiscent of *Gone with the Wind* and listed on the National Register of Historic Places, the Shield House has many dramatic features, including soaring Corinthian columns, wrap-around porches, coffer ceilings with beading, and a large foyer with enclosed columns outlining a grand central-flight staircase. The red-carpeted stairs twist up to a landing and then back to the front of the house. A large guest lounge is naturally lighted through glass doors that open only onto a balcony. Private phones, cable TV. Victorian street lights.

Hosts: Anita Green and Juanita G. McLamb
Rooms: 6 + bungalow (PB) $50-75
Continental Breakfast
Credit Cards: A, B, D
Notes: 2, 5, 7, 8, 10, 12

CLYDE

Windsong: A Mountain Inn

120 Ferguson Ridge, 28721
(704) 627-6111; (704) 627-8080 (FAX)

A romantic, contemporary, log inn high in the breath-taking Smoky Mountains. Intimate rooms are large and bright with high-beamed ceilings, pine log walls, and Mexican tile floors. Fireplaces, tubs for two, separate showers, and private decks or patios. Billiards, swimming, tennis, hiking, and llama trekking. Also, a new deluxe, two-bedroom guest house, tub for two, and woodstove.

Hosts: Donna and Gale Livengood
Rooms: 5 + two-bedroom guest house (PB) $80-120
Full Breakfast (Continental in Guest House)
Credit Cards: A, B
Notes: 2, 7 (over 8), 8, 9, 10, 12 (10%)

DURHAM

Arrowhead Inn

106 Mason Road, 27712
(919) 477-8430 (voice and FAX)

The 1775 Colonial manor house is filled with antiques, quilts, samplers, and warmth. Located on four rural acres, Arrowhead features fireplaces, original architectural details, air conditioning, and homemade breakfasts. A two-room log cabin is also available. Easy access to restaurants, Duke University, University of North Carolina-Chapel Hill, Raleigh, and historic sites, including Duke Homestead Tobacco Museum, Bennett Place. Near I-85.

Hosts: Jerry, Barbara, and Cathy Ryan
Rooms: 8 (6PB; 2SB) $70-140
Full Breakfast
Credit Cards: A, B, C, E
Notes: 2, 5, 7, 8, 9, 10, 12

EAGLE SPRINGS

The Inn at Eagle Springs

Samarland Road, P. O. Box 56, 27242
(919) 673-2722

Previously a private girls' school, the inn is

---

virtually unchanged but completely renovated. Located in the sandhills of North Carolina near Pinehurst, the golf capital of the world, it has access to more than 25 golf courses. One hour off Interstates 95, 85, 40, and 74. Can accommodate small conferences.

Hosts: Wes and Nora Smith
Rooms: 5 (PB) $50
Full Breakfast
Credit Cards: None
Notes: 2, 5, 7, 8, 9, 10, 12

EDENTON

The Lords Proprietors' Inn

300 North Broad Street, 27932
(919) 482-3641; (919) 482-2432 (FAX)

The New York Times called Edenton "The South's prettiest town." The quiet tree-lined streets of the extensive historic district are flanked by fine 18th- and 19th-century homes, three of which comprise The Lords Proprietors' Inn. The Inn's buildings include stately brick Victorian with wrap-around porch; a converted tobacco pack house, boasting Edenton's longest porch; an 1801 frame house, the oldest on the block; and a separate dining building set in the middle of the grounds. Guests enjoy spacious parlors with fireplaces, a library, and large, graciously appointed, guest rooms.

Hosts: Arch, Jane and Martha Edwards
Rooms: 20 (PB) $140-160
Full Breakfast and Dinner
Credit Cards: None
Notes: 2, 4, 5, 7, 8, 9, 10, 12

FRANKLIN

Lullwater Retreat

950 Old Highlands Road, 28734
(704) 524-6532

The 120-year-old farmhouse and cabins are located on a river and creek in a peaceful mountain cove. Hiking trails, river swimming, tubing, and other outdoor activities are on the premises. It serves as a retreat center for church groups and family reunions. Guests cook their own meals or visit nearby restaurants. Chapel, rocking chairs, wonderful views, indoor and outdoor games. Christian videos and reading materials are supplied.

Hosts: Robert and Virginia Smith
Rooms: 11 (5PB; 6SB) $32-46
Self-serve Breakfast
Credit Cards: None
Notes: 2, 7, 8, 9, 10, 11

GLENDALE SPRINGS

Mountain View Lodge and Cabins

Blue Ridge Pkwy. Mile Post 256, P.O. Box 90, 28629
(919) 982-2233

Secluded on the Blue Ridge Parkway, be pampered in our lodge with suites that offer fireplaces and beautiful views. Or enjoy a cabin with kitchenette. Families are welcome and play ground, picnic area, Jacuzzi, hiking, biking, skiing, canoeing are available. Breakfast and dinner are served in the lodge. Scenic and peaceful.

Hosts: George and Nellie Roth
Rooms: 12 (PB) $40-65
Expanded Continental Breakfast
Credit Cards: C
Notes: 2, 4 (limited weekends), 5, 7, 10, 11

NOTES: Credit cards accepted: A Master Card; B Visa; C American Express; D Discover Card; E Diners Club; F Other; 2 Personal checks accepted; 3 Lunch available; 4 Dinner available; 5 Open all

GLENVILLE

Mountain High

Big Ridge Road, 28736
(704) 743-3094

Enjoy mountain views from an elevation of 4,200 feet in a quiet area with no houses nearby. Hike on trails around a private lake. Open July to November.

Hosts: George and Margaret Carter
Rooms: 3 (2 PB; 1 SB) $40
Full Breakfast
Credit Cards: None
Notes: 2, 8, 9, 10

HENDERSONVILLE

Claddagh Inn at Hendersonville

755 North Main Street, 28792
(704) 697-7778; (800) 225-4700 reservations

The Claddagh Inn at Hendersonville is a recently renovated, meticulously clean bed and breakfast that is eclectically furnished with antiques and a variety of collectibles. The inn is located two blocks from the main shopping promenade of beautiful, historic downtown Hendersonville. The friendly, homelike atmosphere is complemented by a safe and secure feeling guests experience while at this lovely inn. The Claddaugh Inn is listed on the National Register of Historic Places.

Hosts: Vicki and Dennis Pacilio
Rooms: 15 (PB) $63-89
Full Breakfast
Credit Cards: A, B, C, D, E
Notes: 2, 5, 7, 8, 9, 10, 12

The Waverly Inn

783 N. Main St., 28792
(800) 537-8195; (704) 693-9193; (704) 692-1010 (FAX)

Listed on the National Register, this is the oldest inn in Hendersonville. Recently renovated, there is something for everyone including: claw-foot tubs, king and queen canopy beds, a suite, telephones, rocking chairs, sitting rooms, and all rooms have private baths. Enjoy our complimentary soft drinks and fresh baked goods. Walk to exceptional restaurants, antique stores, shopping. Biltmore Estate, Blue Ridge Parkway, Connemara nearby. Full country breakfast included in rates. Rated as one of 1993's top 10 bed and breakfasts in the USA by *INNovations*.

Hosts: John and Diane Shiery, Darla Olmstead
Rooms: 15 (PB) $79-99
Full Breakfast
Credit Cards: A, B, C, D
Notes: 2, 5, 7, 8, 9, 10, 12

HICKORY

The Hickory Bed and Breakfast

464 7th Street SW, 28602
(704) 324-0548; (704) 345-1112 (FAX)

1908, two-story, Georgian style house situated in an acre and a half property beautifully landscaped in a residential area. Rest comfortably in one of our four guest rooms decorated with antiques, collectibles, fresh flowers and a country flavor. Homemade iced tea and lemonade with something from the oven are served to our guests in the late afternoon. There is a parlor to sit in and chat, and a library to curl up in with a good book or to play a game. Our full, homemade breakfast is an experience long remembered.

Hosts: Suzanne and Bob Ellis
Rooms: 4 (PB) $55-65
Full Breakfast
Credit Cards: None
Notes: 2, 5, 8, 9, 10, 12

KILL DEVIL HILL

Cherokee Inn Bed and Breakfast

500 N. Virginia Dare Trail, 27948
(919) 441-6127; (800) 554-2764; (919) 441-1072 (FAX)

Our beach house, located at Nags Head Beach on the outer banks of North Carolina, is 600 feet from the ocean. Fine food, history, sports, and adventure galore. We welcome you for a restful, active, or romantic getaway. Enjoy the cypress walls, white ruffled curtains, and wrap-around porch.

Hosts: Bob and Kaye Combs
Rooms: 6 (PB) $55-85
Continental Breakfast
Credit Cards: A, B, C
Notes: 2, 8, 9, 10, 12

LAKE JUNALUSKA

Providence Lodge

207 Atkins Loop, 28745
(704) 456-6486, (704) 452-9588

Providence Lodge is located on the assembly grounds of the United Methodist Church and near the Great Smoky Mountain National Park, Biltmore Estate, and the Cherokee Indian Reservation. The lodge is old, rustic, clean, and comfortable. Meals are especially good—bountiful, delicious food served family style in our large dining room.

Hosts: Ben and Wilma Cato
Rooms: 16 (10PB; 6SB) $45-80
Full Breakfast
Credit Cards: None
Closed September 1-June 1
Notes: 2, 4, 7, 8, 9, 10, 11, 12

Sunset Inn

300 North Lakeshore Drive, 28745
(704) 456-6114; (800) 733-6114

A beautiful mountain inn with large porches, comfortable rooms, and a location that lends itself to sight-seeing, area attractions, or rest. We take pride in maintaining our reputation for excellent food, and we try to make our guests feel pampered. Located on the assembly grounds of the United Methodist Church which schedules daily programs in summer.

Hosts: Norma Wright and Wilma Cato
Rooms: 19 (15 PB; 4 SB) $60-80
Full Breakfast
Credit Cards: None
Notes: 2, 4, 8, 9, 10, 11, 12

LITTLE SWITZERLAND

The Switzerland Inn

P.O. Box 399, 28749
(800) 654-4026; (704) 765-2153

The Switzerland Inn is located directly on the Blue Ridge Parkway, between Asheville and Blowing Rock, near milepost 334 at the Little Switzerland exit. We offer fine accommodations, superb dining, and one of the most spectacular mountain views in the region. Enjoy beautiful Blue Ridge Mountains of North Carolina in a unique and relaxing atmosphere. Our property is ideal for family reunions, weddings, and retreats.

Hosts: The Jensen Family
Rooms: 55 (PB) $75-100
Full Breakfast
Credit Cards: A, B, C
Notes: 2, 3, 4, 7, 8, 9, 10, 12

MAGGIE VALLEY

Smokey Shadows Lodge
Ski Mt. Rd., 28751
(704) 926-0001

We are a "mom and pop" operated rustic mountain lodge accommodation which offers the very best in relaxed atmosphere, home cooked meals and services including everything from casual weekend seminars, informal to formal weddings and receptions, church group gatherings, club sponsored special meetings and weekends, and varieties of other functions. Accommodations include 12 private rooms with baths, a large group dorm type room, a large living room with log beamed ceilings and a large native stone fireplace, a homey dining room that seats 40 to 50 people, all of which are included in the main lodge building. We delight in being able to offer our down home type warmth and real mountain hospitality.

Hosts: Bud and Ginger
Rooms: 12 (PB) $45-60
Continental Breakfast
Credit Cards: A, B
Notes: 2, 3, 4, 5, 7, 8, 9, 10, 11, 12

MARSHALL

Marshall House Bed and Breakfast
5 Hill Street, P.O. Box 865, 28753
(704) 649-9205; (800) 562-9258

Built in 1903, the inn overlooks the peaceful town of Marshall and the waters of the French Broad River. This country inn listed on the National Historic Register is decorated with fancy chandeliers, antiques, and pictures. Four fireplaces, formal dining room, parlor, and upstairs TV/reading room. Storytelling about the house, the town, the people, and the history. Loving house pets, the toot of a choo-choo train, and good service make your visit a unique experience.

Hosts: Ruth and Jim Boylan
Rooms: 9 (2PB; 2SB) $38.50-70
Continental Breakfast (eggs on request)
Credit Cards: A, B, C, D, E
Notes: 3, 4, 5, 6, 7, 9, 10, 11, 12

MEBANE

Spring Run Bed and Breakfast
24 Spring Run, Lake Norman, 28115
(704) 664-6686

Enjoy a three-course breakfast at this bed and breakfast located on a 60 mile long lake. Inside are fine antiques and built-in stain glass. Each guest room has a private bath, free movie channel, ceiling fan, and air conditioning. Amenities include exercise room with card table and games, fireplace, jukebox, paddle boat, lake swimming, boat hook-up available, free beverage cart, early morning newspaper, and coffee. Pier fishing permitted, and golfing across the street. We are 22 minutes north of Charlotte. Three diamond rating from AAA.

Hostess: Mary Farley
Rooms: 17 (PB) $80
Full Breakfast
Credit Cards: None
Notes: 8, 9, 10

NAGS HEAD

First Colony Inn ®

6720 South Virginia Dare Trail, 27959
(919) 441-2343; (800) 368-9390 reservations

Enjoy Southern hospitality in our completely renovated historic inn on the National Register with a boardwalk directly to our private ocean beach. We are the only historic bed and breakfast inn on North Carolina's Outer Banks. The Wright Brothers Memorial, lighthouses, Fort Raleigh (site of the first English colony in the New World) are nearby, or just rock on our two stories of wrap-around verandas.

Hosts: The Lawrences
Rooms: 26 (PB) $60-125 winter; $90-150 spring/fall; $120-200 summer
Continental Breakfast
Credit Cards: A, B, D
Notes: 2 (30 days in advance), 5, 7, 8, 9, 10, 12

NEW BERN

The Aerie

509 Pollock Street, 28562
(919) 636-5553; (800) 849-5533

Just one block from the Tryon Palace in the heart of the historic district, the Aerie offers the closest accommodations to all of New Bern's historic attractions. The Victorian inn is furnished with antiques and reproductions, yet each of the seven individually decorated guest rooms has a modern private bathroom, telephone, and color television. Complimentary beverages are offered throughout your stay, and generous breakfasts await you each morning in the dining room.

Hosts: Gina and David Hawkins
Rooms: 7 (PB) $79-89
Full Breakfast
Credit Cards: A, B, C
Notes: 2, 5, 8, 10, 12

Harmony House Inn

215 Pollock Street, 28560
(919) 636-3810

Enjoy comfortable elegance in an unusually spacious Greek Revival inn built circa 1850 with final additions circa 1900. Guests enjoy a parlor, front porch with rocking chairs and swings, antiques and reproductions, plus a full breakfast in the dining room. Located in the historic district near Tryon Palace, shops, and restaurants. No smoking!

Hosts: A. E. and Diane Hansen
Rooms: 9 (PB) $85
Full Breakfast
Credit Cards: A, B, C
Notes: 2, 5, 8, 10, 12

The King's Arms Colonial Inn

212 Pollock St., 28260
(919) 638-4409; (800) 872-9306

Innkeepers Richard and Pat Gulley uphold the Southern hospitality with spacious rooms, private baths, comfortable decor, and afternoon treats. Enjoy breakfast of coffee, juice, home-baked breads, muffins, ham, biscuits, and fresh fruits served to your room with the morning paper. The King's Arms is located within walking distance of all major attractions in New Bern. Carriage rides available on weekends.

Hosts: Richard and Patricia Gulley
Rooms: 9 (PB) $85
Continental Plus Breakfast
Credit Cards: A, B, C
Notes: 2, 5, 7, 8, 9, 10, 12

The Lighthouse

315 George St., 28562
(919) 633-9488 (Voice and FAX)

Four doors from Tryon Palace, distinctive Italianate-style, Victorian, 1870's, award-winning cottage. Our Irish inn features authentic antique, eighteenth and nineteenth century, Irish and English furnishings. Complimentary tea biscuits. Cozy front porch with rockers. Garden has swing and picnic table. King, queen and/or twin beds with private baths. Breakfast features Irish menu with mid-1880's dishware, crystal, and flatware. Featured on CBS/ENC television.

Hosts: Art and Ruthann Moran-Salinger
Rooms: 2 (PB) $65-74
Full Breakfast
Credit Cards: A, B
Notes: 2, 5, 7, 8, 10, 12

The Lighthouse

New Berne House Inn

709 Broad Street, 28560
(919) 636-2250; (800) 842-7688

Just around the corner from Tryon Palace, New Berne House offers hospitality and comfortable English country decor in a lovingly restored brick Colonial. Seven guest rooms with private vintage baths, high antique beds piled with pillows and lace, air conditioning, phones, and optional TV are available. "Breakfasts that will be served in some small corner of heaven"—*Charlotte Observer*. Afternoon tea is served in the rose parlor or library.

Hosts: David and Gina Hawkins
Rooms: 7 (PB) $55-75
Full Breakfast
Credit Cards: A, B, C, D
Notes: 2, 5, 6 (by arrangement), 7, 8, 9, 10, 12

ORIENTAL

The Tar Heel Inn

205 Church Street, P. O. Box 176, 28571
(919) 249-1078

The Tar Heel Inn is over 100 years old and has been restored to capture the atmosphere of an English country inn. Guest rooms have four-poster or canopy king and queen beds. Patios and bicycles are for guest use. Five churches are within walking distance. Tennis, fishing, and golf are nearby. This quiet fishing village is known as the sailing capital of the Carolinas. Sailing cruises can be arranged, and there are great restaurants. Smoking on porch and patio only. Three-diamond AAA rating.

Hosts: David and Patti Nelson
Rooms: 8 (PB) $60-80
Full Breakfast
Credit Cards: A, B
Notes: 2, 7 (by arrangement), 8, 9, 10, 12

SPARTA

Turby-Villa

East Whitehead Street, Star Route 1, Box 48,
28675
(919) 372-8490

At an altitude of 3,000 feet, this contemporary two-story home is the centerpiece of a 20-acre farm located two miles from town. The house is surrounded by an acre of trees and manicured lawn with a lovely view of the Blue Ridge Mountains. Breakfast is served either on the enclosed porch with white wicker furnishings or in the more formal diningroom with Early American furnishings. Mrs. Mimi Turbiville takes justifiable pride in her attractive, well-maintained bed and breakfast.

Hostess: Maybelline Turbiville
Rooms: 3 (PB) $50
Full Breakfast
Credit Cards: None
Notes: 2, 5, 7, 8, 10

SPRUCE PINE

The Fairway Inn Bed and Breakfast

110 Henry Lane, 28777
(704) 765-4917

A lovely, inviting country home on an 18-hole golf course has a mountain view and five large bedrooms beautifully decorated with soft, appealing colors. Furnishings are eclectic. Your hosts offer tea and cheese in the afternoon. Morning coffee is provided for early risers, and a gourmet breakfast is served at your leisure. Open from April through December.

Hosts: Margaret and John Stevens
Rooms: 5 (PB) $50-70
Full Breakfast
Credit Cards: A, B
Notes: 2, 7, 8, 9, 10, 11

STATESVILLE

Aunt Mae's Bed and Breakfast

532 East Broad Street, 28677
(704) 873-9525

Once through the doors of our century-old home, you know you have stepped back in time. In her 90 years, Aunt Mae collected so many treasures that we cannot display them all at once. Hence, we have an ever-changing decor. Enjoy morning coffee left outside your door, a full breakfast, and homemade snacks. Convenient to I-40, I-77, historic downtown, and tennis courts. Golf and lake close by.

Hosts: Richard and Sue Rowland
Rooms: 2 (PB) $50
Full Breakfast
Credit Cards: A, B
Notes: 2, 5, 8, 9, 10, 12

Cedar Hill Farm Bed and Breakfast

Rt. 1, Box 492, 28677
(704) 873-4332; (800) 484-8457, Ext. 1254

An 1840 farmhouse and private cottage on a 32-acre sheep farm in the rolling hills of North Carolina. Antique furnishings, air conditioning, cable TV, and phones in rooms. After your full country breakfast, swim, play badminton, or relax in a porch rocker or hammock. For a busier day, visit two lovely towns with historic districts, Old Salem, or two larger cities in a

NOTES: Credit cards accepted: A Master Card; B Visa; C American Express; D Discover Card; E Diners Club; F Other; 2 Personal checks accepted; 3 Lunch available; 4 Dinner available; 5 Open all

45-mile radius. Convenient to restaurants, shopping, and three interstate highways.

Hosts: Brenda and Jim Vernon
Rooms: 2 (PB) $55-70
Full Breakfast
Credit Cards: A, B
Notes: 2, 5, 6 (limited), 7, 9, 10, 12

Cedar Hill Farm

Madelyn's Bed and Breakfast

514 Carroll Street, 28677
(704) 872-3973

Relax on one of the most peaceful streets in Statesville, the Crossroads of the Carolinas. When you arrive, fresh fruit, candy, and a plate of home-made cookies await. Take a short walk down tree-lined streets, and shop and eat in historic downtown Statesville. Truly a charming home where John and Madelyn will greet you with a smile. A full gourmet breakfast is served.

Hosts: John and Madelyn Hill
Rooms: 3 (PB) $55-65
Full Gourmet Breakfast
Credit Cards: A, B
Notes: 2, 5, 8, 9, 10, 12

TRYON

Fox Trot Inn

P. O. Box 1561, 800 Lynn Rd. (Rt. #108), 28782
(704) 859-9706

This lovingly restored residence, circa 1915, is situated on six wooded acres within the city limits. It is convenient to everything, yet secluded with a quietly elegant atmosphere. Full gourmet breakfast, afternoon refreshments, heated swimming pool, fully furnished guest house with two bedrooms, kitchen, living room, deck with mountain views. Two guest rooms have sitting rooms.

Hosts: Betty Daugherty and Mimi Colby
Rooms: 4 (PB) $60-110
Guest House: $450 weekly
Full Breakfast
Credit Cards: None
Notes: 2, 7 (in guest house), 8, 9, 10

WAYNESVILLE

The Lodge at the Biodome

184 Shelton Cove Road, 28786
(704) 926-0273

The lodge is an eight-bedroom, four-bath bed and breakfast in the North Carolina biodome eco village. The village has eight homes, a Bunkminster Fuller geodesic dome as a greenhouse, organic gardens, solar and hydro systems, and many other aspects of a self-sufficient village. Rooms have twin, queen, or king beds. Simple but charming.

Host: Hans Keller
Rooms: 8 (SB) $40
Continental Breakfast
Credit Cards: A, B, C
Notes: 4, 5, 6, 7, 8, 9, 10, 11

year; 6 Pets welcome; 7 Children welcome; 8 Tennis nearby; 9 Swimming nearby; 10 Golf nearby; 11 Skiing nearby; 12 May be booked through travel agent

Palmer House Bed and Breakfast

108 Pigeon Street, 28786
(704) 456-7521

Built in the 1880's, the Palmer House is the last of Waynesville's once numerous 19th-century hotels. Located less than one block from Main Street, the Palmer House is also near the Blue Ridge Parkway, the Great Smoky Mountains, Cherokee, and Biltmore Estate. Guests are entitled to a 10% discount off any purchase at the Palmer House Bookshop on Main Street.

Hosts: Jeff Minick and Kris Gillet
Rooms: 7 (PB) $50
Full Breakfast
Credit Cards: A, B, C, D
Notes: 2, 5, 7

WILSON

Miss Betty's Bed and Breakfast Inn

600 West Nash Street, 27893-3045
(919) 243-4447; (800) 258-2058 reservations

Selected as one of the best places to stay in the South, Miss Betty's is located in a gracious setting in the downtown historic section, and comprised of three beautifully restored homes; the National Registered Davis-Whitehead-Harriss House (circa 1858) and the adjacent Riley House (circa 1900), and Green House (circa 1911) is recaptured elegance and style of days gone by. Quiet Victorian charm abounds in an atmosphere of all modern-day conveniences. Guests can browse for antiques in the Inn or visit any of the numerous antique shops that have given Wilson the title "Antique Capital of North Carolina." A quiet eastern North Carolina town also known for its famous barbeque. Wilson, with its four beautiful golf courses and numerous tennis courts, is ideally located midway between Maine and Florida along the main North-South route, I-95.

Hosts: Betty and Fred Spitz
Rooms: 12 (PB) $60-75
Full Breakfast
Credit Cards: A, B, C, D, E
Notes: 2, 5, 8, 9, 10

Miss Betty's B & B Inn

WINSTON-SALEM

Henry F. Shaffner House

150 South Marshall St., 27101
(919) 777-0052; (919) 722-4748 (FAX)

Built in 1907, the Henry F. Shaffner House features eight individually decorated guest rooms complete with cable TV, phones, alarm clocks, and private baths. Conveniently located off Business I-40 two blocks north of historic Old Salem. The

---

NOTES: Credit cards accepted: A Master Card; B Visa; C American Express; D Discover Card; E Diners Club; F Other; 2 Personal checks accepted; 3 Lunch available; 4 Dinner available; 5 Open all

Victorian Tudor style mansion has been converted into the Triad's premiere bed and breakfast inn. Guests enjoy complimentary health club memberships and outdoor hot tub. Two bridal suites are available with whirlpool baths.

Host: David W.F. Regnery
Rooms: 8 (PB) $95-175
Continental Plus Breakfast
Credit Cards: A, B, C
Notes: 2, 5, 7, 8, 9, 10, 12

Lady Anne's Victorian Bed and Breakfast

612 Summit St., 27101
(919) 724-1074

Warm, Southern hospitality surrounds you in this 1890 Victorian home, listed on the National Register of Historic Places. An aura of romance touches each suite or room, all individually decorated with period antiques, treasures, and modern luxuries. Some rooms have two-person whirlpools, cable, HBO, stereo, telephone, coffee, refrigerator, private entrances, and balconies. An evening dessert and full breakfast are served. Lady Anne's is ideally located near downtown attractions, performances, restaurants, shops, and Old Salem Historic Village.

Hostess: Shelley Kirley
Rooms: 4 (PB) $55-110
Full Breakfast
Credit Cards: A, B, C
Notes: 5 8, 10, 12

North Dakota

MCCLUSKY

Midstate Bed and Breakfast

Route 3, Box 28, 58463
(701) 363-2520

In the center of North Dakota, this country home built in 1980 operates under the banner of "The beauty of the house is order, the blessing of the house is contentment, and the glory of the house is hospitality." The guest entrance opens the way to a complete and private lower level with your bedroom, bath, large TV lounge with fireplace, and kitchenette. Three upstairs bedrooms have a bath. Breakfast in your choice of locations: your room, formal dining room, the plant-filled atrium, or on the patio. Very easy to locate: mile marker 232 on ND200. In an area of great hunting of deer, water fowl, and upland game. Our guests are allowed hunting privileges on over 4000 acres. Special rates and provisions for hunting parties. Air conditioned. Children welcome.

Hosts: Allen and Grace Faul
Rooms: 4 (1PB; 3SB) $25-30
Full Breakfast
Credit Cards: None
Notes: 2, 3, 4, 5, 6, 7, 8, 9

NOTES: Credit cards accepted: A Master Card; B Visa; C American Express; D Discover Card; E Diners Club; F Other; 2 Personal checks accepted; 3 Lunch available; 4 Dinner available; 5 Open all

Ohio

BLUE ROCK

McNutt Farm II / Outdoorsman Lodge

6120 Cutler Lake Road, 43720
(614) 674-4555

Country bed and breakfast for overnight travelers in rustic quarters on a working farm in the quiet of the Blue Rock hill country. Only 11 miles from I-70, 35 miles from I-77, and 60 miles from I-71. B&B guests enjoy their own private kitchen, living room with fireplace or woodburner, private bath, porch with swing, and a beautiful view of forests and pastured livestock. Choose either the log cabin or the carriage house. For those who want more than an overnight stay, please ask about our log cabin by the week, or weekend. A cellar-house cabin is available, although it is somewhat primitive. Sleep to the sounds of the whippoorwills and tree frogs. Awake to the ever-crowing rooster, the wild turkey calling, and sometimes the bleating of a new born fawn can be heard. We welcome you by reservation and deposit.

Hosts: Don R. and Patty L. McNutt
Rooms: 2 suites (PB) $30-100
Continental Breakfast
Credit Cards: A, B
Notes: 2, 5, 6 (prearranged), 7 (prearranged), 9, 10

CIRCLEVILLE

Castle Inn B & B

610 S. Court St., 43113
(614) 477-3986

A medieval "castle" in the heart of Ohio features towers, battlements, arches, flying buttresses, stained glass, and a suit of armor named Sir Reginald. Furnished in Victorian antiques, private baths, bedroom fireplaces; full breakfast is served in museum-quality dining room overlooking the walled Shakespeare garden, featuring plants mentioned in Shakespeare's plays. Guests enjoy playing the antique grand piano and perusing the collection of "castle" books, games, and puzzles. Books and magazines available on a wide variety of subjects.

Hosts: Sue and Jim Maxwell
Rooms: 4 (PB) $55-85
Full Breakfast
Credit Cards: A, B
Notes: 2, 5, 7 (over 6), 8, 9, 10, 12

COSHOCTON

1890 Bed and Breakfast

663 N. Whitewoman St., Roscoe Village, 43812
(614) 622-1890

Spend a romantic getaway in a Victorian

---

year; 6 Pets welcome; 7 Children welcome; 8 Tennis nearby; 9 Swimming nearby; 10 Golf nearby;
11 Skiing nearby; 12 May be booked through travel agent

Bed and Breakfast nestled in the heart of historic Roscoe Village. The home is furnished with antiques and features an exquisite touch of hand sponge-painted walls. Restaurants, museums, and exclusive shops are within walking distance of the B&B. Just one and a half hours east of Columbus and two and a half hours south of Cleveland.

Hosts: Curt and Debbi Crouso
Rooms: 4 (PB) $65-75
Expanded Continental
Credit Cards: A, B, C, D
Notes: 2, 5, 9, 10, 12

EAST FULTONHAM

Hill View Acres Bed and Breakfast

7320 Old Town Road, 43735
(614) 849-2728

Old World hospitality and comfort await each of our guests. During your visit, wander over the 21 acres, relax on the deck or patio, use the pool or year-round spa, or cuddle up by the fireplace in the cooler months. A hearty, country breakfast with homemade breads, jams, and jellies is served. We are located ten miles southwest of Zanesville.

Hosts: Jim and Dawn Graham
Rooms: 2 (SB) $37.30-42.60 (Prices include tax)
Full Breakfast weekends; Continental on weekdays.
Credit Cards: A, B
Notes: 2, 3, 4 (by arrangement), 5, 7, 9, 10

FRESNO

Valley View Inn

32327 SR 643 (2.5 miles from New Bedford), 43824
(216) 897-3232

The panoramic view from the back of the Inn is nothing short of breath-taking and is enhanced only by the changing seasons. Guests can enjoy the coziness of the fireplace in the livingroom or relax in the family room. A player piano, checkers, ping pong table, chess, or just comfortable Lazy Boy chair await you. No TV's to interrupt the serenity that abounds as one enjoys gazing at the surrounding fields and farms, woods and wildlife. The Inn is located between Roscoe Village and Sugarcreek and within minutes from all Amish shopping places. We're in the heart of Amish country.

Hosts: Dan and Nancy Lembke
Rooms: 10 (PB) $70-105
Full Breakfast (Continental on Sunday)
Credit Cards: A, B
Notes: 2, 5, 10

GENEVA-ON-THE-LAKE

Otto Court Bed and Breakfast

5653 Lake Road, 44041
(216) 466-8668

Otto Court Bed and Breakfast is a family-run business situated on two acres of lakefront property. There are eight cottages and a 19-room hotel overlooking Lake Erie. Besides a small game room, there is a horseshoe pit, a volleyball court, picnic tables, and plenty of beach with area for a bonfire. Within walking distance is the Geneva State Park and Marina. The Old Firehouse winery, Geneva-on-the-Lake Amusement Center, and the Jennie Munger Museum are nearby.

Hosts: Joyce Otto and Family
Rooms: 12 (8PB; 4SB) $46.50-50
Full Breakfast
Credit Cards: A, B, F
Notes: 2, 4, 5, 7, 9, 10, 12

KELLEY'S ISLAND

Zettlers' Lakefront Bed and Breakfast

207 South Shore Drive, Box 747, 43438
(419) 746-2315

We are located on the lake within walking distance to both ferries and 10 houses from downtown. Zettlers' Lakefront is a turn-of-the-century home with a lovely front porch and a magnificent view of Lake Erie. A full breakfast is served in the front parlor overlooking the lake.

Hosts: Nora and Toby Zettler
Rooms: 4 (SB) $75
Full Breakfast
Credit Cards: A, B
Notes: 2, 9, 12

Zettlers' Lakefront Bed and Breakfast

LAURELVILLE

Hocking House B & B

18597 Laurel Street, 43135
(800) 477-1541

A large turn-of-the-century house tucked into a friendly small village on the edge of Hocking Hills. Guest rooms offer private baths and are furnished in "country Victorian" with antiques and handcrafted pieces, many made locally. Quilts—old, new, and some made by our Amish neighbors—are featured in every room. Two good restaurants are within one block. A new herb garden is being established. Guests are near all Hocking Hills attractions and the studios and shops of many artisans. You can also visit our Amish neighbors for quilts, rugs, baskets, and produce. Spectacular caves, waterfalls, scenery nearby.

Hosts: Max and Evelyn England, Jim and Sue Maxwell
Rooms: 4 (PB) $45-65 (seasonal discount)
Full Breakfast
Credit Cards: A, B
Notes: 2, 5, 12

LEXINGTON

The White Fence Inn

8842 Denman Road, 44904
(419) 884-2356; (800) 628-5793

The White Fence Inn is a beautiful country retreat situated among 73 acres. The 105-year-old farmhouse is decorated in a warm, country style. Common rooms include a large dining room with French doors, a parlor with fireplace and piano, a spacious sitting room with fireplace and TV. Breakfast is served indoors or out-

year; 6 Pets welcome; 7 Children welcome; 8 Tennis nearby; 9 Swimming nearby; 10 Golf nearby; 11 Skiing nearby; 12 May be booked through travel agent

doors. Guest rooms are decorated in individual themes—primitive, baskets and bottles, Victorian, Southwest, Amish, and country. One room has a fireplace and cathedral ceiling.

Hosts: Bill and Ellen Hiser
Rooms: 6 (4PB; 2SB) $51-95
Full Breakfast
Credit Cards: None
Notes: 2, 5, 6, 7, 8, 10, 11

MARION

Olde Towne Manor

245 St. James St., 43302
(614) 382-2402

Elegant stone home nestles on a beautiful acre of land on a quiet street in Marion's historic district. Enjoy a quiet setting in the gazebo or the soothing sauna, or relax reading one of the more than 1,000 books available in the library. A pool table is also available for your enjoyment. A leisurely stroll will take you to the home of President Warren G. Harding and the Harding Memorial. Awarded the 1990 Marion's Beautifications Most Attractive Building.

Hostess: Mary Louisa Rimbach
Rooms: 4 (PB) $55-65
Full Breakfast
Credit Cards: A, B
Notes: 2, 5, 8, 9, 10

MARTINS FERRY

Mulberry Inn B & B

53 North 4th Street, 43935
(614) 633-6058

Victorian frame home built in 1868 by Dr. Ong, the thirteen-room home was also used as his office. In 1911 Dr. Blackford bought the house and also used three rooms for his practice. The Probsts purchased the home in 1971. It became a bed and breakfast in 1987. The guest rooms are done in different periods. The Roosevelt Room (1930's), Victorian, Country, Lucinda have twin beds. All others have double beds. Guests have a beautiful parlor in which to relax and a private dining room. There is a wood-burning fireplace for cold winter nights in the parlor. Homemade quilts, up-down lights, pocket doors, antiques, 3 stairways. 5 minutes from Wheeling, WV, 15 minutes from Olgebay Park, famous for its Festival of Lights November thru February.

Hosts: Charles and Shirley Probst
Rooms: 4 (2PB; 2SB) $45
Full Breakfast
Credit Cards: A, B, D
Notes: 2, 5, 7 (with restrictions), 8, 9, 10, 11, 12

MILLERSBURG

Indiantree Farm Bed and Breakfast

5488 S.R. 515, 44654
(216) 893-2497

Peaceful lodging in guest house on picturesque hilltop farm in the heart of Amish country, a mile from Walnut Creek. Large front porch, farming with horses, hiking trails. Apartments, with kitchen and bath, for the price of a room. An oasis where time slows and the mood is conversation, not television.

Host: Larry Miller
Rooms: 3 (PB) $50-60
Continental Breakfast
Credit Cards: None
Notes: None

NOTES: Credit cards accepted: A Master Card; B Visa; C American Express; D Discover Card; E Diners Club; F Other; 2 Personal checks accepted; 3 Lunch available; 4 Dinner available; 5 Open all

OLD WASHINGTON

Zane Trace Bed and Breakfast

225 Old National Rd, P.O. Box 115, 43768
(614) 489-5970

Brick Victorian built in 1859. Spacious rooms, high ceilings, quiet, comfortable, with in-ground pool available. Home-like environment in a small historical village five miles from Salt Fork State Park, one mile from exit 186 of I-70. Seven miles to Cambridge, Ohio, and I-77 north and south.

Hosts: Ruth and Max Wilson
Rooms: 3 plus suite (1PB; 3SB) $40-45
Continental Breakfast
Credit Cards: None
Notes: 2, 5, 8, 9, 10, 12

OXFORD

The Duck Pond

6391 Morning Sun Rd., S.R. 732 N, 45056
(513) 523-8914

The Duck Pond is situated three miles north of Miami University and uptown Oxford, and two miles south of Hueston Woods State Park, which has an 18-hole golf course, nature trails, boating, swimming, and fishing. Antiquing is just 15 miles away. Come and enjoy the quaintness that only a bed and breakfast can offer. Be our guest and enjoy our famous Hawaiian French Toast. Reservations are required, so please call in advance.

Hosts: Don and Toni Kohlstedt
Rooms: 4 (1PB; 3SB) $50-65
Full Country Breakfast
Credit Cards: None
Notes: 2, 5, 7 (over 12), 8, 9, 10

The Duck Pond

ST. CLAIRSVILLE

My Father's House

173 South Marietta St., 43950
(614) 695-5440

My Father's House Bed and Breakfast combines the old with the new in decor and hospitality. Antique and modern furnishings combine to create a quaint yet comfortable overnight travel experience. Guests enjoy air conditioned queen size bedrooms and private bathrooms. The living room features a romantic open fireplace, while the parlor affords guests the opportunity to relax and watch television. Located just one-half mile from I-70 at the S.R. 9 exit (#216) in St. Clairsville proper, our guests can enjoy a small town stay with the convenience of interstate travel. Fifteen minutes from Wheeling, West Virginia.

Hosts: Mark and Polly Loy
Rooms: 3 (PB) $50-55
Continental Plus Breakfast
Credit Cards: A, B
Notes: 2, 5, 7, 8, 9, 10

My Father's House

year; 6 Pets welcome; 7 Children welcome; 8 Tennis nearby; 9 Swimming nearby; 10 Golf nearby; 11 Skiing nearby; 12 May be booked through travel agent

TIPP CITY

The Willow Tree Inn

1900 West State Route 571, 45371
(513) 667-2957

This restored, pre-Civil War (1830), Federal manor home has a pond and combination springhouse and smokehouse. The original 1830 barn is also on the premises. Four working fireplaces, porches on which to swing and relax, and TV and air conditioning in all rooms; all but one room are suites. Easily located off Exit 68W from N75, just minutes north of Dayton.

Hosts: Tom and Peggy Nordquist
Rooms: 4 (1PB; 3SB) $43-68
Full Breakfast
Credit Cards: A, B
Notes: 1, 7 (over 8) , 8, 9, 10

The Willow Tree Inn

TROY

Allen Villa Bed and Breakfast

434 S. Market Street, 45373
(513) 335-1181

Located 1.5 miles east of I-75 (exit 73) and 15 minutes north of Dayton Airport. Self-serve snack bar, central air conditioning, in-room private bath. Victorian

antiques, TV, telephone, queen, king beds. Four blocks from historic downtown Troy, a pleasant walk to restaurants, shopping, and points of interest.

Hosts: Robert and June Smith
Rooms: 4 (PB) $50-75
Full Breakfast
Credit Cards: A, B, C
Notes: 2, 5, 8, 9, 10, 11

URBANA

At Home in Urbana

301 Scioto St., 43078
(800) 800-0970; (513) 652-4400 (FAX)

Restored 1842 home in historic district. Furnished in Victorian period pieces and family antiques. Two blocks away from downtown shops and restaurants. At the center of the Simon Kenton Historic Corridor. Non-smoking guests only.

Hosts: Grant and Shirley Ingersoll
Rooms: 3 and 1 two-room suite (PB) $50-60
Full Breakfast
Credit Cards: A, B, C, D
Notes: 2, 4, 5, 10, 11

WALNUT CREEK

Troyer's Country View Bed and Breakfast

P.O. Box 91, 4859 Olde Pump St., 44687
(216) 893-3284

The house is over 100 years old, newly remodeled into self-contained suites, each with private bath, country decor, cable TV, air conditioning. Breakfast stocked in your private kitchenette (with oak table and chairs in kitchen area). Couch or bentwood rockers in sitting area. Private deck entrances from beautiful viewing deck, fenced animals to watch in the summer. Honeymoon and anniversary suite has heart-shaped jacuzzi, microwave, and other extras, plus all the amenities mentioned above. Comfortable Amish crafted beds. AAA approved.

Hosts: Owen and Sue Troyer
Rooms: 4 (PB) $65 (slightly less in winter)
Full Self-Serve Breakfast
Credit Cards: A, B
Notes: 2(from Ohio), 5, 7(limited), 8, 9, 10

WAVERLY

Governor's Lodge
171 Gregg Road, 45690
(614) 947-2266

Governor's Lodge is a place like no other. Imagine a beautiful, shimmering lake and an iridescent sunset. A quiet calm in the friendly atmosphere of an eight-room bed and breakfast open all year and situated on a peninsula in Lake White. Every room has a magnificent view. An affiliate of Bristol Village Retirement Community, we offer a meeting room and group rates for gatherings using the whole lodge.

Hosts: David and Jeannie James
Rooms: 8 (PB) $37-62
Expanded Continental Breakfast
Credit Cards: A, B
Notes: 2, 7, 9, 11

AMISH COUNTRY

Oklahoma

ALINE

Heritage Manor

RR 3, Box 33, 73716
(405) 463-2563

Heritage Manor is a country getaway on 80 acres that was settled in the Land Run of 1893 in northwest Oklahoma. Two pre-statehood homes have been joined together and restored by innkeepers using Victorian theme. Beautiful sunrises, sunsets, and stargazing from rooftop deck and relaxing in the hot tub or reading a book from the 5000-volume library. Ostriches, donkeys, and Scotch Highland cattle roam a fenced area. Close to Salenite Crystal digging area and several other attractions.

Hosts: A.J. and Carolyn Rexroat
Rooms: 4 (SB) $50+tax
Full Breakfast
Credit Cards: None
Notes: 2, 4 (by reservation), 5, 7

EDMOND

The Arcadian Inn B & B

328 East First, 73034
(405) 348-6347; (800) 299-6347

With angels watching over you, you are ministered peace and relaxation. The Arcadian Inn is a step back in time to the era of Christian love, and hospitality, and family values. The historical home of Dr. Ruhl, the inn has five luxurious Victorian guest rooms with tubs, and fireplaces, canopy beds, and sunrooms. Sumptuous homemade breakfast served in the sunny dining room beneath cherub paintings. Perfect for romantic getaways, business travelers, or old fashioned family gatherings. Jacuzzi and outdoor spa available.

Hostess: Martha Hall
Rooms: 5 (PB) $65-120
Full Breakfast
Credit Cards: A, B, C
Notes: 2, 4 (by reservation), 5, 8, 9, 10

The Arcadian Inn

OKLAHOMA CITY

The Grandison Bed and Breakfast

1841 N.W. 15th, 73106
(405) 521-0011

This three-story country Victorian sits on a large double lot with beautifully landscaped gardens, trees taller than the house, and a gazebo. Built in 1912, the home has all the original brass and crystal chandeliers and stained glass windows. It is furnished with antiques from the turn-of-the-century throughout. Just 10 minutes from Myriad Gardens and Convention Center, State Fair grounds, Remington Park Raceway, Oklahoma City Zoo, The National Cowboy Hall of Fame, and many wonderful restaurants and shopping facilities.

Hostess: Claudia Wright
Rooms: 5 (PB) $45-90
Full Breakfast
Credit Cards: A, B, C, D
Notes: 2, 3, 4, 5, 6 (by reservation), 7 (by reservation)

year; 6 Pets welcome; 7 Children welcome; 8 Tennis nearby; 9 Swimming nearby; 10 Golf nearby; 11 Skiing nearby; 12 May be booked through travel agent

Oregon

ASHLAND

Cowslip's Belle B & B

159 N. Main St., 97520
(503) 488-2901; (800) 888-6819

Teddy bears and chocolate truffles, roses, antiques, cozy down comforters, and scrumptious breakfasts. Just three blocks to restaurants, shops, and theaters. Nestled in Ashland's historic district, this beautiful 1913 Craftsman bungalow and carriage house was voted one of the top 50 bed and breakfasts in the U.S. by *Inn Times*.

Hosts: Jon and Carmen Reinhardt
Rooms: 4 (PB) $60-110
Full Breakfast
Credit Cards: A, B
Notes: 2, 5, 8, 9, 10, 11, 12

The Redwing Bed and Breakfast

115 N. Main Street, 97520
(503) 482-1807

The Redwing, nestled in Ashland's charming historic district, is a 1911 Craftsman-style home with its original lighting fixtures, beautiful wood, and comfortable decor. Each of our inviting guest rooms enjoys its own distinctive intimacy, queen-size beds, and private bath. We are located one city block from the Shakespeare Festival, Lithia Park, restaurants, and gift shops. In addition, downhill and cross-country skiing, river rafting, and fishing are nearby. Full breakfasts are offered.

Hosts: Mike and Judi Cook
Rooms: 3 (PB) $70-95
Full Breakfast
Credit Cards: None
Notes: 2, 5, 10, 11

ASTORIA

Columbia River Inn Bed and Breakfast

1681 Franklin Ave., 97103
(503) 325-5044

Columbia River Inn is an 1870 Victorian, charming in every way. Come enjoy the new Stairway to the Stars and the unique gardens—lots of flowers. Home is where the heart is, and at Columbia River Inn you'll discover memories really last forever. Two blocks from the mighty Columbia River. My specialty is hospitality.

Hostess: Karen N. Nelson
Rooms: 5 (PB) $70-80
Full Breakfast
Cerdit Cards: A, B
Notes: 2, 5, 7, 10

NOTES: Credit cards accepted: A Master Card; B Visa; C American Express; D Discover Card; E Diners Club; F Other; 2 Personal checks accepted; 3 Lunch available; 4 Dinner available; 5 Open all

Columbia River Inn

CLOVERDALE

Sandlake Country Inn

8505 Galloway Road, 97112
(503) 965-6745

This 1894 farmhouse on the Oregon historic register is the perfect hideaway for making marriage memories. The honeymoon suite offers a four-room sanctuary with private luxury bath, deck, view of Cape Lookout, parlor, and vintage movies. One mile from the beach; private garden spa; bikes and picnic lunches available; forest setting. Honeymoon cottage. Closed-caption TV. Wheelchair accessible.

Hosts: Margo and Charles Underwood
Rooms: 4 (PB) $65-100
Full Breakfast
Credit Cards: A, B
Notes: 2, 3, 4, 5, 12

COTTAGE GROVE

Historic Lea House Inn

433 Pacific Highway, 99 South, 97424
(503) 942-5686

Step back in time to the warmth and charm of this 100-year-old Victorian home.

Located in the historic mining town of Cottage Grove. Also known as the covered bridge capital of Oregon. There are two beautiful lakes and many streams and rivers for fishing, swimming, and other water sports. Located within walking distance to downtown shopping, with many antique stores. For a minimal charge, we will provide a picnic basket lunch and bicycle for that ride to nearby lake, river, or stream. A hearty breakfast is served between 7:30 am and 9:30 am.

Hosts: Michelle and Keith Lawhorn
Rooms: 3 (1PB; 2SB) 55-65
Full Breakfast
Credit Cards: A, B
Notes: 2, 3, 6, 7, 9, 10, 11

Historic Lea House Inn

ELMIRA

McGillivray's Log Home Bed and Breakfast

88680 Evers Road, 97437
(503) 935-3564

Fourteen miles west of Eugene, on the way to the coast, you will find the best of yesterday and the comforts of today. King beds, air-conditioning, and quiet. Old-fashioned breakfasts are usually prepared on an antique, wood-burning cookstove.

year; 6 Pets welcome; 7 Children welcome; 8 Tennis nearby; 9 Swimming nearby; 10 Golf nearby;
11 Skiing nearby; 12 May be booked through travel agent

This built-from-scratch 1982 log home is near Fern Ridge.

Hostess: Evelyn R. McGillivray
Rooms: 2 (PB) $50-70
Full Breakfast
Credit Cards: A, B
Notes: 2, 5

EUGENE

Camille's Bed and Breakfast

3277 Onyx Place, 97405
(503) 344-9576; (503) 484-3138 (FAX)

Camille's Bed and Breakfast is a 60's contemporary home in a quiet, woodsy neighborhood furnished with American country antiques. Rooms offer wonderfully comfortable queen beds, work space, and reading lamps. Guest sitting room with phone and TV. Fax available. Ample breakfast. Laundry facilities. Located just south of the University of Oregon, downtown is minutes away. Bus lines, bike paths, and park with major jogging trail nearby. Excellent restaurant within walking distance. One hour drive to Oregon coast.

Hosts: Bill and Camille Kievith
Rooms: 2 (1PB; 2SB) $55-70
Full Breakfast
Credit Cards: None
Notes: 2, 5, 7, 8, 9, 10

GARIBALDI

Gracy Manor

119 E. Driftwood, P.O. Box 220, 97118
(503) 322-3369

Gracy Manor is a quiet, smoke-free, homey, cheery atmosphere facing hillsides and view of the bay. Three rooms are immaculate, beautifully decorated in ruffled curtains, matching spreads and shams, cushiony carpeting throughout. All have comfortable brass queen size beds. Color TV in each room. Guests share bathroom and are served a full breakfast.

Hostess: Dorothy Gracy
Rooms: 3 (SB) $45-65
Full Breakfast
Credit Cards: None
Notes: 2, 5, 10, 12

GOVERNMENT CAMP

Falcon's Crest Inn

P.O. Box 185, 87287
Government Camp Loop Highway, 97028
(503) 272-3403; (800) 624-7384

Falcon's Crest Inn is a beautiful mountain lodge/chalet-style house, architecturally designed to fit into the quiet natural forest and majestic setting of the Cascades. Conveniently located at the intersection of Highway 26 and The Government Camp Loop Highway, it is within walking distance to Ski Bowl, a year-round playground featuring downhill skiing in the winter and the Alpine Slide in the summer! The Inn has five suites, all with private baths. Each guest room is individually decorated with interesting and unique collectibles and views of mountains and forest. Telephones are available for guest use in each suite.

Hosts: BJ and Melody Johnson
Rooms: 5 (PB) $85-139
Full Breakfast
Credit Cards: A, B, C, D
Notes: 2, 4, 5, 9, 10, 11, 12

NOTES: Credit cards accepted: A Master Card; B Visa; C American Express; D Discover Card; E Diners Club; F Other; 2 Personal checks accepted; 3 Lunch available; 4 Dinner available; 5 Open all

GRANTS PASS

Home Farm Bed and Breakfast

157 Square Creek Rd., 97527
(503) 582-0980

Our 1944 farmhouse bed and breakfast with comfy, country decor invites you to make your stay with us—dozing in our country air, feasting on our hearty breakfasts, playing checkers, pitching horseshoes! There are two lovely guest rooms in the main house and two guest suites in the "bunk house"—one with a western motif (wheelchair accessible) and one with an Americana flavor. All rooms are furnished with queen or king beds, and all have private baths.

Hosts: Bill and Cheri Murray
Rooms: 4 (PB) $50-70
Full Breakfast
Credit Cards: None
Notes: 2, 5, 7 (limited), 9, 10

Martha's Bed and Breakfast Inn

764 Northwest Fourth Street, 97526
(503) 476-4330

Martha's Inn is "a home away from home." A Victorian farmhouse with a large, old-fashioned front porch, furnished with wicker antiques. Located in the historic district. Martha's Inn is five minutes from I-5. Ideal for overnight travelers from Seattle to San Francisco. Close to restaurants. One and one-half hours to Crater Lake or the Oregon coast. Private baths, queen beds, herb garden and English cutting garden. Healthy breakfasts are featured. TV, air conditioning. In the heart of the Rogue River Valley.

Hosts: Evelyn and Glenn Hawkins
Rooms: 3 (PB) $55-75
Full Breakfast
Credit Cards: A, B, D
Notes: 2, 5, 7, 10, 12

Martha's Bed and Breakfast

HEREFORD

Fort Reading Bed and Breakfast

HCR 86, Box 140, 97837
(503) 446-3478

A working cattle ranch located 40 miles southwest of Baker City, in the Burnt River Valley where history abounds. While you're with us, enjoy a stroll around the ranch, the comfort of your own two-bedroom cottage, and a ranch-style breakfast served in the ranch house breakfast room. Fishing and hunting in nearby streams and forests are just a few activities that can be enjoyed. No smoking.

Hosts: Daryl and Barbara Hawes
Rooms: 2 (SB) $40-75
Full Breakfast
Credit Cards: None
Notes: 2, 3, 4 (by arrangement), 6, 7

year; 6 Pets welcome; 7 Children welcome; 8 Tennis nearby; 9 Swimming nearby; 10 Golf nearby; 11 Skiing nearby; 12 May be booked through travel agent

LAGRANDE

The Inn at LaGrande (Stang Manor)

1612 Walnut, 97850
(503) 963-2400 (Voice and FAX)

The Inn is an impressive 1922 lumber baron's Georgian Colonial mansion. The spacious, 10,000-square-foot structure features extraordinary architectural detail, including a basement ballroom and stage. The Manor sits on spacious grounds with a rose garden and magnificent trees. Guest rooms have queen beds and private baths. One room has balcony overlooking the rose garden—the suite features a sitting room with fireplace. Full breakfast in the formal dining room sparkles with silver, crystal, and candles.

Hosts: Marjorie and Pat McClure
Rooms: 4 (PB) $70-90 (includes tax)
Full Breakfast
Credit Cards: A, B
Notes: 2, 5, 10, 11, 12

Pitcher Inn Bed and Breakfast

608 N. Avenue, 97850
(503) 963-9152

The hosts have redecorated their 1925 home to maintain its original flavor. The homey dining room with oak floor and table welcomes you for a full breakfast. The unique, open staircase will lead you to your room. Each of four guest rooms has a touch of romance featuring a different color theme with accents of roses, bows, and pitchers. The honeymoon suite is a spacious room of lace and roses done in pink and black.

Hosts: Carl and Deanna Pitcher
Rooms: 4 (1PB; 3S2B) $55-95
Full Breakfast
Credit Cards: A, B
Closed January 2-15
Notes: 2, 8, 10, 11, 12

LINCOLN CITY

Brey House Ocean View Bed and Breakfast Inn

3725 N.W. Keel, 97367
(503) 994-7123

The ocean awaits you just across the street. Enjoy whale-watching, storm-watching, or just beach-combing. We are conveniently located a short walking distance away from local restaurants and retail shops. Four beautiful rooms to choose from, all private baths, queen beds. Flannel sheets and electric blankets in all rooms. Enjoy Milt and Shirley's talked-about breakfast. Three-story, Cape Cod-style house.

Hosts: Milt and Shirley Brey
Rooms: 4 (PB) $65-85
Full Breakfast
Credit Cards: A, B, D
Notes: 2, 5, 9, 10, 12

NEWBERG

Secluded Bed and Breakfast

19719 Northeast Williamson Road, 97132
(503) 538-2635

This secluded, beautiful, country home on ten acres is an ideal retreat in a wooded setting for hiking, walking in the country,

---

NOTES: Credit cards accepted: A Master Card; B Visa; C American Express; D Discover Card; E Diners Club; F Other; 2 Personal checks accepted; 3 Lunch available; 4 Dinner available; 5 Open all

and observing wildlife. Located near Newberg behind the beautiful Red Hills of Dundee, it is convenient to George Fox College. McMinnville is a 20-minute drive, and the Oregon coast is one hour away. A delectable breakfast varies for your pleasure, tempting you with succulent fresh, farm fruit from the famous Willamette Valley of Oregon. The home has many antiques and collectibles and stained glass in each room.

Hosts: Del and Durell Belanger
Rooms: 2 (1PB; 1SB) $40-50
Full Gourmet Breakfast
Credit Cards: None
Notes: 2, 5, 7, 8, 9, 10

OTIS

Salmon River Bed and Breakfast

5622 Salmon River Hwy., 97368
(503) 994-2639

Deep-woods setting along the Salmon River 10 miles from Lincoln City and the Oregon Coast. Nearby: beaches with seal- and whale-watching possibilities, Factory Outlet Mall, lake with paddle bikes, water skiing, bike rentals, horseback riding, four golf courses, racquetball club, excellent eating emporiums, lake, river, and ocean fishing, biking trails, etc. Breakfast served anytime up to 10:30 am (9:30 am on Sundays). Host is a retired meteorologist; hostess retired Medical Records Supervisor.

Hosts: Marvin and Pawnee Pegg
Rooms: 4 (2PB; 2SB) $45-60
Full Breakfast
Credit Cards: A, B, D
Notes: 2, 5 (except Thanksgiving and Christmas), 7, 8, 9, 10, 12

PORTLAND

John Palmer House

4314 N. Mississippi Ave., 97217
(503) 284-5893; (503) 284-7789 (FAX)

This Victorian inn is run by three generations of the same family, and you become one of the family the moment you enter the door. We are told we serve the best breakfast in town. Close to the ocean and the mountains. Make this your home away from home whether on business or vacation.

Rooms: 7 (2PB; 6SB) $35-125
Full Breakfast
Credit Cards: A, B, C, D
Notes: 2, 5, 7 (by arrangement), 8, 9, 10, 11, 12 (with restrictions)

Trinity House Bed and Breakfast

1956 N.W. Everett St., 97209
(503) 241-6560

This 1906 Victorian has been elegantly renovated with soft colors, many antiques, and Oriental rugs. Centrally located in the City of Roses, we are within walking distance of downtown and Portland's Nob Hill shopping area. We are close to Washington Park, the zoo, and the Convention Center. Both guest rooms are designed with your comfort and relaxation in mind. A full breakfast is served each morning.

Hosts: Carol and Greg Gulliford
Rooms: 2 (PB) $75
Full Breakfast
Credit Cards: None
Notes: 2, 5

---

year; 6 Pets welcome; 7 Children welcome; 8 Tennis nearby; 9 Swimming nearby; 10 Golf nearby; 11 Skiing nearby; 12 May be booked through travel agent

STAYTON

Gardener House Bed and Breakfast

633 N. 3rd Avenue, 97383
(503) 769-6331

Well house suite! This extraordinary suite has coordinated decor, a separate entrance, kitchen, dining room, large bathroom, sitting room, queen size bed, telephone, CATV, and VCR. The Madonna room is in the main house and has much the same as the Well Suite. The dining room is on the same floor in a glassed-in porch. A bright room on any day.

Host: Richard Jungwirth
Rooms: 2 (PB) $55-65
Full Breakfast
Credit Cards: A, B, C, D, E
Notes: 2, 4, 5, 6, 7, 8, 9, 10

Horncroft

42156 Kingston-Lyons Dr., 97383
(503) 769-6287

This private home in a quiet, rural area southeast of Stayton, is 12 miles east of Salem, the center of the Willamette Valley, a rich and scenic agricultrual area. Mt. Jefferson Wilderness Area is one hour east; ocean beaches are one and one-half hours west.

Hosts: Dr. and Mrs. K. H. Horn
Rooms: 3 (1PB; 2SB) $35-45
Full Breakfast
Credit Cards: None
Closed Holidays
Notes: 2, 8, 9, 10, 11

YACHATS

Serenity Bed and Breakfast

5985 Yachats River Road, 97498
(503) 547-3813

Wholesome retreat nestled in the lush Yachats Valley. Gentle place to relax after countryside, forest, and tide pool exploration or bird-watching. Minutes from Cape Perpetua, Sea Lion Caves, and the Oregon Coast Aquarium. Elegant European comfort with private two-person jacuzzi tubs. Centrally located between Newport and Florence, Yachats is the gem of the Oregon Coast. German cooking at its best.

Hosts: Sam and Baerbel Morgan
Rooms: 4 (PB) $69-145
Full German Breakfast
Credit Cards: A, B
Notes: 2, 5, 8, 9, 10

Pennsylvania

ADAMSTOWN

Adamstown Inn

62 West Main Street, 19501-0938
(717) 484-0800; (800) 594-4808

Experience simple elegance in a Victorian home resplendent with leaded-glass windows and door, magnificent chestnut woodwork, and Oriental rugs. All four guest rooms are decorated with family heirlooms, handmade quilts, lace curtains, fresh flowers, and many distinctive touches. Accommodations range from antique to king beds. Two rooms have jacuzzis for two. The inn is located in a small town brimming with antique dealers and only minutes from Reading and Lancaster.

Hosts: Tom and Wanda Berman
Rooms: 4 (PB) $65-95
Expanded Continental Breakfast
Credit Cards: A, B
Notes: 2, 5, 8, 9, 10, 12

AIRVILLE

Spring House

Muddy Creek Forks, 17302
(717) 927-6906

Built in 1798 of warm fieldstone, Spring House is a fine example of colonial architecture with original stenciling. Overlooking a river valley. Now on the National Registry of Historic Places, the house has welcomed guests from around the world who seek a historic setting, tranquility, and access to Amish country and Gettysburg with scenic railroad soon to be open to the public. Regional breakfast specialties and Amish cheeses welcome the traveler.

Hosts: Ray and Constance Hearne
Rooms: 5 (3 PB; 2 SB) $60-85
Full Breakfast
Credit Cards: None
Notes: 2, 5, 7, 8, 9, 10, 12

ANNVILLE

Swatara Creek Inn

Box 692, R.D. 2, 17003
(717) 865-3259

1860's Victorian mansion situated on four acres in the peaceful country. All rooms have private baths, canopied queen-size beds, air-conditioning, and include a full breakfast. Sitting room, dining room, and gift shop on the first floor. Wheelchair accessible. Close to Hershey, Mt. Hope Winery, Mt. Gretna, Reading outlets, and Lancaster Amish area. Close to a lot of historical sites: Cornwall Mines, Ephrata Cloisters, Gettysburg, etc. No smoking in house.

Hosts: Dick and Jeanette Hess
Rooms: 10 (PB) $50-70
Full Breakfast
Credit Cards: A, B, C, D, E
Notes: 2, 5, 7 (limited), 8, 9, 10, 11, 12

ATGLEN

Glen Run Valley View Mennonite Farm

Rural Delivery 1, Box 69, 19310
(215) 593-5656

This is a beautiful cozy farm owned by two likable people who go out of their way to make their guests at home. Hannah's farm breakfasts are enormous, and what guests say about their visits here indicate that it is a very special place. Two guest rooms, one which has a double bed, one with a twin bed. Share bath. In the heart of Pennsylvania Dutch country.

Hosts: Harold and Hanna Stoltzfus
Rooms: 3 (1PB; 2SB) $45-50
Full Breakfast
Credit Cards: None
Notes: 2, 4, 5, 6, 7, 10, 12

Highland View

154C Highland Road, 19310
(610) 593-5066

This country home is in a peaceful setting surrounded by Amish farms. An Amish craft shop is next door. This ranch-style home has central air and a large sunroom to enjoy a full breakfast with this Mennonite couple. Two guest rooms, king and queen beds, share a bath. We are located in an area ideal for touring Pennsylvania Dutch Country and only twenty miles from Longwood Gardens. The village of Intercourse is just 15 minutes away. Stop by for coffee and shoofly pie, a Dutch treat. Dried apple arrangements are Cora's hobbies.

Hosts: Sam and Cora Umble
Rooms: 2 (SB) $40-45
Full Breakfast
Credit Cards: None
Notes: 2, 4, 5, 7, 8, 10, 12

BIRD-IN-HAND

The Village Inn of Bird-in-Hand

Box 253, 2695 Old Phila. Pike, 17505
(717) 293-8369; (717) 768-1511 (FAX)

Listed on the National Historic Register, our Inn is located on Route 340, five miles east of Lancaster in the heart of the Pennsylvania Dutch Country. Each room features its own private bath and includes a continental plus breakfast, free use of indoor and outdoor pools and tennis courts located within walking distance, and a complimentary two-hour tour of the surrounding Amish farmlands. Reservations suggested. Package available.

Hosts: Richmond and Jania Young
Rooms: 11 (PB) $75-149
Continental Breakfast
Credit Cards: A, B, C, D
Notes: 2, 5, 8, 9

NOTES: Credit cards accepted: A Master Card; B Visa; C American Express; D Discover Card; E Diners Club; F Other; 2 Personal checks accepted; 3 Lunch available; 4 Dinner available; 5 Open all

BRADFORD

Bethany Guest House
325 South Main Street, 16403
(814) 398-2046; (800) 777-2046

Relax in the luxury of an 1876 Italianate home built in a Victorian resort community by one of the area's pioneering Christian families. This home on the National Register of Historic Places has been restored and is decorated with period furnishings. It has a parlor, drawing room, Greek Revival dining room, and library. The Covenant Room, with a double-wide whirlpool tub, is ideal for special occasions. Visit nearby Lake Erie, wildlife refuges, bicycle trails, and amusement parks. Christian missionaries stay at no charge Sunday through Thursday, and clergy discounts are available.

Hosts: David and Katie White
Rooms: 4 (PB) $35-55
Full Breakfast
Credit Cards: A, B, D
Notes: 2, 5, 7, 8, 9, 10, 11, 12

Fisher Homestead B & B
253 E. Main St., 16701
(814) 368-3428

The Fisher Homestead is an 1847 farmhouse in a small city setting. It was built by William Fisher, a logger and businessman. It was the third farmhouse built in the city and still maintains its early American charm. Completely remodeled in 1988 to seven guest rooms with private baths, TV, air-conditioning, and telephones. Rooms feature hand-made quilts and antique furnishings. Bradford is adjacent to Allegheny National Forest and Allegheny State Park,

New York, which provides many activities for the area visitors. Included in these are downhill and cross-country skiing, boating, hiking, and bicycling. It is an ideal stay for the business traveler or recreational guest.

Rooms: 8 (PB) $60-68
Full Breakfast (Continental on weekdays)
Credit Cards: A, B, C, E
Notes: 2, 5, 7, 8, 9, 10, 11 Cambridge Springs

CANADENSIS

Brookview Manor
Route 447, R.R. #1, Box 365, 18325
(717) 595-2451

Situated on four picturesque acres, the Inn offers the traveler an ideal retreat from workaday world. Enjoy the simple pleasures of hiking trails or a cozy porch glider on a spacious wrap around porch. Each room offers a panoramic view of the forest, mountains and stream, and all have private baths. Breakfast is served in our cheery dining room and includes fruits, juices, fresh muffins, and a hearty main entree.

Hosts: Nancie and Lee Cabana
Rooms: 6 (PB) $65-145
Full Breakfast
Credit Cards: A, B, C, D
Notes: 2, 5, 8, 9, 10, 11, 12

Dreamy Acres
Route 447 and Seese Hill Road, 18325-0007
(717) 595-7115

Esther and Bill Pickett started Dreamy Acres as a bed and breakfast inn in 1959, doing bed and breakfast before it was in style. Situated on three acres with a stream and a pond, Dreamy Acres is in the heart of the Pocono Mountains vacationland, close to stores, churches, gift shops, and recreational facilities. Guest rooms have air conditioning, color cable TV, and some have VCR's.

Hosts: Esther and Bill Pickett
Rooms: 6 (4PB; 2SB) $36-50
Expanded Continental Breakfast, Continental breakfast served May 1 through October 31.
Credit Cards: None
Notes: 2, 5, 8, 9, 10, 11

CARLISLE

Line Limousin Farmhouse

2070 Ritner Highway, 17013
(717) 243-1281

Relax and unwind in an 1864 brick and stone farmhouse on 100 acres, two miles off I-81, Exit 12. French Limousin cattle are raised here. Enjoy antiques, including a player piano, the use of a golf driving range. Join us for worship at our historic First Presbyterian Church. One suite and two rooms with king/twin extra-long beds. Smoking is not permitted.

Hosts: Bob and Joan Line
Rooms: 3 (2PB; 1SB) $45-60
Full Breakfast
Credit Cards: None
Notes: 2, 5, 7, 10

CHAMBERSBURG

Falling Spring Inn

1838 Falling Spring Road, 17201
(717) 267-3654

Enjoy country living only two miles from I-81, Exit 6 and Route 30, on a working

farm with animals and Falling Spring, a nationally renowned, freshwater, trout stream. A large pond, lawns, meadows, ducks, and birds all make a pleasant stay. Historic Gettysburg is only 25 miles away. Relax in our air-conditioned rooms with queen beds.

Hosts: Adin and Janet Frey
Rooms: 5 (PB) $49-69
Full Breakfast
Credit Cards: A, B
Notes: 2, 7, 5, 8, 9, 10, 11, 12

CHRISTIANA

Winding Glen Farm Guest Home

107 Noble Road, 17509
(215) 593-5535

Winding Glen is located in a beautiful valley, and guests stay in the 250-year-old stone farmhouse. Relax on the front porch swing or walk to the covered bridge. Watch the Amish milk the cows or have an evening meal with an Amish family. Also, Minnie will make you a tour of local, authentic Amish shops. You are invited to visit the Mennonite service Sunday morning.

Hosts: Bob and Minnie Metzler
Rooms: 5 (1PB; 4SB) $45
Full Breakfast
Credit Cards: None
Notes: 2, 5, 7, 9, 10

CLEARFIELD

Victorian Loft

216 S. Front St., 16830
(814) 765-4805; (814) 765-1712; (814) 765-9596 (FAX)

Elegant 1894 Victorian home on the river

NOTES: Credit cards accepted: A Master Card; B Visa; C American Express; D Discover Card; E Diners Club; F Other; 2 Personal checks accepted; 3 Lunch available; 4 Dinner available; 5 Open all

in historic district. Amenities include: memorable breakfast featuring home-baked goods, air conditioned rooms with skylights, private kitchen and dining, guest entertainment center, family movies, and whirlpool bath. Sewing studio featured in *Threads* Magazine—weaving and spinning demonstrations. Hosts are Bible college graduates. Perfect stop on I-80—just three miles off exit 19 in West Central Pennsylvania. Also completely equipped three-bedroom cabin on eight wooded acres nestled in State Forest available for one party only.

Hosts: Tim and Peggy Durant
Rooms: 5 (2PB; 3SB) $45-90
Full Breakfast
Credit Cards: A, B
Rooms: 2, 5, 6, 7, 8, 9, 10, 11, 12

CLEARVILLE

Conifer Ridge Farm

Rural Delivery 2, Box 202A, 15535
(814) 784-3342

Conifer Ridge Farm has 126 acres of woodland, pasture, Christmas trees, and crops. There is a one-acre pond with a pier for swimming, fishing, and boating. The home's rustic exterior opens to a spacious contemporary design. You'll feel its country character in the old barn beams and brick walls that collect the sun's warmth for solar heat. Near Bedford Village and Raystown Dam.

Hosts: Dan and Myrtle Haldeman
Rooms: 2 (1PB; 1SB) $55
Cabin: $30
Full Breakfast
Credit Cards: None
Notes: 2, 4, 5, 7, 9, 10, 11

CLINTON

Country Road Bed and Breakfast

Moody Rd., Box 265, 15026
(412) 899-2528

A peaceful, quiet, farm setting just five miles from Gr. Pittsburgh Airport with pick-up service available, and twenty minutes from downtown. A restored 100-year-old farmhouse with trout pond, in-ground pool, screened-in front porch. Golf course within walking distance, and air tours available in vintage, Piper restored aircraft.

Hosts: Jan and David Cornell
Rooms: 4 (3PB; 1SB) $55-100
Full Breakfast
Credit Cards: A, B, C
Notes: 2, 5, 9, 10

CRESCO

LaAnna Guest House

Rural Route 2, Box 1051, 18326
(717) 676-4225

The 111-year-old Victorian is furnished with Victorian and Empire antiques and has spacious rooms, quiet surroundings, and a trout pond. Walk to waterfalls, mountain views, and wildlife.

Hosts: Julie Wilson and Kay Swingle
Rooms: 3 (SB) $25-30
Continental Breakfast
Credit Cards: None
Notes: 2, 5, 7, 8, 9, 10, 11

EAGLES MERE

Shady Lane Bed and Breakfast

Allegheny Ave., P.O. Box 314, 17731
(717) 525-3394

Surrounded by tall trees on a mountaintop with a mesmerizing view of the endless mountains. A five-minute walk to swimming, boating, canoeing, and fishing on the gorgeous mile-long, spring-fed lake (with groomed path around the perimeter). Minutes' walk to craft and gift shops in small village. All in a Victorian "town that time forgot," a resort town since the late 1800's, with summer theater and winter cross-country skiing, ice skating, and famous toboggan slide.

Hosts: Pat and Dennis Dougherty
Rooms: 7 (PB) $65
Full Breakfast
Credit Cards: None
Notes: 2, 5, 8, 9, 10, 11, 12

EAST BERLIN

Bechtel Mansion Inn

400 West King Street, 17316
(717) 259-7760; (800) 331-1108

This charming Victorian mansion has been tastefully restored and furnished with antiques. Located on the western frontier of the Pennsylvania Dutch country, amid the East Berlin national historic district, the inn is a perfect location for a honeymoon, relaxing getaway, or visiting historic churches and sites in Gettysburg, York, or Lancaster. Gift certificates are available.

Hosts: Ruth Spangler, Chares and Mariam Bechtel
Rooms: 9 (7PB; 2SB) $72.50-130
Expanded Continental Breakfast
Credit Cards: A, B, C, D, E
Notes: 2, 7, 8, 9, 10, 11, 12

ELIZABETHTOWN

West Ridge Guest House

1285 West Ridge Road, 17022
(717) 367-7783

Tucked midway between Harrisburg and Lancaster, this European manor can be found four miles off Route 283 at Rheems-Elizabethtown Exit. Nine guest rooms are each decorated to reflect a different historical style. All nine rooms have private baths. The exercise room with hot tub and large social room are in an adjacent guest house. Twenty to 40 minutes to local attractions, including Hershey Park, Lancaster County Amish community, outlet shopping malls, Masonic homes, Harrisburg—state capital.

Hostess: Alice P. Heisey
Rooms: 9 (PB) $50-80
Full Breakfast
Credit Cards: A, B, C, D
Notes: 2, 5, 7, 8, 12

EMLENTON

Whippletree Inn and Farm

Rural Delivery 3, Box 285, 16373
(412) 867-9543

The inn is a restored, turn-of-the-century home on a cattle farm. The house, barns, and 100 acres of pasture sit on a hill above the Allegheny River. A pleasant trail leads

---

NOTES: Credit cards accepted: A Master Card; B Visa; C American Express; D Discover Card; E Diners Club; F Other; 2 Personal checks accepted; 3 Lunch available; 4 Dinner available; 5 Open all

down to the river. Guests are welcome to use the one-half-mile race track for horses and carriages. Hiking, biking, cross-country skiing, canoeing, hunting, and fishing are nearby. Emlenton offers antique and craft shopping in the restored Old Mill.

Hosts: Warren and Joey Simmons
Rooms: 4 (2PB; 2SB) $45-50
Full Breakfast
Credit Cards: None
Notes: 2, 5, 7, 8, 9, 10

EPHRATA

Clearview Farm Bed and Breakfast

355 Clearview Road, 17522
(717) 733-6333

This restored 1814 limestone farmhouse is surrounded by 200 acres of peaceful farmland that overlook a pond graced by a pair of swans. Although in the country, we are very easy to find and are just minutes from several major highways. Located in the heart of Pennsylvania Dutch Lancaster County, excellent restaurants, antique malls, and outlet shopping are nearby. Featured in *Country Decorating Ideas*; a touch of elegance in a country setting. Four diamond AAA rating.

Hostess: Mildred Wissler
Rooms: 5 (3PB; 2SB) $59-79
Full Breakfast
Credit Cards: A, B
Notes: 2, 5, 8, 10

Historic Smithton Inn

900 West Main Street 17522
(717) 733-6094

Smithton Inn originated prior to the Revo-

lutionary War. The inn is a romantic and picturesque place located in Lancaster County. Its big, square rooms are bright and sunny. Each room has its own working fireplace, and can be candlelighted during evening hours. There is a sitting area in each room with comfortable leather upholstered chairs, reading lamps and a writing desk. Most beds have canopies, soft goose down pillows and bright, hand made Pennsylvannia Dutch quilts. Feather beds are available upon request. Mannerly children and pets are welcome, but please make prior arrangements. Smoking is prohibited. Reservations are prepaid.

Hostess: Dorthy Graybill
Rooms: 8 (PB) $65-135 suites $140-170
Full Breakfast
Credit Cards: A, B, C
Notes: 2, 5, 6 (by prior arrangement) 7, 8, 9, 10, 12

Historic Smithton Inn

The Inns at Doneckers

318-324 North State and 301 West Main, 17522
(717) 733-9502

Relax in country elegance in historic Lancaster County. Four inns of 40 distinctive rooms, decorated in fine antiques, some fireplace/jacuzzi suites. A few steps from The Doneckers Community of exceptional fashion store for the family and home, award-winning gourmet restaurant; art, craft, and quilt galleries and artists'

year; 6 Pets welcome; 7 Children welcome; 8 Tennis nearby; 9 Swimming nearby; 10 Golf nearby; 11 Skiing nearby; 12 May be booked through travel agent

studios; farmer's market. Minutes from antique and collectible markets. Special begin-the-week getaway Sunday thru Thursday. "An oasis of sophistication in Pennsylvania Dutch country"—*Country Inns Magazine*.

Hostess: Jan Grobengieser
Rooms: 40 (38PB; 2SB) $59-175
Continental Breakfast
Credit Cards: A, B, C, D, E
Notes: 2, 3, 4, 5, 7, 8, 9, 10

FRANKLIN

Quo Vadis Bed and Breakfast "Whither Goest Thou?"

1501 Liberty St., 16323
(814) 432-4208

A stately looking home, accented with terracotta tile, Quo Vadis is an 1867, eclectic, Queen Anne house. It is located in an historic district listed on the National Register with a walking tour. The high-ceilinged, spacious rooms, parquet floors, detailed woodworking, moldings, and friezes are from a time of caring craftsmanship and Victorian elegance. The furniture is mahogany, rosewood, oak, walnut, and wicker and has been acquired by the same family for four generations. The quilts, embroidery, and lacework are the handiwork of two beloved ladies. Restaurants, museums, antiques, Barrows-Civic Theatre, bicycle paths, train trip, fishing, Allegheny River Valley are all nearby to enjoy.

Hosts: Kristal and Stanton Bowmer-Vath
Rooms: 6 (PB) $60-70
Continental Breakfast
Credit Cards: A, B, C
Notes: 2, 5, 7 (10 and over), 8, 9, 10, 11, 12

GAP

Ben Mar Farm Bed and Breakfast

5721 Old Phila. Pike, 17527
(717) 768-3309

Come stay with us on our working dairy farm. We are located in the heart of famous "Amish Country." Experience quiet country life while staying in the large, beautifully decorated rooms of our 200-year-old farmhouse. Our efficiency apartment is a favorite including a full kitchen, queen and double bed with private bath. Enjoy a fresh continental breakfast brought to your room. Air conditioned.

Hosts: Herb and Melanie Benner
Rooms: 3 (PB) $38-48
Continental Breakfast
Credit Cards: None
Notes: 2, 5, 7

GETTYSBURG—SEE ALSO HANOVER

The Brafferton Inn

44 York Street, 17325
(717) 337-3423

A truly eclectic bed and breakfast, The Brafferton Inn is the oldest house in Gettysburg's historic district, built in 1786. One of Pennsylvania's finest restorations, the home is furnished with a large collection of eighteenth- and nineteenth-century antiques. Relax in the atrium, lit by a skylight roof, on the deck among flowers and herbs, or in the warm and spacious livingroom.

NOTES: Credit cards accepted: A Master Card; B Visa; C American Express; D Discover Card; E Diners Club; F Other; 2 Personal checks accepted; 3 Lunch available; 4 Dinner available; 5 Open all

Hosts: Jane and Sam Back
Rooms: 10 (10PB) $65-90
Full Breakfast
Credit Cards: A, B
Notes: 2, 7 (over 7), 8, 9, 10, 11

The Brafferton Inn

The Doubleday Inn

104 Doubleday Avenue, 17325
(717) 334-9119

The only B&B directly on the Gettysburg Battlefield, the Inn is beautifully restored, combining a special ambience featuring Civil War furnishings with modern amenities including central air-conditioning. Enjoy afternoon tea with hors d'oeuvres and a candlelight country breakfast. On selected evenings, participate in "Civil War Nights" where a historian brings the battle alive with displays of authentic memorabilia. 50% discount off the second night Sundays through Thursdays completes a gracious combination of history and hospitality.

Hosts: Olga Krossick (Joan and Sal Chandon)
Rooms: 9 (5PB; 4SB) $75-100
Full Breakfast
Credit Cards: A, B
Notes: 2, 5, 8, 10, 11, 12

Hickory Bridge Farm

96 Hickory Bridge Road, Ortanna, 17353
(717) 642-5261

Only eight miles west of historical Gettysburg. Unique country dining and Bed and Breakfast. Cozy cottages with woodstoves and private baths located in secluded wooded settings along a stream. Full farm breakfast served at the farmhouse which was built in the late 1700's. Country dining offered on Fridays, Saturdays, and Sundays in a 130-year-old barn decorated with many antiques. Family owned and operated for 15 years.

Hosts: Dr. and Nancy Jean Hammett
Rooms: 7 (6PB; 1SB) $79-89
Full Breakfast
Credit Cards: A, B
Notes: 2, 4 (on weekends), 5, 7, 8, 9, 10, 11

Keystone Inn

231 Hanover Street, 17325
(717) 337-3888

The Keystone Inn is a large, brick, Victorian home built in 1913. The high-ceilinged rooms are decorated with lace and flowers, and a handsome chestnut staircase rises to the third floor. The guest rooms are bright, cheerful, and air conditioned. Each has a reading nook and writing desk. Choose your own breakfast from our full breakfast menu. One suite available.

Hosts: Wilmer and Doris Martin
Rooms: 4 + suite (3PB; 2SB) $59-100
Full Breakfast
Credit Cards: A, B
Notes: 2, 5, 7, 8, 9, 10, 11

year; 6 Pets welcome; 7 Children welcome; 8 Tennis nearby; 9 Swimming nearby; 10 Golf nearby; 11 Skiing nearby; 12 May be booked through travel agent

Osceola Mill House

GORDONVILLE

Osceola Mill House

313 Osceola Mill Rd., 17529
(717) 768-3758

Built by Jacob Ludwig, a German Mennonite, in 1766, this handsome, limestone mill house rests on the banks of the Pequea Creek adjacent to a 1757 grist mill and a miller's cottage. There are deep-set windows and wide-pine floors. Working fireplaces in the keeping room and in the bedrooms add to the warmth and charm. Amish neighbors farm the picturesque fields adjoining the inn, and their horse and buggies clip-clop past the mill house often. Brimming with antiques. Breakfast alone is worth the trip.

Hosts: Robin and Sterling Schoen
Rooms: 3 (1PB; 2SB) $100
Full Breakfast
Credit Cards: None
Notes: 2, 5, 7 (10 and older), 12

HANOVER

Beechmont Inn

315 Broadway, 17331
(717) 632-3012; (800) 553-7009; (717) 632-3988 (FAX)

An elegant, 1834, Federal Period inn with seven guest rooms, all private baths, fireplaces, air conditioning, afternoon refreshments, and gourmet breakfast. One large suite has a private whirlpool tub, canopy bed, and fireplaces. Gettysburg Battlefield, Lake Marburg, golf, and great antiquing nearby. Convenient location for visits to Hershey, York, or Lancaster. Weekend packages and romantic honeymoon or anniversary packages offered. Picnic baskets available. Great area for biking and hiking. AAA and Mobil approved.

Hosts: Terry and Monna Hormel
Rooms: 7 (PB) $70-125
Full Breakfast
Credit Cards: A, B
Notes: 2, 5, 8, 9, 10

NOTES: Credit cards accepted: A Master Card; B Visa; C American Express; D Discover Card; E Diners Club; F Other; 2 Personal checks accepted; 3 Lunch available; 4 Dinner available; 5 Open all

HERSHEY

Pinehurst Bed and Breakfast

50 Northeast Dr., 17033
(717) 533-2603; (717) 534-2639 (FAX)

Spacious brick home surrounded by lawns and countryside. There is a warm, welcoming, many-windowed living room, or for outdoor relaxing, a large porch with an old-fashioned porch swing. All this within walking distance of all Hershey attractions: Hershey Museum, Rose Gardens, Hersheypark, and Chocolate World. Less than one hour's drive to Gettysburg and Lancaster County. Each room welcomes you with a queen-size bed and a Hershey Kiss on each pillow.

Hostess: Phyllis Long
Rooms: 15 (2PB; 12SB) $45-67
Full Breakfast
Credit Cards: A, B
Notes: 2, 5, 7, 8, 9, 10, 12

HESSTON

Aunt Susie's Country Vacations

Rural Delivery 1, Box 225, 16647
(814) 658-3638

Experience country living in a warm, friendly atmosphere with antiques and oil paintings. Nearby attractions include 28-mile-long Raystown Lake, historic houses, and a restored general store.

Hosts: John and Susan
Rooms: 8 (2PB; 6SB) $45-50
Expanded Continental Breakfast
Credit Cards: None
Notes: 2, 5, 7, 8, 9, 10, 11, 12

INTERCOURSE

Carriage Corner Bed and Breakfast

3705 E. Newport Road, 17534-0371
(717) 768-3059

"A comfortable bed, a hearty breakfast, a charming village, and friendly hosts" has been used to describe our B&B. We have four comfortable rooms, two with private baths and two with a shared bath. Our bed and breakfast offers a relaxing country atmosphere with hand-crafted touches of folk-art and country. Rooms are air-conditioned. We are centered in the heart of beautiful farms and a culture which draws many to nearby villages of Intercourse, Bird-in-Hand, and Paradise. Amish dinners arranged. There is much to learn from these calm and gentle people.

Hosts: Gordon and Gwen Schuit
Rooms: 4 (2PB; 2SB) $55-65
Full Breakfast
Credit Cards: A, B
Notes: 2, 5, 7, 12

JIM THORPE

The Inn at Jim Thorpe

24 Broadway, 18229
(717) 325-2599; (717) 325-9145 (FAX)

The Inn rests in a unique and picturesque setting in the heart of historic Jim Thorpe. Our elegant, restored guestrooms are complete with private baths, remote-controlled, color TV's and air-conditioning. While in town, take historic walking tours, shop in over 50 quaint shops and galleries, go mountain biking on the northeast's best trails, or raft the turbulent Lehigh River.

---

year; 6 Pets welcome; 7 Children welcome; 8 Tennis nearby; 9 Swimming nearby; 10 Golf nearby; 11 Skiing nearby; 12 May be booked through travel agent

It's all right outside our door!

Host: David Drury
Rooms: 22 (PB) $65-100
Continental Breakfast
Credit Cards: A, B, C, D, E
Notes: 3, 4, 5, 7, 8, 9, 10, 11, 12

KENNETT SQUARE

Meadow Spring Farm Bed and Breakfast

201 East Street Road, Rt. 926, 19348
(215) 444-3903

1836 farmhouse on a 150-acre working farm. Guests can participate in gathering eggs for breakfast. The house is filled with family antiques, quilts, and a doll collection including Santa and cows. The hosts will prepare a full country breakfast before the guests start touring the area, swimming in the pool, or just walking the farm. Minutes from Longwood, Brandywine River Museum, and Winterthur.

Hosts: Anne Hicks and Debbie Hicks Axelrod
Rooms: 7 (4PB; 3SB) $55-100
Full Breakfast
Credit Cards: None
Notes: 2, 5, 7, 8, 9, 10

KINZERS

Sycamore Haven Farm

35 South Kinzer Road, 17535
(717) 442-4901

We have approximately 40 milking cows and many young cattle and cats for children to enjoy. Our farmhouse has three guest rooms, all with double beds and one single. We also have cots and a playpen.

Located 15 miles east of Lancaster on Route 30.

Hosts: Charles and Janet Groff
Rooms: 3 (SB) $30-40
Continental Breakfast
Credit Cards: None
Notes: 2, 5, 6, 7, 8, 10

LAMPETER

Bed and Breakfast— The Manor

830 Village Rd., Box 416, 17537
(717) 464-9564

This cozy farmhouse is minutes away from Lancaster's historical sites and attractions. Guests delight in Mary Lou's home-made breakfasts featuring Eggs Mornay, crepes, stratas, fruit cobblers, and home-made breads and jams. A swim in the pool and a nap under a shade tree is the perfect way to cap your day of touring. Dinner, an overnight stay, and a buggy ride with an Old Order Amish family can be arranged. Children welcome. We cater to groups that are welcomed to use our meeting room.

Hosts: Mary Lou Paolini and Jackie Curtis
Rooms: 5 (2PB; 3SB) $65-75
Full Breakfast
Credit Cards: A, B
Notes: 2, 3, 4, 5, 7, 8, 9, 10

LANCASTER

The Apple Bin Inn Bed and Breakfast

2835 Willow Street Pike, Willow Street, 17584
(717) 464-5881; (800) 338-4296

Southern Lancaster County's finest bed

NOTES: Credit cards accepted: A Master Card; B Visa; C American Express; D Discover Card; E Diners Club; F Other; 2 Personal checks accepted; 3 Lunch available; 4 Dinner available; 5 Open all

and breakfast. Minutes from Lancaster's oldest home, The Hans Herv House, Amish historic buildings, shopping outlets and antiques. Bring your bike and see the area at a slow pace. We have storage. Picnic lunches available (additional cost). Don't forget the wonderful food of the area. We will help you plan your visit wisely. Color cable TV in guest room. Your home away from home. Spend the weekend and join us for church Sunday morning following breakfast.

Hosts: Debbie and Barry Hershey
Rooms: 4 (2PB; 2SB) $55-75
Full Breakfast
Credit Cards: A, B, C
Notes: 2, 4, 5, 8, 9, 10

The King's Cottage, A Bed and Breakfast Inn
1049 East King St., 17602
(717) 397-1017; (800) 747-8717

Traditionally styled elegance, modern comfort, and warm hospitality in Amish country. King and queen beds, private baths, gourmet breakfasts, and personal service create a gracious friendly atmosphere at this award-winning Spanish-style mansion. Relax by the fire and enjoy afternoon tea in the library while chatting with innkeepers about directions to restaurants and attractions. Special Amish dinners or personal bus tours arranged. Near farmers' markets, Gettysburg, and Hershey. On National Register, AAA, and Mobil listed EXCELLENT!

Hosts: Karen and Jim Owens
Rooms: 8 (PB) $75-120
Full Breakfast
Credit Cards: A, B, D
Notes: 2, 5, 6, 8, 9, 10, 12

Lincoln Haus Inn
1687 Lincoln Highway East, 17602
(717) 392-9412

Lincoln Haus Inn is the only inn in Lancaster County with a distinctive hip roof. It is furnished with antiques and rugs on gleaming, hardwood floors, and it has natural oak woodwork. I am a member of the Old Order Amish Church, serving family-style breakfast with a homey atmosphere. Convenient location, close to Amish farmlands, malls, historic Lancaster; five minutes from Route 30 and Pennsylvania Dutch Visitors Bureau.

Hostess: Mary K. Zook
Rooms: 6 (PB) $45-65
Apartment: 2 (PB)
Full Breakfast
Credit Cards: None
Notes: 2, 5, 7, 8, 9, 10, 12

New Life Homestead Bed and Breakfast
1400 East King Street (Route 462), 17602-3240
(717) 396-8928

In the heart of the Amish area is a stately, brick Victorian close to all attractions, markets, farms, and outlets. Each room is decorated with family heirlooms and antiques. Full breakfast and evening refreshments are served. Tours and meals are arranged with local families. Worship with us in our Mennonite church. Private baths and air-conditioning.

Hosts: Carol and Bill Giersch
Rooms: (PB) $40-70
Full Breakfast
Credit Cards: None
Notes: 2, 5, 7, 8, 9, 10, 12

Old Road Guest Home

2501 Old Phila. Pike, 17576
(717) 393-8182

Old Road Guest Home is nestled in the rolling farmlands in the heart of PA Dutch country. Comfortable air conditioned rooms with TV. Ground floor rooms available. Spacious shaded lawn to enjoy picnics. Easy parking. Private and shared baths. Near fine restaurants. Alcoholic beverages and indoor smoking prohibited.

Hostess: Marian Buckwalter
Rooms: 6 (3PB; 3SB) $28-35
No Breakfast
Credit Cards: None
Notes: 2, 5, 7, 9, 10

The Walkabout Inn

Walkabout Inn

837 Village Road, 17537
(717) 464-0707

This 1925, brick, Mennonite farmhouse features large wrap-around porches, balconies, English gardens, and antique furnishings. The inn takes its name from the Australian word which means to go out and discover new places. Australian-born host Richard will help you explore the Amish country surrounding the home. An elegant, full breakfast is served by candle-light. The honeymoon and anniversary suites are beautiful.

Hosts: Richard and Margaret Mason
Rooms: 4 (PB) $79-99
Suites: 1 (PB) $179 for five adults
Full Breakfast
Credit Cards: A, B, C
Notes: 2, 3, 4, 5, 7, 8, 9, 10, 12

Cornerstone Inn

LANDENBERG

Cornerstone Inn Bed and Breakfast

Rd. 1, Box 155, 19350
(215) 274-2143

Cornerstone dates back to 1704, the time when early records document a land grant from William Penn of England to William Penn's son in Philadelphia. The original house was built in the early 1700's, with additions constructed at three later times. Then, in 1820, Cornerstone was completed as the proud, gracious structure that will soon welcome you. Each bedroom's quaint decor is surrounded by a sense of timeless romance. Bringing together the unhurried pace of the past and the conveniences of today. For long term guests, Cornerstone's renovated barn is the home of two furnished guest apartments. Come to your home in the country. Call today for reservations or information. It's a place

---

NOTES: Credit cards accepted: A Master Card; B Visa; C American Express; D Discover Card; E Diners Club; F Other; 2 Personal checks accepted; 3 Lunch available; 4 Dinner available; 5 Open all

with a long history of pampered guests.

Hosts: Linda and Marty Mulligan
Rooms: 7 (PB) $85-150
Full Breakfast
Credit Cards: A, B, D
Notes: 2, 5, 7, 8, 9, 10, 12

LEWISBURG

Pineapple Inn

439 Market Street, 17837
(717) 524-6200

In the American tradition of genuine hospitality, the Pineapple Inn greets you. This elegant, Federal-style home built in 1857 by the eminent architect Louis Palmer is located in the heart of the lovely historical town of Lewisburg, Pennsylvania, near Bucknell University. All rooms beautifully finished in fine antiques, many of historical interest. Full country breakfast and complimentary afternoon tea in parlor included in tariff. Unique facilities available for wedding receptions, anniversary celebrations, formal and informal parties. Catering available. Businessmen and women enjoy the friendly, relaxing, homelike atmosphere.

Hosts: Deborah and Charles North
Rooms: 6 (2PB; 4SB); $59-85
Full Breakfast
Credit Cards: A, B, C, D, E
Notes: 2, 5, 7 (limited), 8, 9, 10

LIMA

Hamanassett

P.O. Box 129, 19037
(610) 459-3000

This early 19th-century country manor house is on 48 secluded and peaceful acres of woodlands, gardens, and trails in Pennsylvania and Delaware's Brandywine Valley: Winterthur, Hagley, Nemours Brandywine (Wyeth) museums, and Longwood Gardens. Well-appointed, large rooms prevail: queen, doubles, twins, canopied king beds, TV's, private baths and amenities. Beautiful Federalist living room and extensive library. Full country breakfast, sophisticated cuisine. Near tennis, golf, and excellent dining opportunities. Great for quiet weekend escape. Two-night minimum stay.

Hostess: Evelene H. Dohan
Rooms: 6 (PB) $85-120
Full Breakfast
Credit Cards: None
Notes: 2, 5, 8, 10, 12

LITITZ

The Alden House

62 East Main Street, 17543
(717) 627-3363; (800) 584-0753

Fully restored townhouse in the heart of the town's historic district. All local attractions within walking distance. Relax on one of three spacious porches and watch Amish buggies or experience a whiff of fresh chocolate from the local candy factory. Home of the nation's oldest pretzel factory. Family suites, Amish dining, bicycle storage available, and only 10 minutes north of Lancaster. Enjoy our "OLD-FASHIONED HOSPITALITY."

Hostess: Leanne Schweitzer
Rooms: 7 (5PB; 2SB) $65-95
Expanded Continental Breakfast
Credit Cards: A, B, C
Notes: 2, 5, 7 (over 6), 8, 9, 10

---

year; 6 Pets welcome; 7 Children welcome; 8 Tennis nearby; 9 Swimming nearby; 10 Golf nearby; 11 Skiing nearby; 12 May be booked through travel agent

Banner House Bed and Breakfast

37 E. Lincoln Avenue, 17543
(717) 626-REST

We have been pampering guests in the European tradition since 1986. We customize breakfast to suit your taste and time. Located in the heart of Lancaster County where you can explore the richness of the Amish, Mennonite, and Moravian cultures. Lititz hosts the Wilbur Chocolate Factory, Sturgis Pretzel, and the home of General Sutter. Banner House also offers retreat facilities for seven, plus one scholarship situation.

Hosts: Kay Garrity-Roth and Vincent Roth
Rooms: 3 (SB) $45-55
Both Continental and Full Breakfast
Credit Cards: None
Notes: 2, 5, 7

Swiss Woods Bed and Breakfast

500 Blantz Road, 17543
(717) 627-3358; (800) 594-8018; 717-627-3483 (FAX)

A visit to Swiss Woods is reminiscent of a trip to one of Switzerland's quaint, charming guest houses. Located in beautiful Lancaster County, this inn was designed with comfort in mind. Breakfast is a memorable experience of inn specialties. The gardens are a unique variety of flowering perennials and annuals. A massive sandstone fireplace dominates the sunny common room. Rooms feature natural woodwork and queen beds with down comforters, some with jacuzzis, patios, and balconies. Enjoy our spectacular view and special touches. German spoken.

Hosts: Debrah and Werner Mosimann
Rooms: 7 (PB) $75-115
Full Breakfast
Credit Cards: A, B
Notes: 2, 9, 12

MANHEIM

Herr Farmhouse

2256 Huber Drive, 17545
(717) 653-9852

Historic, circa 1750, stone farmhouse nestled on 11.5 acres of scenic farmland. The Inn has been fully restored and retains all original trim, flooring, and doors. Of the six working fireplaces, two are located in guest rooms. Take a step into yesteryear amidst the Colonial furnishings. Breakfast served in country kitchen with walk-in fireplace. Amish dining, family suite, and indoor bicycle storage available. Nine miles west of Lancaster outside of Mount Joy. Excellent dining nearby.

Host: Berry Herr
Rooms: 4 (2PB; 2SB) $70-95
Expanded Continental
Credit Cards: A, B
Notes: 2, 5, 8, 9, 10

The Inn at Mt. Hope

2232 E. Mt. Hope Rd., 17545-0155
(717) 664-4708; (717) 270-2688 (FAX)

An 1850's stone home with high ceilings and magnificent pine floors. The Inn sits on four and one-half acres of woodland and grass bordered by a stream. Convenient to all Lancaster County attractions as well as Hershey and adjacent to the Mt. Hope Winery and Pennsylvania Renaissance

---

NOTES: Credit cards accepted: A Master Card; B Visa; C American Express; D Discover Card; E Diners Club; F Other; 2 Personal checks accepted; 3 Lunch available; 4 Dinner available; 5 Open all

Faire. Ideal setting for a small couples retreat or getaway. Screened porch and swimming pool are available for relaxation.

Rooms: 8 (5PB; 3SB) $50-115
Full Breakfast
Credit Cards: A, B
Notes: 2, 7, 9

The Inn at Mt. Hope

Manheim Manor Bed and Breakfast Inn

140 S. Charlotte St., 17545
(717) 664-4168

Come experience Victorian hospitality in elegantly appointed 1856 historic home. Rooms with private bath, air conditioning, CATV, porch, balcony, refrigerator, and clock radios. Bedtime cordials, mints, and chocolate. Amish dinner, buggy rides, and winter sleigh rides available. Bountiful breakfast. Minutes from Pennsylvania Renaissance Faire and other attractions.

Hosts: Al and Alice Avella
Rooms: 6 (PB) $85-115+tax
Full Breakfast
Credit Cards: C
Notes: 2, 5, 8, 9, 10, 11, 12

Wenger's Bed and Breakfast

571 Hosslen Road, 17545
(717) 665-3862

Relax and enjoy your stay in the quiet countryside of Lancaster County. Our ranch-style house is within walking distance of our son's 100-acre dairy farm. The spacious rooms will accommodate families. You can get a guided tour through the Amish farmland. Hershey, the chocolate town, Pennsylvania's state capital at Harrisburg, and the Gettysburg Battlefield are all within one hour's drive.

Hosts: Arthur and Mary K. Wenger
Rooms: 2 (PB) $40-45
Full Breakfast
Credit Cards: None
Notes: 2, 5, 7

MILFORD

Cliff Park Inn and Golf Course

RR 4, Box 7200, 18337
(800) 225-6535; (717) 296-3982 (FAX)

Historic country inn on secluded 600-acre estate. Spacious rooms with private bath, telephone, and climate control. Victorian-style furnishings. Fireplaces. Golf at the door on one of America's oldest golf courses (1913). Hike or cross-country ski on seven miles of marked trails. Golf and ski equipment rentals. Golf school. Full service restaurant rated 3-stars by Mobil Guide. MAP or B&B plans available. Specialists in business conferences

year; 6 Pets welcome; 7 Children welcome; 8 Tennis nearby; 9 Swimming nearby; 10 Golf nearby; 11 Skiing nearby; 12 May be booked through travel agent

and country weddings.

Host: Harry W. Buchanan III
Rooms: 18 (PB) $90-145
Full Breakfast
Credit Cards: A, B, C, D, E
Notes: 2, 3, 4, 5, 7, 8, 9, 10, 11, 12

MONTOURSVILLE

The Carriage House at Stonegate

Road 1, Box 11A, 17754
(717) 433-4340

The Carriage House at Stonegate is the original carriage house for one of the oldest farms in the beautiful Loyalsock Valley. It offers 1,400 square feet of space on two levels and is totally self-contained and separate from the main house. It is located within easy access to I-80, I-180, and U.S. 15 and on the edge of extensive forests offering a wide range of outdoor activities in all seasons.

Hosts: Harold and Dena Mesaris
Rooms: 2 (SB) $50
Continental Breakfast
Credit Cards: None
Notes: 2, 5, 6, 7, 8, 9, 10, 11

MOUNT JOY

Cedar Hill Farm

305 Longenecker Road, 17552
(717) 653-4655

This 1817 stone farmhouse overlooks a peaceful stream and was the birthplace of the host. Stroll the acreage or relax on the wicker rockers on the large front porch. Enjoy the singing of the birds and serene countryside. A winding staircase leads to

the comfortable rooms, each with a private bath and centrally air conditioned. A room for honeymooners offers a private balcony. Breakfast is served daily by a walk-in fireplace. Located midway between the Lancaster and Hershey areas where farmers' markets, antique shops, and good restaurants abound. Gift certificates for anniversary or holiday giving. Open all seasons.

Hosts: Russel and Gladys Swarr
Rooms: 5 (PB) $60-65
Expanded Continental Breakfast
Credit Cards: A, B, C, D
Notes: 2, 5, 7, 8, 10

Green Acres Farm Bed and Breakfast

1382 Pinkerton Road, 17552
(717) 653-4028; 717-653-2840 (FAX)

Our 1830 farmhouse is furnished with antiques and offers a peaceful haven for your getaway. The rooster, chickens, wild turkey, Pigmy goats, lots of kittens, pony, and 1,000 hogs give a real farm atmosphere on this 160-acre grain farm. Children love the pony cart rides, and everyone enjoys the trampoline and swings. We offer tour information in the Amish country.

Hosts: Wayne and Yvonne Miller
Rooms: 7 (PB) $55
Full Breakfast
Credit Cards: A, B
Notes: 2, 5, 6, 7, 8, 9, 10, 12

Hillside Farm B & B

607 Eby Chiques Road
(717) 653-6697

Quiet, secluded, two-acre 1863 farm

NOTES: Credit cards accepted: A Master Card; B Visa; C American Express; D Discover Card; E Diners Club; F Other; 2 Personal checks accepted; 3 Lunch available; 4 Dinner available; 5 Open all

homestead overlooking Chickies Creek. Comfortable cozy country furnishings and antiques. Private and semi-private baths, children 10 and over welcome, full, country, all-you-can-eat breakfast, strictly non-smoking, air conditioned. First-floor and second-floor porches for guests' use. Second-floor refrigerator for guests' use. All rooms decorated differently. No TV or phone in guest rooms. Phone for guests' use in foyer. TV, VCR, movies, tapes, baby grand piano for guests' use in living room. Small library on second floor. Large barn to explore. On biking trail.

Hosts: Gary and Deb Lintner/Bob and Wilma Lintner
Rooms: 5 (3PB; 2SB) $53-66.25
Full Breakfast
Credit Cards: None
Notes: 2, 5, 7 (over 10), 8, 9, 10, 12

MUNCY

The Bodine House

307 South Main Street, 17756
(717) 546-8949

The Bodine House, featured in the December 1991 issue of *Colonial Homes* magazine, is located on tree-lined Main Street in the historic district. Built in 1805, the house has been authentically restored and is listed on the National Register of Historic Places. Most of the furnishings are antiques. The center of Muncy, with its shops, restaurants, library, and churches, is a short walk down the street. No smoking.

Hosts: David and Marie Louise Smith
Rooms: 4 (PB) $55-70
Full Breakfast
Credit Cards: A, B, C
Notes: 2, 5, 7 (over 6)

NEWFOUNDLAND

Buena Vista

Rt. 447 (Panther Rd), Box 195, 18445
(717) 676-3800; (717) 676-5826 (FAX)

Come and relax with us in rural northeastern Pennsylvania. High above the valley floor, we overlook the village of Newfoundland. Our buildings began as a Moravian farm in the 1800's and have been converted to a country inn. Our location in the Lake Wallenpaupack Watershed region offers natural beauty and ample opportunities for recreation, shopping, and dining. A pool is located on our property. Breakfast is served, other meals may be available. Reservations required.

Hosts: Dave and Denise Keevil
Rooms: 15 (9PB; 6SB) $30-45
Full Breakfast
Credit Cards: A, B
Notes: 2, 3, 4, 5, 7, 10, 11

NEWVILLE

Nature's Nook Farm

740 Shed Rd., 17241
(717) 776-5619

Nature's Nook Farm is located in a quiet, peaceful setting along the Blue Mountains. Warm Mennonite hospitality and clean, comfortable lodging await you. Enjoy freshly brewed garden tea in season. Home-made cinnamon rolls, muffins or coffee cake a specialty. Stroll along the flower gardens, close to Colonel Denning State Park with hiking trails, fishing, and swimming. Two hours to Lancaster, one hour to Harrisburg, one and a half hours to Gettysburg and Hershey. Wheelchair

year; 6 Pets welcome; 7 Children welcome; 8 Tennis nearby; 9 Swimming nearby; 10 Golf nearby; 11 Skiing nearby; 12 May be booked through travel agent

accessible.

Hosts: Don and Lois Leatherman
Rooms: 1 (PB) $40
Continental Breakfast
Credit Cards: None
Notes: 2, 5, 7, 8, 9, 10

NORTH WALES

Joseph Ambler Inn

1005 Horsham Rd., 19454
(215) 362-7500; (215) 361-5924 (FAX)

The Joseph Ambler Inn is an historical Colonial estate featuring exceptional evening dining. Beautifully appointed guest rooms are furnished with antiques and reproductions, all with private baths. Full, country breakfast is included. The Inn offers exclusive facilities for banquets, meetings, and private parties. Set on 13 acres of lawns and gardens, it is perfect for small wedding receptions and rehearsal dinners. Please call for a tour or reservations.

Hosts: Steve and Terry Kratz
Rooms: 28 (PB) $95-140
Full Breakfast
Credit Cards: A, B, C, D, E
Notes: 2, 4, 5, 7, 8, 9, 10, 12

OXFORD

Log House Bed and Breakfast

15225 Limestone Road, 19363
(215) 932-9257

Clean, quiet, country, Chester County log home, away from city and traffic noises. Midway between Lancaster (Amish coun-

try), Philadelphia, Wilmington. Air-conditioned rooms, private baths. Family room available. Picnic area, hiking, biking, no smoking, full breakfast, no limit to your stay. Open Year round.

Hosts: E. E. and Arlene E. Hershey
Rooms: 3 (PB) $45
Full Breakfast
Credit Cards: None
Notes: 2, 5, 7, 8, 9, 10, 11

PARADISE

Maple Lane Farm Bed and Breakfast

505 Paradise Lane, 17562
(717) 687-7479

Clean, comfortable, air-conditioned rooms have antiques, quilts, poster and canopy beds. This working dairy farm has a winding stream, woodland, and a 40-mile view. Real Amish country, near museums, craft shops, antique shops, and farmers' markets.

Hosts: Edwin and Marion Rohrer
Rooms: 4 (2PB; 2SB) $45-55
Expanded Continental Breakfast
Credit Cards: None
Notes: 2, 5, 7, 8, 9, 10, 12

PAUPACK

The Lampost Bed and Breakfast at Lake Wallenpaupak

HCR Box 154, Route 507, 18451
(717) 857-1738

An assortment of lamposts line the

driveway leading to this white Colonial home on two acres overlooking Lake Wallenpaupak. This is an ideal stopover for those who love waterfront activities like swimming, boating, fishing, and water skiing. If you'd rather stay high and dry, there are facilities for golfing, tennis, and horseback riding nearby. Other recreational activities include scenic train excursions and balloon rides. Located in the Pocono Mountains.

Hosts: Lily, Karen and David
Rooms: 5 (2PB; 3SB) $50-125
Continental Breakfast
Credit Cards: A, B
Notes: 7, 8, 9, 10, 11

PEACH BOTTOM

Pleasant Grove Farm
368 Pilottown Road, 17563
(717) 548-3100

Located in beautiful, historic Lancaster County, this 160-acre dairy farm has been a family-run operation for 110 years, earning the title of Century Farm by the Pennsylvania Department of Agriculture. As a working farm, it provides guests the opportunity to experience daily life in a rural setting. Built in 1814, 1818, and 1820, the house once served as a country store and post office. Full country breakfast served by candlelight.

Hosts: Charles and Labertha Tindall
Rooms: 4 (SB) $45-60
Full Breakfast
Credit Cards: None
Notes: 2, 5, 7, 9

PHILADELPHIA

Bed and Breakfast—The Manor and Reservation Service
830 Village Rd., Box 416, 17537
(717) 464-9564

This reservation service covers Lancaster County/Philadelphia area. An example inn —cozy farmhouse in the heart of Amish country, minutes away from Lancaster's attractions. Full gourmet breakfast, deluxe in-ground pool. A dinner, overnight stay, and a buggy ride with an Old Order Amish family can be arranged. In nearby Philadelphia enjoy your stay at a B&B in the historic district as well as the famous Philadelphia art museum area. Children welcome. We cater to groups. Meeting room available.

POINT PLEASANT (NEW HOPE)

Tattersall Inn
Cafferty and River Road, Box 569, 18950
(215) 297-8233

This 18th-century, plastered, fieldstone home with its broad porches and manicured lawns resembles the unhurried atmosphere of a bygone era. Enjoy the richly wainscoted entry hall, formal dining room with marble fireplace, and a collection of vintage phonographs. Step back in time when you enter the Colonial common room with beamed ceiling and walk-in fireplace. The spacious, antique-furnished guest

---

year; 6 Pets welcome; 7 Children welcome; 8 Tennis nearby; 9 Swimming nearby; 10 Golf nearby; 11 Skiing nearby; 12 May be booked through travel agent

rooms are a joy. Air conditioned. Private baths.

Hosts: Gerry and Herb Moss
Rooms: 6 (PB) $75-99
Continental Breakfast
Credit Cards: A, B
Notes: 2, 5, 7, 8, 9, 12

QUARRYVILLE

Runnymede Farm Guest House Bed and Breakfast

1030 Robert Fulton Highway, 17566
(717) 786-3625

Enjoy our comfortable farmhouse in south Lancaster County. The rooms are clean and air conditioned, and the lounge has a TV. Close to tourist attractions, but not in the main stream. Country breakfast is optional.

Hosts: Herbert and Sara Hess
Rooms: 3 (SB) $35-40
Full Breakfast
Credit Cards: None
Notes: 2, 5, 7, 8, 9, 10

SAINT THOMAS

Heavenly Sent (No Longer Easy Does It Farm)

7886 LWW, 17252
(717) 369-5882

Even a traveler without wings can easily find Heavenly Sent, located just west of St. Thomas on Route 30. This five-acre haven will lift the spirits of its guests with its panoramic view of the Appalachian Mountains and easy access to White Trail Ski Resort, Ski Liberty, historic Gettysburg, Cowans Gap State Park, Wilson College, and many other attractions. Breakfast is tailored to the guests' wishes. House is beautifully restored and contains many antique furnishings. The are three resident, beautiful, caged parrots.

Hosts: Gregg and Karen Brady
Rooms: 2 (PB) $80-120
Continental Breakfast
Credit Cards: A, B
Notes: 2, 3 & 4 (for additional charge), 5, 7 (limited), 9, 10, 11, 12 (restricted)

SCOTTDALE

Pine Wood Acres Bed and Breakfast

Rural Route 1, Box 634, 15683-9567
(412) 887-5404

A country home surrounded by four acres of woods, wildflowers, and herb and flower gardens. Ten miles from the Pennsylvania Turnpike and I-70, New Stanton exits; 25 miles from Frank Lloyd Wright's Falling Water. Full breakfasts and warm hospitality are yours to enjoy at Pine Wood Acres. Hosts are members of the Mennonite Church.

Hosts: Ruth and James Horsch
Rooms: 3 (SB) $58.30-79.50
Full Breakfast
Credit Cards: None
Notes: 2, 5, 6, 7, 8, 9, 10, 11, 12

SHIPPENSBURG

Field and Pine Bed and Breakfast

2155 Ritner Highway, 17257
(717) 776-7179

Surrounded by stately pine trees, Field and Pine is a family-owned bed and breakfast with the charm of an early American stone house on an 80-acre gentleman's farm. Built in 1790, the house has seven working fireplaces, original wide-pine floors, and stenciled walls. Bedrooms are furnished with antiques, quilts, and comforters. A gourmet breakfast is served in the formal dining room. Three miles from I-81 between Carlisle and Shippensburg.

Hosts: Mary Ellen and Allan Williams
Rooms: 3 (1PB; 2SB) $65-75
Full Breakfast
Credit Cards: A, B
Notes: 2, 5, 8, 9, 10, 12

SMOKETOWN (LANCASTER COUNTY)

Homestead Lodging

184 East Brook Road, Route 896, 17576
(717) 393-6927

Welcome to Homestead Lodging where

quiet, country living and a homey atmosphere await you. After a leisurely morning coffee and danish, enjoy a walk down the lane to the scenic farmland around us. You can tour the countryside or go on a shopping spree in one of our many markets, quilt shops, antique shops, and craft shops. Restaurants are within walking distance.

Hosts: Robert and Lori Kepiro
Rooms: 4 (PB) $28-49
Continental Breakfast
Credit Cards: A, B
Notes: 2 (deposit only), 5, 7, 8, 9, 10, 11

SOMERSET

H.B.'s Cottage

231 West Church Street, 15501
(814) 443-1204; (814) 443-4313 (FAX)

In the borough of Somerset, this 1920's stone and frame cottage has an oversize fireplace in the livingroom and is furnished in the traditional manner with accent pieces and collectibles from overseas travels by this retired Naval Officer and his wife. The guest room is warmly decorated and has a private porch. Located close to Seven Springs, Falling Water, Hidden Valley, biking and hiking trails, and whitewater sports. No smoking.

Hosts: Hank and Phyllis Vogt
Rooms: 1 (PB) $65
Extended Continental Breakfast
Credit Cards: A, B
Notes: 2, 6 (limited), 8, 9, 10, 11

---

year; 6 Pets welcome; 7 Children welcome; 8 Tennis nearby; 9 Swimming nearby; 10 Golf nearby; 11 Skiing nearby; 12 May be booked through travel agent

SPRUCE CREEK

Cedar Hill Farm of Spruce Creek Valley

HC-01, Box 26, Rte 45 east, 16683
(814) 632-8319

This early 1800's farmhouse is located in Huntingdon County on an active livestock farm. Individual and family activities are available at Old Bedford Village, Horse Shoe Curve, Bland's Park, Raystown Lake, Lincoln and Indian Caverns, and Penn State University. Member Pennsylvania Farm Vacation Association. Fishing and hunting available on private and state game lands during stated seasons; proper licenses required.

Hostess: Sharon M. Dell
Rooms: 4 (SB) $35-50
Full Breakfast
Credit Cards: A, B
Notes: 2, 5, 7, 11

STAHLSTOWN

Thorn's Cottage Bed and Breakfast

R.D. #1, Box 254, 15687
(412) 593-6429

Located in the natural, cultural, and historic Ligonier Valley area of Pennsylvania's scenic Laurel Mountains, PA turnpike eight miles away, fifty miles east of Pittsburgh, the secluded three-room cottage offers guests a homey, woodland privacy. In addition, the hosts offer one bedroom, shared bath in their cozy, arts-and-crafts bungalow. Porches and herb garden complement the European, country-inspired ambience. Breakfast includes homebaked muffins and scones to complement country, gourmet-style dishes.

Hosts: Larry and Beth Thorn
Rooms: 1 cottage (PB); 1 room (SB) $40-55
Full Breakfast
Credit Cards: None
Notes: 2, 5, 7, 9, 10, 11

STARRUCCA

Nethercott Inn Bed and Breakfast

P.O. Box 26, 18462
(717) 727-2211

This lovely, 1893 Victorian home is nestled in a small village in the Endless Mountains and furnished in antiques. All rooms have queen size beds and private baths. A full breakfast is included. Located three and one-half hours from New York City and Philadelphia, and eight hours from Toronto, Canada.

Hosts: Ned and Ginny Nethercott
Rooms: 5 (PB) $65
Full Breakfast
Credit Cards: A, B, C, D
Notes: 2, 5, 7, 10, 11, 12 (10%)

Nethercott Inn

NOTES: Credit cards accepted: A Master Card; B Visa; C American Express; D Discover Card; E Diners Club; F Other; 2 Personal checks accepted; 3 Lunch available; 4 Dinner available; 5 Open all

The Decoy Bed and Breakfast

STRASBURG (LANCASTER COUNTY)

The Decoy Bed and Breakfast

958 Eisenberger Road, 17579
(717) 687-8585; (800) 726-2287; (717) 687-8585 (FAX)

This former Amish home is set in farmland with spectacular views and an informal atmosphere. Craft shops and attractions are nearby, and bicycle tours can be arranged. Two cats in residence.

Hosts: Debby and Hap Joy
Rooms: 5 (PB) $42.40-63.60 (taxes included)
Full Breakfast
Credit Cards: None
Notes: 2, 5, 7, 8, 10

SWIFTWATER

Britannia Country Inn

P.O. Box 8, 18370
(717) 839-7243

A taste of England in the heart of the Poconos. Set on 12 acres with pool, tennis courts, and lawn sports. Four individual cottages with fireplaces. Nine, English, Laura Ashley-decorated inn rooms. Eight family "Pocono's Rustic" cottages. Quaint porch and log fires in the restaurants. American and English cuisine.

Hosts: Bob and Joan Matthews, Barry and Mary Webster
Rooms: 21 (PB) $50-90
Full Breakfast
Credit Cards: A, B, C, E
Notes: 4, 5, 6, 7, 8, 9, 10, 11, 12

THOMPSON

Jefferson Inn

Route 171, Rural Delivery 2, Box 36, 18465
(717) 727-2625

Built in 1871, the inn offers reasonably priced accommodations and a full-service restaurant. Situated in the rolling hills of northeast Pennsylvania, there are thousands of acres available nearby for fishing, boating, and some of the best deer and turkey hunting around. Other seasonal activities include skiing, snowmobiling,

year; 6 Pets welcome; 7 Children welcome; 8 Tennis nearby; 9 Swimming nearby; 10 Golf nearby; 11 Skiing nearby; 12 May be booked through travel agent

horseback riding, and golf. Good, Gospel-preaching churches are nearby.

Hosts: Douglas and Marge Stark
Rooms: 6 (3PB; 3SB) $30-50
Continental Breakfast (full available for extra fee)
Credit Cards: A, B
Notes: 2, 3, 4, 5, 6, 7, 8, 9, 10, 11 (XC), 12

TOWANDA

The Victorian Guest House

118 York Avenue, 18848
(717) 265-6972

Considered one of the grandest homes in Bradford County, this elegant 1897 structure is classic Victorian, with porches, arches, tower rooms, and a host of period architectural splendors. Bedrooms and open areas of the home are furnished with 19th-century antiques. Warm, cozy, Christian atmosphere.

Hosts: Tom and Nancy Taylor
Rooms: 10 (PB) $50-60
Continental Breakfast
Credit Cards: A, B, C, E
Notes: 2, 5, 7, 8, 9, 10, 11, 12

VALLEY FORGE

Valley Forge Mountain Bed and Breakfast

Box 562, 19481
(800) 344-0123; (215) 783-7783 (FAX)

George Washington headquartered here! Centrally located between Philadelphia, Lancaster County, Reading outlets, and the Brandywine Valley, this French Colonial is on three wooded acres adjacent to Valley Forge Park. Air conditioning,

phones, TV/VCR, computer, printer, FAX, fireplaces, and bridle and hiking trails. Near fine shopping, antiquing, restaurants, cross-country skiing, horseback riding, golf. Two guest suites—one double Victorian, one California king.

Hosts: Dick and Carolyn
Suites: 2 (PB) $50-65
Full or Continental Breakfast
Credit Cards: A, B, C, E
Notes: 2, 5, 7, 8, 9, 10, 11, 12

WELLSBORO

Kaltenbach's B & B

Stony Fork Road, Rural Delivery 6, Box 106A, 16901
(717) 724-4954; (800) 722-4954

This sprawling, country home with room for 32 guests offers visitors comfortable lodging, home-style breakfasts, and warm hospitality. Set on a 72-acre farm, Kaltenbach's provides ample opportunity for walks through meadows, pastures, and forests, picnicing, and watching the sheep, pigs, rabbits, and wildlife. All-you-can-eat country-style breakfasts are served. Honeymoon suites have tubs for two. Hunting and golf packages are available. Pennsylvania Grand Canyon. ABBA 2 crown award-winner.

Host: Lee Kaltenbach
Rooms: 11 (9PB; 2SB) $60-125
Full Breakfast
Credit Cards: A, B
Notes: 2, 3, 4, 5, 7, 8, 9, 10, 11

Kaltenbach's Bed and Breakfast

WEST ALEXANDER

Saints' Rest

P.O. Box 15, 77 Main Street, 15376
(412) 484-7950

Saints' Rest Bed and Breakfast, a home
away from home. Victorian gingerbread
outside, interior decorated with liveable
antiques. Saints' Rest is located 45 miles
west of Pittsburgh on the Old National
Pike. One minute from I-70, east or west,
or Main Street in historical borough of
West Alexander. Fifteen minutes from
Wheeling, West Virginia, and Washington, Pennsylvania. Attractions include nationally known Oglebay Park, 20 minutes
away, and Jamboree USA. Non-smoking
residence.

Hosts: Myrne and Earl Lewis
Rooms: 3 (2PB; 1 SB) $60 + tax
Full Breakfast
Credit Cards: None
Notes: 2, 5, 7 (over 8)

WHITE OAK

Easlers Bed and Breakfast

3401 Foster Road, 15131
(412) 673-1133

Encircled by silver maples on the highest
hill in Allegheny County, this 1929 English
Tudor mansion welcomes family travelers
with four restful guest rooms. White Oak is
located about 17 miles southeast of Pittsburgh and seven miles from the Pennsylvania Turnpike (Exits 6 and 7). Gourmet
breakfasts are a specialty. Children under
ten stay free in parents' room. New
solarium with hot tub.

Hostess: Kathleen Easler
Rooms: 4 (2PB; 2SB) $40-60
Full Breakfast
Credit Cards: None
Notes: 2, 5, 6, 7, 8, 9, 12

WILKES-BARRE

Ponda-Rowland Bed and Breakfast Inn and Farm Vacations

Rural Route 1, Box 348, Dallas, 18612
(717) 639-3245; (800) 854-3286

The farmhouse, circa 1850, features a
large stone fireplace, beamed ceilings, and
museum-quality country antiques. On this
large, scenic farm in the Endless Mountain
region of Pennsylvania, guests can see and
touch pigs, goats, sheep, cows, rabbits,
and a horse. They also can enjoy 34 acres
of a private wildlife refuge, including six
ponds, walking and skiing trails, canoeing,
swimming, and ice skating. Nearby are
horseback riding, air tours, state parks,
trout fishing, hunting, restaurants, county
fairs, downhill skiing.

Hosts: Jeanette and Cliff Rowland
Rooms: 5 (PB) $55-85
Full Breakfast
Credit Cards: A, B, C, D
Notes: 2, 5, 7, 9, 10, 11, 12

---

year; 6 Pets welcome; 7 Children welcome; 8 Tennis nearby; 9 Swimming nearby; 10 Golf nearby;
11 Skiing nearby; 12 May be booked through travel agent

WRIGHTSVILLE

Roundtop Bed and Breakfast

6995 Roundtop Lane, 17368
(717) 252-3169; (800) 801-0184

Roundtop is situated high above the Susquehanna River on more than 100 acres of woodland. Built in 1880, this German stone house has been renovated to take full advantage of the spectacular views. Its many porches and fireplaces, as well as its spacious, attractive rooms, make it a romantic weekend getaway any time of the year. It is halfway between York and Lancaster.

Hosts: Jodi and Tyler Sloen
Rooms: 6 (1PB; 4SB) $50-75
Full Breakfast
Credit Cards: A, B
Notes: 2, 5, 7

YORK

Smyser-Bair House Bed and Breakfast

30 South Beaver Street, 17401
(717) 854-3411

A magnificent Italianate townhouse in the historic district. Rich in history and architectural details with crystal chandeliers and stained glass windows. Enjoy our antiques, warm hospitality, and player piano. Near Lancaster, Gettysburg, and Baltimore. Walk to farmer's markets. Convenient parking.

Hosts: The King Family
Rooms: 4 (1PB; 3SB) $60-80
Full Breakfast
Credit Cards: A, B
Notes: 2, 5, 7, 10, 12

Roundtop Bed and Breakfast

NOTES: Credit cards accepted: A Master Card; B Visa; C American Express; D Discover Card; E Diners Club; F Other; 2 Personal checks accepted; 3 Lunch available; 4 Dinner available; 5 Open all

Rhode Island

BLOCK ISLAND

Hotel Manisses

1 Spring Street, 02807
(401) 466-2421; (401) 466-2858 (FAX)

Restored Victorian hotel with authentic turn-of-the-century furnishings and today's comforts. All rooms with private bath and telephone; some have jacuzzis. Fine dining in our dining room overlooking the fountains and gardens. After-dinner drinks and flaming coffees served in upstairs parlor.

Hosts: Justin and Joan Abrams; Steve and Rita Draper
Rooms: 17 (PB) $100-350
Full Breakfast
Credit Cards: A, B, C
Notes: 2, 4, 7 (over 10), 8, 9, 12

The Sheffield House

High Street, 02807
(401) 466-2494; (401) 466-5067 (FAX)

1888 Queen Anne Victorian in quiet setting—a five-minute walk to ferry dock, beaches, shops, restaurants in quaint Old Harbor. Guests enjoy complimentary breakfast of fresh fruit, juices, granola and cereals, yogurt, home-baked muffins, and coffee and teas served from antique Irish sideboard. Guests have use of the house, wrap-around porch, and secluded garden. Afternoon tea is served.

Hosts: Steve and Claire McQueeny
Rooms: 7 (5PB; 2SB) $50-140
Continental Plus Breakfast
Credit Cards: A, B, C
Notes: 2, 5, 8, 9, 12

The White House

Spring Street, 02807
(401) 466-2653

Large island mansion with French Provencal antique furniture throughout. Sea vistas all rooms. Gourmet breakfast. Transportation to and from ferry/airport. Library. President's room with authentic autographs from presidents.

Hosts: Joseph V. and Violette M. Connolly
Rooms: 3 (1PB; 2SB) $100-120 (off-season rates available)
Full Breakfast
Credit Cards: A, B, C
Notes: 2, 5, 8, 9, 12

Willows

P.O. box 1260, 5310 Route 1, 02813
(401) 364-7727; (401) 364-3290 (FAX)

Visit this 15-acre estate beside a salt water pond with boating, outdoor pool, and tennis court. Enjoy quiet, relaxing surroundings—very well maintained. All

year; 6 Pets welcome; 7 Children welcome; 8 Tennis nearby; 9 Swimming nearby; 10 Golf nearby; 11 Skiing nearby; 12 May be booked through travel agent

rooms have air-conditioning and telephone.

Host: Scott Duhamel
Rooms: 30 (PB) $50-120
Full Breakfast
Credit Cards: A, B
Notes: 4, 5, 8, 9, 10

GREEN HILL

Fairfield-By-The-Sea Bed and Breakfast

527 Green Hill Beach Road, 02879-6215
(401) 789-4717

An artist's contemporary home in an intimate, country setting offers beauty and seclusion. Stress reduction is the order of the day at this comfortable, airy house with an eclectic collection of art and an interesting library. Day trips are possible to Block Island, Martha's Vineyard, Cape Cod, Boston, Newport, Plymouth, and Mystic Seaport. Golf, bird-watching, tennis, sailing, nature trails, fine shops, museums, historical sights, antiques, restaurants are all nearby.

Hostess: Jeanne A. Lewis
Rooms: 2 (SB) $45-60
Expanded Continental Breakfast
Credit Cards: C
Notes: 2, 5, 7, 8, 9, 10, 11, 12

KINGSTON

Hedgerow Bed and Breakfast

1747 Mooresfield Road, P.O. Box 1586, 02881
(401) 783-2671; (800) 486-4587

A lovely Colonial built in 1933 on two and one-quarter acres with tennis courts and formal gardens. Conveniently located 15 miles from Newport, 30 miles south of Providence, and next to the University of Rhode Island. The ferry to Block Island, beaches, and Mystic and Connecticut's seaport are within easy reach. Call for price information.

Hosts: Ann and Jim Ross
Rooms: 4 (SB) $60
Full Breakfast
Credit Cards: D
Notes: 2, 5, 7, 8, 9, 10

MIDDLETOWN

Lindsey's Guest House

6 James St., 02842
(401) 846-9386

Walk to beaches and restaurants. Five minutes to Newport's famous mansions, Ocean Drive, Cliff Walk, boat and bus tours, and bird sanctuary. Quiet residential neighborhood with off-street parking. Large yard and deck with hostess available for information about events and discounts. Split-level, owner-occupied home with expanded continental breakfast. One room is wheelchair accessible for 28 inch wheelchair.

Hostess: Anne Lindsey
Rooms: 3 (1PB; 2SB) $45-85
Continental Plus Breakfast
Credit Cards: A, B
Notes: 2, 5, 7, 8, 9, 10, 12

NEWPORT

Admiral Farragut Inn

31 Clarke Street
Mailing address: 8 Fair Street, 02840
(401) 846-4256; (800) 343-2863

The Admiral Farragut Inn, circa 1702, is a

most unique colonial inn. Everywhere, in our guest rooms, great room, foyer, and halls, there are fresh interpretations of colonial themes, and even a bit of whimsy, to make anyone's stay a delight. Our personal favorites are the Shaker-style, four-poster beds made by our in-house carpenter. There are painted armoires, gaily colored stencils, imported English antiques, faux-marble mantels with real Delft tiles. Located in one of Newport's historic areas and central to attractions. Afternoon tea is served.

Hostess: Deanna Shinnick
Rooms: 10 (PB) $50-110
Full Breakfast
Credit Cards: A, B, C, E
Notes: 7 (over 12), 8, 9, 10, 12

Bed and Breakfast Rhode Island, Inc.

P.O. Box 3291, 02840
(401) 849-1298; (800) 828-0000; (401) 849-1306 (FAX)

This is a professional, full-time reservation service representing historic inns, guest houses, and homestays throughout Rhode Island and New England. Quality accommodations are offered at elegant Victorian and historic Colonial inns and homes located in towns, villages, on the ocean, and in great rural settings. All are closely quality controlled and personally inspected for cleanliness and desirability. Individual, and group packages, and tours available. Barbara and Rodney Wakefield, owners.

Cliffside Inn

2 Seaview Avenue, 02840
(800) 845-1811; (401) 848-5850

Built in 1880 by the Governor of Maryland as a summer getaway, this elegant Victorian is located in a quiet neighborhood near the beach and Newport's famous Cliff Walk. The house was also home of eccentric artist Beatrice Turner who painted over 1,000 self-portraits during her lifetime. Rooms may include whirlpool tubs, a steam bath, and period antiques. All rooms are air conditioned.

Host: Stephen Nicolas
Rooms: 12 (PB) $135-325
Full Breakfast
Credit Cards: A, B, C, D, E
Notes: 2, 5, 8, 9, 12

Halidon Hill Guest House

Halidon Avenue, 02840
(401) 847-8318

Location is everything in Newport, and we are a ten-minute walk from Hammersmith Farm, minutes from the beach, convenient to shopping areas, restaurants, and mansions. Our rooms are modern and spacious, and we have a deck and in-ground pool for your enjoyment.

Hosts: Helen and Ginger Burke
Rooms: 4 (2PB; 2SB) $55-125
Continental Breakfast
Credit Cards: C, D, E
Notes: 5, 7, 8, 10, 12

---

year; 6 Pets welcome; 7 Children welcome; 8 Tennis nearby; 9 Swimming nearby; 10 Golf nearby; 11 Skiing nearby; 12 May be booked through travel agent

John Easton House

23 Catherine Street, 02840
(401) 849-6246 (Voice and FAX)

This gracious Victorian inn is listed on the National Historic Register and is situated in the heart of Newport. Each room is spacious, elegantly furnished, and has a sparkling private bathroom, air-conditioning , and color television. Some rooms have kitchenettes, and some have working fireplaces for that autumn or off-season chill. Our off-season rates are lower, too. Excellent location within walking distance to the beach and waterfront boutiques. Ample off-street parking. All rooms are non-smoking.

Hosts: Ted and Carmen Gloria Critz
Rooms: 6 (PB) $65-125
Continental Breakfast
Credit Cards: A, B, D
Notes: 5, 7, 8, 9, 10, 12

Spring Street Inn

353 Spring Street, 02840
(401) 847-4767

Spring Street Inn is a charming restored Victorian home, circa 1858. We have seven double guestrooms and private baths, a harbor-view apartment for two to four people, and a comfortable guest sitting room with CATV. We serve a home-cooked, full breakfast and have off-street parking. The Inn is within walking distance to all Newport's highlights, only one block from the harbor.

Hosts: Parvin and Damian Latimore
Rooms: 8 (6PB; 2SB) $45-140
Full Breakfast
Credit Cards: A, B
Notes: 2, 5, 7, 8, 9, 12

Stella Maris Inn

91 Washington St., 02840
(401) 849-2862

French Victorian mansion, built in 1862 on one and one-half acres of lawns and gardens overlooking Newport Harbor. Large wrap-around porch. Five rooms with water view. Four rooms with working fireplaces. Quiet residential neighborhood —short walk to town—parking on premises. Antique furnishings. Homemade muffins and breads baked daily.

Hosts: Dorothy and Ed Madden
Rooms: 8 (PB) $50-150
Upgraded Continental Breakfast
Credit Cards: None
Notes: 2, 5, 7, 8, 9, 10, 12

PROVIDENCE

The Old Court B & B

144 Benefit Street, 02903
(401) 751-2002; (401) 272-6566 (FAX)

The Old Court is filled with antique furniture, chandeliers, and memorabilia from the nineteenth century, with each room designed to reflect period tastes. All rooms have private baths, and the antique, Victorian beds are comfortable and spacious. Just a three-minute walk from the center of downtown Providence, near Brown University and Rhode Island School of Design.

Hostess: Becky Aijala
Rooms: 11 (PB) $95-160
Continental Breakfast
Credit Cards: A, B, C, D
Notes: 8

NOTES: Credit cards accepted: A Master Card; B Visa; C American Express; D Discover Card; E Diners Club; F Other; 2 Personal checks accepted; 3 Lunch available; 4 Dinner available; 5 Open all

State House Inn

43 Jewett Street, 02908
(401) 785-1235; (401) 351-4201 (FAX)

A country inn usually means peace and quiet, friendly hosts, comfort and simplicity, with beautiful furnishings. The State House Inn has all of these qualifications, but just happens to be located in the city of Providence. Our inn has fireplaces, hardwood floors, Shaker or Colonial furnishings, canopy beds, and modern conveniences such as FAX, TV, and phone. Located near downtown and local colleges and universities.

Hosts: Frank and Monica Hopton
Rooms: 10 (PB) $59-99
Full Breakfast
Credit Cards: A, B, C
Notes: 5, 7, 12

WAKEFIELD

Larchwood Inn

521 Main St., 02879
(401) 783-5454; (401) 783-1800 (FAX)

Watching over the main street of this quaint New England town for over 160 years, this grand old house, surrounded by lawns and shaded by stately trees, dispenses hospitality and good food and spirits from early morning to late at night. Historic Newport, picturesque Mystic Seaport, and salty Block Island are a short ride away.

Hosts: Francis and Diann Browning
Rooms: 19 (12PB; 7SB) $30-90
Full Breakfast
Credit Cards: A, B, C, D, E
Notes: 2, 3, 4, 5, 6, 7, 8, 9, 10, 12

WYOMING

The Cookie Jar Bed and Breakfast

64 Kingstown Road (Rte. 138 off I-95), 02898
(401) 539-2680; (800) 767-4262

The heart of our home, the living room, was built in 1732 as a blacksmith's shop. Later, the forge was removed and a large granite fireplace was built by an American Indian stonemason. The original wood ceiling, hand-hewn beams, and granite walls remain today. The property was called the Perry Plantation, and, yes, they had two slaves who lived above the blacksmith's shop. We offer friendly, home-style living in a comfortable, country setting. On Route 138 just off I-95.

Hosts: Dick and Madelein Sohl
Rooms: 3 (1PB; 2SB) $60-65
Full Breakfast
Credit Cards: None
Notes: 2, 5, 7, 8, 9, 10, 12

---

year; 6 Pets welcome; 7 Children welcome; 8 Tennis nearby; 9 Swimming nearby; 10 Golf nearby; 11 Skiing nearby; 12 May be booked through travel agent

South Carolina

BEAUFORT

TwoSuns Inn B & B

1705 Bay Street, 29902
(803) 522-1122 (Voice and FAX); (800) 532-4244

Southern charm in Historic Beaufort (*Prince of Tides* film site) and informal ambience in a three-story, 1917, grand home right on the bay await TwoSun's guests. Visit our quaint downtown, enjoy a carriage ride through our historic waterfront community, and relax in our newly restored home, complete with Carrol's weavings, collectibles, period decor, wheelchair accessibility and business amenities.

Hosts: Carrol and Ron Kay
Rooms: 5 (PB) $89-109
Full Breakfast
Credit Cards: A, B, C
Notes: 2, 5, 8, 9, 10, 12

BENNETTSVILLE

The Breeden House Inn and Carriage House

404 East Main Street, 29512
(803) 479-3665

Built in 1886, the romantic Breeden House is a beautifully restored Southern mansion on two acres. Provides very comfortable and liveable surroundings which will capture your interest and inspire your imagination. Listed on the National Register of Historic Places, the Inn is located 20 minutes off I-95. A great half-way point between Florida and New York. Both houses have inviting porches with wicker, rockers, swings, and ceiling fans. Beautiful antique decor, pool, cable TV in each room, phone in most rooms. Great country kitchen in Carriage House. A haven for antique lovers, runners, and walkers. Owned and operated by a Christian family. No smoking. Retreats and reunions welcome.

Hosts: Wesley and Bonnie Park
Rooms: 7 (PB) $50-55
Full Breakfast
Credit Cards: A, B, D
Notes: 2, 5, 7, 9, 10, 12

CHARLESTON

1837 Bed and Breakfast

126 Wentworth Street, 29401
(803) 723-7166

Enjoy accommodations in a wealthy cotton planter's home and brick carriage house centrally located in Charleston's historic district. Canopied, poster, rice beds. Walk to boat tours, the old market, antique shops, restaurants, and main attractions. Near the Omni and College of

Charleston. Full gourmet breakfast is served in the formal dining room and includes sausage pie, Eggs Benedict, ham omelets, and home-baked breads. The 1837 Tea Room serves afternoon tea to our guests and the public. Off-street parking.

Hosts: Sherri and Richard Dunn
Rooms: 8 (PB) $59-99
Full Breakfast
Credit Cards: A, B, C
Notes: 2, 5, 8, 9, 10

Ashley Inn Bed and Breakfast

201 Ashley Avenue, 29403
(803) 723-1848; (803) 723-9080 (FAX)

Stay in a stately, historic, circa 1835 home. So warm and hospitable, the Ashley Inn offers seven intimate bedrooms featuring canopy beds, private baths, fireplace, and air conditioning. Delicious breakfasts are served on a grand columned piazza overlooking a beautiful Charleston garden, or in the formal dining room. Relax with tea and cookies after touring nearby historic sites or enjoying the complimentary touring bicycles. Simple elegance in a warm, friendly home noted for true Southern hospitality.

Hosts: Sally and Bud Allen
Rooms: 7 (PB) $59-105
Full Breakfast
Credit Cards: A, B
Notes: 2, 5, 7 (over 12), 8, 9, 10, 12

The Belvedere

40 Rutledge Avenue, 29401
(803) 722-0973

A late 1800's Colonial mansion in the downtown historic district on Colonial Lake has an 1800 Georgian interior with mantels and woodwork. Three large bedrooms have antiques, Oriental rugs, and family collections. Easy access to everything in the area.

Hosts: David Spell and Rick Zender
Rooms: 3 (PB) $110-125
Continental Plus Breakfast
Credit Cards: None
Closed December 1-February 15
Notes: 2, 7 (over 8), 8, 9, 10

Cannonboro Inn Bed and Breakfast

184 Ashley Avenue, 29403
(803) 723-8572; (803) 723-9080 (FAX)

Stay in a gracious, historic, Charleston, single house. Over 150 years old, the Cannonboro Inn lies in the heart of a section of Charleston's historic district. Shaded by crepe myrtles and palmettos, guests enjoy a full breakfast overlooking the garden and fountain. The parlor welcomes guests to visit, read, or play games; complimentary bicycles provided for touring.

Hosts: Bud and Sally Allen
Rooms: 6 (PB) $69-125
Full Breakfast
Credit Cards: A, B
Notes: 2, 5, 7 (over 12), 8, 9, 10, 12

Country Victorian Bed and Breakfast

105 Tradd Street, 29401-2422
(803) 577-0682

Come relive the charm of the past. Relax in a rocker on the piazza of this historic home and watch the carriages go by. Walk to antique shops, churches, restaurants, art galleries, museums, and all historic points

year; 6 Pets welcome; 7 Children welcome; 8 Tennis nearby; 9 Swimming nearby; 10 Golf nearby; 11 Skiing nearby; 12 May be booked through travel agent

of interest. The house, built in 1820, is located in the historic district south of Broad. Rooms have private entrances and contain antique iron and brass beds, old quilts, antique oak and wicker furniture, and braided rugs over heart-of-pine floors. Homemade cookies will be waiting. Many extras!

Hostess: Diane Deardurff Weed
Rooms: 2 (PB) $65-90
Expanded Continental Breakfast
Credit Cards: None
Notes: 2, 5, 7, 8, 9, 10, 12

King George IV Inn and Guests

32 George Street, 29401
(803) 723-9339

A 200-year-old, circa 1790, Charleston Historic House located in the heart of historic district. The inn is Federal style with three levels of Charleston side porches. All rooms have decorative fireplaces, 10-12 foot ceilings, wide-planked hardwood floors, old furnishings, and antiques. Private baths, parking, AC, TV's. One-minute walk to historic King Street, five-minute walk to historic market. A step back in time!

Hosts: Jean, Lynn, Sara, BJ, and Mike
Rooms: 8 (PB) $55-85
Continental Breakfast
Credit Cards: A, B
Notes: 2, 5, 6 (by arrangement), 7, 8, 9, 10, 12

The Kitchen House, Circa 1732

126 Tradd Street, 29401
(803) 577-6362

Nestled in the heart of the historic district,

the Kitchen House is a completely restored, 18th-century, kitchen dwelling. Southern hospitality, absolute privacy, cozy fireplaces, antiques, patio, and colonial herb garden await you. The refrigerator and pantry are stocked for breakfast. The pre-Revolutionary War house was featured in *Colonial Homes* magazine and written up in the *New York Times*.

Hostess: Lois Evans
Rooms: 3 (PB) $75-150
Full Breakfast
Credit Cards: A, B
Notes: 2, 5, 7, 8, 9, 10, 12

Rutledge Victorian Inn and Guest House

114 Rutledge Avenue, 29401
(803) 722-7551

Welcome to the past! This century-old Victorian house in Charleston's downtown historic district is quaint but elegant, with large, decorative porches, columns, and antique gingerbread. The authentic Old Charleston house has decorative fireplaces, hardwood floors, 12-foot ceilings, 10-foot doors and windows, old furnishings, and antiques. Modern amenities include air conditioning, TV, private or shared baths, ice machine, and refrigerator. Walking distance to all historic attractions. Homemade goodies served in continental breakfast.

Hosts: Jean, Sara, BJ, Lynn, and Mike
Rooms: 11 (6PB; 5SB) $45-85
Continental Breakfast
Credit Cards: A, B
Notes: 2, 5, 6 (some), 7, 8, 9, 10, 12

NOTES: Credit cards accepted: A Master Card; B Visa; C American Express; D Discover Card; E Diners Club; F Other; 2 Personal checks accepted; 3 Lunch available; 4 Dinner available; 5 Open all

CLIO

The Henry Bennett House
301 Red Bluff Street, 29525

The Henry Bennett House is a turn-of-the-century Queen Anne Victorian and is located in the historic district of Clio. Built in 1903 by Mr. Bennett, who was a cotton farmer. The exterior is most striking with the enormous wrap-around veranda and pillars. The interior has wide-board paneled wainscoting and paneled-beaded, board ceilings. There are fireplaces throughout the house. The walls are plaster, and the floors are heart pine. Must be seen to appreciate.

Hosts: Connie and Dennis Hodgkinson
Rooms: 2 $50
Full Breakfast
Credit Cards: A, B
Notes: 2, 4, 5, 7, 9, 10

COLUMBIA

Claussen's Inn
2003 Greene Street, 29205
(803) 765-0440; (800) 622-3382; (803) 799-7924 (FAX)

This AAA four diamond rated inn is listed on the National Register of Historic Places. Located near the heart of Columbia next to the University of South Carolina, Claussen's offers a vast array of restaurants and night life within walking distance. With amenities that include complimentary breakfast served to your room, newspaper delivered daily to your door, and turndown service, Claussen's unique decor and service are designed for that "at-home" ambience.

Host: Dan Vance
Rooms: 29 (PB) $85-110
Continental Plus Breakfast
Credit Cards: A, B, C
Notes: 2, 3, 4, 5, 7, 10, 12

GEORGETOWN

1790 House
630 Highmarket Street, 29440
(803) 546-4821

Meticulously restored, 200-year-old plantation-style inn located in the heart of historic Georgetown. Spacious, luxurious rooms, fireplaces, central air and heat. Lovely gardens to enjoy. Stay in the "slave quarters," "rice planters'" rooms, our beautiful honeymoon cottage with jacuzzi tub, or one of our other lovely rooms. Walk to shops, restaurants, and historic sites. Short drive to Myrtle Beach and the Grandstrand, Brokgreen Gardens, Pawley's Island, and Charleston. A golfer's paradise! Rated by ABBA, AAA, and Mobil Travel.

Hosts: Patricia and John Wiley
Rooms: 6 (PB) $70-125
Full Breakfast
Credit Cards: A, B, C
Notes: 2, 5, 7, 8, 10, 12

Ashfield Manor
3030 S. Island Rd., 29440
(803) 546-0464

This Christian home offers southern hospitality in the style of a real southern plantation. Ashfield Manor offers an elegant country setting. All rooms are oversized and redecorated with period furnishings; private entrance and color TV. Continental breakfast is served in your room, the parlor, or on the 57-foot screened porch.

year; 6 Pets welcome; 7 Children welcome; 8 Tennis nearby; 9 Swimming nearby; 10 Golf nearby; 11 Skiing nearby; 12 May be booked through travel agent

Georgetown is quaint and historic with many attractions.

Hosts: Dave and Carol Ashenfelder
Rooms: 4 (SB) $45-65
Continental Breakfast
Credit Cards: A, B, C, D, E
Notes: 2, 5, 7, 8, 9, 10, 12

The Shaw House

613 Cypress Court, 29440
(803) 546-9663

After ten years, we are still excited about everyone who visits. We have a wonderful location overlooking a beautiful marsh, seen from a spacious den with an all-glass view. Large bedrooms; many antiques; well-stocked with books and magazines; wonderful nooks to relax and read; piano. Only five blocks from downtown and great restaurants. Our guests always leave with a recipe or prayer tied with a ribbon. Great bird-watching and bikes available. AAA approved.

Hosts: Mary and Joe Shaw
Rooms: 3 (PB) $55
Full Breakfast
Credit Cards: None
Notes: 2, 5, 7, 8, 9, 10

Shipwright's Bed and Breakfast

609 Cypress Ct., 29440
(803) 527-4475

Three thousand plus square feet of beautiful, quiet, clean home is yours to use when you stay. It's nautically attired and tastefully laced with family heirlooms. Guests say they feel like they just stayed at their best friend's home. The bedrooms and baths are beautiful and very comfortable. You'll never get "Grandma Eicker's Pancakes" anywhere else (the inn is famous for them). There's a great story behind the pancakes! The view from the large porch is breath-taking. Five minutes from Ocean Beach.

Hostess: Lea Wright
Rooms: 2 (1PB; 1SB) $50
Full Breakfast
Credit Cards: None
Notes: 2, 5, 7, 8, 9, 10

GREENWOOD

Inn on the Square

104 Court Street, 29646
(803) 223-7067

Each of the 48 rooms at the Inn is spacious and filled with lovely antique reproductions including rice-carved or pencil post beds with genuine Bates spreads, writing desks, armoires, all in solid mahogany. The Inn is convenient to shopping and has a quiet atmosphere of privacy and service. A small inn with lots of big city services!

Rooms: 48 (PB) $59.95-79.95
Full Breakfast (Continental on the weekend)
Credit Cards: A, B, C, D, E
Notes: 2, 3, 4, 5, 7, 8, 9, 10, 12

HONEA PATH

Sugarfoot Castle

211 S. Main St., 29654
(803) 369-6565

Enormous trees umbrella this 19th-century, brick ,Victorian home. Fresh flowers grace the 14-inch thick walled rooms furnished with family heirlooms. Enjoy the livingroom's interesting collections or the library's commfy chairs, TV, VCR, books, fireplace, desk, and game table. Upon arising, guests find coffee and juice outside their doors, followed by breakfast of hot breads, cereal, fresh fruit, and beverages served by candlelight in the dining room. Rock away the world's cares on a screened porch overlooking peaceful grounds.

Hosts: Gale and Cecil Evans
Rooms: 3 (SB) $44-48
Continental Breakfast
Credit Cards: A, B
Notes: 2, 5, 8, 9, 10

LANCASTER

Wade-Beckham House

3385 Great Falls Highway, 29720
(803) 285-1105

A circa 1832 plantation house listed on the National Register of Historic Places. Rural setting offering the Rose Room, the Summer House Room, the Wade Hampton Room. Antique and craft stores on premises. Peaceful homey environment.

Hosts: Bill and Jane Duke
Rooms: 3 (SB) $60
Full Breakfast
Credit Cards: None
Notes: 2, 8, 10

MCCLELLANVILLE

Laurel Hill Plantation

8913 North Highway 17, P. O. Box 190, 29458
(803) 887-3708

Laurel Hill faces the Atlantic Ocean and Intracoastal Waterway. Wrap-around porches provide a spectacular view of creeks and marshes. The reconstructed house is furnished with country and primitive antiques that reflect the Low Country lifestyle. Boating on the waterway depends on the tide, weather, and availability of the captain. Only 45 minutes north of Charleston, 1 hour and fifteen minutes south of Myrtle Beach.

Hosts: Jackie and Lee Morrison
Rooms: 4 (PB) $65-75
Full Breakfast
Credit Cards: None
Notes: 2, 5, 7 (over six), 9, 10, 12

MONCKS CORNER

Rice Hope Plantation Inn

206 Rice Hope Dr., 29461
(800) 569-4038; (803) 884-0223

Rice Hope Plantation was a working rice plantation in the 1790's. The beautiful grounds are graced with live oak trees, Spanish moss, and 200-year-old terraced formal gardens, with the Cooper River in the background. Because it is everything you think of when you picture a Southern plantation, Tri-Star Pictures filmed the movie *Consenting Adults* here. A friendly, relaxed atmosphere makes Rice

Hope the perfect place to get away from everything.

Hostess: Doris Kaspeak
Rooms: 5 (2PB; 3SB) $60-75
Continental Breakfast
Credit Cards: A, B
Notes: 2, 3, 4, 5, 7, 8, 12

MYRTLE BEACH

Serendipity, an Inn

407 North 71st Avenue, 29577
(803) 449-5268

An award-winning, mission-style inn is just 300 yards from the ocean beach and has a heated pool and Jacuzzi. All rooms have air conditioning, color TV, private baths, and refrigerators. Secluded patio, Ping-Pong, and shuffleboard. Over 70 golf courses nearby, as well as fishing, tennis, restaurants, theaters, and shopping. Ninety miles to historic Charleston. Near all country music theaters.

Hosts: Cos and Ellen Ficarra
Rooms: 12 (PB) $65-85
Expanded Continental Breakfast
Credit Cards: A, B, C, D
Notes: 7, 8, 9, 10, 12

ROCK HILL

East Main Guest House

600 E. Main St., 29730
(803) 366-1161

After extensive renovations, the upstairs contains three professionally decorated guest rooms with private baths, TV, and sitting room. The honeymoon suite features a canopy bed, fireplace, and whirlpool bath. A gourmet continental breakfast is served in the gracious dining room, and weather permitting under the patio garden percola. We are located 20 minutes from downtown Charlotte, NC.

Hosts: Jerry and Melba Peterson
Rooms: 3 (PB) $59-79
Expanded Continental Breakfast
Credit Cards: A, B, C
Notes: 2, 5, 8, 9, 10, 11, 12

East Main Guest House

South Dakota

BRYANT

The Big Brown Country Inn Bed-n-Breakfast

RR 1, Box 186, 57221-9793
(605) 628-2049

This 100-year-old, Victorian-style home is decorated in country crafts and Early American-style furniture. It sits on a tree-lined street in a small town. It is close to a Laura Wilder Museum and several small lakes for fishing. Laundry facilities are available and you may play the piano or ride bikes. Breakfast consists of home-made breads, jams, and jellies.

Hosts: Floyd and Myrta Rossel
Rooms: 3 (SB) $25
Both Full and Continental Breakfast
Credit Cards: None
Notes: 2, 5, 6, 7, 8, 9, 10

CANOVA

Skoglund Farm

Route 1, Box 45, 57321
(605) 247-3445

Skoglund Farm brings back memories of Grandpa and Grandma's home. It is furnished with antiques and collectibles. A full, home-cooked evening meal and break-fast are served. You can sight-see in the surrounding area, visit Little House on the Prairie Village, hike, horseback ride, or just relax. Several country churches are located nearby.

Hosts: Alden and Delores
Rooms: 5 (SB) $30 each adult; $20 each teen; $15 each child; children 5 and under free
Full Breakfast
Credit Cards: None
Notes: 2, 3, 4 (included), 5, 6, 7, 8, 9, 10, 12

CHAMBERLAIN

Riverview Ridge

HC69, Box 82A, 57325
(605) 734-6084

Modern home with queen and king beds. Beautiful view of the Missouri River. Lots of country peace and quiet with ample parking for your recreational vehicles. Full breakfasts with homemade breads and jellies. Enjoy fishing and golfing nearby. Make our home your home. Just 3 1/2 miles north of Chamberlain on Highway 50.

Hosts: Frank and Alta Cable
Rooms: 3 (1PB; 2SB) $45-55
Full Breakfast
Credit Cards: None
Notes: 2, 5, 7, 9, 10, 12

year; 6 Pets welcome; 7 Children welcome; 8 Tennis nearby; 9 Swimming nearby; 10 Golf nearby; 11 Skiing nearby; 12 May be booked through travel agent

CUSTER

Custer Mansion Bed and Breakfast

35 Centennial Drive, 57730
(605) 673-3333

Historic, 1891, Victorian Gothic home listed on the National Register of Historic Places features a blend of Victorian elegance and country charm with Western hospitality. Clean, quiet accommodations and delicious home-cooked breakfast. Central to all Black Hills attractions such as Mt. Rushmore, Crazy Horse Memorial, and many others. Recommended by *Bon Appetit*, AAA, and *Mobil Travel Guide*.

Hosts: Mill and Carole Seaman
Rooms: 6 (2PB; 4SB) $45-70
Full Breakfast
Credit Cards: None
Notes: 2, 5, 7, 8, 9, 10, 11

FREEMAN

Golden Robin Nest

1210 E. 4th Street, 57029
(605) 925-4410

Enjoy quiet Christian atmosphere, hosted by mature couple in small town. Enter via the Family Room—play games, piano, watch TV. Stairs from this room lead to guest rooms. Freeman is 35 miles north of Yankton (Gavin's Point Dam) and 45 miles from Sioux Falls (winter skiing). Mitchell (balloon races, Doll Museum, Corn Palace) is 55 miles away. I-29 is 31 miles east and I-90 is 29 miles north of Freeman. We are just off of State High-

way 81. No smoking.

Hosts: Goldie and Bob Boese
Rooms: 2 (SB) $25-30
Continental Breakfast
Credit Cards: None
Notes: 2, 5, 6 (outside only), 7, 8, 9, 10, 11

MILESVILLE

Fitch Farms

Box 8, 57553
(605) 544-3227

Fitch Farms is located three miles east and one mile north of the junction of highways 34 and 73. Western farm home. Lady of the house quilts and weaves on a floor loom. Two baths, full breakfast served family-farm style. Joggers and walkers welcome, also campers. Free ballroom dance lessons.

Hosts: Ed and Frances Fitch
Rooms: 2 (PB) $35
Full Breakfast
Credit Cards: None
Notes: 2, 5, 6, 7

RAPID CITY

Abend Haus Cottage and Audrie's Cranbury Corner Bed and Breakfast

23029 Thunderhead Falls Rd., 57702
(605) 342-7788

The ultimate in charm and Old World hospitality, our country home and five-acre estate is surrounded by thousands of acres

---

NOTES: Credit cards accepted: A Master Card; B Visa; C American Express; D Discover Card; E Diners Club; F Other; 2 Personal checks accepted; 3 Lunch available; 4 Dinner available; 5 Open all

of national forest in a secluded, Black Hills setting. Each quiet, comfortable suite and cottage has private entrance, hot tub, patio, cable TV, and refrigerator. Free trout fishing, hiking, biking available on property.

Hosts: Hank and Audry Kuhnhauser
Rooms: 6 (PB) $85
Full Breakfast
Credit Cards: None
Notes: 2, 5, 8, 9, 10, 11

SENECA

Rainbow Lodge
HC 78, Box 81, 57473
(605) 436-6795

Spend a quiet, relaxing day or evening by the lake on the prairie. Beautiful landscaping and trees, meditation areas, and chapel. You will enjoy country charm and hospitality on this oasis on the prairie; handicapped accessible; full, country-style breakfast; four miles off Highway 212. Reservations required.

Hosts: Ralph and Ann Wheeler
Rooms: 3 (SB) $30-45
Full Breakfast
Credit Cards: None
Notes: 2, 4, 5, 7

YANKTON

Mulberry Inn
512 Mulberry Street, 57078
(605) 665-7116

The beautiful Mulberry Inn offers the ultimate in comfort and charm in a traditional setting. Built in 1873, the inn features parquet floors, six guest rooms furnished with antiques, two parlors with marble fireplaces, and a large porch. Minutes from the Lewis and Clark Lake and within walking distance of the Missouri River, fine restaurants, and downtown. The inn is listed on the National Register of Historic Places.

Hostess: Millie Cameron
Rooms: 6 (2PB; 4SB) $35-51 May-September;
$32-45 October-April
Continental Breakfast (Full breakfast available with extra charge)
Credit Cards: A, B, C
Notes: 2, 5, 7, 8, 9, 10

Mulberry Inn

Tennessee

CHATTANOOGA

Alford House

5515 Alford Hill Dr., Rt. 4, 37419
(615) 821-7625

A 17-room, traditional-style home with antique decor located on the side of Lookout Mountain. Ten minutes to downtown Tennessee Aquarium and major attractions, and hiking trails are nearby. Coffee is served at wake-up, and breads, muffins, fresh fruits, cheeses, and juice start your day off right. Relax in the gazebo while enjoying the sounds of God's creation.

Hostess: Rhoda Alford
Rooms: 2 (SB) 1 suite (PB) $50-75
Expanded Continental Breakfast
Credit Cards: B
Notes: None

CHRISTIANA

Cedar Thicket Bed and Breakfast

3552 Rock Springs Rd., 37037
(615) 893-4015

Built on its original foundation dating back to the Civil War, this Victorian farmhouse was reconstructed in 1895 and is in the ownership of the sixth generation. The two-story home, complete with many of the original furnishings, is located on a 180-acre farm which is listed as a Century Farm. Area attractions include Stones River Battlefield, Nashville, and Opryland. Also available is a quaint house with kitchen and bathroom, a great place for those who prefer a more private atmosphere.

Hosts: Gilbert and Ginny Gordon
Rooms: 2 (PB) $50-60
Full Breakfast
Credit Cards: None
Notes: 2, 5, 7

Cedar Thicket

DANDRIDGE

Mill Dale Farm Bed and Breakfast

140 Mill Dale Road, 37725
(615) 397-3470; (800) 767-3471

Nineteenth-century farmhouse located in Tennessee's second oldest town. Floating staircase leads to three guest rooms, all with private baths. Nearby is fishing, boating, swimming, tennis, golf, the Great Smoky Mountains, Gatlinburg, and Pigeon Forge. Delicious country breakfast.

Hostess: Mrs. T. Hood (Lucy C.) Franklin
Rooms: 3 (PB) $65+tax
Full Breakfast
Credit Cards: None
Notes: 2, 5, 7, 8, 9, 10, 11

KODAK

Grandma's House

734 Pollard Road, 37764
(615) 933-3512; (800) 676-3512; (615) 933-0748 (FAX)

Colonial-style home on three acres at the base of the Great Smoky Mountains. Only two miles off I-40 at the 407 exit. Owners live on premises and are both native East Tennesseans. Country decor with handmade quilts and crafts. Farm-style "loosen your belt" breakfast begins when guests gather around the big oak table and Hilda says the blessing.

Hosts: Charlie and Hilda Hickman
Rooms: 3 (PB) $65
Full Breakfast
Credit Cards: A, B
Notes: 2, 5, 10, 11, 12

LEBANON

Rockhaven Bed and Breakfast

126 Timber Trail, 37987
(800) 647-4144

Lovely Cape Cod with private, luxurious three-room suite. Living room/kitchenette with refrigerator, microwave, and cable TV. Office area with library and phone.

Master bedroom has king-size bed, ceiling fan, and skylight. The 10 by 20 master bath offers jacuzzi, double-sink vanity, and marble shower. Delicious breakfast and Southern hospitality. The Inn can accommodate up to four people traveling together, and is only 20 minutes from Opryland and Nashville. This is a non-smoking environment. Special rates for senior citizens.

Hostess: Rhonda Anthamatten
Rooms: One Suite (PB) $85
Full Breakfast (continental available upon request)
Credit Cards: A, B
Notes: 2, 5, 10, 12

LIMESTONE

Snapp Inn B & B

1990 Davy Crockett Pk. Rd., 37681
(615) 257-2482

Your hosts will welcome you into this gracious 1815 Federal home furnished with antiques and set in farm country. Enjoy the peaceful mountain view from the full back porch, or play a game of pool. Located close to Davy Crockett State Park; 15 minutes to historic Jonesborough or Greenville.

Hosts: Dan and Ruth Dorgan
Rooms: 2 (PB) $50
Full Breakfast
Credit Cards: None
Notes: 2, 5, 6, 7 (1 only), 8, 9, 10, 12

MONTEAGLE

Adams Edgeworth Inn

Monteagle Assembly, 37356
(615) 924-2669; (615) 924-3236 (FAX)

Circa 1896, Adams Edgeworth Inn has

year; 6 Pets welcome; 7 Children welcome; 8 Tennis nearby; 9 Swimming nearby; 10 Golf nearby; 11 Skiing nearby; 12 May be booked through travel agent

provided fine lodging for almost 100 years and is still the region's leader in elegance and quality. Recently refurbished in English Manor decor, the inn is a showcase for fine antiques, important original paintings and sculptures, and a prize-winning rose garden. Stroll through the 96-acre Victorian Village which surrounds the inn, or drive 6 miles to the Gothic campus of Sewanee, University of the South. Cultural activities are year round; 150 miles of hiking trails, scenic vistas, waterfalls. Tennis, swimming, golf, riding nearby. Gourmet meals by special arrangement. "One of the best inns I've ever visited anywhere ..." (Sara Pitzer, *Recommended Country Inns* in *Country Inns Magazine*).

Hosts: Wendy and David Adams
Rooms: 12 (PB) $55-95; 1 suite $140
Full Breakfast
Credit Cards: A, B
Notes: 2, 4, 5 (by special arrangement), 8, 9, 10, 12 (by special arrangement)

North Gate Lodge

Monteagle Assembly #103, 37356
(615) 924-2799

Sleep on antique iron beds and custommade mattresses; wake with the birds for an early morning cup of coffee followed by a sumptuous full breakfast. Settle into a restful day at the inn or explore the walks and byways of the Monteagle Sunday School Assembly grounds, a 112-year-old Chautauqua with 160 Victorian summer homes. Nearby is a 90-year-old bakery, the Gothic campus of the University of the South, mountain vistas, waterfalls, hundreds of hiking trails, and innumerable shopping forays.

Hosts: Nancy and Henry Crais
Rooms: 7 (PB) $65-80
Full Breakfast
Credit Cards: None
Notes: 2, 5, 7, 8, 9, 10, 12

MURFREESBORO

Clardy's Guest House

435 East Main Street, 37130
(615) 893-6030

This large Victorian home was built in 1898 and is located in Murfreesboro's historic district. You will marvel at the ornate woodwork, beautiful fireplaces, and magnificent stained glass overlooking the staircase. The house is filled with antiques, as are local shops and malls. The hosts will help you with dining, shopping, and touring plans.

Hosts: Robert and Barbara Deaton
Rooms: 3 (2PB; 1SB) $35-50
Continental Breakfast
Credit Cards: None
Notes: 2, 5, 8, 9, 10

Clardy's Guest House

NATCHEZ TRACE—SEE NATCHEZ TRACE, MISSISSIPPI

PIGEON FORGE

Day Dreams Country Inn

2720 Colonial Drive, 37863
(615) 428-0370 (Voice and FAX)

Delight in the true country charm of this antique-filled, two-story log home with its six uniquely decorated bedrooms. Enjoy an evening by our cozy fireplace or relax on the front porch to the soothing sound of Mill Creek dancing by. Treat your taste buds to our bountiful country breakfast each morning. Perfect for family reunions and retreats. From Parkway, take 321 S., go one block, turn left on Florence Dr., go three blocks, and turn right on Colonial Dr.

Hosts: Yvonne and Mark Trombley
Rooms: 6 (PB) $79-99
Full Breakfast
Credit Cards: A, B
Notes: 2, 5, 7, 8, 9, 10, 11, 12

Hilton's Bluff Bed and Breakfast Inn

2654 Valley Heights Dr., 37863
(615) 428-9765; (800) 441-4188, (Ext. 8)

Truly elegant country living. Secluded hilltop setting only 1/2 mile from heart of Pigeon Forge. Minutes from outlet shopping, Dollywood, and Smoky Mountain National Park. The honeymoon, executive, and deluxe rooms, all with private baths, five with two-person jacuzzis, king beds, and waterbeds. Tastefully decorated in romantic mingling of the old and new. Private balconies, covered decks with rockers and checkerboard tables. Den with mountain-stone fireplace, game room/conference room. Southern gour-

met breakfast. Group rates for corporate seminars and church groups.

Hosts: Jack and Norma Hilton
Rooms: 10 (PB) $69-104
Full Breakfast
Credit Cards: A, B, C
Notes: 2, 3 & 4 (to groups reserving entire inn), 5, 7 (by arrangement), 8, 9, 10, 11, 12 (certain restrictions apply)

RED BOILING SPRINGS

Armour's Red Boiling Springs Hotel

321 East Main, 37150
(615) 699-2180

Armour's Hotel is one of three remaining historical hotels from a well-known booming mineral resort era of Red Boiling Springs heydey. The newly renovated building is furnished with antiques reflecting the turn of the century. Mineral baths are available on premises. Family-style meals are served by reservations only. Group retreats are welcome. No television or telephones in rooms will interrupt your visits.

Hosts: Brenda and Bobby Thomas
Rooms: 20 (PB) $65
Full Breakfast and Dinner included
Credit Cards: None
Notes: 2, 3, 4, 5, 7, 8

RUGBY

Newbury House Bed and Breakfast

P.O. Box 8, Hwy 52, 37733
(615) 628-2441

Restored 1880 Newbury House bedrooms are furnished with Victorian antiques, guest

year; 6 Pets welcome; 7 Children welcome; 8 Tennis nearby; 9 Swimming nearby; 10 Golf nearby; 11 Skiing nearby; 12 May be booked through travel agent

parlor, front veranda, complimentary tea and coffee. Pioneer and Percy cottages sleep from one to ten; kitchen facilities. Historic Rugby is listed on the National Register of Historic Places. Daily guided tours include: School House Visitor Centre; Thomas Hughes Library 1882, Kingstone Lisle (the founder's home), 1884, and the Christ Church Episcopal, 1887, with original hanging lamps and 1849 rosewood organ still played for Sunday services.

Rooms: 5 + 2 cottages (3PB; 2SB) $58-68
Full Breakfast
Credit Cards: A, B
Notes: 2, 3, 4, 5, 7 (at cottages), 9, 10

SEVIERVILLE

Blue Mountain Mist Country Inn
1811 Pullen Rd., 37862
(615) 428-2335

Experience the silent beauty of mountain scenery while rocking on the big wrap-around porch of this Victorian-style farmhouse. Common rooms filled with antiques lead to twelve individually decorated guest rooms. Enjoy many special touches such as old-fashioned claw-foot tubs, high antique headboards, quilts, and jacuzzis. Nestled in the woods behind the inn are five country cottages designed for romantic getaways. The Great Smoky Mountains National Park and Gatlinburg are only twenty minutes away.

Hosts: Norman and Sarah Ball
Rooms: 12 and 5 cottages (PB) $79-125
Full Breakfast
Credit Cards: A, B
Notes: 5, 7, 10, 11

TOWNSEND

Richmont Inn
220 Winterberry Lane, 37882
(615) 448-6751

Situated on "the peaceful side of the Smokies," this Appalachian barn is beautifully furnished with eighteenth-century English antiques and French paintings. Breathtaking mountain views, graciously appointed rooms with sitting areas, wood-burning fireplaces, spa tubs for two, and balconies. French and Swiss cuisine are served at breakfast with flavored coffees and gourmet desserts by candlelight in the evenings. The Smoky Mountains, art/craft shops, outlet shopping, and historic Cades Cove are all nearby. "A special place for couples."

Hosts: Susan and Jim Hind
Rooms: 10 (PB) $85-115
Full Breakfast
Credit Cards: None
Notes: 2, 5, 9, 10, 12

Richmont Inn

Texas

ALTO

Lincrest Lodge

Alto/Rusk Texas, P.O. Box 799, 75925
(409) 858-2223; (409) 858-2232 (FAX)

A charming, spacious, newly built, country mansion set on the side of a hill with a 16-acre park located in the green hills and forests of central east Texas and a 35-mile view. Featuring fine food and hospitality including romantic gourmet dinners—the perfect country retreat. Twenty miles west of Nacogdochos, the oldest town in Texas.

Hosts: Chet and Charlie Wej
Rooms: 6 (2PB; 4SB) $69
Full Breakfast
Credit Cards: A, B, C
Notes: 2, 4, 5

AUSTIN

Peaceful Hill Bed and Breakfast

10817 Ranch Road 2222, 78730-1102
(512) 338-1817

Country inn on ranch land high in rolling hills west of Austin, 15 minutes to city, five minutes to Lake Travis. Great porch—rocking chairs, porch swing, big breakfast table—soak up countryside and view of city skyline. Hammock for two; hiking and bicycling; two miles to golf, tennis, and swimming. Huge living room looks out to countryside and city view. Grand stone fireplace—crackling fire. Full home-cooked breakfast. Peaceful is the name, Peaceful is the game.

Hostess: Mrs. Peninnah Thurmond
Rooms: 2 (PB) $60+
Full Breakfast
Credit Cards: A, B, C (executive)
Notes: 2, 5, 6 (in cage), 7, 8, 9, 10

BRENHAM

Heartland Country Inn and Retreat

Rt. 2, Box 446, 77883
(409) 836-1864

Perched on a hilltop overlooking a spectacular panoramic view of country church, rolling hills, cows, trees, lakes, 158 acres, peaceful stress-free getaway to promote R&R. Two two-story inns offer 14 bedrooms tastefully furnished with antiques in country, traditional, Victorian, French, Primitive decor. Comfortable king, queen, and twin beds. Conference room for 40 people. Experience a delightful step back in time—more gentle lifestyle with a touch of the past and luxuries of the present. Perfect for retreats as guests feel it's a spiritual landscape.

Hostess: Shirley Sacks
Rooms: 14 (5PB; 9SB) $65
Full Breakfast
Credit Cards: None
Notes: 2, 3&4 (by arrangement), 5, 7, 12

CANTON

Bed and Breakfast Country Style

P.O. Box 1101, 75103
(800) 725-2899

A reservation service for 31 bed and breakfast homes in the area. Canton is known worldwide for First Monday Trade Days—the world's oldest and largest flea market.

CANYON

Country Home Bed and Breakfast

Route 1, Box 447 (1 mile south of Canyon on 8th Street), 79015
(806) 655-7636

Welcome to country relaxation, lovely West Texas sunsets, bountiful breakfasts including sausage, quiche, and baked french toast. Country Home's antique decor blends comfortable hominess with understated elegance. You will feel right at home among the quilts, original artwork, perennial flower beds, wedding gazebo, and hot tub. The honeymoon suite includes a whirlpool bath. We're close to Palo Duro Canyon, Panhandle Plains Museum, Texas musical drama, and West Texas State University. Twenty

miles south of Amarillo.

Hostess: Tammy Money
Rooms: 3 (1PB; 2SB) $70-110
Full Breakfast
Credit Cards: A, B, C, D
Notes: 2, 5, 10, 12

CHAPPELL HILL

The Browning Plantation

Rt. 1, Box 8, 77426
(409) 836-6144

Southern hospitality flourished in the Browning Plantation Home, which was built in 1857. The Chappell Hill area became known as the "Athens of Texas" because of its large plantation homes and its reputation for being a "nucleus of literature and culture." The Browning Plantation was the focus of the Chappell Hill social life. Every effort has been made during the thirty-one month restoration to maintain the historical integrity of the house. Sixty miles from Houston on a major highway. House sits on 220 acres and has a model train with one and one-half miles of track. There is fishing nearby.

Hosts: R.P. and Mildred Ganchan
Rooms: 6 (2PB; 4SB) $90-120
Full Breakfast
Credit Cards: None
Notes: 2, 5, 8

COLUMBUS

Raumonda

1100 Bowie, P.O. Box 112, 78934
(409) 732-2190; (409) 732-5135; (409) 732-8730
(FAX a tn Buddy Rau)

In this Victorian home, built in 1887, you

willbe greeted with warmth and hospitality reminiscent of the Old South. Three fireplaces with white marble mantles, original, grained, painted woodwork, and Victorian bronze hardware make this one of the most outstanding houses in Texas. We also manage the Gant Guest House.

Host: R.F. "Buddy" Rau
Rooms: 3 (PB) $80
Continental Breakfast
Credit Cards: None
Notes: 2, 3& 4 (by special arrangement), 5, 8, 9, 10, 12

Raumonda

CROSBYTON

Smith House Bed and Breakfast Inn

306 West Aspen, 79322
(806) 675-2718

The Inn was built in 1921 by J. Frank Smith, a cowboy from the nearby Two Buckle Ranch. The original oak furniture and iron beds highlight the early West Texas charm. The Inn has a large dining room, a separate meeting room, a parlor for entertaining. Guests can enjoy a rocking chair on the large front porch or just relax in the hot tub. Available for groups, retreats, or dinners.

Hosts: Linda and Kenny Jones
Rooms: 12 (8PB; 4SB) $50-85
Full Breakfast
Credit Cards: A, B, D
Notes: 2, 5, 7, 8, 9, 12

ENNIS

Raphael House

500 W. Ennis Avenue, 75119
(214) 875-1555

This elegant, 1906 Neoclassic Revival mansion is on the National Register and for the last two years was voted one of the top B&B's in the USA. The 19-room mansion is a showcase of quality antiques, rich wall coverings, and luxurious fabrics. Amenities include large baths with antique claw-foot tubs, down comforters and pillows, scented soaps and toiletries, afternoon refreshments and turn down service. Swedish massage, honeymoon packages, and corporate deals available. Very romantic!

Hosts: Brian and Danna Cody Wolf
Rooms: 7 (PB) $58-160
Full Breakfast
Credit Cards: A, B, C, E, F
Notes: 2, 3, 4, 5, 8, 9, 10

FREDERICKSBURG

Magnolia House

101 East Hackberry, 78624
(210) 997-0306; (800) 880-4374

Circa 1925; restored 1991. Enjoy Southern hospitality in a grand and gracious manner. Outside, lovely magnolias and a bubbling fish pond and waterfall set a soothing mood. Inside, beautiful living

---

year; 6 Pets welcome; 7 Children welcome; 8 Tennis nearby; 9 Swimming nearby; 10 Golf nearby; 11 Skiing nearby; 12 May be booked through travel agent

room, game room, and formal dining room provide areas for guests to mingle. Four romantic rooms and two suites have been thoughtfully planned, appointed with antiques and original paintings by the owner. A Southern-style, seven-course breakfast completes a memorable experience.

Hostess: Geri Lilley
Rooms: 4 (2PB; 2SB) $68-98
Suites: 2 (PB)
Full Breakfast
Credit Cards: A, B, C, D
Notes: 2, 5, 8, 9, 10, 12

Schmidt Barn

Route 2, Box 112A3, 78624
(210) 997-5612 — Ask for Schmidt Barn

The Schmidt Barn is located one and one-half miles outside historic Fredericksburg. This 130-year-old limestone structure has been turned into a charming guest house with loft bedroom, living room, bath, and kitchen. The hosts live next door. German-style breakfast is left in the guest house for you. The house has been featured in *Country Living* and is decorated with antiques.

Hosts: Dr. Charles and Loretta Schmidt
Guest House: 1 (PB) $73-103
Continental Breakfast Plus
Credit Cards: A, B, D
Notes: 2, 5, 6, 7, 8, 9, 10, 12

GALVESTON

The Gilded Thistle

1805 Broadway, 77550
(409) 763-0894; (800) 654-9380

An oasis on Galveston Island. Enter a wonderland of Victorian collectibles, superb service, and bountiful amenities. Take tea with Blanche, Black Bart, and the other bears, and see their pretties. Be pampered by hosts who endeavor to share a feeling of history and that special sense of graciousness of times gone by. Featured in the *New York Times* and *Country Inns, Southern Living, House Beautiful,* and other magazines. Call or write for brochure. Teddy bears are free. Tradition of excellence since 1985.

Hosts: Helen and Pat Hanemann
Rooms: 3 (1 PB; 2 SB) $135-145
Full Breakfast
Credit Cards: A, B
Notes: 2, 3, 4, 5, 7, 8, 9, 10

The Victorian Bed and Breakfast Inn

511 17th Street, 77550
(409) 762-9944

Galveston's first bed and breakfast, this 1899 home exudes Victorian romantic charm. A wrap-around veranda, bird's eye maple floors, tiled fireplaces, and unique built-in benches welcome guests once they pass by 90-year-old palm and magnolia trees. Extremely large bedrooms offer guests king beds, porches, antiques, and warm, personal touches. Located in a historic district, the home is less than one mile from the Gulf beach and an easy walk to museums, shopping, restaurants, and theaters.

Hostess: Marcy Hanson
Rooms: 6 (2PB; 4SB) $85-125
Continental Breakfast
Credit Cards: A, B, C
Notes: 2, 5

GEORGE WEST

Country Estates Bed and Breakfast

Rt. 1, Box 285, 78022
(512) 566-2335

You'll enjoy a peaceful, relaxing atmosphere when you pass through the gate on this 85-acre South Texas, family-owned, cattle ranch. Ranch tours, birds and wildlife, or roaming and hiking at leisure. Fish in stock tanks for bass and catfish. Country home furnished with antiques and collectibles, mesquite-burning fireplaces, three guest rooms: Wicker and Old Lace, Quilt, and Cactus. Large porches, swimming pool, game room with pool table. Full ranch breakfast with homemade jams and jellies. Other meals optional with home-grown vegetables and fruit in season. Texas mesquite BBQ, picnics. Golf, fishing, and antiques nearby. Located between San Antonio and Corpus Christi. Dinner and luncheon parties and hunting packages available. Warm Christian atmosphere. No smoking.

Hosts: Fred and Evelyn
Rooms: 3 (1PB; 2SB) $75-85
Full Breakfast
Credit Cards: None
Notes: 2, 3, 4, 5, 7 (by arrangement), 9, 10, 12

GRANBURY

Dabney House Bed and Breakfast

106 South Jones, 76048
(817) 579-1260; evenings (817) 823-6867

Craftsman-style one-story home built in

1907 by local banker. Furnished with antiques, hardwood floors, and original woodwork. Long-term business rates available per request, and romance dinner by reservation only. We offer custom special occasion baskets in room upon arrival by advance order only. Book whole house for family occasions, staff retreats, or Bible retreats at discount rate.

Hosts: John and Gwen Hurley
Rooms: 4 (PB) $55-95
Full Breakfast
Credit Cards: A, B, C
Notes: 2, 5, 8, 9, 10, 12

Nutt House Hotel and Bed and Breakfast Inn

Town Square, 76048
(817) 573-5612

The Nutt House Hotel, located on the square, was built in 1893. Furnishings are from the 1880's with air conditioning and ceiling fans. The inn, a log cabin, is located one block from the square on a beautiful wooded lot on the water. The buffet-style restaurant specializes in country cooking, serving specialties of chicken and dumplings, bite-size cornbread, and homemade cobblers. After the ringing of the dinner bell, period-costumed waitresses will serve the fabulous meal.

Hostess: Sylvia "Sam" Overpeck
Rooms: 17 (8PB; 9SB) $39-85
Continental Breakfast
Credit Cards: A, B, C, D, E, F
Notes: 3, 4, 5, 7, 9, 10

---

year; 6 Pets welcome; 7 Children welcome; 8 Tennis nearby; 9 Swimming nearby; 10 Golf nearby; 11 Skiing nearby; 12 May be booked through travel agent

HILLSBORO

Tarlton House of 1895

211 N. Pleasant, 76645
(817) 582-7216

Turn-of-the-century Victorian home provides guests with modern comfort of private baths and king size beds. Enjoy front porch swings, parlor, and music room. Healthy country breakfast. Over 150 antique dealers, Southwest Outlet Mall, Lake Witney, golf and canoeing. No smoking.

Hosts: Gene and Mary Smith
Rooms: 8 (PB) $89-125
Full Breakfast
Credit Cards: A, B
Notes: 2, 5, 7 (over 12), 10, 12

JEFFERSON

McKay House Bed and Breakfast Inn

306 East Delta, 75657
(903) 665-7322; (214) 348-1929

Jefferson is a town where one can relax, rather than get tired. The McKay House, an 1851 Greek Revival cottage, features a pillared front porch and many fireplaces, offering genuine hospitality in a Christian atmosphere. Heart-of-pine floors, 14-foot ceilings, and documented wallpapers complement antique furnishings. Guests enjoy a full "gentleman's" breakfast. Victorian nightshirts and gowns await pampered guests in each bed chamber.

Hosts: Alma Ann and Joseph Parker
Rooms: 4 + 3 suites (PB) $75-125
Full Breakfast
Credit Cards: A, B
Notes: 2, 5, 10, 12

Pride House

409 Broadway, 75657
(903) 665-2675

Luscious interiors, luxurious amenities, and legendary breakfasts! Filled with heirlooms, antiques, lush plants and slick magazines. Air-conditioned, private baths, claw-foot tubs, showers for two, big beds, fireplaces, porch swings, private balcony. Phones and TV's on request. Romantic Victorian dreamhouse in historic steamboat port with brick streets, picket fences, National Register houses, noteworthy restaurants, dozens of antique shops, steam train, and daily tours of gorgeous houses, the river, and this town of 2,100 Texans.

Hostesses: Christel and Carol
Rooms: 10 (PB) $55-100
Full Breakfast
Credit Cards: A, B
Notes: 2, 5, 7, 8, 9, 10, 12

LEANDER

Trail's End Bed and Breakfast

12223 Trail's End Rd. #7, 78641
(512) 267-2901

Trail's End Bed and Breakfast has an elegant Main House with two guest rooms upstairs. The Guest House is in the woods in a wooded country setting on six acres within easy driving distance from Austin and other quaint Hill Country towns. The many porches, decks, and patios with garden areas provide lots of inviting outdoor spaces. The two fireplaces, lots of seating areas in both houses provide romantic and cozy togetherness inside. You may also shop in the B&B store in the Main

---

NOTES: Credit cards accepted: A Master Card; B Visa; C American Express; D Discover Card; E Diners Club; F Other; 2 Personal checks accepted; 3 Lunch available; 4 Dinner available; 5 Open all

House. We provide business people a comfortable lodging alternative, a great place to have that getaway and work or play. We look forward to serving you and hope you'll try our B&B. I know you will not be disappointed.

Hosts: JoAnn and Tom Patty
Rooms: 4 (2PB; 2SB) $65-95
Full Breakfast
Credit Cards: A, B
Notes: 2, 4, 5, 7, 9, 10, 12 (10%)

Trail's End

NEW BRAUNFELS

Antik Haus Bed and Breakfast

118 S. Union Avenue, 78130
(210) 625-6666

Step back in time with a visit to a wonderful, two-story, restored Victorian home complete with a gazebo, strombella, and hot-water spa. We are located next to Landa Park where you can enjoy a two-hour tube ride on the Comal River, a bicycle built-for-two ride through the park, or walk to the Schlitterbahn Water Park. A full gourmet breakfast is served.

Hosts: Donna and Jim Irwin
Rooms: 4 (1PB; 3SB) $65-85
Full Breakfast
Credit Cards: None
Notes: 2, 5, 7 (over 12), 8, 9, 10

Aunt Nora's B & B

120 Naked Indian Trail, Canyon Lake, 78132-1865
(210) 905-3989

In the Texas hill country, minutes from New Braunfels, Guadalupe River at Canyon Lake is a country house with a touch of Victorian, nestled on a hillside amid oak and cedar trees. Breathe fresh country air from the front porch swing, enjoy patio hot tub and handmade furnishings. Tastefully decorated queen rooms in main house and separate cottages all in a delightful scenic setting.

Hosts: Alton and Iralee Haley
Rooms: 3 (1PB; 2SB) $65-125
Full Breakfast on weekends, Continental Breakfast on weekdays
Credit Cards: None
Notes: 2, 5, 7, 8, 9, 10, 12

Historic Kuebler-Waldrip Haus

1620 Hueco Springs Loop, 78132
(210) 625-8372 (Voice and FAX); (800) 299-8372 (reservations only)

A restored pioneer German home and original schoolhouse on 43 acres just five minutes from historic Gruene New Braunfels, museums, river and water park activities, bicycling, and horse stables. Watch a variety of wildlife or play croquet. Maggy Waldrip and son, Darrell Waldrip will create a "down-home" welcome. Eight private rooms and private baths (one wheelchair accessible and 2 with whirl-pool) sleep 14-25 people and include a full breakfast. Meeting rooms also available to seat 45-50 people. Perfect for romantic getaways, weddings, honeymoons, reunions, conferences, etc. Children are welcome. Just 30 minutes from San Antonio and 45 minutes from Austin.

Hosts: Maggy Kuebler Waldrip and son, Darrel Waldrip
Rooms: 8 (PB) $79-105
Full Family-style Sit-Down Breakfast
Credit Cards: A, B, C, D
Notes: 2, 5, 7, 8, 9, 10

The Rose Garden

195 South Academy, 78130
(210) 629-3296

Come to our Rose Garden with designer bedrooms, fluffy towels, scented soaps, and potpourri-filled rooms. Our half-century old home is only one block from downtown. Enjoy a movie, browse our antique shops, or stroll along the Comal Springs—all within walking distance. We offer two guest rooms. The Royal Rose Room has a four-poster rice-queen bed with a crystal chandelier and country French decor. The Country Rose Room has a Victorian-style, iron-and-brass queen bed with pine walls also done in country French. A full gourmet breakfast is served in the formal dining room.

Hostess: Dawn Mann
Rooms: 2 (1PB; 1SB) $65-80
Full Breakfast
Credit Cards: None
Notes: 2, 5, 8, 9, 10, 12

SAN ANTONIO

The Belle of Monte Vista

505 Belknap Place, 78212
(210) 732-4006

J. Riely Gordon designed this 1890 Queen Anne Victorian home located conveniently in this famous Monte Vista historic district, one mile from downtown San Antonio. The house has eight fireplaces, stained-glass windows, hand-carved oak interior, and Victorian furnishings. Near zoo, churches, river walk, El Mercado, arts, and universities. Transportation to and from airport, bus, and train station upon request. Easy access from all major highways.

Host: Jim Davis
Rooms: 8 (4PB; 4SB) $60+tax
Full Breakfast
Credit Cards: None
Notes: 2, 5, 7, 8, 9, 10

Falling Pines Bed and Breakfast

300 West French Pl., 78212
(210) 733-1998; (800) 880-4580; (210) 736-2340 (FAX)

Built in 1911-12, three-story 9,000-square-feet, restored and updated for modern conveniences (air conditioning, new baths, etc.) in 1980-82. Eclectic decor includes Civil War era Steinway piano, hardwood floors, Oriental rugs, antique furniture. Two rooms with an antique double bed, one room with twin beds, the suite (Persian) is 2,000-square-feet in a single room with a unique decor and bath. Grounds enclose one acre of towering pines, oaks, and pecan trees. We are one and one-half miles from

---

NOTES: Credit cards accepted: A Master Card; B Visa; C American Express; D Discover Card; E Diners Club; F Other; 2 Personal checks accepted; 3 Lunch available; 4 Dinner available; 5 Open all

Riverwalk; we are ten minutes from the airport.

Hosts: Grace and Bob Daubert
Rooms: 3 + 1 suite (PB) $100-150
Full Breakfast
Credit Cards: None
Notes: 2, 5, 8, 9, 10

TEXARKANA

Mansion on Main Bed and Breakfast Inn
802 Main, 75501
(903) 792-1835

"Twice as Nice," the motto of Texarkana, USA (Texas and Arkansas), is standard practice at Mansion on Main. The 1895 Neoclassic Colonial mansion, surrounded by 14 tall columns, was recently restored by the owners of McKay House, the popular bed and breakfast in nearby Jefferson. Six bed chambers vary from the Governor's Suite to the Butler's Garret. Guests enjoy Southern hospitality, period furnishings, fireplaces, and a gentleman's breakfast. Thirty miles away is the town of Hope, birthplace of President Clinton.

Hosts: Carolyn and Bill White
Rooms: 4 and 2 suites (PB) $55-110
Full Sit-Down Breakfast
Credit Cards: A, B
Notes: 2, 5, 10, 12

WIMBERLY

Delafield's Delight
16 Chisolm Trail, 78676
(800) 859-8574

Large one-bedroom house with full kitchen, living room, and bathroom. A 12-by 30-foot deck overlooks a beautiful shaded yard. Located in the rolling hills of Texas 18 miles off I-35 between Austin and San Antonio. Close to golf course, river activities, etc., or just relax at our home and be close to God!

Hostess: Sue Farrar
Rooms: 1 (PB) $65-85
Continental Breakfast
Credit Cards: None
Notes: 2, 5, 7, 8, 9, 10

WINNSBORO

Thee Hubbell House
307 West Elm, 75494
(903) 342-5629; (800) 227-0639; (903) 342-6627 (FAX)

Located in beautiful North East Texas with Southern hospitality at its best. Ten uniquely decorated rooms five of which are located in a carriage house, and a newly added play house spa.

Hosts: Dan and Laurel Hubbell
Rooms: 10 (PB) $65-175
Full Breakfast (Continental Breakfast available)
Credit Cards: A, B, C, D, E, F
Notes: 2, 4, 5, 7, 8, 9, 10, 11, 12

Thee Hubbell House

---

year; 6 Pets welcome; 7 Children welcome; 8 Tennis nearby; 9 Swimming nearby; 10 Golf nearby; 11 Skiing nearby; 12 May be booked through travel agent

Utah

EPHRAIM

Ephraim Homestead Bed and Breakfast

135 W. 100 North (43-2), 84627
(801) 283-6367

This peaceful and private retreat offers lodging in the three main structures that make up a typical historic Mormon pioneer homestead: house, barn and grainery (log cabin). A charming, one-of-a-kind bed and breakfast, Ephraim Homestead provides a most unique and memorable experience. Located in the Sanpete Valley in Central Utah, it is a short drive to refreshing mountain glories and other places of recreation, history and adventure.

Hosts: McKay and Sherron Andersen
Rooms: 4 (2PB; 2SB) $35-75+tax
Full Breakfast
Credit Cards: None
Notes: 2, 5, 7, 8, 9, 10

ST. GEORGE

Greene Gate Village

76 W. Tabernacle St., 84770
(801) 628-6999; (800) 350-6999; (801) 628-5068 (FAX)

Behind the green gates, nine beautifully restored homes provide modern comfort in pioneer elegance. Our guests love the nostalgic charm of the Bentley House with elegant Victorian decor—and the quaint Tolley House, where eleven children were born and raised. The Grainery sleeps three in rooms where early settlers loaded supplies for their trek to California. The Orson Pratt Home, built by another early Mormon leader, is on the National Register of Historic Places. Green Hedge, with one of the village's two bridal suites, was originally built in another part of town but was moved to Green Gate Village in 1991. Family reunions or other large groups (up to 22) may share the comfort and charm of the Greenehouse, built in 1872. The Greenehouse has all the modern conveniences of a full kitchen, swimming pool, and tennis court.

Hosts: John, Sheri and Barbara Green
Rooms: 17 (PB) $45-110
Full Breakfast
Credit Cards: A, B, C
Notes: 2, 4, 5, 7, 8, 9, 10, 11, 12

NOTES: Credit cards accepted: A MasterCard; B Visa; C American Express; D Discover Card; E Diners Club; F Other; 2 Personal checks accepted; 3 Lunch available; 4 Dinner available; 5 Open all year; 6 Pets

Seven Wives Inn

217 N. 100 West, 84770
(801) 628-3737; (800) 600-3737

The Inn consists of two adjacent pioneer
adobe homes with massive handgrained
moldings framing windows and doors.
Bedrooms are furnished with period antiques and hand-made quilts. Some rooms
have fireplaces; two have a whirlpool tub.
Swimming pool on premises.

Hosts: Donna and Jay Curtis; Alison and Jon
Bowcutt
Rooms: 13 (PB) $50-70, suites $100
Full Breakfast
Credit Cards: A, B, C, D, E
Notes: 2, 5, 7, 8, 9, 10, 12

Bluff St. Exit
St. George Blvd.
Left   217 N.
          100 W.

Caroline

8-9
Breakfast

welcome; 7 Children welcome; 8 Tennis nearby; 9 Swimming nearby; 10 Golf nearby; 11 Skiing nearby; 12
May be booked through travel agent

Vermont

ALBURG

Thomas Mott Homestead Bed and Breakfast

Blue Rock Road on Lake Champlain
Route 2, Box 149-B, 05440
(802) 796-3736; (800) 348-0843

Hosted by a criminology/American history major who enjoys gourmet cooking, this completely restored 1838 farmhouse has a guest living room with TV and fireplace overlooking the lake; game room with bumper pool and darts; quilt decor. Full view of Mt. Mansfield and Jay Peak. One hour to Montreal/Burlington; one and one-half hours to Lake Placid, New York, and Stowe. Lake activities winter and summer. Amenities include Ben and Jerry's ice cream, lawn games, and horseshoes.

Host: Patrick J. Schallert, Sr., M.A., B.A.
Rooms: 4 (PB) $55-70
Full Breakfast
Credit Cards: A, B, D
Notes: 2, 4 (gourmet dinners w/advance notice), 5, 7 (over 6), 9, 10, 11, 12

Thomas Mott Homestead

ARLINGTON

Hill Farm Inn

Rural Route 2, Box 2015, 05250
(802) 375-2269; (800) 882-2545

Hill Farm is one of Vermont's original farmsteads granted from King George III in 1775. It has been an inn since 1905 and still retains the character of an old farm vacation inn on 60 beautiful acres between the Taconic and Green Mountains with a mile frontage on the Battenkill River. We offer hearty home cooking, charming rooms, and hiking, biking, canoeing, and relaxing with spectacular views.

Hosts: Regan and John Chichester
Rooms: 13 (8PB; 5SB) $60-95
Full Country Breakfast
Credit Cards: A, B, C, D
Notes: 2, 4, 5, 6 (limited), 7, 8, 9, 10, 11, 12

Shenandoah Farm

Battenkill Rd., 05250
(802) 375-6372

Experience New England in this lovingly restored 1820 Colonial overlooking the Battenkill River. Wonderful "Americana" year-round. Full "farm-fresh" breakfast is

---

NOTES: Credit cards accepted: A Master Card; B Visa; C American Express; D Discover Card; E Diners Club; F Other; 2 Personal checks accepted; 3 Lunch available; 4 Dinner available; 5 Open all

served daily and is included.

Host: Woody Masterson
Rooms: 5 (1PB; 4SB) $$60-75
Full Breakfast
Credit Cards: A, B
Notes: 2, 5, 8, 10, 11, 12

BELLOWS FALLS

Blue Haven Christian Bed and Breakfast

227 Westminister Road, 05101
(802) 463-9008

Explore Vermont's beauty from our 1830 restored schoolhouse. Experience canopy beds, hand-painted touches, and a big country kitchen where hearth-baked Vermont breakfasts elicit oohs and aahs. Have tea time treats at the antique glass, laden sideboard, or in the ruddy pine common room. Expect a peaceful and pleasant time here. Christian fellowship and prayer are always available. Open to one and all in God's love. Please come!

Hostess: Helene Champagne
Rooms: 6 (4PB; 2SB) $58-70
Full Breakfast (weekends); Continental Breakfast (weekdays)
Credit Cards: A, B, C
Notes: 2, 7, 8, 9, 10, 11, 12

BRANDON

The Moffett House B & B

69 Park St., 05733
(802) 247-3843; (800) 752-5794

While experiencing the special beauty of Vermont, come to historic Brandon, one of the state's loveliest towns. Park Street has been referred to as "one of the most beautiful streets in New England" and we heartily agree! The Moffett House, located on Park Street, is a fine example of 1860 Victorian elegance. Its large cheery rooms seem to relect the special warmth of its namesake, the late, former owner Hugh Moffett, famed Time-Life Editor and Vermont Legislator. We know you will enjoy the Moffett House hospitality. Please come visit us!

Hosts: Mary Bowers and Doug Flanagan
Rooms: 7 (3PB; 4SB)) $65-125
Full Breakfast
Credit Cards: A, B,
Notes: 2, 4, 5, 6, 7, 8, 9, 10, 11, 12

The Moffett House

Rosebelle's Victorian Inn

31 Franklin St., Route 7, 05733
(802) 247-0098

Elegantly restored, non-smoking, 1830's Victorian Mansard is listed on the National Register of Historic Places. Six spacious rooms, with private and semi-private baths, full gourmet breakfast, afternoon tea, and candlelight dining available to our guests. Only minutes to Killington, Pico, and Sugarbush downhill and cross-country skiing. A true four-season inn to enjoy the

year; 6 Pets welcome; 7 Children welcome; 8 Tennis nearby; 9 Swimming nearby; 10 Golf nearby; 11 Skiing nearby; 12 May be booked through travel agent

foliage, enter activities, hiking, biking, or visit museums, antique shops, or read a good book. Not suggested for children under twelve. Sorry, no pets allowed. Cash preferred, Visa and Mastercard accepted. Ici on parle Francais. Gift certificates and summer and winter packages available.

Hosts: Ginette and Norm Milot
Rooms: 6 (4PB; 2SB) $50-85
Full Breakfast
Credit Cards: A, B
Notes: 4, 5, 7 (under 12), 8, 9, 10, 11

BURLINGTON—SEE ESSEX

CALAIS

Evergreen's Chalet

HC 32, Box 41, 05648
(802) 223-5156

Charming "Nature Lover's Paradise." Located on 140 private acres. Furnished in Colonial Maple. Dining/living room, all electric kitchen, three bedrooms with Posturpedic beds, two baths, large deck with grill, private tika, carport. Miles of nature trails provide hours of pleasure, nature pond, hiking, cross country skiing, snowmobiling. Many lakes and ponds nearby. No smoking or pets. Free guided tours available. Rates by day, weekend, or week. Brochure available.

Hosts: Elizabeth and Wayne Morse
Rooms: 3 (1PB; 2SB) $35.75
Continental Breakfast
Credit Cards: A, B
Notes: 2, 5, 7(12 years and up), 9, 10, 11

CHELSEA

Shire Inn

8 Main Street, P. O. Box 37, 05038
(802) 685-3031; (800) 441-6908

The Shire Inn was built in 1832, and the Federal brick facade is an architectural gem of the period. The inn still operates five of the original fireplaces, four of which are in guest bedrooms. At the inn, guests enjoy cycling, cross-country skiing, and hiking. Nearby they can swim, canoe, fish, hunt antiques, downhill ski, and go sleigh riding. Chelsea is within 30 to 34 miles of Woodstock/Quechee, Montpelier, or Hanover, New Hampshire, home of Dartmouth College.

Hosts: Jay and Karen Keller
Rooms: 6 (PB) $80-170
Full Breakfast
Credit Cards: A, B
Notes: 2, 4, 5, 7 (over 8), 8, 9, 10, 11

CHESTER

Henry Farm Inn

P. O. Box 646, Green Mountain Turnpike, 05143
(802) 875-2674; (800) 723-8213

The Henry Farm Inn supplies the beauty of Vermont with old-time simplicity. Nestled on fifty acres of rolling hills and meadows, assuring peace and quiet. Spacious rooms, country sitting areas, and a sunny dinning room all guarantee a feeling of home. Come and visit for a day or more!

Hosts: Jean and Ken Tande
Rooms: 7 (PB) $40-90
Full Breakfast
Credit Cards: A, B, C
Notes: 2, 5, 7, 8, 9, 10, 11, 12

NOTES: Credit cards accepted: A Master Card; B Visa; C American Express; D Discover Card; E Diners Club; F Other; 2 Personal checks accepted; 3 Lunch available; 4 Dinner available; 5 Open all

The Hugging Bear Inn and Shoppe

Main Street, 05143
(802) 875-2412; (800) 325-0519

Teddy bears peek out the windows and are tucked in all the corners of this beautiful Victorian house built in 1850. If you love teddy bears, you'll love the Hugging Bear. There are six guest rooms with private shower baths and a teddy bear in every bed. Full breakfast and afternoon snack are served.

Hosts: Georgette, Paul, and Diane Thomas
Rooms: 6 (PB) $55-90
Full Breakfast
Credit Cards: A, B, C, D
Notes: 2, 5, 7, 8, 9, 10, 11

CUTTINGSVILLE

Buckmaster Inn

Lincoln Hill Road, Rural Route 1, Box 118,
Shrewsbury, 05738
(802) 492-3485

The Buckmaster Inn (1801) was an early stagecoach stop in Shrewsbury. Standing on a knoll overlooking a picturesque barn scene and rolling hills, it is situated in the Green Mountains. A center hall, grand staircase, and wide-pine floors grace the home, which is decorated with family antiques and crewel handiwork done by your hostess. Extremely large, airy rooms, wood-burning stove, four fireplaces, two large porches.

Hosts: Sam and Grace Husselman
Rooms: 4 (2PB; 2SB) $50-60
Full Breakfast
Credit Cards: None
Notes: 5, 7, 8, 9, 10, 11

Maple Crest Farm

Lincoln Hill, Box 120, 05738
(802) 492-3367

This 27-room 1808 farmhouse has been preserved for five generations and is located in the heart of the Green Mountains in Shrewsbury. It has been a bed and breakfast for 23 years. Ten miles north of Ludlow and ten miles south of Rutland, an area that offers much to visitors. Pico, Killington, and Okemo are nearby for downhill skiing. Cross-country skiing and hiking are offered on the premises.

Hosts: William, Donna and Russell Smith
Rooms: 4 (SB) $25-35 per person
Full Breakfast
Credit Cards: None
Notes: 2, 5, 7, 8, 9, 10, 11, 12

DANBY

Quail's Nest Bed and Breakfast

P.O. Box 221, Main St., 05739
(802) 293-5099 (Voice and FAX)

Nestled in a quiet mountain village, our inn offers the guests friendly conversation around the fireplace, rooms filled with cozy quilts and antiques, and a hearty, home-cooked breakfast in the morning. Hiking, skiing, swimming, and outlet shopping are all very close by as well as our local craft and antique shops. Our guests are all treated as part of the family, which is what makes a real difference.

Hosts: Chip and Anharad Edson
Rooms: 5 (3PB; 2SB)) $66-75
Full Breakfast
Credit Cards: A, B,
Notes: 2, 5, 7, 8, 9, 10, 11

year; 6 Pets welcome; 7 Children welcome; 8 Tennis nearby; 9 Swimming nearby; 10 Golf nearby; 11 Skiing nearby; 12 May be booked through travel agent

Silas Griffith Inn

South Main Street, Rural Route 1, Box 66F,
05739
(802) 293-5567

Built by Vermont's first millionaire, this
Victorian inn was built in 1891 in the heart
of the Green Mountains, with spectacular
mountain views. It features 17 delightful,
antique-furnished rooms and a fireplace in
the living and dining room. Hiking, skiing,
antiquing nearby. Come and enjoy our
elegant meals and New England hospitality.

Hosts: Paul and Lois Dansereau
Rooms: 17 (11PB; 6SB) $69-86
Full Breakfast
Credit Cards: A, B, C
Notes: 2, 4, 5, 7, 9, 10, 11, 12

DERBY LINE

Derby Village Inn

46 Main St., 05830
(802) 873-3604

Enjoy this charming, old, Victorian mansion situated in the quiet village of Derby
Line, within walking distance of the Canadian border and the world's only international library and opera house. The nearby
countryside offers year-round recreation—
downhill and cross-country skiing, water
sports, cycling, fishing, hiking, golf,
snowmobiling, sleigh rides, antiquing, and
most of all peace and tranquility. We are
a non-smoking facility.

Hosts: Tom and Phyllis Moreau
Rooms: 8 (5PB; 3SB) $50-60
Full Breakfast
Credit Cards: A, B, D
Notes: 2, 5, 7, 8, 9, 10, 11

ENOSBURG FALLS

Berkson Farms

RR1, Box 850, 05450
(802) 933-2522

Relax in our 150-year-old farmhouse on a
working dairy farm. Located on 600 acres
of meadowland surrounded by a variety of
animals, nature, and warm hospitality. Picnic, hike, bike in the warmer months;
cross-country ski and sled in the winter.
Enjoy our hearty home-style meals using
our maple syrup and farm-fresh dairy products. Close to Canada and major ski
areas. Children and pets welcome. Reservations suggested.

Hosts: Susan and Terry Spoonire
Rooms: 4 (1PB; 3SB) $50-60
Full Breakfast
Credit Cards: None
Notes: 2, 3, 4, 5, 6, 7, 9, 10, 11

ESSEX

The Inn at Essex

70 Essex Way, 05452
(802) 878-1100; (800) 727-4295; (802) 878-0063
(FAX)

The Inn at Essex is a Colonial-style inn on
the outskirts of Burlington, Vermont. It is
the only AAA Four Diamond inn/hotel in
Burlington. The Inn is nestled between the
beautiful Green Mountains of Vermont
and New York's Adirondack Mountains.
The Inn offers 97 elegantly furnished and
spacious rooms, 30 with woodburning
fireplaces. All of the rooms have direct-
dial phones, computer modem and fax
hook-ups, desks, TV's, radios, and sitting
areas. You will be able to savor the
glorious food of our two restaurants pre-

pared by 18 chefs and over 100 students of the New England Culinary Institute. You can enjoy patio dining or have lite fare by our new outdoor pool and waterfall, rock garden. Stroll through the gardens, take an invigorating hike, or bike ride on the recreation path. 10 minutes from Burlington International Airport. We offer complimentary airport shuttle.

Hosts: Jim and Judi Lamberti
Rooms: 97 (PB) $73-185
Continental Breakfast with room (full available at extra charge)
Credit Cards: A, B, C, D, E
Notes: 2, 3, 4, 5, 7, 8, 9, 10, 11, 12

FAIR HAVEN

Maplewood Inn

Route 22A South, 05743
(802) 265-8039; (800) 253-7729 (outside VT)

Exquisite 1843 Greek Revival on the Vermont Register of Historic Places and a romantic, antique-filled haven! Keeping room with fireplace, gathering room with books and games, parlor with complimentary cordials. Elegant rooms and suites are air conditioned, have fireplaces, color cable TV's, radios, and in-room phone available. Near everything! Bikes, canoes, and antique shop on site. Lakes Region. Pet boarding arranged. A true four-season experience! Guidebook and Mobil recommended.

Hosts: Doug and Cindy Baird
Rooms: 5 (PB) $70-105
Continental Plus Breakfast
Credit Cards: A, B, D
Notes: 2, 5, 7 (over 5), 8, 9, 10, 11, 12

FAIRLEE

Rutledge Inn and Cottages

Lake Morey Drive, 05045
(802) 333-9722

An outstanding lakeside resort offers genuine hospitality and excellent New England dining. It is located in the lovely Connecticut Valley on a spring-fed lake with a sandy beach and 1,000 feet of waterfront. No phones or TV! We have all kinds of activities for adults and young people that you can take part in, or just plain ignore. A place to step back in time to enjoy summer the way it was meant to be enjoyed.

Hosts: Bob and Nancy Stone
Rooms: 38 (33PB; 5SB) $67-93
Continental or Full Breakfast
Credit Cards: None
Open May to October
Notes: 2, 3, 4, 7, 8, 9, 10, 12

Silver Maple Lodge and Cottages

Rural Route 1, Box 8, 05045
(802) 333-4326; 800-666-1946

A historic bed and breakfast country inn is located in a four-season recreational area. Enjoy canoeing, fishing, golf, tennis, and skiing within a few miles of the lodge. Visit nearby flea markets and country auctions. Choose a newly renovated room in our antique farmhouse or a handsome, pine-paneled cottage room. Many fine restaurants are nearby. Darmouth College is 17 miles away. Also offered are hot air balloon packages, inn-to-inn bicycling, canoeing, and walking tours. Brochure available.

Hosts: Scott and Sharon Wright
Rooms: 14 (12PB; 2SB) $48-68
Continental Breakfast
Credit Cards: A, B, C, D
Notes: 2, 5, 7, 8, 9, 10, 11, 12

JERICHO

Henry M. Field Victorian Bed and Breakfast

R.R. 2, Box 395, 05465
(802) 899-3984

A Victorian Italianate c.1875 renovated and restored by the current owners in the heart of the village of Jericho. The house features tall ceilings, ornamental plaster, etched glass, and paneled doors, and molding of mahogany and chestnut. Three large parlors decorated with period furnishings are for guests use. The area features skiing, cycling, hiking, golf, tennis, trail-riding, and antiques. Convenient to Mount Mansfield and Lake Champlain. Burlington is only 12 miles. Non-smoking residence.

Hosts: Mary Beth and Terrance L. Horan
Rooms: 3 (PB) $60-70
Full Breakfast (holidays and weekends)
Continental Breakfast (weekdays)
Credit Cards: A, B
Closed December 22 through January 2
Notes: 2, 7 (limited), 8, 9, 10, 11, 12 (no commision)

LOWER WATERFORD

Rabbit Hill Inn

Pucker Street and Route 18, 05848
(802) 748-5168; (800) 76-BUNNY;
(802) 748-8342 (FAX)

Full of whimsical and charming surprises,

this Federal-period inn, established in 1795, has been lavished with love and attention. Many guest rooms have fireplaces and canopied beds. Chamber music, candlelit gourmet dining, and turn-down service make this an enchanting and romantic hideaway in a tiny, restored village overlooking the mountains. Award-winning, nationally acclaimed inn. Our service is inspired by Philippians 2:7.

Hosts: John and Maureen Magee
Rooms: 18 (PB) $78-199
Full Breakfast
Credit Cards: A, B
Closed first two weeks of November and all of April
Notes: 2, 4, 8, 9, 10, 11, 12

LUDLOW

The Combes Family Inn

RFD #1, Box 275, 05149
(802) 228-8799

Bring your family home to ours here in Vermont at The Combes Family Inn. The Inn, a century-old farmhouse, located on a country back road offers a quiet respite from the hustle and bustle of today's lifestyle! Relax and socialize (BYOB) in our Vermont Barnboard "Keeping Room" furnished with turn-of-the-century oak. Sample Bill's country breakfasts and Ruth's delicious home-cooking. Our lush Green Mountains invite you to join us for a relaxing, casual vacation. Eleven, cozy, country-inspired guest rooms—all with private baths.

Hosts: Ruth and Bill Combes
Rooms: 11 (PB) $78-90
Full Breakfast
Credit Cards: A, B, C, D
Closed April 15 through May 15
Notes: 2, 4, 6, 7, 8, 9, 10, 11, 12

LYNDONVILLE

Wildflower Inn

Darling Hill Road, 05851
(802) 626-3427; (800) 627-8310

Located on over 500 acres with spectacular views, this 12-room and 10-suite inn is
a perfect Christian retreat. Whether as a
family or by yourself, you'll find a little
piece of heaven at the Wildflower. Visit
our Blue Cross, take a walk on our nature
trails, enjoy God's handiwork in our gardens, stop in at our petting barn to see the
animals, or head out to explore our beautiful Northeast Kingdom.

Hosts: Jim and Mary O'Reilly and Family
Rooms: 22 (20PB; 2SB) $80-130 ($140-200
m.a.p.)
Full Breakfast
Credit Cards: A, B
Notes: 2, 4, 5, 7, 8, 9, 10, 11

MIDDLEBURY

Middlebury Inn

14 Courthouse Square, 05753
(802) 388-4961; (800) 842-4666

This 1827, historic, 75-room landmark
overlooks the village green in a picturesque New England college town. Discover Middlebury, Vermont—the splendor of its historic district—Vermont State
Craft Center, Middlebury College, boutique shopping, and four season recreation. Elegantly restored rooms, private
bath, telephone, color TV, and air-conditioning (in season). The inn offers breakfast, lunch, dinner, seasonal porch dining,
afternoon tea, and Sunday brunch. Recommended by AAA and a Member of

Historic Hotels of America.

Hosts: Jane and Frank Emanuel, Innkeepers
Rooms: 22 (20PB; 2SB) $80-130 ($140-200
m.a.p.)
Full Breakfast
Credit Cards: A, B, C
Notes: 3, 4, 5, 6 (limited), 7, 8, 9, 10, 11, 12

MONTGOMERY

Eagle Lodge

Rt. 1, Box 900, Montgomery Center, 05471
(802) 326-4518

While in Vermont, the Green Mountain
State, plan to stay with a Methodist family
as you enjoy your hiking, biking,
snowmobiling, or just restful, leisurely vacationing at Eagle Lodge. "There have
never been strangers here, only friends
who had not yet met." We, the Scotts, are
true Vermonters and the lodge and its food
are all of pure Vermont flavor—that's
simple and with our guests', of any faith,
comfort in mind.

Hosts: The Scott Family (contact Irene)
Rooms: 15 (7PB; 8SB) $35-55 (winter) $25 +
tax (summer)
Full Breakfast
Credit Cards: A, B
Notes: 2, 4 (in winter), 5, 7, 8, 9, 10, 11 (Jay
Peak)

MORETOWN

Camel's Hump View

Box 720, 05660
(802) 496-3614

Camel's Hump View is an 1831 farmhouse complete with white-faced Hereford cows, chickens, and Lassie, a Sheltie
dog. The inn accommodates sixteen guests.

You can sleep in an antique rope bed with handmade quilts and braided rugs. Meals prepared with fruits and vegetables from our garden to give you country cooking at its best. Skiing, hiking, biking, golf, canoeing, or horseback riding either on premises or nearby.

Hosts: Jerry and Wilma Maynard
Rooms: 8 (1PB; 7SB) $50-60
Full Breakfast
Credit Cards: F
Notes: 2, 4, 5, 7, 8, 9, 10, 11,

MT. HOLLY

The Hortonville Inn

Box 14, 05758
(802) 2.)-2587

The Hortonville Inn sits on a hilltop on thirteen acres, in an area known for its snow and reliable skiing. The inn was recently renovated and now has a porch dining area with fireplace and wonderful mountain views. In-room movies are available, with over 250. Complimentary wine and hors d'oeuvres are served by the fire at the end of the day, herbal tea and homemade cookies are always available. Breakfast is country-style with four courses.

Hosts: Ray and Mary Maglione
Rooms: 5 (2PB; 3SB) $50-75
Full Breakfast
Credit Cards: A, B
Notes: 2, 5, 9, 10, 11,12

The Hortonville Inn

NORTH TROY

The 1893 House Bed and Breakfast

30A Highland Ave., Rt. 105, 05859
(802) 988-9614

Come visit us in our 1893 Victorian home in North Troy, Vermont, a quaint valley town surrounded by beautiful mountains. We are eight miles from Jay Peak, and one and one-half hours from Montreal. Lots of hiking trails, biking routes, skiing, antiquing, or just relaxing in the quiet country.

Hosts: Rick and Pat Shover
Rooms: 3 (1PB; 2SB) $50
Full Breakfast
Credit Cards: None
Notes: 2, 5, 7, 9, 11

ORLEANS

Valley House Inn

4 Memorial Square
(802) 754-6665; (800) 545-9711

One quarter mile off I-91, Exit 26. An 1800's country inn in the center of the Northeast Kingdom's lakes region. Easy access to scenic hiking, biking, hunting, and lake and river fishing. Cocktail lounge on premises. The grand lobby with pressed metal ceiling and walls, with half-moon front desk make you feel like you are stepping back to the turn of the century. Staying at a nice Vermont country inn doesn't have to be expensive.

Hosts: David and Louise Bolduc
Rooms: 22 (20PB; 2SB) $35-70
Breakfast not included (restaurant on premises)
Credit Cards: A, B, C, D
Notes: 2, 3, 4, 5, 7, 8, 9, 10, 11,12

NOTES: Credit cards accepted: A Master Card; B Visa; C American Express; D Discover Card; E Diners Club; F Other; 2 Personal checks accepted; 3 Lunch available; 4 Dinner available; 5 Open all

PITTSFIELD

Swiss Farm Lodge

P.O. Box 630, Rt. 100 North, 05762
(802) 746-8341; (800) 245-5726

Working Hereford beef farm. Enjoy the
casual, family-type atmosphere in our living room with fireplace and TV or in the
game room. Home-cooked meals and
baking served family style. Our own maple
syrup, jams, and jellies. Walk-in cooler
available for guests' use. Cross-country
trails on site. B&B available all year.
M.A.P. November to April only. Mountain bike trails close by. Owned and
operated by the same family for 45 years.
Lower rates for children in same room as
parents.

Rooms: 17 (14PB; 3SB) $40-50
Full Breakfast
Credit Cards: None
Notes: 2, 5, 7, 8, 9, 10, 11

RANDOLPH

Placidia Farm B & B

R.D. 1, Box 275, 05060
(802) 728-9883

Beautiful log home on 81 tranquil acres
with brook, pond, hiking, cross-country
skiing on property. Four-season sports
nearby. Private apartment includes bedroom, living room, equipped kitchen, bath,
private entrance, and deck. Comfortable
country furnishings. Linens provided.
Hearty breakfast.

Host: Viola Frost-Laitinen
Rooms: 1 apartment (PB) $75-85
Full Breakfast
Credit Cards: None
Notes: 2, 5, 7, 8, 9, 10, 11

STOWE

Inn at the Brass Lantern

717 Maple Street, 05672
(802) 253-2229; (800) 729-2980; (802) 253-7425
(FAX)

This traditional, Vermont, bed and breakfast, country inn in the heart of Stowe is an
award-winning restoration of an 1810 farmhouse and carriage barn overlooking Mt.
Mansfield, Vermont's most prominent
mountain. The inn features period antiques,
quilts, and planked floors. The entire inn is
air conditioned. Most rooms have views,
and some have fireplaces. Special packages include honeymoon, skiing, golf, sleigh
and surrey rides, and more. No smoking.

Host: Andy Aldrich
Rooms: 9 (PB) $65-120
Full Breakfast
Credit Cards: A, B, C
Notes: 2, 5, 8, 9, 10, 11, 12

The Siebeness Inn

3681 Mountain Rd., 05672
(800) 426-9001; (802) 253-8942; (802) 253-9232
(FAX)

A warm welcome awaits you at our charming country inn nestled in the foothills of Mt.
Mansfield. Romantic rooms have country
antiques, private baths, air conditioning.
Awake to the aroma of freshly baked
muffins, which accompany your hearty
New England breakfast. Relax in our
outdoor hot tub in winter, or our pool with
mountain views in summer. Fireplace in
lounge. Bike, walk, or cross-country ski
from inn on recreation path. Honeymoon,
golf, and ski packages.

Hosts: Sue and Nils Anderson
Rooms: 11 (PB) $60-100
Full Breakfast
Credit Cards: A, B, C, D, E
Notes: 2, 4 (winter), 5, 7, 8, 9, 10, 11, 12

year; 6 Pets welcome; 7 Children welcome; 8 Tennis nearby; 9 Swimming nearby; 10 Golf nearby;
11 Skiing nearby; 12 May be booked through travel agent

Timberhölm Inn

452 Cottage Club Road, 05672
(802) 253-7603; (800) 753-7603

This delightful country inn in a quiet,
wooded setting serves afternoon tea and
cookies in the summer, and après ski soup
in the winter. We have ten individually
decorated rooms with quilts and antiques,
and a spacious, sunny great room with a
large fieldstone fireplace. Game room
with shuffleboard; deck overlooking the
Worchester Mountains; outdoor hot tub;
cable TV.

Hosts: The Hildebrand family
Rooms: 10 (PB) $60-100
Full Breakfast
Credit Cards: A, B
Notes: 2, 5, 7, 8, 9, 10, 11, 12

Strong House Inn

VERGENNES

Strong House Inn

82 West Main St., 05491
(802) 887-3337

Comfortable and elegant lodging in an
1834 Federal home. Listed on the
Register of Historic Places. Perfectly located in the heart of the Lake Champlain
Valley with fine views of the Green Mountains and Adirondack ranges. The area
offers some of the finest cycling in Ver-

mont. Nearby is a lake, hiking, golf, skiing,
and Shelburne Museum. The Inn offers 7
rooms, 2 suites, private baths, and working fireplaces. A full country breakfast is
included.

Hosts: Mary and Hugh Bargiel
Rooms: 7 (5PB; 2SB) $65-140
Full Breakfast
Credit Cards: A, B, C
Notes: 2, 4, 5, 7, 8, 9, 10, 11, 12

WAITSFIELD

Mad River Barn

Route 17, 05673
(802) 496-3310

This classic Vermont lodge has spacious
rooms, some with TV's and kitchenettes.
There are three meeting rooms on the
premises. Dinner is served by reservation.
We are near skiing, hiking, and biking, and
have an outdoor pool, white perennial
garden, and grand, stone fireplace in the
pub.

Hostess: Betsy Pratt
Rooms: 15 (PB) $24-48 per person
Full Breakfast
Credit Cards: A, B, C
Notes: 2, 4, 5, 7, 8, 9, 10, 11, 12

Mountain View Inn

Rural Free Delivery Box 69, Route 17, 05673
(802) 496-2426

The Mountain View Inn is an old farmhouse, circa 1826, that was made into a
lodge in 1948 to accommodate skiers at
nearby Mad River Glen. Today it is a
country inn with seven rooms. Meals are
served family style around the antique
harvest table where good fellowship pre-
vails. Sip mulled cider around a crackling
fire in our living room when the weather

turns chilly.

Hosts: Fred and Suzy Spencer
Rooms: 7 (PB) $35-65 per person
Full Breakfast
Credit Cards: None
Notes: 2, 4, 5, 7, 8, 9, 10, 11, 12

Newtons' 1824 House Inn

Route 100, Box 159, 05673
(802) 496-7555; (800) 426-3986;
(802) 496-7558 (FAX)

Enjoy relaxed elegance in one of six beautiful guest rooms at this quintessential farmhouse on 52 acres. The inn features antiques, chandeliers, fireplaces, and classical music. Breakfast by the fire includes such whimsical gourmet delights as soufflés, crepes, blueberry buttermilk pancakes, and freshly squeezed orange juice. Cross-country skiing and swimming hole are nearby. AAA three-diamond rated.

Hosts: Nick and Joyce Newton
Rooms: 6 (PB) $75-115
Full Breakfast
Credit Cards: A, B, C
Notes: 2, 5, 8, 9, 10, 11, 12

WALLINGFORD

White Rocks Inn

R.R. 1, Box 297, Route 7, 05773
(802) 446-2077

Circa 1840's, elegant farmhouse inn. Listed on the National Register of Historic Places. Five antique-filled guest rooms with canopy beds and private baths. Delicious full breakfast included. Non-smokers only. Milkhouse cottage with living/dining area, king-sized bed, kitchen, whirlpool bath, French doors to deck, and more. Horseback riding is also nearby along with golf, tennis, swimming, and skiing.

Hosts: June and Alfred Matthews
Rooms: 5 + cottage (PB) $70-90 (cottage $130 and up) (higher peak season prices)
Full Breakfast
Credit Cards: A, B, C
Notes: 2, 7 (over age 10), 8, 9, 10, 11,

WARREN

Beaver Pond Farm Inn

Golf Course Road, RD Box 306, 05674
(802) 583-2861

Beaver Pond Farm Inn, a small, gracious country inn near the Sugarbush ski area, is located 100 yards from the first tee of the Sugarbush Golf Course, transformed into 40 kilometers of cross-country ski trails in the winter. *Bed & Breakfast in New England* calls it "The best of the best." Rooms have down comforters and beautiful views. Hearty breakfasts are served, and snacks are enjoyed by the fireplace. Continental dinners are offered three times a week during the winter. Hiking, biking, soaring, and fishing nearby. Ski and golf packages are available.

Hosts: Bob and Betty Hansen
Rooms: 6 (4PB; 2SB) $64-90
Full Breakfast
Credit Cards: A, B, C
Notes: 2, 4, 7 (over 5), 8, 9, 10, 11, 12

Beaver Pond Farm

year; 6 Pets welcome; 7 Children welcome; 8 Tennis nearby; 9 Swimming nearby; 10 Golf nearby; 11 Skiing nearby; 12 May be booked through travel agent

WATERBURY

Grünberg Haus Bed and Breakfast

Route 100 South, Rural Route 2, Box 1595, 05676
(802) 244-7726; Reservations (800) 800-7760

Spontaneous, personal attention in a hand-built, Austrian mountain chalet with a huge fieldstone fireplace, sauna, jacuzzi, grand piano, cross country ski center, tennis court, and imaginative full breakfasts. Cozy, Old World chalet guest rooms feature balconies and antiques. Innkeeper and musician Chris entertains at the piano and Innkeeper Mark takes care of the chickens, cats, and Ike, the pet turkey. "Like visiting a pal," *Hudson Dispatch*. "Quiet, romantic," *Vermont* magazine. Central to Stowe, Waitsfield, Sugarbush, Burlington, Montpelier. Home of Ben & Jerry's!

Hosts: Christopher Sellers and Mark Frohman
Rooms: 10 (5PB; 5SB) $55-130
Imaginative Full Musical Breakfast
Credit Cards: A, B, C, D, F
Notes: 2, 4 (for 10 or more), 5, 7, 8, 9, 10, 11, 12

Grünberg Haus

Inn at Blush Hill

Blush Hill Road, Rural Route 1, Box 1266, 05676
(802) 244-7529; (800) 736-7522

This Cape Cod bed and breakfast, circa 1790, sits on five acres with spectacular mountain views. The inn has a large common room, library, antiques, and four fireplaces, one in a guest room. Enjoy a breakfast of Vermont products at a ten-foot farmhand's table in front of a bay window overlooking the Worcester Mountains. Afternoon refreshments are served. We are adjacent to Ben and Jerry's ice cream factory, and skiing at Stowe and Sugarbush are only minutes away.

Hosts: Gary and Pamela Gosselin
Rooms: 6 (4PB; 2SB) $55-115 seasonal
Full Breakfast
Credit Cards: A, B, C, D, F
Notes: 2, 5, 7, 8, 9, 10, 11, 12

WESTON

The Colonial House

287 Route 100, Box CBB, 05161
(802) 824-3934; (800) 639-5033

Family oriented with old-fashioned hospitality, a comfortable inn and motel. "Vermont's Favorite Breakfast" with dinners to match. Conveniently located on Route 100 outside Weston, with summer theater, shops, museums, and 7 minutes from Weston Priory. Three downhill ski areas and 400 km of cross-country within 20 minutes. The place to stay while visiting southern Vermont. 2-Star Mobil Travel Guide. 2 Diamond AAA.

Hosts: John and Betty Nunnikhoven
Rooms: 15 (9PB; 6SB) $50-84
Full Breakfast
Credit Cards: A, B, D
Notes: 2, 4, 5, 7, 8, 9, 10, 11,

The Wilder Homestead Inn

Lawrence Hill Road, Rural Route 1, Box 106D, 05161
(802) 824-8172

Built in 1827 with Rumford fireplaces and

original Moses Eaton stenciling, the inn has been carefully restored by us and has quiet surroundings and antique furnishings. Walk to village shops, museums, summer theater. Nearby are Weston Priory, fine restaurants, skiing. Weston is a village that takes you back in time. Craft Shoppe on premises. No smoking.

Hosts: Peggy and Roy Varner
Rooms: 7 (5PB; 2SB) $60-100
Full Breakfast
Credit Cards: A, B (deposit only)
Notes: 2, 7 (over 6), 8, 9, 10, 11

The Wilder Homestead Inn

WILMINGTON

Shearer Hill Farm Bed and Breakfast

P.O. Box 1453, 05363
(802) 464-3253; (800) 437-3104

Pristine farm setting on country road, large rooms (king, queen, twin), private baths, delicious Vermont breakfast. Cross-country trails on property. Near downhill skiing, shopping, swimming, fishing, horseback riding. Only 210 miles from New York, 120 miles from Boston, 90 miles

from Hartford, and 70 from Albany.

Hosts: Bill and Patti Pusey
Rooms: 4 (PB) $70-80
Full Breakfast
Credit Cards: A, B, D
Notes: 2, 5, 8, 9, 10, 11

WOODSTOCK

Kedron Valley Inn

Route 106, South Woodstock, 05071
(802) 457-1473

1822 country inn, 7 minutes south of Woodstock on Route 106. Private baths, fireplaces, queen-sized, canopy beds, heirloom quilts, and private decks. Award-winning, air-conditioned dining. Swimming lake with 2 white sand beaches, stables, tennis, golf, and downhill and cross-country skiing are nearby. Featured in *Country Living* and *Yankee* and *Country Home*. Voted "Inn of the Year" by inn-goers. Substantial savings midweek, non-peak, and all spring.

Hosts: Max and Merrily Comms
Rooms: 27 (PB)
Full Breakfast
Credit Cards: A, B, D
Notes: 2, 4, 5, 6, 7, 8, 9, 10, 11, 12

Shearer Hill Farm

year; 6 Pets welcome; 7 Children welcome; 8 Tennis nearby; 9 Swimming nearby; 10 Golf nearby; 11 Skiing nearby; 12 May be booked through travel agent

Virginia

ARLINGTON

Memory House

6406 North Washington Boulevard, 22205
(703) 534-4607

In a prime location is this charming, ornate, restored 1899 Victorian with period antiques, wall stenciling, prize-winning handicrafts, and collectibles. The subway, one block away, quickly takes you to the mall area of Washington, D.C. By car, it is ten minutes to the White House, museums, and monuments. Two guest rooms and child's nook; air conditioning; TV; antique clawfoot tub and shower. Relax on wicker furniture on the porch or in double parlors. Share in old-fashioned comfort and friendship.

Hosts: John and Marlys McGrath
Rooms: 2 (PB) $69-85
Expanded Continental Breakfast
Credit Cards: None
Notes: 2, 5, 7, 8, 9, 12

Memory House

CHARLOTTESVILLE

The Clifton Country Inn

Route 13, Box 26, 22901
(804) 971-1800; (804) 971-7098 (FAX)

Built in 1799, this nationally recognized inn was originally owned by Thomas Mann Randolph, an early governor of Virginia. Only five miles from Charlottesville, Clifton is nestled on 48 acres and offers 14 luxurious rooms and suites all with working fireplaces and private baths. Room rates include both afternoon tea and breakfast. Named one of the top twelve inns in America by *Country Inns* magazine in February, 1993. New heated pool, spa, and tennis court.

Host: Craig Hartman, Chef and Innkeeper
Rooms: 14 (PB) $143-193
Full Breakfast
Credit Cards: A, B, C
Notes: 2, 4, 5, 7, 8, 9, 10, 11, 12

CULPEPER

Fountain Hall

609 South East Street, 22701
(703) 825-8200; (800) 476-2944

Fountain Hall is a charming 1859 Colonial Revival bed and breakfast. All of our rooms are tastefully restored and most are furnished with antiques. Three guest rooms

---

NOTES: Credit cards accepted: A Master Card; B Visa; C American Express; D Discover Card; E Diners Club; F Other; 2 Personal checks accepted; 3 Lunch available; 4 Dinner available; 5 Open all year; 6 Pets

have private porches overlooking the grounds. Fireplaces can be found in the common rooms along with books, local literature, board games, music, and TV/VCR. Fountain Hall is within walking distance to Historic Downtown Culpeper and Amtrak. Charlottesville and Dulles airports are nearby.

Hosts: Steve, Kathi and Leah-Marie Walker
Rooms: 5 (PB) $65-115
Expanded Continental Breakfast
Credit Cards: A, B, C, D
Notes: 2, 5, 7, 8, 9, 10

FREDRICKSBURG

La Vista Plantation

4420 Guinea Station Rd., 22408
(703) 898-8444; (703) 898-1041

This Classical revival-style manor house, circa 1838, is situated on ten quiet, country acres and is surrounded by farm fields and mature trees. Stocked pond, six fireplaces, antiques, rich Civil War past, radio, phone, TV, and bicycles. Fresh eggs and homemade jams are served for breakfast; air conditioned; close to historic attractions.

Hosts: Edward and Michele Schiesser
Rooms: 2 (PB), $85
Full Breakfast
Credit Cards: A, B
Notes: 2, 5, 7, 9, 10, 12

HARRISONBURG

Kingsway B & B

3581 Singers Glen Road, 22801
(703) 867-9696

Enjoy the warm hospitality of your hosts who make your comfort their priority. This private home is in a quiet rural area with a view of the mountains in the beautiful Shenandoah Valley. Carpentry and home-making skills, many house plants and outdoor flowers, a large lawn, and the in ground pool help to make your stay restful and refreshing. Just four and one-half miles from downtown; nearby is Skyline Drive, caverns, historic sites, antique shops, and flea markets.

Hosts: Chester and Verna Leaman
Rooms: 2 (PB) $50-55
Expanded Continental Breakfast
Credit Cards: D
Notes: 2, 5, 6, 9, 10, 12

HILLSVILLE

Bray's Manor B & B

Route 3, Box 210, 24343
(703) 728-7901; 800-753-BRAY

Conveniently located just off Highway 58 four miles east of I-77. The porch and two decks offer cool breezes and lovely views of the surrounding countryside. The sitting room provides TV, VCR, and books before a warm fire in season. Large air conditioned rooms, queen beds, private baths, sitting area, TV, and full country breakfast.

Hosts: Dick and Helen Bray
Rooms: 4 (PB) $65
Full Breakfast
Credit Cards: A, B, D
Notes: 2, 5, 7, 8, 10, 12

welcome; 7 Children welcome; 8 Tennis nearby; 9 Swimming nearby; 10 Golf nearby; 11 Skiing nearby; 12 May be booked through travel agent

LURAY

Shenandoah River Roost

Route 3, Box 566, 22835
(703) 743-3467

Sit on the front porch of this two-story log
home and enjoy beautiful views of the
mountains and the Shenandoah River.
Located three miles west of Luray Caverns, and ten miles west of Skyline Drive
and Shenandoah National Park. Swimming, tubing, canoeing, and golf are all
nearby. No smoking.

Hosts: Rubin and Gerry McNab
Rooms: 2 (SB) $65+tax
Full Breakfast
Credit Cards: None
Closed November 1-May 1
Notes: 2, 8, 9, 10

MEADOWS OF DAN

Spangler B & B

Route 2, Box 108, 24120
(703) 952-2454

The Spangler Bed and Breakfast borders
the National Parkway at milepost 180,
four miles south of Mabry Mill, elevation
3,000 feet. The farmhouse dates from
1904 with four large bedrooms, living room
with piano, dining room, and kitchen. There
is an old log cabin for one couple and a new
log cabin for two couples with shared bath.
These face a three and one-half-acre lake
with fishing, boating, and swimming. No
smoking. Groups welcome.

Hosts: Trudy and Harold Spangler
Rooms: 7 (1 PB; 6 SB) $50-60
Full Breakfast
Credit Cards: None
Notes: 2, 5, 7, 8, 9, 10, 11

MIDDLEBURG

Welbourne

Route 1, Box 300, 22117
(703) 687-3201

A seventh generation antebellum home in
Virginia hunt country, on a 550 acre farm.
Home to Colonel R.H. Dulany, C.S.A.,
founder of America's oldest horse show
and oldest fox hunt. Welbourne has many
Civil War stories and is a Virginia Landmark. Beth Thomas Wolfe and F. Scott
Fitzgerald stayed here, and each published
a story using the house as a setting. Somewhat worn, its "faded elegance" is reminiscent of the Old South.

Hosts: Nat and Sherry Morison
Rooms: 8 (PB) $85.20-95.85
Full Breakfast
Credit Cards: None
Notes: 2, 5, 6, 7

Welbourne

NATURAL BRIDGE

Burger's Country Inn

Route 2, Box 564, 24578
(703) 291-2464

This historic inn is furnished in antiques and
country collectibles. The rambling farmhouse with wrap-around porch and large
columns is on ten wooded acres. Four
guest rooms and three baths are available.
Enjoy croquet in summer and relax by the
fire in winter. Special continental breakfast is included. Visit the Natural Bridge

---

NOTES: Credit cards accepted: A MasterCard; B Visa; C American Express; D Discover Card; E Diners
Club; F Other; 2 Personal checks accepted; 3 Lunch available; 4 Dinner available; 5 Open all year; 6 Pets

and historic Lexington. Beautiful Blue Ridge Parkway nearby. Call or write for brochure/reservations.

Host: Frances B. Burger
Rooms: 4 (2PB; 2SB) $45-50
Expanded Continental Breakfast
Credit Cards: None
Notes: 2, 5, 6, 7, 10, 12

NELLYSFORD

Trillium House

P.O. Box 280, 22958
(804) 325-9126, 800-325-9126 (for reservations);
(804) 325-1099 (FAX)

Designed and built in 1983 to meet today's standards while retaining the charm of yesteryear. Outstanding library and sunroom. In the heart of Wintergreen's Devil's Knob Village, a year-round, 11,000 acre resort. An assortment of activities and recreation available to guests. Mountain country with trees and birds and a golf course can be seen from the breakfast table.

Hosts: Ed and Betty Dinwiddie
Rooms: 12(PB) $90-120, ($105-150 weekends and holidays)
Full Breakfast
Credit Cards: A, B
Notes: 2, 4 (on Friday and Saturday), 5, 7, 8, 9, 10, 11, 12

The Garden and the Sea Inn

NEW CHURCH/EASTERN SHORE

The Garden and the Sea Inn

Virginia Eastern Shore, Route 710, P.O. Box 275, 23415
(804) 824-0672

This elegant, European-style country inn with French-style gourmet restaurant is near Chincoteague and Assateague Islands. Five large, luxurious guest rooms, beautifully designed; spacious private baths; Victorian detail; stained glass; Oriental rugs; antiques; bay windows; library; and patio. Beautiful beach and wildlife refuge are nearby; afternoon tea; romantic escape package; and chamber music dinner-concerts. Mobil three-star and AAA three-diamond rated.

Hosts: Jack Betz and Victoria Olian
Rooms: 5 (PB) $85-135
Expanded Continental Breakfast
Credit Cards: A, B, C, D, E
Notes: 2, 4, 7, 8, 9, 10, 12

ONANCOCK

The Spinning Wheel Bed and Breakfast

31 North Street, 23417
(804) 787-7311

This 1890's Folk Victorian home, in the historic waterfront town of Onancock on Virginia's Eastern Shore, has antiques and spinning wheels throughout. All guest rooms have queen beds, private baths, and air-conditioning. Guests can visit Kerr

welcome; 7 Children welcome; 8 Tennis nearby; 9 Swimming nearby; 10 Golf nearby; 11 Skiing nearby; 12 May be booked through travel agent

Place (1799 museum), cruise to Tangier Island from Onancock Wharf, and walk to restaurants. Bicycles, tennis, and golf are available. A calm Eastern Shore getaway from D.C., Maryland, Virginia, Delaware, and New Jersey on the Chesapeake Bay, five miles from the Atlantic.

Hosts: David and Karen Tweedie
Rooms: 5 (PB) $75-85
Full Breakfast
Credit Cards: A, B
Notes: 2, 8, 9, 10, 12

RICHMOND

The William Catlin House

2304 East Broad Street, 23223
(804) 780-3746

Richmond's first and oldest bed and breakfast features antique, canopy poster beds, and working fireplaces. A delicious full breakfast is served in the elegant dining room. Built in 1845, this richly appointed home is in the Church Hill historic district and was featured in *Colonial Homes* and *Southern Living* magazines. Directly across from St. John's Church, where Patrick Henry gave his famous Liberty or Death speech. Just two minutes from I-95 and Route 64.

Hosts: Robert and Josie Martin
Rooms: 5 (3 PB; 2 SB) $89.50 (price includes all taxes)
Full Breakfast
Credit Cards: A, B, D
Notes: 2, 5, 7, 12

SMITH MOUNTAIN LAKE

The Manor at Taylor's Store

Route 1, Box 533, 24184
(703) 721-3951; 800-248-6267

This historic 120-acre estate with an elegant manor house provides romantic accommodations in guest suites with fireplaces, antiques, canopied beds, private porches, and use of hot tub, billiards, exercise room, guest kitchen, and many other amenities. A separate three-bedroom, two-bath cottage is ideal for a family. Enjoy six private, spring-fed ponds for swimming, canoeing, fishing, and hiking. Full heart-healthy, gourmet breakfast is served in the dining room with panoramic views of the countryside.

Hosts: Lee and Mary Lynn Tucker
Rooms: 6 (4 PB; 2 SB) $80-115
Full Breakfast
Credit Cards: A, B
Notes: 2, 3, 5, 7, 8, 9, 10, 11, 12

STANLEY

Jordan Hollow Farm Inn

Rt. 2, Box 375, 22851
(703) 778-2285; (703) 778-1759 (FAX)

A 200-year-old Colonial farm restored into a full service country inn. There are 150 acres with five miles of walking trails, horseback riding, swimming, and a game room. A fully equipped meeting room can accommodate groups. AAA, Mobile, IIA, and ABBA approved. Featured in *Country Magazine, Southern Living,*

Condé Host and more.

Hosts: Jetze and Marley Beers
Rooms: 21 (PB) $140-180
Full Breakfast (and dinner)
Credit Cards: A, B, D, E
Notes: 2, 3, 4, 5, 7, 8, 9, 10, 11, 12

STAUNTON

Ashton Country Home

1205 Middlebrook Avenue, 24401
(800) 296-7819; (703) 885-7819

Ashton is a delightful blend of town and country. This 1860 Greek revival home is located on 24 acres, yet one mile from the center of Staunton. There are four comfortable and attractive bedrooms, each with a private bath. A graduate of the New York Restaurant School, innkeeper Shiela Kennedy greets guests each morning with a hearty breakfast of eggs, bacon, homefries, muffins, fruit, juice, and coffee. Innkeeper Stanley Polanski provides the music of Gershwin and Porter on the grand piano.

Hosts: Shiela Kennedy and Stanley Polanski
Rooms: 4 (PB) $75-90
Full Breakfast
Credit Cards: None
Notes: 2, 5, 8, 9, 10

Thornrose House at Gypsy Hill

531 Thornrose Avenue, 24401
(703) 885-7026

Outside, this turn-of-the-century Georgian residence has a wrap-around veranda, Greek colonnades, and lovely gardens. Inside, a fireplace and grand piano create a formal but comfortable atmosphere. Five attractive bedrooms with private baths are on the second floor. Your hosts offer afternoon tea, refreshments, and conversation. Adjacent to a 300-acre park that is great for walking, with tennis, golf, and ponds. Other nearby attractions include the Blue Ridge National Park, natural chimneys, Skyline Drive, Woodrow Wilson's birthplace, and the Museum of American Frontier Culture.

Hosts: Suzanne and Otis Huston
Rooms: 5 (PB) $55-70
Full Breakfast
Credit Cards: None
Notes: 2, 5, 7, 8, 9, 10

TANGIER ISLAND

Sunset Inn

Box 156, 23440
(804) 891-2535

Enjoy accommodations one-half block from the beach with a view of the bay. Deck, air conditioning, bike riding, and nice restaurants.

Hosts: Grace and Jim Brown
Rooms: 9 (8PB; 1SB) $50-$60
Continental Breakfast
Credit Cards: None
Notes: 2, 5, 7, 9

VIRGINIA BEACH

Barclay Cottage Bed and Breakfast

400 16th St., 23451
(804) 422-1956

Casual sophistication in a warm, historic,

inn-like atmosphere. Designed in turn-of-the-century style, the Barclay Cottage is two blocks from the beach in the heart of the Virginia Beach recreational area. The inn itself is completely restored with antique furniture to bring the feeling of yesterday with the comfort of today. Formerly the home of Lillian S. Barclay, the inn has been a guest home for many years. We have kept the historic ambience of the old inn while modernizing it significantly to meet today's needs. We look forward to welcoming you to the Barclay Cottage where the theme is "We go where our dream lead us."

Hosts: Peter and Claire
Rooms: 6 (3PB; 3SB) $65-80
Full Breakfast
Credit Cards: A, B, C
Notes: 9, 10, 12

WASHINGTON

Caledonia Farm Bed and Breakfast

Route 1, Box 2080, Flint Hill, 22627
(703) 675-3693

Enjoy ultimate hospitality, comfort, scenery, and recreation adjacent to Virginia's Shenandoah National Park. This romantic getaway to history and nature includes outstanding full breakfasts, fireplaces, airconditioning, hayrides, bicycles, lawn games, VCR, and piano. World's finest dining, caves, Skyline Drive, battlefields, stables, antiquing, hiking, and climbing are all nearby. Washington, D.C., is 68 miles away; Washington, Virginia, just four miles. A Virginia historic landmark, the farm is listed on the National Register of Historic Places. AAA three diamond rated.

Host: Phil Irwin
Rooms: 2 and 1 suite (1 PB; 2 SB) $80-140
Full Breakfast
Credit Cards: A, B, D
Notes: 2, 5, 7 (over 12), 8, 9, 10, 11, 12

Caledonia Farm

WAYNESBURG

The Iris Inn

191 Chinquapin Dr., 22980
(703) 943-1991

The charm and grace of Southern living in a totally modern facility, nestled in a wooded tract on the western slope of the Blue Ridge, overlooking the historic Shenandoah Valley—that's what awaits you at the Iris Inn in Waynesboro. It's ideal for a weekend retreat, a refreshing change for the business traveler, and a tranquil spot for the tourist to spend a night or a week. Guest rooms are spacious, comfortably furnished, and delightfully decorated in nature and wildlife motifs. Each room has private bath and individual temperature control.

Hosts: Wayne and Iris Karl
Rooms: 7 (PB) $80-95
Full Breakfast
Credit Cards: A, B
Notes: 2, 5, 8, 9, 10

NOTES: Credit cards accepted: A MasterCard; B Visa; C American Express; D Discover Card; E Diners Club; F Other; 2 Personal checks accepted; 3 Lunch available; 4 Dinner available; 5 Open all year; 6 Pets

WILLIAMSBURG

Applewood Colonial Bed and Breakfast

605 Richmond Road, 23185
(804) 229-0205; (800) 899-2753

The owner's unique apple collection is evidenced throughout this restored colonial home. Four elegant guest rooms (one suite with fireplace) are conveniently located four short blocks from Colonial Williamsburg and very close to the College of William and Mary campus. Antiques complement the romantic atmosphere. The dining room has a beautiful built-in corner cupboard and a crystal chandelier above the pedestal table where homemade breakfast is served. Afternoon tea. No smoking.

Host: Fred Strout
Rooms: 4 (PB) $70-120
Continental Deluxe Breakfast
Credit Cards: A, B
Notes: 2, 5, 7, 8, 10, 12

Fox Grape

701 Monumental Avenue, 23185
(804) 229-6914; (800) 292-3699

Genteel accommodations just five blocks north of Virginia's restored colonial capital. Furnishings include canopied beds, antiques, counted cross stitch, a duck decoy collection, and a cup-plate collection. Points of interest include Colonial Williamsburg, Carters Grove Plantation, Jamestown, Yorktown, and the College of William and Mary.

Hosts: Pat and Bob Orendorff
Rooms: 4 (PB) $70-78
Continental Breakfast
Credit Cards: A, B, D
Notes: 2, 5, 7, 8, 9, 10, 12

Hite's Bed and Breakfast

704 Monumental Avenue, 23185
(804) 229-4814

An attractive Cape Cod B & B just a seven-minute walk to Colonial Williamsburg. Large rooms cleverly furnished with antiques and collectibles. Each room has TV, phone, radio, coffeemaker, robes, and private baths. You will especially like the suite with its large sitting room and old-fashioned bathroom with claw-foot tub. In the parlor for your enjoyment is an antique pump organ and hand-crank Victrola. You can swing in the back yard and enjoy the squirrels, birds, and gold fish pond.

Hosts: Faye and James Hite
Rooms: 2 (PB) $65-75
Continental Plus Breakfast
Credit Cards: None
Notes: 2, 5, 7

Newport House B & B

710 South Henry Street, 23185-4113
(804) 229-1775

A reproduction of an important 1756 home, Newport House has museum-standard period furnishings, including canopy beds. A five-minute walk to the historic area. Full breakfast with Colonial recipes; Colonial dancing in the ballroom every Tuesday evening (beginners welcome). The host is a historian/author (including a book on Christ) and former museum director. The hostess is a gardener, beekeeper, 18th-century seamstress, and former nurse. A pet rabbit entertains at breakfast. No smoking.

Hosts: John and Cathy Millar
Rooms: 2 (PB) $100-120
Full Breakfast
Credit Cards: None
Notes: 2, 5, 7, 10, 12

---

welcome; 7 Children welcome; 8 Tennis nearby; 9 Swimming nearby; 10 Golf nearby; 11 Skiing nearby; 12 May be booked through travel agent

The Travel Tree B&B Reservation Service

P.O. Box 838, 23187
(800) 989-1571

Searching for lodging in an historic estate, small inn, or private homestay becomes a one-step process when you make your reservations through The Travel Tree, Williamsburg's Bed and Breakfast Reservation Service. We offer a select variety of accommodations, with rates ranging from $50-150, double occupancy. Office hours are from 6pm to 9pm, Monday through Thursday. Please send a SASE for a brochure. Gift certificates available.

Williamsburg Sampler Bed and Breakfast

922 Jamestown Road, 23185
(804) 253-0398

This 18th century plantation-style three-story brick Colonial was awarded AAA Three Diamond Award. Located in the heart of Williamsburg and within walking distance to historic Colonial Williamsburg. Richly furnished bedrooms with private baths and king- or queen-size beds. Collection of antiques, pewter, and samplers are displayed throughout the house. A "Skip Lunch" breakfast is served. Internationally recognized as a favorite spot for a romantic honeymoon and for the special care to guests.

Hosts: Helen and Ike Sisanc
Rooms: 4 (PB) $85-90
Full Breakfast
Credit Cards: A, B, C
Notes: 2, 5, 8, 9, 10, 12

Williamsburg Sampler

WOODSTOCK

Azalea House Bed and Breakfast

551 South Main Street, 22664
(703) 459-3500

A large Victorian house built in 1892 featuring family antiques and stenciled ceilings. It was used as a parsonage initially, serving a church three blocks away for about 70 years. Located in the historic Shenendoah Valley, it is close to Skyline Drive and the mountains. Many Civil War sites are within short driving distance. Nearby activities include antiquing, hiking, and horseback riding.

Hosts: Price and Margaret McDonald
Rooms: 3 (PB) $45-70
Full Breakfast
Credit Cards: None
Notes: 2, 7 (over 5), 9, 10, 11

Azalea House

NOTES: Credit cards accepted: A MasterCard; B Visa; C American Express; D Discover Card; E Diners Club; F Other; 2 Personal checks accepted; 3 Lunch available; 4 Dinner available; 5 Open all year; 6 Pets

Washington

ANACORTES

Albatross Bed and Breakfast

5708 Kingsway West, 98221
(206) 293-0677

Our 1927 Cape Cod-style home offers king and queen beds and private baths in all guest rooms. The quiet, relaxing living room, patio, and deck areas view waterfront, islands, and mountains. You can walk to Washington Park, Skyline marina, fine dining, and inspirational beaches. We also offer sightseeing cruises aboard a 46-foot sailboat and have 2-speed cross bikes available. We are close to the State Ferry Boat terminal for access to the San Juan Islands and Victoria, B.C. We are also close to over 25 churches.

Hosts: Ken and Barbie
Rooms: 4 (PB) $75-85
Full Breakfast
Credit Cards: A, B
Notes: 2, 5, 7, 8, 9, 10, 11, 12

Blue Rose Bed and Breakfast

1811 9th St., 98221
(206) 293-5175

Blue Rose Bed and Breakfast offers you near-the-water old town charm, top quality service, warmth, and comfort. We know how to make your stay in Anacortes memorable and things to do often easier. A charming turn-of-the-century craftsman's dream. Beamed ceilings and hardwood floors highlight ornate period built-ins. Discover a place in which sea, woods, and snow mountains are so united in a landscape.

Hostess: Creamy Wilkins
Rooms: 2 (SB) $69
Full Breakfast
Credit Cards: A, B
Notes: 5, 7, 8, 9, 10, 11, 12

Sunset Beach Bed and Breakfast

100 Sunset Beach, 98221
(800) 359-3448

Hosts: Joann and Hal Harker
Rooms: 3 (1PB; 2SB) $69-79
Full Breakfast
Credit Cards: A, B
Notes: 2, 5, 9, 10, 11, 12

ANDERSON ISLAND

The Inn at Burg's Landing

8808 Villa Beach Road, 98303
(206) 884-9185; (206) 488-8682

Catch the ferry from Steilacoom to stay at

---

welcome; 7 Children welcome; 8 Tennis nearby; 9 Swimming nearby; 10 Golf nearby; 11 Skiing nearby; 12 May be booked through travel agent

this contemporary log homestead built in 1987. It offers spectacular views of Mt. Rainier, Puget Sound, and the Cascade Mountains and is south of Tacoma off I-5. Choose from three guest rooms. The inn has a private beach. Collect seashells and agates, swim on two freshwater lakes nearby, tennis or golf. Tour the island by bicycle or on foot and watch for sailboats and deer. Hot tub. Full breakfast. Families welcome. No smoking.

Hosts: Ken and Annie Burg
Rooms: 3 (2PB; 1SB) $65-90
Full Breakfast
Credit Cards: A, B, C
Notes: 2, 5, 7, 8, 9, 10, 11

ASHFORD

Mountain Meadows Inn Bed and Breakfast

28912 S.R. 706 E, 98304
(206) 569-2788

Built in 1910, as a mill superintendent's house, Mountain Meadows Inn Bed and Breakfast has made a graceful transition to quiet country elegance. An era of Northwest logging passed by and was seen in vivid detail from the vantage point of spring board and misery whip. Old growth stumps scattered around the house and pond still wear spring board notches as witness to a time when trees, men, and the stories of both were tall. The innkeeper says guests tell him its the best B&B they have ever stayed in. Model railroad museum.

Host: Chad Darrah
Rooms: 5 (PB) $55-95
Full Breakfast
Credit Cards: A, B
Notes: 2, 5, 7, 9, 10, 11

BELLEVUE

Petersen B & B

10228 Southeast Eighth Street, 98004
(206) 454-9334

We offer two rooms five minutes from Bellevue Square with wonderful shopping and one-half block from the bus line to Seattle. Rooms have down comforters, and we have a hot tub on the deck. Children are welcome. No smoking.

Hosts: Eunice and Carl Petersen
Rooms: 2 (SB) $50-55
Full Breakfast
Credit Cards: None
Notes: 5, 7

BELLINGHAM

Bed and Breakfast Service (BABS)

P.O. Box 5025, 98226
(206) 733-8642

We are a reservation service with host homes all over the United States. Call and let us set up your next stay at a bed and breakfast. Our rates are reasonable in the European tradition. Coordinators are Dolores and George Herrmann.

Circle F Bed and Breakfast

2399 Mt. Baker Highway, 98226
(206) 733-2509; (206) 734-3816 (FAX)

Circle F Bed and Breakfast is a home away from home for all of our guests. The Victorian-style ranch house was built in 1892 and is located on 330 acres of pasture and woodlands. We are a work-

NOTES: Credit cards accepted: A MasterCard; B Visa; C American Express; D Discover Card; E Diners Club; F Other; 2 Personal checks accepted; 3 Lunch available; 4 Dinner available; 5 Open all year; 6 Pets

ing farm, and you can enjoy hiking trails and visits with the farm animals. A hearty breakfast is served by a friendly farm family who enjoys the company of all visitors.

Host: Guy J. Foster
Rooms: 4 (1 PB; 3 SB) $45-55
Full Breakfast
Credit Cards: None
Notes: 2, 5, 7

CAMANO ISLAND

Willcox House Bed and Breakfast

1462 Larkspur Lane, 98292
(206) 629-4746

This island retreat, a short drive from Seattle, is designed for relaxing! Enjoy the panoramic view of the Cascade Mountains. Named for the owner's great aunt, early 1900's illustrator, Jesse Willcox Smith, and decorated with her works. It's a step back in time to a less stressful pace. Leisurely, country breakfast of Willcox House blended coffee, assorted omelettes, Swedish pancakes, muffins, and fresh fruits in season, with sun streaming into a cozy breakfast room.

Hosts: Esther Harmon, Madelyn, and Joe Braun
Rooms: 4 (PB) $65
Full Breakfast
Credit Cards: A, B
Notes: 2, 5, 8, 9, 10, 11

CATHLAMET

The Gallery Bed and Breakfast

Little Cape Horn, 98612-9544
(206) 425-7395; (206) 425-1351 (FAX)

The Gallery is a contemporary elegant country home with sweeping views of the majestic Columbia River ship channel. The large deck has a hot tub for relaxing while watching tug boats, seals, eagles, and windsurfers. It is surrounded by tall cedar and fir trees and a tall cliff with waterfalls. A private beach is a few steps away. Breakfast is served with fine china, crystal, and warm Christian hospitality.

Hosts: Eric and Carolyn Feasey
Rooms: 4 (2PB; 2SB) $60-80
Full Breakfast
Credit Cards: C
Notes: 2, 5, 7 (over 6)

CLE ELUM, SOUTH

The Moore House Country Bed and Breakfast

P.O. Box 629, 526 Marie Avenue, 98943
(509) 674-5939; (800) 2-2-TWAIN (WA or Canada only)

Relive the grand era of railroading at this former Chicago, Milwaukee, St. Paul, and Pacific Crewman's Hotel. Now restored as a unique tearoom inn filled with railroad memorabilia and artifacts. Our rooms range from economical to exquisite. We also offer two genuine cabooses as guest rooms. Located adjacent to Iron Horse State Park, a non-motorized recreational

welcome; 7 Children welcome; 8 Tennis nearby; 9 Swimming nearby; 10 Golf nearby; 11 Skiing nearby; 12 May be booked through travel agent

trail. Located five miles from historic Roslyn, a.k.a Cicely, Alaska, in the CBS television series *Northern Exposure*.

Hosts: Eric and Cindy Sherwood
Rooms: 12 (5PB; 6SB) $45-105 + tax
Full Breakfast
Credit Cards: A, B, C
Notes: 2, 5, 7, 9, 10, 11, 12

COSMOPOLIS

Cooney Mansion

1705 Fifth Street, 98537
(206) 533-0602

This 1908 National Historic Register home, situated in wooded seclusion, was built by Neil Cooney, owner of one of the largest sawmills of the time. It captures the adventure of the Northwest. Share the lumber baron's history and many of his original "craftsman" style antiques. Enjoy 18 holes of golf (in back yard) or a leisurely walk around Mill Creek Park. Relax in the sauna and jacuzzi, curl up with one of the many books from the library, or watch TV in the ballroom.

Hosts: Judi and Jim Lohr
Rooms: 9 (5PB; 4SB) $49-115
Full Breakfast
Credit Cards: A, B, D
Notes: 2, 5, 8, 10

COUPEVILLE

The Victorian Bed and Breakfast

602 N. Main, P.O. Box 761, 98239
(206) 678-5305

This Italianate Victorian home was built in 1889 by Jacob Jenne, now the Victorian Bed and Breakfast proudly provides accommodations throughout the year to Whidbey Island visitors. Guests at the Victorian may choose from either the charming upstairs bedrooms with private baths, queen beds, or hideaway in the cottage. Also available are a tea room with TV and tapes and a private patio to relax in.

Hosts: Al and Marion Sasso
Rooms: 2 plus 1 cottage (PB) $65-100
Full Breakfast
Credit Cards: A, B
Notes: 2, 5, 6 (limited), 7, 8, 9, 10

DARRINGTON

Sauk River Farm Bed and Breakfast

32629 State Route J30 NE, 98241
(206) 436-1794

The wild and scenic Sauk River runs through this farm nestled in a valley of the North Cascades. All-season recreational opportunities await you. Wildlife abounds year round. The Native American Loft Room is a collector's delight; The Victorian Room offers pastoral privacy. Hallmarks of the farm are its views of rugged mountains, intimate atmosphere, comfortable accommodations, and solitude for those seeking relaxation. Step back in time and sample Darrington hospitality with its Bluegrass music and crafters. No smoking.

Hosts: Leo and Sharon Mehler
Rooms: 2 (SB) $40-60
Full Breakfast
Credit Cards: None
Notes: 2, 5, 11

NOTES: Credit cards accepted: A MasterCard; B Visa; C American Express; D Discover Card; E Diners Club; F Other; 2 Personal checks accepted; 3 Lunch available; 4 Dinner available; 5 Open all year; 6 Pets

DEER HARBOR—ORCAS ISLAND

Palmer's Chart House

P.O. Box 51, 98243
(206) 376-4231

Hosts: Don and Mayjean Palmer
Rooms: 2 (PB) $60 + tax
Full Breakfast
Credit Cards: None
Notes: 2, 5, 7 (over 12), 8, 10, 11, 12

ELLENSBURG

Murphy's Country Bed and Breakfast

Route 1, Box 400, 98926
(509) 925-7986

Two large guest rooms in a lovely 1915 country home with a sweeping view of the valley. Full breakfast. Close to fly fishing and golfing.

Hostess: Doris Callahan-Murphy
Rooms: 2 (S1.5B) $60
Full Breakfast
Credit Cards: A, B, C
Notes: 2, 5, 10

FERNDALE

Slater Heritage House Bed and Breakfast

1371 W. Axton Rd., 98248
(206) 384-4273

The home is an old Victorian house that has been completely restored to its original beauty and charm. It features four guest rooms with antiques. Queen-sized beds and private baths. It is located less that a mile from I-5 and 12 miles from the Canadian Border. It is close to golfing, hiking, skiing, and water. It is five miles from Bellis Fair, the largest shopping mall in the Pacific Northwest. Rates include full country breakfast. Come spend a night in another era!

Host: Rickie Prink
Rooms: 4 (PB) $52-65
Full Breakfast
Credit Cards: A, B, C, E
Notes: 2, 5, 7, 10, 11

FRIDAY HARBOR

States Inn

2039 West Valley Road, 98250
(206) 378-6240; (206) 378-6241 (FAX)

A Three Diamond AAA rated inn. A nine-room country inn located in a quiet valley on the west side of San Juan Island, close to British Camp and Roche Harbor. We offer warm hospitality and a relaxing environment. Our rooms are tastefully decorated with a slight flavor of each of the states for which they are named. A full and hearty breakfast is served. We are situated on a 44-acre horse boarding ranch.

Hosts: Kevin and Lynn Taylor
Rooms: 8 plus 2 bedroom suite (PB) $80-110
Full Breakfast
Credit Cards: A, B
Notes: 2, 5, 7 (limited), 12

States Inn

GRAPEVIEW

Llewop Retreat

Box 97, 98546
(206) 275-2287

Bed and breakfast is provided in the large
contemporary home on a wooded knoll
that overlooks Case Inlet and Stretch Island. Many windows, skylights, and decks
allow a feeling of oneness with the incred-
ible beauty of the environment. Guests are
welcome to explore the property, play
pickleball, or unwind in the whirlpool spa.
No pets. Families welcome. Smoking on
outside decks only; TV; extra beds; excellent golf course and restaurants just four
miles away. Clergy discount.

Host: Kris Powell
Rooms: 3 (PB) $78-98
Full Breakfast
Credit Cards: None
Notes: 2, 5, 7, 10

LANGLEY—WHIDBEY ISLAND

Log Castle Bed and Breakfast

3273 East Saratoga Road, 98260
(206) 221-5483

A log house on a private, secluded beach
features turret bedrooms, wood-burning
stoves, porch swings, and panoramic views
of the beach and mountains. Relax before
a large stone fireplace or listen to the call of
gulls as you watch for bald eagles and sea
lions.

Hosts: Senator Jack and Norma Metcalf
Rooms: 4 (PB) $80-105
Full Breakfast
Credit Cards: A, B
Notes: 2, 8

LEAVENWORTH

All Seasons River Inn Bed and Breakfast

8751 Icicle Rd., 98826
(509) 548-1425

River front guest rooms, magnificent Cascade views and warm hospitality are but a
few reasons why All Seasons River Inn
was selected as one of the 50 most romantic getaways in the Pacific Northwest, and
it is why a stay here will call you back again
and again. Built as a bed and breakfast, all
guest rooms are very spacious with antique decor, river-view deck, and private
bath; some with jacuzzi tub and fireplace.
Full gourmet breakfast, adults only. No
smoking on premises.

Hosts: Kathy and Jeff Falconer
Rooms: 5 (PB) $85-125
Full Breakfast
Credit Cards: A, B
Notes: 2, 5, 8, 9, 10, 11, 12 (with exceptions)

Run of the River Bed and Breakfast

9308 E. Leavenworth Rd., P.O. Box 285, 98826
(800) 288-6491

Imagine the quintessential log Northwest
bed and breakfast inn right on the river and
surrounded on two sides by a bird refuge.

Guests enjoy the peacefulness of expansive decks, offering stunning views of the river and the Cascade Mountains that tower above. Each room is provided with every imaginable amenity including binoculars to view the wildlife. All rooms feature hand-hewn log beds and furniture crafted by Washington artisians. For outdoor enthusiasts, the Icicle Valley is world famous for its rock climbing, hiking, and biking. Guests also enjoy use of the inn's complimentary mountain bikes.

Hosts: Monty and Karen Turner
Rooms: 6 (PB) $90-140
Full Breakfast
Credit Cards: A, B, C
Notes: 2, 5, 8, 10, 11, 12

LOPEZ ISLAND

Aleck Bay Inn

Aleck Bay Road, Route 1, Box 1920, 98261
(206) 468-3535; (206) 468-3533 (FAX)

The Aleck Bay Inn is located on the south end of Lopez Island. It has seven acres bounded by the beaches and offshore islands. It provides facilities for vacation, weekend hide-away, travelers, honeymooners, weddings, business meetings, and family gatherings. Our rooms contain small fireplaces, queen-size beds, floral linens, etc. Two of them have private baths with jacuzzi tub. A large 600 sq. ft. meeting room with panoramic view of the strait is available for special needs.

Hosts: May and David Mendez
Rooms: 4 (2PB; 2SB) $75-135
Full Breakfast
Credit Cards: A, B, C
Notes: 2, 5, 9, 10, 12

MacKaye Harbor Inn

Route 1, Box 1940, 98261
(206) 468-2253; (206) 468-9555

This Victorian beachfront bed and breakfast in the San Juan Islands is an ideal getaway, full of warmth and nostalgia. There is a sandy beach and extensive grounds on a tree-lined harbor. Wildlife frequents the area. Kayak and bicycle rental. Quiet, excellent location for small groups or couples. The kitchen is available for guest use. No smoking.

Hosts: Robin and Mike Bergstrom
Rooms: 5 (1PB; 4SB) $69-109
Full Breakfast
Credit Cards: A, B
Notes: 2, 3, 5, 8, 10, 12

LYNDEN

Century House Bed and Breakfast

401 So. B.C. Avenue, 98264
(206) 354-2439; (206) 354-6910 (FAX)

Located on 35 acres at the edge of town, Century House is a 105-year-old Victorian home. You'll find this completely restored home a quiet retreat with spacious gardens and lawns for your enjoyment. The quaint Dutch village of Lynden is within an easy walk boasting the best museums in the area and gift shops galore …but sorry; the town is closed on Sunday. Take day trips to the Cascade Mountains and Mount Baker, the sea, Seattle, Vancouver, or Victoria, British Columbia.

Hosts: Jan and Ken Stremler
Rooms: 4 (2PB; 2SB) $60-85
Full Breakfast
Credit Cards: A, B
Notes: 2, 5, 7, 8, 9, 10, 11

---

welcome; 7 Children welcome; 8 Tennis nearby; 9 Swimming nearby; 10 Golf nearby; 11 Skiing nearby; 12 May be booked through travel agent

MAPLE FALLS

Yodier Inn

7425 Mt. Baker Hwy, P.O. Box 222, 98266
(206) 599-2156; (800) 642-9033

The Yodier Inn is a countrified bed and breakfast, located 26 miles east of Bellingham, Washington, and 25 miles west of the Mount Baker Recreational Area. Located in the village of Maple Falls, The Yodier Inn is the perfect place to come and stay while enjoying the many recreational activities the Mount Baker Foothills have to offer.

Hosts: Bethnie and Jeff Morrison
Rooms: 2 (PB) $65
Full Breakfast
Credit Cards: A, B
Notes: 2, 5, 6, 7 (over 12), 10, 11

MONTESANO

Sylvan House

P.O. Box 416, 98563
(206) 241-3453

A country hideaway that is only a ten-minute hike to Lake Sylvia State Park, hunting, fishing, and swimming. The three story, 1970, family home has been used as B&B for six years. High on a hilltop with a sweeping view of the valley below. Gourmet food. Charter member of Washington State Bed and Breakfast Guild. In Washington's State magazine *Destination Washington*. Four rooms; two queen, one twin, two baths. No smoking. High decks. Limited to older children. No pets.

In several cookbooks and B&B books on the West Coast.

Hosts: Mike and Jo Anne Murphy
Rooms: 4 (2PB; 2SB) $55-65
Full Breakfast
Credit Cards: None
Notes: 2, 5, 7 (older), 9, 11, 12

PORT TOWNSEND

Belmont Restaurant and Inn

925 Water St., 98368
(206) 385-3007

Hosts: Rudy Valiani, Joanne Moliskey, and Jeff Fragchineuud
Rooms: 4 (PB) $69-89
Full Breakfast
Credit Cards: A, B, C, D
Notes: 2, 3, 4, 5, 6, 7, 8, 9, 10, 12

The English Inn

718 F St., 98368
(206) 385-5302 (voice and FAX)

The English Inn was built in 1885 in the Italianate style. It is one of the more gracious Victorian mansions in Port Townsend. It has five large, sunny bedrooms, three of which have views of the Olympic Mountains. Beautiful scenery, hiking, antiquing, and only two hours from Seattle. A lovely garden, hot tub, and lots of comfort, but best of all, fresh scones for breakfast!

Hostess: Juliette Swenson
Rooms: 5 (PB) $65-95
Full Breakfast
Credit Cards: A, B
Notes: 2, 8, 10

NOTES: Credit cards accepted: A MasterCard; B Visa; C American Express; D Discover Card; E Diners Club; F Other; 2 Personal checks accepted; 3 Lunch available; 4 Dinner available; 5 Open all year; 6 Pets

Lizzie's Victorian Bed and Breakfast

731 Pierce St., 98368
(206) 385-4168

Elegant, yet invitingly comfortable, Victorian mansion in a quiet, historic district. Two parlors, with fireplaces and pianos, enveloped with quiet music, and the ever-present coffee and tea. Breakfast in the sunny kitchen around 11-foot oak table is a special treat and the "Lizzie" replica doghouse may itself be worth the whole trip. Walking distance to theaters, restaurants, shopping, and beaches. Quite simply, the finest!

Hosts: Bill and Patti Wickline
Rooms: 8 (5PB; 3SB) $58-105
Full Breakfast
Credit Cards: A, B, D
Notes: 2, 5, 8, 10

Lizzie's Victorian Bed and Breakfast

Trenholm House

2037 Haines, 98368
(206) 385-6059

An 1890 Victorian farmhouse inn. Original woodwork. Five guest rooms and cottage furnished in country antiques. Gourmet breakfast, beautiful lagoon, and bay views make every stay memorable. Members of the Washington Bed and Breakfast Guild, Olympic Peninsula Bed and Breakfast Association, National Bed and Breakfast Association, and the Chamber of Commerce.

Hosts: Michael and Patricia Kelly
Rooms: 6 (2PB; 4SB) $62-95
Full Breakfast
Credit Cards: A, B
Notes: 2, 5, 7 (over 12), 8, 9, 10, 12

SEATTLE

Chambered Nautilus Bed and Breakfast Inn

5005 22nd Avenue Northeast, 98105
(206) 522-2536

A gracious 1915 Georgian Colonial that is nestled on a hill and furnished with a mixture of American and English antiques and fine reproductions. A touch of Mozart, Persian rugs, a grand piano, two fireplaces, four lovely porches, and national award-winning breakfasts help assure your special comfort. Excellent access to Seattle's theaters, restaurants, public transportation, shopping, bike and jogging trails, churches, Husky Stadium, and the University of Washington campus.

Hosts: Bill and Bunny Hagemeyer
Rooms: 6 (4 PB; 2 SB) $77.50 - 97.50
Full Breakfast
Credit Cards: A, B, C, E, F
Notes: 2, 5, 8, 9, 10, 11, 12

Chambered Nutilus B & B

welcome; 7 Children welcome; 8 Tennis nearby; 9 Swimming nearby; 10 Golf nearby; 11 Skiing nearby; 12 May be booked through travel agent

Chelsea Station B & B

4915 Linden Avenue North, 98103
(206) 547-6077 (voice and FAX)

Chelsea Station consistently provides the peaceful surroundings travelers enjoy. Lace curtains, ample breakfasts, and comfy king beds share warm feelings of "Grandma's time." The nearby Seattle Rose Garden contributes beauty to the human spirit. With a cup of tea in the afternoon, Chelsea Station is a perfect place for relaxation and renewal. No smoking.

Hosts: Dick and Mary Lou Jones
Rooms: 5 (PB) $59-114
Full Breakfast
Credit Cards: A, B, C, D, E
Notes: 2, 5, 8, 9, 10, 12

The Shafer-Baillie Mansion Guest House

907 14th Avenue East, 98112
(206) 322-4654; (206) 329-4654 (FAX)

Antiques of yesteryear; a quiet and enjoyable atmosphere; formal living room and fireplace with comfortable seating for our guests; full library with TV and VCR; formal dining room seats 50; billiard room with copper fireplace; spacious grounds and garden for summer parties and weddings; port cochere and gazebos on north and south lawns with tables and seating; great food in your price range; casual buffet or gourmet sumptuous fare. With your event in mind, we will help you plan your occasion, whether it's a breakfast, luncheon, or meeting all day with both. There are telephones in every room.

Host: Erv Olssen
Rooms: 13 (10PB; 3SB) $59-115
Continental Breakfast
Credit Cards: A, B, C
Notes: 2, 5, 6 (on request), 8, 9, 10, 11, 12

SEQUIM

Greywolf Inn

395 Keeler Road, 98382
(206) 683-5889

Nestled in a crescent of towering evergreens, this Northwest country estate overlooking the Dungeness Valley is the ideal starting point for year round light adventure on the Olympic peninsula…hiking, fishing, biking, boating, bird watching, sightseeing, and golf. Enjoy Greywolf's sunny decks, Japanese style hot tub, and meandering five-acre woodswalk, or curl up by the fire with a good book. Then, retire to one of the inn's cozy comfortable theme rooms. It is the perfect ending to an exciting day.

Hosts: Peggy and Bill Melang
Rooms: 6 (PB) $58-98
Full Breakfast
Credit Cards: A, B, C
Notes: 2, 3, 5, 7 (over 12), 8, 9, 10, 11, 12

Margie's Inn on the Bay

120 Forest Road, 98382
(206) 683-7011; (800) 730-7011

Sequim's only waterfront bed and breakfast. A contemporary ranch-style home with 180 feet on the water. Five well-appointed bedrooms with private baths. A large sitting room with VCR and movies. Two Persian cats and a talking parrot. Close to the marina, fishing, Dungeness National Wildlife Refuge and Spit, Olympic Game Farm, hiking and biking, Hurricane Ridge, gift shops, and much more. Great restaurants in the area. AAA inspected.

Hosts: Margie and Don Vorhies
Rooms: 5 (PB) $69-125
Full Breakfast
Credit Cards: A, B
Notes: 2, 5, 7 (over 12), 8, 9, 10, 11, 12

NOTES: Credit cards accepted: A MasterCard; B Visa; C American Express; D Discover Card; E Diners Club; F Other; 2 Personal checks accepted; 3 Lunch available; 4 Dinner available; 5 Open all year; 6 Pets

Seabreeze Beach Cottage

SILVERDALE

Seabreeze Beach Cottage

16609 Olympic View Road, NW, 98383
(206) 692-4648

Challenged by lapping waves at high tide, this private retreat will awaken your five senses with the smell of salty air, a taste of fresh oyster and clams, views of the Olympic Mountains, and the exhilaration of sun, surf, and sand. Free brochure. Hot at the water's edge.

Host: Dennis Fulton
Rooms: 2 (PB) $119-149
Continental Breakfast
Credit Cards: A, B
Notes: 2, 5, 6, 7, 9, 10, 12

SNOHOMISH

Victorian Rose

124 Avenue D, 98290

A 1900 pink Victorian home appointed with period furnishings. Two rooms with private baths are available. The Rose and Lace Room is a very romantic room and the Grandma Rose Room is just like a grandma's house with fireplace. We are one block away from the downtown antique capital of Northwest (Snohomish). Relax on the deck or in the gardens, and you're right below parachutists and hot air balloons. Hot air balloon rides can be arranged. It has been rumored that breakfast has been served in bed, and of course our lavish breakfast in the dining room is one you won't forget.

Hosts: Dave and Sheri Kelnhofer
Rooms: 2 (PB) $60-65
Full Breakfast
Credit Cards: B
Notes: 2, 5, 7 (over 12), 9, 10

SPOKANE

Marianna Stoltz House Bed and Breakfast

E. 427 Indiana Avenue, 99207
(509) 483-4316

Our 1908 historic home is situated five minutes from downtown. Furnished with antiques, old quilts, and Oriental rugs. We

welcome; 7 Children welcome; 8 Tennis nearby; 9 Swimming nearby; 10 Golf nearby; 11 Skiing nearby; 12 May be booked through travel agent

offer a wrap-around veranda, sitting room, and parlor which provide relaxation and privacy. Enjoy king, queen or single beds with private or shared baths, air-conditioning and TV. A tantalizing, unique, and hearty breakfast is prepared each morning. Close to shopping, opera house, convention center, Centennial Trail, riverfront park, and bus.

Hosts: Jim and Phyllis Maguire
Rooms: 4 (2PB; 2SB) $60-65+tax
Full Breakfast
Credit Cards: A, B, C, D, E
Notes: 2, 5, 7 (over 10), 9, 11, 12

WHITE SALMON

Llama Ranch Bed and Breakfast

1980 Highway 141, 98672
(509) 395-2786; (800) 800-LAMA

Hospitality plus unforgettable delight. Jerry and Rebeka share their love of llamas on free llama walks through the woods with each guest walking a "llovable" llama. There are stunning views of both Mt. Adams and Mt. Hood. The ranch is located between the Mt. Adams wilderness area and the Columbia Gorge national scenic area with many varied activities close by. Picturesque views and photographic memories abound along with the serenity, dignity, and beauty of llamas.

Hosts: Jerry and Rebeka Stone
Rooms: 7 (2 PB; 5 SB) $55-75
Full Breakfast
Credit Cards: A, B, D
Notes: 2, 5, 6, 7, 10, 11, 12

Marianna Stoltz House

West Virginia

BERKELEY SPRINGS

The Country Inn
207 S. Washington Street, 25411
(304) 258-2210; (800) 822-6630 (Reservations);
(304) 258-3986 (FAX)

Just over the mountain. . .less than 100 miles from Balto. Enjoy the warmth and service of a unique and charming country inn. 70 distinctive rooms, creative cuisine, and light specialties. Relax in our full service spa, art gallery, and serene gardens. Many irresistible packages available. Call for reservations.

Hosts: Mr. and Mrs. Jack Barker
Rooms: 70 (57PB; 13SB) $35-80
Full Breakfast
Credit Cards: A, B, C, D, E
Notes: 2, 3, 4, 5, 7, 8, 9, 10, 11, 12

HUTTONSVILLE

Hutton House
Route 219-250, 26273
(304) 335-6701

Meticulously restored and decorated, this Queen Anne Victorian on the National Register of Historic Places is conveniently located near Elkins, Cass Railroad, and Snowshoe Ski Resort. It has a wrap-around porch and deck for relaxing and enjoying the view, TV, game room, lawn for games, and a friendly kitchen. Breakfast and afternoon refreshments are served at your leisure; other meals are available with prior reservation or good luck! Come see us!

Hosts: Loretta Murray and Dean Ahren
Rooms: 7 (3PB; 4SB) $50-65
Full Breakfast
Credit Cards: A, B, C
Notes: 2, 5, 7, 8, 10, 11, 12

LEWISBURG

General Lewis Inn
301 E. Washington St., 24901-1425
(800) 628-4454

Come rock in a chair on the veranda of the General Lewis Inn. See passengers alight from a horse-drawn carriage. On chilly days dream by the fireplace, solve one of the puzzles, or play a fascinating game. Don't miss Memory Lane's display of ancient tools for home and farm. Antiques furnish every room, including comfortable canopy, spool, and poster beds. The dining room in the 1834 wing features Southern cooking. Nestled in beautiful Greenbrier Valley, the Inn offers nearby walking tours. Check out the Lewisburg historical district and browse the antique shops. Outdoor recreational activities

---

year; 6 Pets welcome; 7 Children welcome; 8 Tennis nearby; 9 Swimming nearby; 10 Golf nearby; 11 Skiing nearby; 12 May be booked through travel agent

abound throughout the Valley.

Hostess: Janine Zanecki
Rooms: 25 (PB) $55-80
Full Breakfast
Credit Cards: A, B, C
Notes: 2,3, 4, 5, 6, 7, 8, 9, 10, 11, 12

MARTINSBURG

Boydville, The Inn at Martinsburg

601 South Queen St., 25401
(304) 263-1448

1812 stone manor house on ten park-like acres in town limits. Rich in Civil War history. Walk to Blue Ridge Outlets. On National Register. Six bedrooms, private baths, large public rooms, fireplace, and TV. Rates include expanded continental breakfast, featuring native products. Restaurants nearby. Rocking porch overlooking century-old trees and boxwoods. Private and quiet. Antiquing in area. Personal checks preferred. Closed during the month of August.

Hosts: La Rue Frye, Bob Boege, and Carolyn Snyder/Pete Bailey
Rooms: 6 (4PB; 2SB) $100-125
Expanded Continental Breakfast
Credit Cards: A, B
Notes: 2, 10, 11, 12

PARKERSBURG

Harmony House Bed and Breakfast

710 Ann St., 26101
(304) 485-1458

This 1901 Queen Anne home is on the National Register of Historic Places. It is conveniently located downtown within walking distance of the art museum, live theatres, movie theaters, and the departure point to historic Blennerhassett Island. The guest rooms are decorated with antiques, Victorian light fixtures, and Oriental rugs. Original oak woodwork, unique fireplaces, and stained glass adorn the home. At least one music box can be found in each room and a player piano welcomes guests to the formal parlor.

Hosts: Deborah and Rich Shaffer
Rooms: 3 (1PB; 2SB) $40-48
Expanded Continental Breakfast
Credit Cards: A, B, C, D, E
Notes: 2, 5, 8, 9, 10

VALLEY CHAPEL / WESTON

Ingeberg Acres

Millstone Rd., P.O. Box 199, 26446
(304) 269-2834

A unique experience can be yours at this scenic 450-acre horse and cattle farm. Ingeberg Acres is located in the heart of West Virginia seven miles from Weston, overlooking its own private valley. Hiking, swimming, hunting, and fishing or just relaxing can be the orders of the day. Observe or participate in numerous farm activities.

Hosts: Inge and John Mann
Rooms: 3 (SB) $59
Full Breakfast
Credit Cards: None
Notes: 2, 5, 7, 9, 10

NOTES: Credit cards accepted: A Master Card; B Visa; C American Express; D Discover Card; E Diners Club; F Other; 2 Personal checks accepted; 3 Lunch available; 4 Dinner available; 5 Open all

Wisconsin

ALBANY

Albany Guest House

405 South Mill Street, 53502
(608) 862-3636

An experience in tranquility, just 30 miles south of the capital dome in Madison. Enjoy king and queen beds in air-conditioned rooms in a restored 1908 home. Relax on the wide, flower-filled front porch or light the fireplace in the master bedroom. Canoe, tube, or fish the Sugar River; bike, hike, or cross-country ski the Sugar River Trail. Visit nearby New Glarus, America's Little Switzerland, or Monroe, The Swiss Cheese Capital.

Hosts: Bob and Sally Braem
Rooms: 4 (PB) $50-70
Full Breakfast
Credit Cards: None
Notes: 2, 5, 7, 9, 10, 11

Oak Hill Manor

401 E. Main Street, 53502
(608) 862-1400

A 1908 brick manor house on the Sugar River Bicycle Trail. Spacious sunny corner rooms are air-conditioned and all have queen-size beds. Choose a room with a fireplace, a porch, or a canopy bed. Stroll the acre of gardens or sit by the fire in the guest parlor. Gourmet fireside breakfast served daily. Hike, bike, canoe, golf, and cross country ski. Bicycles available at no charge.

Hosts: Lee and Mary DeWolf
Rooms: 4 (PB) $55-60
Full Breakfast
Credit Cards: A, B
Notes: 2, 5, 8, 10, 11, 12

Sugar River Inn

304 South Mill St., 53502
(608) 862-1248

Our turn-of-the-century inn, with many original features, has the charm of yesteryear, and Christian fellowship. We are located in a quiet village in southern Wisconsin along the Sugar River. We have spacious lawn, canoeing, and fishing in the back yard. We are minutes away from the bike trail. Comfortable and light airy rooms await you, queen-size beds, fine linens, afternoon refreshments, and wake up coffee. We are near New Glarus, House on the Rock, Little Norway, and the state capital in Madison. Cash or check. Children allowed by arrangement.

Hosts: Jack and Ruth Lindberg
Rooms: 4 (1PB; 3SB) $50-60
Full Breakfast
Credit Cards: None
Notes: 2, 5, 7 (by arrangement), 10

---

year; 6 Pets welcome; 7 Children welcome; 8 Tennis nearby; 9 Swimming nearby; 10 Golf nearby; 11 Skiing nearby; 12 May be booked through travel agent

ALGOMA

Amberwood Inn

N7136 Hwy. 42, 54201
(414) 487-3471

Luxury Lake Michigan beachfront accommodations. Located on two and one-half private acres with 300 feet of beach. Each suite is large, romantic, and very private. Private baths, whirlpool tubs, sauna, and private decks open to water. Awaken to sunrise over water; sleep to the sound of the waves. Ten minutes to Door County.

Rooms: 5 (PB) $55-85
Full Breakfast
Credit Cards: A, B
Notes: 2, 7, 9, 10

CEDARBURG

The Washington House Inn

W62 N573 Washington Avenue, 53012
(414) 375-3550; (800) 554-4717

Built in 1884 and listed on the National Register of Historic Places, 29 guest rooms feature antiques, down comforters, whirlpool baths, fireplaces, and cable TV. Located in the heart of the Cedarburg historic district, within walking distance of area antique shops, fine dining, and historic Cedar Creek settlement.

Hostess: Wendy Porterfield
Rooms: 29 (PB) $59-159
Expanded Continental Breakfast
Credit Cards: A, B, C, D, E
Notes: 2, 5, 7, 8, 9, 10, 11

CHETEK

Trails End Bed and Breakfast

641 Ten Mile Lake Drive, 54728
(715) 924-2641

Peace and tranquility await you in this modern spacious log lodge, situated on our private island. The 4,000-square-foot, three-level log home houses antiques of every sort, with stories behind most every unique feature of the home from an 1887 jail door to a 300 pound, seven-foot wagon wheel and a huge stone fireplace. Each guest's bedroom—the Romantic, Indian, and Western Rooms—are decorated with antiques of yesteryear.

Hosts: Richard and Bonnie Flood
Rooms: 3 (1PB; 2SB) $70-90
Full Breakfast
Credit Cards: A
Notes: 5, 9, 10

EAGLE RIVER

Brennan Manor—Old World Bed and Breakfast

1079 Everett Rd., 54521
(715) 479-7353

This castle in the forest evokes images of King Arthur with its suit of armor, arched windows, hand hewn wood work, and a 30-foot stone fireplace. You'll stay in one of four antique-decorated rooms (private baths) that opens onto a balcony overlooking the Great Rooms. There, wintertime guests gather to sip hot chocolate and munch popcorn after cross-country skiing in the Nicolet National Forest or

---

NOTES: Credit cards accepted: A Master Card; B Visa; C American Express; D Discover Card; E Diners Club; F Other; 2 Personal checks accepted; 3 Lunch available; 4 Dinner available; 5 Open all

snowmobiling on 500 miles of trails. Situated on the largest freshwater chain of lakes in the world, the inn's frontage includes a beach, boathouse, and piers for warm weather fun. A three bedroom guest house is also available. No smoking.

Hosts: Connie and Bob Lawton
Rooms: 4 (PB) $69-89
Full Breakfast
Credit Cards: A, B
Notes: 2, 5, 8, 9, 10, 11, 12

The Inn at Pinewood

P.O. Box 549, 1800 Silver Forest Lane, 54521
(715) 479-4114

Northwoods elegance at its finest. Warmest hospitality awaits you the minute you arrive at this delightful 21 room bed and breakfast. Eight romantic guest rooms, all with king-size beds, private baths, and balconies. Many with double whirlpool baths and fireplaces. Summers: swim, hike, fish, play tennis. Winters: ski, snowmobile, then relax by the fire in the huge stone fireplace. Reserve the entire inn for conferences and retreats. Scrumptious full breakfasts. Gift certificates available.

Hosts: Edward and Nona Soroosh
Rooms: 8 (PB) $65-95
Full Breakfast
Credit Cards: A, B
Notes: 2, 5, 7, 8, 9, 10, 11, 12

EAU CLAIRE

Otter Creek Inn

2536 Hwy. 12, 54701
(715) 832-2945

Enjoy breakfast in bed amid the antiques of yesteryear in this 6,000-square-foot, three-story, country Victorian inn. Pamper yourself in amenities of today with double whirlpools, phones, air conditioning, and cable television. Venture outside to stroll the wooded grounds or snuggle up inside near the fire to watch the deer and wildlife saunter by on their way to the creek. All this country charm is less than three minutes from numerous restaurants, shops, and museums.

Hosts: Randy and Shelley Hansen
Rooms: 4 (PB) $59-129
Expanded Continental Breakfast
Credit Cards: A, B, C
Notes: 2, 5, 8, 9, 10, 11

ELLISON BAY

Wagon Trail Resort, Restaurant and Conference Center

1041 Hwy. 22, 54210
(414) 854-2385; (414) 854-5278 (FAX)

Wagon Trail's homestyle hospitality begins with comfortable year-round accommodations, from a large Scandinavian lodge to secluded vacation homes and cozy bayside cottages. Tensions melt in our indoor pool, sauna, and whirlpool. Homemade specialties and a delectable buffet distinguish our restaurant, while Grandma's Swedish Bakery serves famous pecan rolls and Scandinavian treats. Miles of groomed hiking and ski trails criss-cross two hundred wooded acres.

Hosts: Mike and Miriam Dorn
Rooms: 80 (PB)
Both Full and Continental Breakfast
Credit Cards: A, B, C, D, E
Notes: 2, 3, 4, 5, 7, 8, 9, 10, 11, 12

year; 6 Pets welcome; 7 Children welcome; 8 Tennis nearby; 9 Swimming nearby; 10 Golf nearby; 11 Skiing nearby; 12 May be booked through travel agent

FERRYVILLE

Mississippi Humble Bush Bed and Breakfast

Box 297, 54628
(608) 734-3022

Located in Ferryville, Wisconsin, on the Mississippi River between LaCrosse and Prairie du Chien. Good fishing, excellent turkey and deer hunting, many rustic biking roads. All rooms overlook the river and have a private bath. Enjoy luxurious comfort and a full farm breakfast.

Hostess: Elisabeth Atwell
Rooms: 4 (PB) $65
Full Farm Breakfast
Credit Cards: A, B
Notes: 2, 7

FISH CREEK

Thorp House Inn and Cottages

4135 Bluff Road, P. O. Box 490, 54212
(414) 868-2444

A turn-of-the-century historic home with a bay view. Four romantic guest rooms (one with whirlpool), parlor with stone fireplace, and cozy library—all furnished with fine antiques and lots of authentic detail. Home-baked continental breakfast. Fireplace cottages furnished in country antiques are also available. We are located in the village of Fish Creek, the heart of the Door County Peninsula, just blocks from Peninsula State Park.

Hosts: Christine and Sverre Falck-Pedersen
Rooms: 4 (PB) $70-130; 7 cottages (PB)
Continental Breakfast
Credit Cards: None
Notes: 2, 5, 7 (cottages only), 8, 9, 10, 11

FORT ATKINSON

The Lamp Post Inn

408 South Main, 53538
(414) 563-6561

We welcome you to the charm of our 115-year-old Victorian home filled with beautiful antiques. Five grammophones for your listening pleaure. For the modern, one of our baths features a large jacuzzi. We are located 7 blocks from the famous Fireside Playhouse. You come a stranger, but leave here a friend. No smoking.

Hosts: Debbie and Mike Rusch
Rooms: 3 (2PB; 1SB) $60-85
Full Breakfast
Credit Cards: None
Notes: 2, 5, 7, 8, 9, 10, 11

HAZEL GREEN

Wisconsin House Stage Coach Inn

2105 E. Main St., 53811-0071
(608) 854-2233

Built as a stage coach inn in 1846, the Inn now offers six rooms and two suites for your comfort. Join us for an evening's rest. Dine and be refreshed in the parlor where General Grant spent many an evening with his friend Jefferson Crawford. Most conveniently located for all the attractions of the Tri-State Area. Galena, Illinois, is ten minutes away, Dubuque, Iowa, 15 miles, and Platteville is 20 miles away.

Hosts: Ken and Pat Disch
Rooms: 8 (6PB; 2SB) $55-100
Full Breakfast
Credit Cards: A, B
Notes: 2, 3, 4, 5, 7, 9, 10, 11, 12

NOTES: Credit cards accepted: A Master Card; B Visa; C American Express; D Discover Card; E Diners Club; F Other; 2 Personal checks accepted; 3 Lunch available; 4 Dinner available; 5 Open all

HUDSON

Phipps Inn

1005 3rd. St., 54016
(715) 386-0800

Listed on the National Registry of Historic Places, this 1884 Queen Anne Victorian inn offers comfort, romance and elegance. Authentic antiques, six whirlpools, and nine fireplaces make it a must to experience. Close to St. Paul, Minneapolis, and Mega Mall activities.

Hosts: Cyndi and John Berglund
Rooms: 6 (PB) $99-179
Full Breakfast
Credit Cards: A, B, C
Notes: 2, 5, 8, 9, 10, 11, 12

IOLA

Taylor House B & B

210 E. Iola St., 54945
(715) 445-2204

Turn-of-the-century Victorian home. Antique-furnished rooms. Parlor with fireplace. Queen-size beds. Paved country roads are ideal for biking. Fifteen minutes from Waupaca Chain O' Lakes. Full Breakfast.

Hosts: Crystal and Richard Anderson
Rooms: 4 (1PB; 3SB) $46-50
Full Breakfast
Credit Cards: None
Notes: 2, 5, 7, 9, 10, 11

Trillium

LA FARGE

Trillium

Rt. 2, Box 121, 54639
(608) 625-4492

A fully furnished private cottage on our diversified farm. Cottage has complete bath, full kitchen, porch with swing, and a stone fireplace in the living room. The cottage has two double beds plus a crib and highchair. Located in Southwestern Wisconsin, offering a wide variety of seasonal recreational opportunities.

Hostess: Roasanne Boyett
Rooms: 2 (PB) $60-70
Full Breakfast
Credit Cards: None
Notes: 2, 5, 7, 8, 9, 10, 11

LAKE DELTON

The Swallow's Nest Bed and Breakfast

141 Sarrington, P.O. Box 418, 53940
(608) 254-6900

The unique decor is English in taste with period collectibles. New home with cathedral windows and ceiling. Offers seclusion among the trees and bird's-eye view of the lake. Relax in the library or by the fireplace. Fine restaurants nearby. Close to Wisconsin Dells, Devils Head, two state parks, and Circus World Museum. Full Breakfast, four rooms, and four private baths. No pets and no smoking. Gift certificates available.

Hosts: Rod and Mary Ann Stemo
Rooms: 4 (PB) $60-70
Full Breakfast
Credit Cards: A, B
Notes: 2, 5, 8, 9, 10, 11

year; 6 Pets welcome; 7 Children welcome; 8 Tennis nearby; 9 Swimming nearby; 10 Golf nearby; 11 Skiing nearby; 12 May be booked through travel agent

LODI

Victorian Treasure Bed and Breakfast Inn

115 Prairie Street, 53555
(800) 859-5199 (voice and FAX)

Experience timeless ambience, thoughtful amenities, and caring innkeepers at a classic bed and breakfast inn. Timeless ambience. . .1897 Queen Anne architecture, wrap-around front porch, stained and leaded glass, pocket doors, gas and electric chandeliers, and more. Thoughtful amenities. . .turn down service, cotton terry robes, glycerine soaps, down pillows and comforters, dual control electric blankets. Caring innkeepers. . .educated and experienced in hotel and restaurant management, gourmet cooks, fussy about details, and genuinely interested in exceeding guest's expectations. Located in the scenic Lake Wisconsin recreational area, between Madison and Wisconsin Dells. Call toll-free for a brochure, and to learn more about this exceptional inn.

Hosts: Todd and Kimberly Seidl
Rooms: 4 (PB) $65-110
Full Breakfast
Credit Cards: A, B
Notes: 2, 5, 8, 9, 10, 11

Victorian Treasure Inn

MADISON

Annie's Bed and Breakfast

2117 Sheridan Drive, 53704
(608) 244-2224; (608) 242-9611 (FAX)

When you want the world to go away, come to Annie's, the quiet inn on Warner Park with the beautiful view. Luxury accommodations at reasonable rates. Close to the lake and park, it is also convenient to downtown and the University of Wisconsin campus. There are unusual amenities in this charming setting, including a romantic gazebo surrounded by butterfly gardens, a shaded terrace, and pond. Two beautiful two-bedroom suites. Double jacuzzi. Full air conditioning. Winter cross-country skiing, too!

Hosts: Anne and Larry Stuart
Suites: 2 (PB) $80-95
Full Breakfast
Credit Cards: A, B, C
Notes: 2, 5, 7 (over 12), 8, 9, 10, 11

MEQUON

Port Zedler Motel

10036 North Port Washington Road, 53092
(414) 241-5850

AAA approved; air-conditioned; convenient to downtown and excellent restaurants (12 minutes from downtown Milwaukee); free cable, color TV (HBO and Showtime); touch tone in-room phones; free ample parking; free ice; children under 12 stay free; senior/AARP/AAA discounts; in-room refrigerator on request, if available; German is spoken. I-43 northbound one-half mile NW of exit 83; I-43 southbound exit 28A, 1 block east and

---

NOTES: Credit cards accepted: A Master Card; B Visa; C American Express; D Discover Card; E Diners Club; F Other; 2 Personal checks accepted; 3 Lunch available; 4 Dinner available; 5 Open all

one and one-half mile north on Port Washington Rd. (Hwy. W)

Hostess: Sheila
Rooms: 16 (PB) $34.95-49.95
Continental Breakfast
Credit Cards: A, B, C
Notes: 5, 6, 7, 8, 9, 10, 11, 12

OSCEOLA

St. Croix River Inn

305 River St., 54020
(800) 645-8820

A meticulously restored 80-year-old stone home nestled in one of the region's finest recreational areas. Ski at Wild Mountain or Trollhaugen. Canoe or fish in the lovely St. Croix River, or visit the scenic Taylors Falls area. Then relax in the bed and breakfast suites of the St. Croix River Inn. They're elegantly furnished—some with fireplaces, all with jacuzzi, whirlpool baths. So, whether it's a honeymoon or an occasion you want to be special, get started—give us a call.

Host: Ben Johnson
Rooms: 7 (PB) $100-200
Full Breakfast (continental on weekdays)
Credit Cards: A, B, C
Notes: 5, 8, 9, 10, 11, 12

PLYMOUTH

Yankee Hill Bed and Breakfast

405 Collins Street., 53073
(414) 892-2222

Yankee Hill Bed and Breakfast, with its two historic homes, welcomes you into the solitude of a quiet, small Wisconsin agricultural town in the heartland of the scenic Kettle Moraine recreational area. Our home is an 1891 Queen Anne-style, while the second home is listed on the National Register of Historic Places with a modified Italianate Gothic architectural styling. Both homes have great common rooms to meet and socialize with friends. Rooms have individualized decor with period and unique antiques for your enjoyment. Nuture your relationships at Yankee Hill and walk to excellent dining experiences in Plymouth. Peg and Jim, resident hosts, will be happy to assist you in planning a relaxing visit in Wisconsin.

Hosts: Peg and Jim Stahlman
Rooms: 11 (6PB; 5SB) $61-93
Full Breakfast (continental available)
Credit Cards: None
Notes: 2, 5, 7 (limited), 8, 9, 10, 11, 12

PORT WASHINGTON

The Inn at Old Twelve Hundred

806 West Grand Avenue, 53074
(414) 284-6883

Midway between Milwaukee and Sheboygan, Port Washington is a quaint fishing village on the shores of Lake Michigan. Only minutes to historic Cedarburg. Elegant late 1800's grand, Victorian inn offering authentic decor and furnishings. Beautifully appointed guest rooms. In-room fireplace and/or whirlpools available. Spacious enclosed porches. Enjoy croquet, horseshoes, tandem bicycle, and picturesque gazebo in large private yard. Air-conditioned. Restricted smoking.

Hostesses: Stephanie and Ellie Bresette
Rooms: 3(PB) $65-145
Both Full and Continental Breakfast
Credit Cards: A, B, C
Notes: 2, 5

Yankee Hill Bed and Breakfast

RIVER FALLS

Knollwood House Bed and Breakfast

N8257-950th Street-Knollwood Drive, 54022
(715) 425-1040, 800-435-0628

Old-fashioned country charm with a touch of today. 80 restful acres with hiking, cross-country ski trails, outdoor pool, golf green (three tees), hot tub, and sauna. Only 45 minutes from the Mall of America

and 15 minutes from the Great River Road.

Hosts: Jim and Judy Tostrud
Rooms: 4 (2PB; 2SB) $80-95
Full Breakfast
Credit Cards: None
Notes: 2, 5, 7(10 and over), 8, 9, 10, 11, 12

SPARTA

The Franklin Victorian Bed and Breakfast

220 East Franklin Street, 54656
(608) 269-3894; (800) 845-8767

This turn-of-the-century home welcomes you to by-gone elegance with small-town quiet and comfort. The four spacious bedrooms provide a perfect setting for ultimate relaxation. Full home-cooked breakfast is served before starting your day of hiking, biking, skiing, canoeing, antiquing, or exploring this beautiful area.

Hosts: Lloyd and Jane Larson
Rooms: 4 (2 PB; 2 SB) $60-80
Full Breakfast
Credit Cards: A, B
Notes: 2, 5, 7 (over 10), 8, 9, 10, 11

Just-n-Trails Bed and Breakfast

R. 1, Box 274, 54656
(608) 269-4522; (800) 488-4521

Enjoy three luxurious cottages each with a double whirlpool bath, fireplace, and porch. Five rooms in the 1920 farmhouse, cross-country ski on 10 miles of state-of-the-art groomed trails. Enjoy the lodge with indoor bathrooms. Located near four bicycle trails, five canoeable rivers, the largest and finest cranberry museum, Amish shops, and a Norwegian immigrant settlement. This is a lovely working dairy farm and guests of all ages are welcome to pet the calves and watch the milking.

Hosts: Don and Donna Justin
Rooms: 8 (6PB; 2SB) $60-195
Full Breakfast
Credit Cards: A, B, C, D
Notes: 2, 5, 7, 8, 9, 10, 11, 12

STEVENS POINT

Dreams of Yesteryear Bed and Breakfast
1100 Brawley Street, 54481
(715) 341-4525

Dreams of Yesteryear

Featured in *Victorian Homes Magazine* and listed on the National Register of Historic Places. Your hosts are from Stevens Point and enjoy talking about the restoration of their turn-of-the-century home which has been in the same family for three generations. All rooms are furnished in antiques. Guests enjoy use of parlors, porches, and gardens. Two blocks from the historic downtown, antique and specialty shops, picturesque Green Circle Trails, the university, and more. Dreams of Yesteryear is truly "a Victorian dream come true."

Hosts: Bonnie and Bill Maher
Rooms: 4 (2PB; 2SB) $55-75
Full Breakfast
Credit Cards: A, B, C, D
Notes: 2, 5, 7 (over 12 or with approval), 8, 9, 10, 11, 12

Victorian Swan on Water
1716 Water Street, 54481
(715) 345-0595

Enjoy our city's central location. From here you can see the rest of Wisconsin. This restored 1889 home showcases crown moldings, beautiful woodwork, and antiques, with comfort as the main ingredient. Stroll our riverwalks. Visit our university, local brewery, the many golf courses, parks, and bike and ski trails, but don't forget our delicious breakfast. Private baths, air-condition, and gift certificates.

Hostess: Joan Ouellette
Rooms: 4 (PB) $50-95
Full Breakfast
Credit Cards: A, B, C, D
Notes: 2, 5, 10, 11, 12

STURGEON BAY

Hearthside Inn

2136 Taube Rd., 54235
(414) 746-2136

This remodeled 1800's farmhouse has a pleasant blend of contemporary and antique furnishings. Lake Michigan can be seen in the distance. The old barn still stands nearby. Within easy driving distance are fantastic state parks, beaches for swimming in summer, or skiing in the winter. Lighthouses, U.S. Coast Guard Station, lake cruises, airport, ship building, and weekend festivals. The rooms are charming, three with queen beds. The upper east wing room has three twin beds. Customers may use TV's, VCR's, living and sun rooms, plus group meeting rooms.

Hosts: Don and Lu Lussendorf
Rooms: 4 (PB) $45-65
Full Breakfast
Credit Cards: A, B
Notes: 2, 5, 7, 8, 9, 10, 11

WISCONSIN DELLS

Historic Bennett House Bed and Breakfast

825 Oak Street, 53965
(608) 254-2500

The 1863 home of an honored pioneer photographer is listed on the National Register of Historic Places. We'll pamper you with elegant lace, crystal, antiques, romantic bedrooms, and luscious fireside breakfast. The private suite has a parlor, Eastlake bedroom, and shower bath. The English room has a walnut and lace canopy bed. And the garden room has a brass bed. Walk to river tours, antiques, and crafts. Minutes to hiking, biking, canoeing, four golf courses, five ski areas, five state parks, greyhound racing, bird watching, and Indian culture. Bennett, Rockwell, circus, and railroad museums are also near by. Gift certificates are available.

Hosts: Gail and Rich Obermeyer
Rooms: 3 (1 PB; 2 SB) $65-85
Full Breakfast
Credit Cards: None
Notes: 2, 5, 8, 9, 10, 11, 12

Wyoming

BIG HORN

Spahn's Big Horn Mountain Bed and Breakfast

Box 579, 82833
(307) 674-8150

Towering log home and secluded guest cabins on the mountainside in whispering pines. Borders one million acres of public forest with deer and moose. Gracious mountain breakfast served on the deck with binoculars to enjoy the 100-mile view. Owner is former Yellowstone ranger. Ten minutes from I-90 near Sheridan.

Hosts: Ron and Bobbie Spahn
Rooms: 4 (PB) $65-100
Full Breakfast
Credit Cards: A, B
Notes: 2, 3, 4, 6, 7

CHEYENNE/LARAMIE

A. Drummond's Ranch
399 Happy Jack Rd., (State Highway 210), 82007
(307) 634-6042

Quiet, gracious retreat of casual elegance on 1200 acres near state park and national forest. Home-made snacks, beverages, and fresh fruit always available. Terrycloth robes provided during visits. Outdoor hot tub. Adventure at your pace on mountain bikes, cross-country skis, hikes, or fishing nearby. Reservations required; no smoking, please. Horses in transit boarded, or vacation with your horse.

Hosts: Kent and Taydie Drummond
Rooms: 4 (2PB; 2SB) $60-125
Full Breakfast
Credit Cards: None
Notes: 2, 3, 4, 5, 7, 11

ENCAMPMENT

Platt's Rustic Mountain Lodge
Star Route 49, 82325
(307) 327-5539

A peaceful mountain view, located on a working ranch with wholesome country atmosphere and lots of western hospitality. Horseback riding, pack trips, youth programs, photograhic safaris, wilderness fishing, hiking, and rock hounding. Fully guided tours available to ranch recreational activities and scenic mountain areas. Enjoy the flora and fauna, historic trails, and old mining camps, plus snowmobiling, ice fishing, and cross-country skiing in the winter. By reservation only. Private fishing cabin rentals available May through September.

Hosts: Mayvon and Ron Platt
Rooms: 3 (SB) $55
Full Breakfast
Credit Cards: None
Closed Thanksgiving and Christmas
Notes: 5, 6, 7, 11

A. Drummond's Ranch

NOTES: Credit cards accepted: A Master Card; B Visa; C American Express; D Discover Card; E Diners Club; F Other; 2 Personal checks accepted; 3 Lunch available; 4 Dinner available; 5 Open all

Alberta

CANMORE

Cougar Creek Inn
PO Box 1162, T0L 0M0
(403) 678-4751

Quiet, rustic, cedar chalet with mountain views in every direction. Grounds border on Cougar Creek and are surrounded by rugged mountain scenery which invites all types of outdoor activity. Hostess has strong love for the mountains and can assist with plans for local hiking, skiing, canoeing, mountain biking, back-packing, etc., as well as scenic drives. The bed and breakfast has a private entrance with sitting area, fireplace, games, TV, sauna and numerous reading materials for guests' use. Breakfasts are hearty and wholesome with many home-baked items.

Hostess: Mrs. Patricia Doucette
Rooms: 4 (SB) $55-60 (Canadian)
Full Breakfast
Credit Cards: None
Notes: 2, 3, 5, 7, 8, 9, 10, 11

NANTON

The Squire Ranch
Rural Route 1, T0L 1R0
(403) 646-5789

Welcome to our ranch in the lovely foothills of the Rocky Mountains. We have horses, cattle, goats, sheep, llamas, miniature donkeys, and bantam chickens. Yard, playground, and indoor activities are available. This is good country for riding, walking, hunting, and fishing. We have easy access to Fort MacLeod, Kananaskis, Waterton, and Banff.

Hosts: Sam and Rosemary Squire
Rooms: 3 plus cabin (1 PB; 2 SB) $25-60 (Canadian)
Full Breakfast (other meals upon request)
Credit Cards: None
Notes: 2, 3 (restricted), 4 (restricted), 5, 6 (restricted), 7, 8, 9, 10

Timber Ridge Homestead
Box 94, T0L 1R0
(403) 646-2480 (winter); (403) 646-5683 (summer)

Timber Ridge Homestead is a rustic establishment in beautiful foothills ranching country about 70 miles SW of Calgary. We have good, quiet horses to help you see abundant wild flowers, wild life, and wonderful views of the Rockies. Good plain cooking if you want it. To get here, go to Nanton, 50 miles south of Calgary, drive West on highway 533 for 4 miles, turn south and follow winding road into hills for twelve miles, and the gate is on the right.

Hostess: Bridget Jones
Rooms: 3 (SB) $25 per person
Full Breakfast
Credit Cards: None
Notes: 2, 3, 4, 7

---

welcome; 7 Children welcome; 8 Tennis nearby; 9 Swimming nearby; 10 Golf nearby; 11 Skiing nearby; 12 May be booked through travel agent

British Columbia

ABBOTSFORD

The Cliff House
36050 Southridge Place, V3G 1E2
(604) 852-5787

Our bed and breakfast is two miles from the U.S. Border. Set in a quiet location, The Cliff House Bed and Breakfast offers visitors a restful spot to spend the night or longer, in a mountain village at the home of Walter and Ina Friesen. The home away from home with its elegant traditional decor is equipped with a luxurious full bathroom, queen-size beds, and the use of our family room. Hot breakfast is served, as is a courtesy bedtime snack. No pets. No smoking!

Hosts: Walter and Ina Friesen
Rooms: 2 (SB) $55
Full Breakfast
Credit Cards: None
Notes: 5, 9, 10, 11

DUNCAN

Fairburn Farm Country Manor
3310 Jackson Rd., RR#7, V9L 4W4
(604) 746-4637

Victorian manor house, pastoral views, and family farm. We grow organic fruit, vegetables, and meat, grind wheat for flour and churn golden butter from brown swiss cows. Bedrooms with queen or twin beds, private bathrooms, and fireplaces. Library, sitting room, and south-facing veranda. One hundred and thirty acres, trails, mountain stream, fields, virgin timber, reforestation, working sheepdogs, antique sawmill, and barns. Approved by Fodor Canada's *Great Country Inns and Sanctuaries*.

Hosts: Darrel and Anthea Archer
Rooms: 6 (PB) $85-130
Full Breakfast
Credit Cards: A
Notes: 2, 7, 8, 9, 10, 12

FORT STEELE

Wild Horse Farm Bed and Breakfast
Box 7, V0B 1N0
(604) 426-6000

Step back into a time of leisure and luxury at Wild Horse Farm, a secluded, historic, park-like 80-acre estate in the Canadian Rocky Mountains adjoining Fort Steele Historic Town. The log covered home was built by the New York Astors in the early 1900's with spacious high ceilinged

---

NOTES: Credit cards accepted: A MasterCard; B Visa; C American Express; D Discover Card; E Diners Club; F Other; 2 Personal checks accepted; 3 Lunch available; 4 Dinner available; 5 Open all year; 6 Pets

rooms, five fieldstone fireplaces, and antique furnishings. Screened verandas invite you to relax in a setting which reflects generations of tradition and comfort. Awaken to hot tea or coffee brought to your room. Enjoy a leisurely gourmet breakfast later in the dining room.

Hosts: Bob and Orma Termuende
Rooms: 5 (2PB; 3SB) $48-87
Full Breakfast
Credit Cards: None
Notes: 5, 7 (by arrangement), 8, 9, 10, 11, 12 (10%)

MILL BAY/VANCOUVER ISLAND

Pine Lodge Farm Bed and Breakfast

3191 Muatter Road, V0R 2P0
(604) 743-4083; (604) 743-7134 (FAX)

Our beautiful antique-filled lodge is located 25 miles north of Victoria. It is situated on a 30-acre farm overlooking ocean and islands. Arbutus trees, walking trails, farm animals, and wild deer add to the idyllic setting. Each room has en suite baths and shower. Also, a delightful cottage with two bedrooms and baths, living room, dinette, kitchen, and hot tub is available. Full farm breakfast. No smoking.

Hosts: Cliff and Barb Clarke
Rooms: 7 (PB) $75-85
Cottage: 1 (PB) $110-160
Full Breakfast
Credit Cards: A, B
Notes: 2, 5, 10, 12

NORTH DELTA

Sunshine Hills Bed and Breakfast

11200 Bond Blvd., V4E 1M7
(604) 596-6496

Private entrance. Two cozy bedrooms with TV, shared bathroom, and a beautiful sunroom. Close to U.S. Border, airport, and ferries (20 minutes). Kitchenette. We are originally Dutch, very European. Breakfast includes fresh fruit, orange juice, and much more. Your host knows the city very well and can be of help to all the guests.

Hostess: Patzi Wein Honrug
Rooms: 2 (SB) $50
Full Breakfast
Credit Cards: None
Notes: 7, 8, 10

SIDNEY

Graham's Cedar House Bed and Breakfast

1825 Lands End Road, V8L 5J2
(604) 655-3699; (604) 655-1422 (FAX)

We offer air-conditioned chalet luxury on a woodsey country estate with tall trees and magnificent ferns all around. Relish the quiet walk among the trees or to the beach. Enjoy the romantic executive suite or a one or two bedroom apartment suite with kitchen and family room. All rooms feature private baths, private entrances, patio deck, and TV. Breakfast served at your convenience. Close to Butchaat Gardens, Victoria marinas, and USA and Canadian ferries. See you soon.

Hosts: Dennis and Kay Graham
Rooms: 3 (PB) $75-105 (Canadian funds)
Full Breakfast
Credit Cards: A, B
Notes: 5, 7 (over 10), 8, 10, 12

Graham's Cedar House

SOOKE

Ocean Wilderness Guest Accommodations

11009 West Coast Road, V0S 1N0
(604) 646-2116

Ocean Wilderness, an oceanfront jewel, is open year round. The elegant rooms have antiques, comfortable sitting areas, and canopied beds. Wander the gardens or soak in the jacuzzi tub overlooking the ocean and Olympic Mountains. A full country breakfast for two is included. This is served in the dining room or in the privacy of your room. Browse the gift shop for a special remembrance of your restful holiday. Beach access via sloping trail.

Hostess: Marion Paine
Rooms: 7 (PB) $85-210 (Canadian)
Full Breakfast
Credit Cards: A, B
Notes: 2, 4, 5, 8, 10, 12

UCLUELET

B & B at Burley's

Box 550, 1078 Helen Road, V0R 3A0
(604) 726-4444

A waterfront home on a small "drive to" island at the harbor mouth. Watch the ducks and birds play, heron, and king-fisher work, and eagles soar. In the harbor, trollers, draggers, and seiners attract the gulls. Loggers work in the distant hills. There is a view from every window, a large living room, fireplace, books, and recreation room with pool table.

Hosts: Ron Burley and Micheline Burley
Rooms: 6 (SB) $40-50
Continental Breakfast
Credit Cards: A, B
Notes: 8, 9, 10

Beautiful B & B

428 West 40 Avenue, V5Y 2R4
(604) 327-1102

Gorgeous colonial home furnished with antiques, fresh flowers, and views from bedrooms. Great central location five minutes to Downtown. Walking distance to tennis, golf, Queen Elizabeth Park, Van Dusen Gardens, swimming, the X, three cinemas, and a major shopping center. Friendly helpful host, quiet street, comfortable beds, and a generous breakfast served in a formal dining room. Luxurious suite with pink, marble fireplace, large balcony, views (north and south), double sinks, and extra large tub.

Hosts: Corinne and Ian Sanderson
Rooms: 5 (1PB; 4SB) $70-150 (Canadian)
Full Breakfast
Credit Cards: None
Notes: 7 (over 14), 8, 9, 10, 11, 12

VERNON

The Windmill House

5672 Learmouth Rd., RR#1, 519A, C2, V1T 6L4
(604) 549-2804

Sleep in a beautiful windmill in the country setting of the Coldstream Valley. All rooms have a view of the low mountains across the pastures of the valley. We are fifteen minutes east of Vernon off of Hwy. #6, close to beaches, and 45 minutes from the ski hill. There are three choices of full cooked breakfasts served with homemade muffins and jams. Smoke free residence with small house dog.

Hosts: Cor and Mary Manders
Rooms: 5 (2PB; 3SB) $45-65 (canadian)
Full Breakfast
Credit Cards: A, B
Notes: 3, 4, 5, 6, 7, 9, 10, 11

The Windmill House

VICTORIA

AA—Accommodations West B&B Service

660 Jones Terrace, V8Z 2L7
(604) 479-1986; (604) 479-9999 (FAX)

No reservation fee. Over seventy choice locations. Inspected and approved. Ocean view, farm tranquility, cozy cottage, city convenience, historic heritage! Assistance with itineraries includes Victoria, Vancouver Island, and some adjacent islands. For competent, caring service, call Doreen. C.P. 7 days. Open 7am-10pm Monday thru Saturday and 2pm-9pm on Sundays.

Battery Street Guest House

670 Battery Street, V8V 1E5
(604) 385-4632

Newly renovated guesthouse, built in 1898 with four bright comfortable rooms, two with bathrooms. Centrally located within walking distance to Downtown, Beacon Hill Park, and Victoria's scenic Marine Drive only one block away. A full hearty breakfast served by a Dutch hostess. No smoking.

Hostess: Pamela Verduyn
Rooms: 4 (2 PB; 2 SB) $55-80
Full Breakfast
Credit Cards: None
Notes: 2

Dashwood Seaside Manor

Number One Cook Street, V8T 5A7
(604) 385-5517

Enjoy the comfort and privacy of your own elegant suite in one of Victoria's traditional Tudor mansions. Gaze out your window at the ocean and America's Olympic Mountains. If you're an early riser, you may see seals, killer whales, or sea otters frollicking offshore. Watch an eagle cruise by. Help yourself to breakfast from your private, well-stocked kitchen. You're

welcome; 7 Children welcome; 8 Tennis nearby; 9 Swimming nearby; 10 Golf nearby; 11 Skiing nearby; 12 May be booked through travel agent

minutes away from the attractions of town. Stroll there through beautiful Beacon Hill Park.

Host: Derek Dashwood
Rooms: 14 (PB) $65-240
Self-catered, Full Breakfast
Credit Cards: A, B, C
Notes: 2, 5, 6 (small), 7, 8, 10, 12

Elk Lake Lodge Bed and Breakfast

5259 Pat Bay Hwy (Route 17), V8Y 1S8
(604) 658-8879

Originally built as a chapel in 1910, the Elk Lake Lodge now offers 5 very comfortable and attractive guest rooms, catering to an informal, warm Victorian hospitality. Located just 10 minutes from downtown Victoria. Across the road from beautiful Elk Lake, guests can enjoy the outdoor hot tub, a view from every bedroom, fresh flowers, and comforters. Fresh baking daily. Coffee and tea served each evening with a charming fireplace on those chilly nights.

Hosts: Marty and Ivan Musar
Rooms: 5 (3PB; 2SB) $75-95 (off season rates available)
Full Breakfast
Open May 1- October 15
Credit Cards: A, B
Notes: 7 (Over 12), 9, 10, 12

Oak Bay Guesthouse

1052 Newport Avenue, V8S 5E3
(604) 598-3812

Built from designs by famous architect Samuel McLure. This classy, 1912 inn, established since 1922, has your comfort at heart. Set in beautiful gardens in the prime peaceful location c f Oak Bay, only one block from the water and minutes from Downtown. Ten rooms with private bathrooms, antiques; sitting room with Inglenook fireplace; sunroom with Library and TV. Home-cooked breakfast. Golf, shopping, and city bus at door.

Hosts: Pam and Dave Vandy
Rooms: 10 (PB) $59-135 (Canadian)
Full Breakfast
Credit Cards: A, B
Notes: 8, 9, 10, 12

Peggy's Cove Bed and Breakfast

279 Coal Point Lane, R.R. #1, Sidney, V8L 3R9
(604) 656-5656; (604) 655-3118 (FAX)

Spoil yourself! Come join me in my beautiful home surrounded by ocean on three sides. Imagine a gourmet breakfast on the sundeck, watching sea lions at play, eagles soaring, and if you are lucky a family of killer whales may appear. Canoe into the sunset in the evening; spend a romantic moment relaxing in the **hot tub** under the stars. World famous Butchart Gardens and BC and Anacortes Ferries are only minutes away. Many consider Peggy's Cove a honeymoon paradise.

Hostess: Peggy Waibel
Rooms: 3 (1PB; 2SB) $95-150 (US)
Full Breakfast
Credit Cards: None
Notes: 2, 5, 6, 7, 8, 9, 10, 12

Sonia's Bed and Breakfast by the Sea

175 Bushby St., V8S 1B5
(604) 385-2700; (800) 667-4489; (604) 744-3763 (FAX)

Sonia has queen- and king-size beds,

NOTES: Credit cards accepted: A Master Card; B Visa; C American Express; D Discover Card; E Diners Club; F Other; 2 Personal checks accepted; 3 Lunch available; 4 Dinner available; 5 Open all year; 6 Pets

private bathrooms with a big, hot breakfast. The new suite looks out over the Straits of Juan de Fuca. A lovely walk to the Inner Harbour—Empress Hotel. Close to everything—shopping, good restaurants, Beacon Hill Park, and bus at door. No smoking. Adults only.

Hosts: Sonia McMillan and Brian
Rooms: 3 (PB) 1 suite(PB) $55-125 (US)
Full Breakfast
Credit Cards: None
Notes: 2, 8, 9, 10

Top O'Triangle Mountain

3442 Karger Terr, V9C 3K5
(604) 478-7853

Our home, built of solid cedar construction, boasts a spectacular view of Victoria, the Juan de Fuca Strait, and the Olympia Mountains in Washington. We are a relaxed household with few rules, lots of hospitality, and clean, comfortable rooms. A hearty breakfast is different each morning.

Hosts: Pat and Henry Hansen
Rooms: 3 (PB) $60-85 Canadian
Full Breakfast
Credit Cards: A, B
Notes: 5, 7, 8, 9, 10, 12

WEST VANCOUVER

Beachside Bed and Breakfast

4208 Evergreen Avenue, V7V 1H1
(604) 922-7773; (604) 926-8073 (FAX)

Guests are welcomed to this beautiful waterfront home with a basket of fruit and fresh flowers. Situated on a quiet cul-de-sac in an exclusive area of the city, the house, with Spanish architecture accented by antique stained-glass windows, affords a panoramic view of Vancouver's busy harbor. There are private baths, a patio leading to the beach, and a large jacuzzi at the seashore, where you can watch seals swim by daily. Near sailing, fishing, hiking, golf, downhill skiing, and antique shopping.

Hosts: Gordon and Joan Gibbs
Rooms: 3 (PB) $75-150 (U.S.)
Full Breakfast
Credit Cards: A, B
Notes: 2, 5, 8, 10, 11, 12, 13

WHISTLER

Golden Dreams Bed and Breakfast

6412 Easy Street, V0N 1B6
(604) 932-2667; 800-668-7055; (604) 932-7055 (FAX)

Uniquely decorated Victorian, Oriental and Aztec theme rooms feature sherry decanter, cozy duvets. Relax in the luxurious private jacuzzi and awake to a nutritious vegetarian breakfast including homemade jams and fresh herbs served in the country kitchen. A short walk to the valley trail to village activities and restaurants.

Hostess: Ann Spence
Rooms: 3 (1PB; 2SB) $65-95
Full Breakfast
Credit Cards: A, B
Notes: 2, 5. 7, 8, 9, 10, 11

welcome; 7 Children welcome; 8 Tennis nearby; 9 Swimming nearby; 10 Golf nearby; 11 Skiing nearby; 12 May be booked through travel agent

Manitoba

WINNIPEG

Bed and Breakfast of Manitoba Reservation Service

533 Sprague Street, R3G 2R9
(204) 783-9797

Organized in 1980, B&B of Manitoba has a variety of hosts who add a unique flavor of ethnic and cultural heritage along with warm, friendly, Manitoba hospitality. The inspected homes are located in urban, rural, and popular resort areas. Call or write for a full color brochure, with detailed listing and description of each home.

New Brunswick

FREDERICTON

Appelot Bed and Breakfast

R.R. 4 (Located on Hwy. 105), E3B 4X5
(506) 444-8083

Attractive farmhouse overlooking the St. John River. Three bedrooms with a view in a restful country atmosphere. Full homemade breakfast served on the spacious sunporch. Orchards and woodlands with walking trails, "a bird watchers delight." Board games, TV, VCR, books, and piano inside; picnic table, gas BBQ, and lawn swing outside. Area attractions include several golf courses, Mactaquac Park, Kings Landing Historical Village, museums in Fredericton, the Beaverbrook Art Gallery, and the Provincial Archives.

Hosts: Ed and Elsie Myshrall
Rooms: 3 (1PB; 2SB) $50
Full Breakfast
Credit Cards: None
Notes: 2, 9, 10, 12
Open May 1 through October 31

welcome; 7 Children welcome; 8 Tennis nearby; 9 Swimming nearby; 10 Golf nearby; 11 Skiing nearby; 12 May be booked through travel agent

Nova Scotia

AMHERST

Amherst Shore Country Inn

RR 2 Amherst (Highway 366), B4H 3X9
(902) 661-4800

Escape to the quiet natural beauty of Nova Scotia's Northumberland Strait. This renovated century-old farmhouse offers comfortable rooms, suites, cottages, and country style gourmet meals. Enjoy a walk on our 600-foot long private beach before having dinner served at 7:30 pm (with reservation) each night. Curried potato soup, sole stuffed with crab, chicken with brandied cream sauce, and meringue torte with almond butter are representative of what dinner is like each night. Open May 1 to October 13, 1994.

Hosts: Donna and Jim Laceby
Rooms: 4 plus 1 cottage (PB) $99-119
Full Breakfast (additional fee)
Credit Cards: A, B
Notes: 4 (by reservation), 9, 10, 12

WOLFVILLE

Blomidon Inn

P.O. Box 839, 127 Main St., B0P 1X0
(902) 542-2291; (902) 542-7461 (FAX)

Today, this 19th century sea captain's mansion features 26 charming guest rooms, all with baths in suite, telephones, handmade quilts, and most with four-poster beds. Working fireplaces and a baby grand piano can be found in the front sitting rooms while two dining rooms and a large terrace feature the freshest fare the valley and sea have to offer. Open daily for lunch between 11:30 and 2:00 pm; brunch is offered on Saturdays and Sundays; and dinner is served each evening between 5:00 and 9:30 pm.

Hosts: Jim and Donna Laceby
Rooms: 26 (PB) $74-125
Continental Buffet Breakfast
Credit Cards: A, B
Notes: 3, 4, 5 (except Christmas), 7 (limited), 8, 10, 11, 12

Amherst Shore Country Inn

Blomidon Inn

NOTES: Credit cards accepted: A MasterCard; B Visa; C American Express; D Discover Card; E Diners Club; F Other; 2 Personal checks accepted; 3 Lunch available; 4 Dinner available; 5 Open all year; 6 Pets

Ontario

BRAESIDE

Glenroy Farm
Bed and Breakfast

Rural Route 1, K0A 1G0
(613) 432-6248

Beautiful, quiet farm setting just a one-hour drive from Ottawa. Situated in historic McNab township of Renfrew County in the heart of the Ottawa Valley, halfway between the towns of Renfrew and Arnprior. We live in an 1884, stone house that has been well-maintained by three generations of McGregors, the family who built the home and lived in it. We have a farming operation growing strawberries and corn and raising beef cattle. Located within driving distance of the Ottawa River raft rides, Storyland, Logos Land, Bonnechere Caves, and other attractions. Home of the 1994 International Plowing Match. No smoking or alcoholic beverages.

Hosts: Noreen and Steve McGregor
Rooms: 5 (1PB; 4SB) $35-50
Full Breakfast
Credit Cards: None
Notes: 2, 4, 5, 7, 9, 10, 11

CARDINAL

Roduner Farm

R.R. 1, K0E 1E0
(613) 657-4830

Enjoy true country hospitality at our 300-acre active dairy farm. We are located just three miles north of Cardinal, one and one-half miles north of Trans Canada Route 401, about one-half hour drive from Ogdensburg, New York. During your stay here observe some of the farm activities, relax on our spacious lawn or in our comfortable home, or explore the surroundings. We also speak Schweizer-deutsch and a little French.

Hosts: Walter and Margareta Roduner
Rooms: 2 (1PB; 2SB) $30-38
Full Breakfast
Credit Cards: None
Notes: 2, 4 (by arrangement), 5, 6, 7, 8, 9, 10, 11

ELMIRA

Teddy Bear Bed
and Breakfast

Wyndham Hall, RR 1, N3B 2Z1
(519) 669-2379

Hospitality abounds in our gracious countryside 1907 schoolhouse, minutes from Elmira. The elegance and charm of our

welcome; 7 Children welcome; 8 Tennis nearby; 9 Swimming nearby; 10 Golf nearby; 11 Skiing nearby; 12 May be booked through travel agent

home is enhanced by Canadian and Old Order Mennonite quilts and rugs. Beautifully decorated bedrooms. Lounge; complimentary refeshments; and full breakfasts.

Hosts: George and Vivian Smith
Rooms: 3 (1PB, 2SB) $65 (Canadian)
Full Breakfast
Credit Cards: A, B, C
Notes: 2, 5, 10

Windmere Farm

KAWARTHA LAKES

Windmere Farm Bed and Breakfast

Selwyn, RR3, Lakefield, K0L 2H0
(705) 652-6290; (705) 652-6949 (FAX)

Windmere is located in the heart of the Kawartha Lakes, a water skier's and fisherman's paradise. Joan and Wally have an air-conditioned 1845 stone farmhome, set amid shaded lawns and a huge spring-fed swimming-pond. The older part of the house has high ceilinged rooms decorated with fine art and Victorian antiques. In the new wing, the accent is on wood, warmth, and informality. Fresh-baked bran muffins and home-made jams are served each morning; in the evening, tea and snacks are offered in the family room. Walking trails, golf courses, and parks are nearby. No smoking.

Hosts: Joan and Wally Wilkins
Rooms: 4 (2PB, 2SB) $45-65
Full Breakfast
Credit Cards: None
Notes: 3, 5, 7, 9, 10, 11, 12 (10%)

LEAMINGTON

Home Suite Home Bed and Breakfast

115 Erie Street South, N8H 3B5
(519) 326-7169

Near Point Pelee National Park. Home Suite Home features 2 honeymoon suites, 2 additional rooms, and large inground pool. Large, traditional home decorated Victorian Country. Four and one-half baths, plush carpet, and fine linen. In house air-conditioning, hearty, full, country breakfast. Area attractions include dinner theaters, cycling and canoeing, tropical gardens, and trips to Pelee Island. Log burning fireplace for cool winter evenings. No smoking. No pets. Agatha is coordinator for Point Pelee Bed and Breakfast Association.

Hosts: Harry and Agatha Tiessen
Rooms: 4 (2 PB; 2 SB) $40-60
Full Breakfast
Credit Cards: None
Notes: 2, 5, 7, 8, 9, 10

Home Suite Home

NOTES: Credit cards accepted: A MasterCard; B Visa; C American Express; D Discover Card; E Diners Club; F Other; 2 Personal checks accepted; 3 Lunch available; 4 Dinner available; 5 Open all year; 6 Pets

Home Suite Home Bed and Breakfast Reservation Service

115 Erie St. S, N8H 3B5
(519) 326-7169

The hosts of the Home Suite Home Bed and Breakfast are also coordinators of a reservation service for all of your travel needs in the Leamington area. With over 70 rooms and cottages to choose from, they are sure to have what you are looking for. Attractions in the area include dinner theaters, cycling, and canoeing, Pelee Winery tours, trips to Pelee Island, etc. Agatha Tiessen, coordinator.

MADOC

Camelot Country Inn

R.R. 5, K0K 2K0
(613) 473-0441

Relax in the quiet, country setting of our 1853 brick and stone home. It is surrounded by plantings of red and white pine on 25 acres of land in the heart of Hastings County. Original woodwork and oak floors have been lovingly preserved. There are three guest rooms available, two doubles and one twin. The full breakfast may be chosen by guests from the country breakfast or one of two gourmet breakfasts.

Hostess: Marian Foster
Rooms: 3 (SB) $45
Full Breakfast
Credit Cards: None
Notes: 2, 4 (by arrangement), 5, 7, 9, 10, 11

Camelot Country Inn

NEW HAMBURG

The Waterlot Inn

17 Huron St., N0B 2G0
(519) 662-2020

Spend a night with us sometime. Two large and very comfortably appointed rooms, one under each of the 1840 peaks at the front of the house. These share a memorable, marble shower, bidet, water closet, wet vanity, and a sitting area lit by the cupola. A white, iron double bed, a queen-size sleeper in the living room and a large three-piece bathroom. In the morning we'll feed you something, but you must catch the kitchen first—but not too early!

Host: Gordon Elkeer
Rooms: 3 (1PB; 2SB) $65-85
Continental Breakfast
Credit Cards: A, B, C
Notes: 2, 3, 4, 5, 8, 9, 10, 11

welcome; 7 Children welcome; 8 Tennis nearby; 9 Swimming nearby; 10 Golf nearby; 11 Skiing nearby; 12 May be booked through travel agent

Gretna Green Bed and Breakfast

NIAGARA FALLS

Gretna Green Bed and Breakfast

5077 River Rd., L2E 3G7
(905) 357-2081

A warm welcome awaits you in this Scots-Canadian home overlooking the Niagara River Gorge. All rooms are air-conditioned and have their own TV. Included in the rate is a full breakfast with home-made scones and muffins. We also pick up at the train or bus stations. Many people have called this a "home away from home."

Hosts: Stan and Marg Gardiner
Rooms: 4 (PB) $45 (Oct-April), $55 (May-Sept.) (Canadian funds)
Full Breakfast
Credit Cards: None
Notes: 5, 7, 8, 10

OTTAWA

Australis Guest House

35 Marlborough Avenue, K1N 8E6
(613) 235-8461

We are the oldest, established, and still operating bed and breakfast in the Ottawa area. Located on a quiet, tree-lined street one block from the Rideau River, with its ducks and swans, and Strathcona Park. We are a 20-minute walk from the parliament buildings. This period house boasts leaded-glass windows, fireplaces, oak floors, and unique eight-foot-high stained-glass windows overlooking the hall. Hearty, home-cooked breakfasts with home-baked breads and pastries. Winner of the Ottawa Hospitality Award for April 1989. Recommended by *Newsweek*, January 1990, and featured in the *Ottawa Sun* newspaper, January 1992 for our Australian bread. Baby sitting is available.

Hosts: Carol and Brian Waters
Rooms: 3 (1 PB; 2 SB) $45-65 Canadian
Full Breakfast
Credit Cards: None
Notes: 2, 5, 7, 8

Beatrice Lynn Guest House

Home is new and air-conditioned. Three large guest rooms tastefully decorated, one private bathroom, one shared. Lounge for guest use. Bicycles provided for guest use. Transportation to and from marina available for those arriving by boat, also to and from dining and theater. Parking for all guests. Non-smoking home. Beautiful scenery, theaters, historic sites, golf, shop-

---

NOTES: Credit cards accepted: A MasterCard; B Visa; C American Express; D Discover Card; E Diners Club; F Other; 2 Personal checks accepted; 3 Lunch available; 4 Dinner available; 5 Open all year; 6 Pets

ping, boating, and dining.

Rooms: 3 (1PB; 2SB) $45
Full Breakfast
Credit Cards: None
Notes: 2, 5, 6, 7, 8, 9, 10, 11

Burnside Guest Home

STRATFORD

Burnside Guest Home

139 William Street, N5A 4X9
(519) 271-7076; (519) 393-5239 (FAX)

Burnside is a turn-of-the-century home on the north shore of Lake Victoria, the site of the first Stratford logging mill. The home features many family heirlooms and antiques and is centrally air-conditioned. Our rooms have been redecorated with light and cheery colors. Relax in the gardens overlooking the Avon River on hand-crafted furniture amid the rose, herb, herbaceous, and annual flower gardens. Within walking distance of Shakespearean theaters. Stratford is the home of a world renowned Shakespearean festival from May 4 to November 14, 1994. Also enjoy farmers' market, Mennonite coun-try, art and craft shops, outstanding architecture, and the outdoor Art in the Park.

Host: Lester J. Wilker
Rooms: 5 (SB) $50-60 Canadian; (student rates available)
Full Breakfast
Credit Cards: B
Notes: 2, 5, 7, 8, 9, 10, 11

TRENTON

Devonshire House

R.R #4 (Highway #2), K8V 5P7
(613) 394-4572

Relax the moment you arrive! We'll pamper you. Tea and coffee anytime with home-made cookies and pies on hand most evenings at no extra charge. An eclectic mix of antique and modern provides an interesting an attractive design for the interior of an Italianate style, red brick farmhouse, circa 1875. We have over 18 acres for you to explore: woods, stream, and nature trails to investigate. Located on Highway #2, halfway between Brighton and Trenton.

Host: Brian Greene
Rooms: 4 (SB) $38
Full Breakfast
Credit Cards: None
Notes: 2, 4 (with reservation), 5, 6, 8, 9, 10, 12

TORONTO

Beaches Bed and Breakfast

124 Waverly Road, M4L 3T3
(416) 699-0818

Out of season special rates for business travelers. Facilities include Lake Ontario,

welcome; 7 Children welcome; 8 Tennis nearby; 9 Swimming nearby; 10 Golf nearby; 11 Skiing nearby; 12 May be booked through travel agent

beach and boardwalk, a tasty breakfast, and direct transportation to the city center. Swimming, galleries and great cafes within walking distance. Some parking. Non-smoking. Air-conditioning. TV.

Host: Enid Evans
Rooms: 4 (2PB; 2SB) $58-68
Full Healthy Breakfast
Credit Cards: None
Notes: 2, 5, 6, 7

Burken Guest House

322 Palmerston Blvd., M6G 2N6
(416) 920-7842; FAX (416) 960-9529

Lovely, non-smoking home located in Downtown close to all attractions. Eight guest rooms furnished with antiques, washbasin, telephone, and ceiling fans. Continental breakfast served on deck in summer. TV-lounge, parking, and maid-service.

Hosts: Burke and Ken
Rooms: 8 (SB) $60-65 (Canadian)
Continental Breakfast
Credit Cards: A, B
Notes: 5, 12

Toronto Bed and Breakfast

Box 269, 253 College St., M5T 1R5
(416) 588-8800; (416) 961-3676; (416) 964-1756 (FAX)

Let us simplify your travel plans throughout Metro Toronto, Ottawa, Kingston, and Niagara Falls! Now in its 15th year, Toronto's oldest and original bed and breakfast registry is serving the entire area. Our reservation service of quality inspected B&B homes provides a high level of safety, comfort, cleanliness, and hospitality. Advance reservation recommended; free brochure on request. Traveler's checks, Visa, MC, AE, DC.

Burken Guest House

Prince Edward Island

MURRAY RIVER

Bayberry Cliff Inn

Rural Route 4, Little Sands, C0A 1W0
(902) 962-3395

Located on the edge of a 40-foot cliff are two uniquely redecorated post-and-beam barns, antiques, and marine art. Seven rooms have double beds, three with extra sleeping lofts. One room has two single beds. Two rooms, including the honeymoon suite, have private bath. Seals, occasional whale sightings, restaurants, swimming, innertubing, and craft shops are all nearby.

Hosts: Don and Nancy Perkins
Rooms: 8 (2PB; 6SB) $35-75
Full Breakfast
Credit Cards: A, B
Notes: 2, 9, 10

O'LEARY

Smallman's Bed and Breakfast

Knutsford, Rural Route 1, C0R 1V0
(902) 859-3469; (902) 859-2664

We have a split-level house with a garage on the west end and brick gate posts. We have a racetrack behind the house where some guests like to go for a walk. There are churches, stores, craft shops, tennis, golf, and lovely beaches for relaxing. We live in a quiet, country area on Route 142 off Highway 2. Come into O'Leary and go four miles west. Three-star rating.

Hosts: Arnold and Eileen Smallman
Rooms: 4 (SB) $25-35
Full or Continental Breakfast
Credit Cards: None
Notes: 5, 7, 8, 9, 10, 11

welcome; 7 Children welcome; 8 Tennis nearby; 9 Swimming nearby; 10 Golf nearby; 11 Skiing nearby; 12 May be booked through travel agent

Quebec

MONTREAL

Armor Inn

151 Sherbrooke Est, H2X 1C7
(514) 285-0140; (514) 284-1126 (FAX)

The Armor Inn is a small hotel with a typical European character. In the heart of Montreal, it offers a warm family atmosphere and is ideally situated close to Métro, Saint Denis, and Prince Arthur streets. It is a 15-minute walk to Old Montreal, the Palais of Congress, and numerous underground shopping centers.

Host: Annick Morvan
Rooms: 15 (7 PB; 8 SB) $38-55
Continental Breakfast
Credit Cards: A, B
Notes: 5, 7, 12

Auberge de la Fontaine

1301 Rachel St., East, H2J 2K1
(514) 597-0166; (514) 597-0496 (FAX)

The Auberge de la Fontaine is a nice stone house, newly renovated, where the 21 rooms, in a warm and modern decor, are of unique style in Montréal. Comfortable, friendly atmosphere and attentive, personal service are greatly appreciated by our corporate and leisure travelers. Each room is tastefully decorated. The suites with whirlpool baths, as well as the luxurious rooms, have brick walls and exclusive fabrics. It will settle you in an elegant and quiet environment. Duvet and decorative pillows will ensure you a cozy comfort. Breakfast is a given at the Auberge. A delicious variety of breakfast foods are set out each morning and you have access to the kitchen at any time for snacks. There are no parking fees. We want our guests to feel comfortable and be entirely satisfied with their stay.

Hostesses: Céline Bordeau and Jean Lamothe
Rooms: 21 (PB) $105-175 (canadian)
Full Buffet Breakfast
Credit Cards: A, B, C, E, F
Notes: 5, 7, 8, 9, 12

Auberge de la Fontaine

NOTES: Credit cards accepted: A MasterCard; B Visa; C American Express; D Discover Card; E Diners Club; F Other; 2 Personal checks accepted; 3 Lunch available; 4 Dinner available; 5 Open all year; 6 Pets

Bed and Breakfast à Montréal

PO Box 575, Snowdon Station, H3X 3T8
(514) 738-9410; (514) 735-7493 (FAX)

B&B Montréal is the city's oldest reservation service, established in 1980. This agency specializes in quality private homes, most offering private bathrooms. Locations are Downtown or up to 10 minutes away with excellent public transit. All hosts speak English and will enhance your visit with their suggestions. Full breakfasts are served and free parking is available. Marian Kahn, coordinator. Room rates range from $30-85. Visa, Mastercard, and American Express accepted.

Casa Bella Hotel

264 Sherbrooke West, H2X 1X9
(514) 849-2777; (514) 849-3650 (FAX)

The same owner has operated this charming hotel for 21 years. The 100-year-old European-style house has been renovated and is located Downtown, near "La Place Des Arts," U.S. Consulate, Metro, bus, and within walking distance of Old Montreal, Prince Arthur Street, and shopping center. Rooms are comfortable for a low price. Parking is available.

Rooms: 20 (14 PB; 6 SB) $45-80
Continental Breakfast
Credit Cards: A, B, E
Notes: 5, 7

Manoir Ambrose

3422 Stanley, H3A 1R8
(514) 288-6922; (514) 288-5757 (FAX)

A small, Victorian-style mansion, comfortable and quiet at reasonable rates, right in the heart of the action. Downtown Montreal at the slope of the Mount Royal. Restaurants, theatres, shopping, and business districts. Near Peel Subway.

Hostess: Lucie Seguine
Rooms: 22 (15PB; 7SB) $50-70
Continental Breakfast
Credit Cards: A, B
Notes: 5, 9, 12

Manoir Ambrose

Manoir Sherbrooke

157 Sherbrooke Est, H2X 1C7
(514) 845-0915; (516) 284-1126 (FAX)

The Manoir Sherbrooke is a small hotel with a European character offering a family atmosphere. It is convenient to Métro and Saint Denis and Prince Arthur streets. It is within walking distance of Old Montreal, the Palais of Congress, and numerous shopping centers.

Host: Annick Legall
Rooms: 22 (14 PB; 8 SB) $42-70
Continental Breakfast
Credit Cards: A, B
Notes: 5, 7, 12

welcome; 7 Children welcome; 8 Tennis nearby; 9 Swimming nearby; 10 Golf nearby; 11 Skiing nearby; 12 May be booked through travel agent

Bay View Farm

NEW CARLISLE WEST

Bay View Farm

337 Main Highway, Route 132, Box 21, G0C 1Z0
(418) 752 2725; (418) 752-6718

On the coastline of Quebec's picturesque Gaspé Peninsula, guests are welcomed into our comfortable home located on Route 132, Main Highway. Enjoy fresh sea air from our wrap-around veranda, walk, or swim at the beach. Visit natural and historic sites. Country breakfast, fresh farm, garden and orchard produce, home baking, and genuine Gaspesian hospitality. Light dinners by reservation. Craft, quilting, and folk music workshops. August Folk Festival. Also a small cottage for $350 per week. English and French spoken.

Hostess: Helen Sawyer
Rooms: 5 (SB) $35
Full Breakfast
Credit Cards: None
Notes: 3, 4, 5, 7, 8, 9, 10, 11

QUEBEC

Au Petit Hôtel des Ursulines Enr. (Au Petit Hotel)

3, Ruelle des Ursulines, G1R 3Y6
(418) 694-0965; (418) 692-4320 (FAX)

True to its name, the Au Petit Hotel provides the ideal mix between the intimacy of a family operated bed and breakfast and a full service hotel. Located near the St. Louis gate in the small Ursulines street within the old city of Quebec, the Au Petit Hotel opens its doors to you, offering the kind of lodging which effectively combines a quiet surrounding within the warm and hospitible atmosphere of the Old City.

Hosts: The Tims Family
Rooms: 16 (PB) $55-85 (Canadian)
Continental Breakfast
Credit Cards: A, B, C, E
Notes: 2 (for deposit only), 5, 7

Au Petit Hotel

NOTES: Credit cards accepted: A Master Card; B Visa; C American Express; D Discover Card; E Diners Club; F Other; 2 Personal checks accepted; 3 Lunch available; 4 Dinner available; 5 Open all year; 6 Pets

Hayden's Wexford House

450 Rue Champlain, G1K 4J3
(418) 524-0525; (418) 648-8995 (FAX)

Ancestral home built in the beginning of the
18th century, at the heart of our heritage
and located in the Old Quebec, and very
near the main points of interest. In the
summer, relax in the flower garden and in
the winter, by the fireside. Enjoy breakfast
in a warm decor and relaxed atmosphere.

Host: Michelle Paquet Riviere
Rooms: 3 (SB) $62
Full Breakfast
Credit Cards: B
Notes: 5, 7, 9, 10, 11

ST-MARC-SUR-LE-RICHELIEU

Hostellerie Les Trois Tilleuls

290 Rue Richelieu, J0L 2E0
(514) 584-2231

The Hostellerie Les Trois Tilleuls is a
charming inn on the banks of the Richelieu
River. The dining room features authentic
French cuisine with an extensive wine list
of exceptional vintages.

Host: Michel Aubriot
Rooms: 24 (PB) $84-350 (Canadian)
Full Breakfast
Credit Cards: A, B, C, D, E
Notes: 3, 4, 5, 7, 8, 9, 10, 12

STE-PETRONILLE

Auberge La Goeliche

22 Rue Du Quai, G0A 4C0
(418) 828-2248; (418) 828 2745 (FAX)

Overhanging the St. Lawrence River, this
castle-like inn offers a breathtaking view of
Quebec City, a 15-minute drive away. It
is also close to famous Mont. Ste. Anne
Ski Center. Its 22 rooms are warmly
decorated in rustic French-Canadian style.
Outdoor swimming pool. English and continental breakfasts. Guided tours of historic surroundings available.

Hosts: Janet Duplain, Andree Marchmand, and
Alain Turgeon
Rooms: 22 (PB) $100
Full Breakfast (Continental available)
Credit Cards: A, B, C
Notes: 3, 4, 5, 7, 8, 9, 10, 11, 12

---

welcome; 7 Children welcome; 8 Tennis nearby; 9 Swimming nearby; 10 Golf nearby; 11 Skiing nearby; 12
May be booked through travel agent

Puerto Rico

CABO ROJO

Parador Perichi's

HC-01, Box 16310, Carr 102, Joyuda, 00623
(809) 851-3131; (809) 851-0560 (FAX)

Parador Perichi's Hotel in Joyuda, Cabo Rojo, site of Puerto Rico's resorts on the West. Excellence has distinguished Perichi's in its 12 years of hospitality and service. Our 30 air-conditioned rooms are covered with wall to wall carpeting, private baths and balconies, color TV, and telephone. Perichi's award-winning restaurant features the finest foods—not to be missed. After sunset meet friends in our cozy lounge. Live music on weekends at the pool area. Comfortable banquet room for 300 persons, those who like to combine business with pleasure and much more.

Rooms: 30 (PB) call for rates
Full Breakfast
Credit Cards: A, B, C, D, E
Notes: 3, 4, 5, 7, 8, 9, 10, 11, 12

MARICAO

Parador La Hacienda Juanita

Road 105, KM 23-5, P.O. Box 777, 00606
(809) 838-2550; (809) 838-2551 (FAX)

1830. This hacienda-style building once served as the main lodge for a coffee plantation. Twenty-four acres, 1,600 feet above sea level in the cool tropical mountains of a Puerto Rican rain forest. Bird watchers' paradise.

Hosts: Radamés and Abraham Rivera
Rooms: 21 (PB) $65
Continental Breakfast
Credit Cards: A, B, C
Notes: 2, 3, 4, 5, 7, 8, 9, 12

SAN JUAN

El Canario Inn

1317 Ashford Avenue-Condado, 00907
(809) 722-3861; (809) 722-0391 (FAX)

San Juan's most historic and unique B&B inn. All 25 guest rooms are air-conditioned with private baths, cable TV, and telephone, and come with complimentary continental breakfast. Our tropical patios and sundeck provide a friendly and informal atmosphere. Centrally located near beach, casinos, restaurants, boutiques, and public transportation.

Hosts: Jude and Keith Olson
Rooms: 25 (PB) $65-90
Continental Breakfast
Credit Cards: A, B, C, D, E
Notes: 5, 7, 8, 9, 12

NOTES: Credit cards accepted: A Master Card; B Visa; C American Express; D Discover Card; E Diners Club; F Other; 2 Personal checks accepted; 3 Lunch available; 4 Dinner available; 5 Open all year; 6 Pets

Tres Palmas Guest House

2212 Park Boulevard, 00913
(809) 727-4617

Remodeled in 1990, all rooms include air-conditioners, ceiling fans, CATV with remote control, AM/FM clock radio, small decorative refrigerators, and continental breakfast. Oceanfront, beautiful sandy beach; daily maid service; newspapers; magazines; games; ocean-view sun deck; fresh beach towels; and chairs. Tourist information available. Centrally located ten minutes from the airport and Old San Juan.

Hosts: Jeannette Maldonado and Elving Torres
Rooms: 9 plus 3 apartments (11 PB; 1 SB)
$45-85; $45-60 off-season
Continental Breakfast
Credit Cards: A, B, C
Notes: 3, 4, 5, 7, 9

VIEQUES

La Esparanza Sugar Plantation Hotel Corporation

P.O. Box 1569, 00765-1569
(809) 741-8675; (809) 741-1313 (FAX)

Our twenty-four rooms are located on the southern side of the picturesque island of Vieques. Our lovely gardens take you directly to the tropical and aquamarine waters of the Carribbean Sea. You can swim, fish, scuba, kayak, or snorkel. Some of our rooms are large enough for a family of four. We provide an excellent restaurant with a veranda overlooking the sea.

Host: Lic. Charlie Ruiz Cox
Rooms: 24 (PB) $76-96
Full Breakfast
Credit Cards: A, B, C
Notes: 2, 3, 4, 5, 7, 8, 9, 12

welcome; 7 Children welcome; 8 Tennis nearby; 9 Swimming nearby; 10 Golf nearby; 11 Skiing nearby; 12 May be booked through travel agent

Virgin Islands

ST. CROIX

Pink Fancy Inn

27 Prince Street, 00820
(809) 773-8460; (800) 524-2045;
(809) 773-6448 (FAX)

A small, unique historic inn located a block and a half away from the town of Christiansted. From our inn, there are 20 restaurants, duty-free shopping, and historic sites. All our rooms are on a courtyard with a tropical garden, a pool, hammocks, and gazebo. Our rooms all consist of kitchenettes, CATV, telephone, fridge, air-conditioning and ceiling fans. And to top it off, we have a twenty-four hour complimentary bar and expanded continental breakfast.

Hostess: Dixie Ann Tang-innkeeper
Rooms: 12 (PB) $90
Expanded Continental Breakfast
Credit Cards: A, B, C, E
Notes: 5, 7, 8, 9, 10, 12

ST. THOMAS

Danish Chalet

P.O. Box 4319, 00803-4319
800-635-1531; (809) 777-4886 (FAX)

Ten minutes from the Cyril King Airport, overlooking Charlotte Amalie Harbor with cool mountain and bay breezes. Five-minute walk to town with duty-free shopping, restaurants, and waterfront activities. Complimentary, continental breakfast, sundeck; jacuzzi; $1 honor bar; free beach towels; in-room phones; air-conditioning or ceiling fans. Can arrange day sails, sight-seeing trips, car rental, etc. Special honeymoon packages available. We have been in the hospitality profession for nearly fifty years and welcome your visit.

Hosts: Frank and Mary Davis
Rooms: 13 (5PB; 8SB) $60-95
Continental Breakfast
Credit Cards: A, B
Notes: 2, 5, 6, 7, 8, 9, 10, 12

Villa Elaine

44 Water Island, 00802
(809) 774-0290; (809) 776-0890 (FAX)

Rental includes continental breakfast, supplies and snorkel from property. Walk or hike 500-acre water island 10-minute ferry ride to St. Thomas. Lovely Honeymoon Beach is a five-minute walk. A beautiful, peaceful, secure retreat. Courtesy service to and from ferry. Minimum stay of three days.

Hostess: Elaine Grissom
Rooms: 2 (PB) $100
Continental Breakfast
Credit Cards: None
Notes: 2, 5, 8, 9, 10

NOTES: Credit cards accepted: A MasterCard; B Visa; C American Express; D Discover Card; E Diners Club; F Other; 2 Personal checks accepted; 3 Lunch available; 4 Dinner available; 5 Open all year; 6 Pets

The Christian Bed and Breakfast Directory

P.O. Box 719
Uhrichsville, OH 44683

INN EVALUATION FORM

Please copy and complete this form for each stay and mail to the address
above. Since 1990 we have maintained files that include thousands of
evaluations from inngoers. We value your comments. These help us to keep
abreast of the hundreds of new inns that open each year and to follow the
changes in established inns.

Name of inn: _____

City and State: _____

Date of stay: _____

Length of stay: _____

Please use the following rating scales for the next items.
A: Outstanding. B: Good. C: Average. D: Fair. F: Poor.

Attitude of innkeepers: _____   Attitude of helpers: _____

Food Service: _____   Handling of Reservations: _____

Cleanliness: _____   Privacy: _____

Beds: _____   Bathrooms: _____

Parking: _____   Worth of price: _____

Comments on the above: _____
_____
_____
_____
_____

What did you especially like? _____
_____
_____
_____

Suggestions for improvements: _____
_____

Christian Bed & Breakfast Directory

Listing Reservation Form

You will receive a complimentary copy of the Directory upon publication.

PLEASE TYPE OR PRINT CLEARLY, answering all questions. Return with your check, money order, or credit card information for the **$25.00 fee** to *The Christian Bed & Breakfast Directory,* P.O. Box 719, 1810 Barbour Drive, Uhrichsville, OH 44683. **All materials must be in by October 7, 1994, to be included in the 1995-1996 edition.**

NAME OF INN _____

ADDRESS _____

CITY_____ STATE_____ ZIP_____

TELEPHONE _____ FAX _____

___Enclosed is my check for $25.00 United States Dollars.

___Charge $25.00 to my credit card: Visa___MC___American Express___Discover

Credit Card Number_____ Exp. Date _____

Signature _____

PLEASE ATTACH A DESCRIPTION OF YOUR BED AND BREAKFAST OF 50 TO 70 WORDS.

Host(s)/Hostess _____
Number of guest rooms _____
Number with private baths_____ Number with shared baths _____
Rate range for two people sharing one room (lowest to highest) _____
Full or continental breakfast? _____

Circle those that apply:

1. Credit Cards
   A. MasterCard
   B. Visa
   C. American Express
   D. Discover Card
   E. Diners Club
   F. Other
2. Personal checks accepted
3. Lunch available
4. Dinner available
5. Open all year
6. Pets welcome
7. Children welcome
8. Tennis nearby
9. Swimming nearby
10. Golf nearby
11. Skiing nearby
12. May be booked by a travel agent